The Complete Guide to Competitive Walking

~>~>~>~>~>~>~>~>~>~>~>~>~>~>~>~>

Racewalking, Power Walking, Nordic Walking and More!

By Dave McGovern

World Class Publications
Locust Valley, NY

Library of Congress cataloging in publication data available.
1st printing, November 2020 10 9 8 7 6 5 4 3 2 1

ISBN 978-0-9662176-3-6

Cover photos: 1, 2 Library of Congress; 3, 4 Dave McGovern, 5 Emmanuel Tardi, 6 Karen Asp, 7 Jeff Salvage, 8 Mike Madigan
Additional photography: Loretta McGovern, Michael Bartholomew
Proofreading: Greg Page

World Class Publications
20 High Street
Locust Valley, NY 11560

Printed in the United States of America
First Edition

DEDICATION

This book is dedicated to the many thousands of walkers who have allowed me the honor and pleasure of coaching them at my clinics and camps, and one-on-one, since 1991—especially the one I married, Loretta Schuellein-McGovern. ☺

FOREWORD

One of the first times I raced Dave McGovern, he tried to puke on me. You read that right; he tried to throw up on me with less than one kilometer to go in my first US National 20km Championship race. "Well," I thought, "here is a guy who takes his racing seriously; I could probably learn a thing or two from him." Now, most of us like to do our learning in a safer environment. So, if you want to learn to be the best walker you can be without getting puked on, this is the book for you. McGovern has crafted an encyclopedic volume summing up all he knows about competitive walking. Race walking? He's got that covered. Power walking? Got it. Nordic walking? Yep. It is all here; it is amazing and it has definitely been worth the wait.

The first time I remember meeting Dave was at the 1991 US World Racewalk Cup Trials in San Jose, CA. He was battling a case of non-viral hepatitis and wasn't having his best day; I was only racing the 20km distance for the second time (with no clue what I was doing) but we made a great pair for a large chunk of that race. As I remember it, despite his own suffering, McGovern kept giving me advice and coaching me along until before I knew it I was walking a huge personal best. A few years later—after the puking incident—we both had good days at the 1995 US World Racewalking Cup Trials, made the team and got to travel together to Beijing, China. He has been a great friend, competitor and a source of constant inspiration ever since.

In fact, I have to give McGovern a ton of credit for helping me make three Olympic teams in the 50k racewalk. One reason I made my first team in 2000 was because he was so darn fast at 20k. I doubted I could ever break into the top three in the US at the "sprint" distance, so I shifted my focus to the longer 50k shortly before the 2000 Olympic Trials. I made my third team in part because McGovern never wavered in his support of me and numerous other young walkers in the US. By 2007, I had decided to retire and not try for the 2008 Olympics. Thankfully, Dave talked me out of it, supported me in many ways along the journey—including as my personal aid station guru at a pivotal race in Cheboksary, Russia—and I made the team as the sole US representative in the 50k in Beijing. Thanks, Dave!

In this book, McGovern shares incredible information he has lived and learned as a world-class athlete and a world-class coach. He has taken beginning walkers and turned them into Olympic Trials qualifiers and National Masters Champions. For decades, he has traveled the globe teaching people how to walk faster and more efficiently at distances from 1,500 meters to 100 miles. He likes to joke that he gets paid to teach grown-ups how to put one foot in front of the other. I contend he doesn't get paid nearly enough for the masterful job he does.

Along my Olympic journey, I learned about a few other types of walking, too (not enough to write a book about it, though—good job, McGovern!). While preparing for the 2008 Olympic

Trials in the 50k racewalk, I planned to walk the 2007 Portland Marathon. Race organizer Judy Heller had included an official race walk division, but I wound up with a hamstring injury a few weeks before my planned trip and I had to call and tell her I wasn't able to compete. She said, "Why not try the 'Nordic Walking' division?" My response was, "What's Nordic Walking?" I had two weeks to teach myself a new walking sport. (I wish I had the book you are holding in your hands back then!) At first I found it inefficient and awkward to walk with poles in each hand, but I soon figured it out and to my surprise ended up winning the race. That's another thing McGovern will teach you in this book: Winning is Fun!

I hope I've convinced you that you have a treasure trove of walking information in your hands. You'll learn more than you thought you ever could about how to put one foot in front of the other from one of the world's best coaches. And as far as the puking thing goes? Do what he says, not what he does!

—Philip Dunn 3x Olympian, 50-kilometer Race Walk,
Nordic Walking Marathon World Champion

PREFACE

If you've picked up this book, chances are you've been bitten by the competitive walking bug. Perhaps you're training to walk in a local charity 5k, or your first half-marathon, or even a full marathon. Maybe you're a competitive racewalker, or Nordic walker, or possibly even a triathlete considering walking in the "run" portion of an upcoming sprint, half or full Ironman event. If any of these scenarios describe your situation, you've come to the right place! Competitive walking presents unique physiological and biomechanical challenges, yet good technique and training information can be hard to come by. *The Complete Guide to Competitive Walking* will help you to achieve your goals, whatever they may be, by providing you with the technique and training tools you will need to walk faster, more efficiently, and with fewer injuries (in the already low-risk sport of competitive walking!)

Technique is perhaps the most critical element for those who want to walk far and fast. The human body is very well designed for walking long distances at a moderate pace, but less so for walking those distances *fast*. The inherent mechanical limitations of "normal" walking technique can make moving at speeds faster than about four to five miles per hour unimaginable for most people. But with some technique changes, it is possible to walk *much* faster. Olympic-style racewalking is the ultimate in high-speed walking, but it's not necessarily for everyone. Even so, adding at least some elements of this fast, efficient style to your present gait will allow you to get to the finish line of your next race before the water tables are packed away and the beer truck heads back to the brewery. Section II of *The Complete Guide to Competitive Walking* will show you tips and tricks to improve your walking, making you more efficient, faster, and less likely to sustain injuries, whether you're a power walker, racewalker, Nordic walker or "just" a regular walker working toward completing a marathon or Ironman triathlon.

Although improving your walking technique is a very effective shortcut to faster times, it's not the only thing you'll need to work on. You'll also need to get out the door and put in some miles/kilometers! Section III delves into training. Each chapter in this section will show you exactly how to prepare for almost every imaginable race, or series of races, from sprints in the 1,500-meter to 5-kilometer (.93 to 3.1 miles) range, to ultra-marathons as well as multi-day events like the Disney Marathon's "Goofy Challenge" (half- and full marathons on consecutive days) or track meets with two or more walks held over a number of days, like the US National Masters Track & Field Championships, the World Masters Athletics World Championships or St. George, Utah's Huntsman Games. My previous two books, *The Complete Guide to Racewalking* and *The Complete Guide to Marathon Walking,* both came in a 6" x 9" format. This tome comes in a larger, 8.5" x 11" format, not just because I was trying to keep the page count under a ridiculous 330+ pages (!) but because the larger page size is better suited for displaying detailed training schedules. A necessary step, because *The Complete Guide to Competitive Walking* is chock full of them! Section III contains nearly 60 different beginning, intermediate and advanced training schedules for just about any possible racing scenario.

To round it all out, chapters on stretching, strength training, nutrition, psychology and more will guide you to walking healthfully and injury-free for years to come. All told, *The Complete Guide to Competitive Walking* provides you with everything you could possibly need to know in order to walk far and fast, no matter which style of walking you choose to use!

CONTENTS

SECTION I: BEFORE GETTING STARTED

Before moving on to sections on technique, training schedules, and racing tips, a little background is in order. Section I will introduce you to the long and colorful history of competitive walking, a bit about shoes and equipment, some basic background physiology, tips on nutrition and hydration, and hints on where to train. Obviously, you're eager to jump ahead to the training schedules, but please don't! You'll have a much better appreciation for *why* you'll need to do a particular workout or supplemental exercise if you take things one step at a time. Read on!

CHAPTER 1: FROM SAHELANTHROPUS TO SUZUKI: A NOT-SO-BRIEF HISTORY OF COMPETITIVE WALKING

Bipedal locomotion evolved as a way for our early hominid ancestors to reduce the energy costs of foraging for nuts and berries, allowed them to scan the horizon for predators, and perhaps helped them to map out shortcuts to the nearest Taco Bell. In 1978 a fossilized trail of 3.6-million-year-old hominid footprints was uncovered at Laetoli, Tanzania. The impressions were left by a pair of *Australopithecus afarensis,* walking upright, side-by-side, through wet volcanic ash. Far earlier, *Sahelanthropus tchadensis* was likely our first ancient ancestor to perambulate bipedally across the African plains.

Competition is the driving force behind all evolutionary advancement; it is in our bones and in our DNA. It is also in our soul. Once human beings—or our pre-human ancestors—began walking upright, it probably didn't take long for them to challenge one another to walking competitions.

The ascent of walking.

Fast forward several million years… Although the earliest recorded walking races may have been depicted in Egyptian hieroglyphics chiseled into stone around 2,500BC,[1] competitive walking's lineage can be reliably dated back to at least the late 16th century as English noblemen bet fortunes on races arranged between their footmen. Eventually, solitary endurance feats and challenge races between two competitors over very long distances became increasingly—and some might say

[1] Jeff Salvage mentioned the racewalking glyphs in his first book, *Walk Like an Athlete*. In all of my research for this and other books, I haven't found a single mention of it anywhere else. I'm pretty sure he made it up. ☺

absurdly—popular. These exhibitions and foot races, usually between 100 and 2,000 miles in length, took place as town-to-town road walks, or on short loop courses set up at fairgrounds.

The Pedestrian Era

Fast-forward to the 18th and 19th centuries as long-distance "pedestrian" races in Europe and the US began attracting gushing press coverage and throngs of spectators. Robert Barclay Allardice ("Captain Barclay") was the most celebrated pedestrian of the early 19th century. His most famous feat—walking 1,000 miles in 1,000 consecutive hours in 1809—gave birth to the sport of pedestrianism. Many others followed suit attempting ever more challenging feats of endurance. Betting on the outcome of the spectacles was rampant, which was likely responsible for much of the popularity of the events—that, and the lack of anything more interesting going on in the days before Wi-Fi. In the US, pedestrianism got its start in 1861 when Edward Payson Weston, having lost a bet on the outcome of the 1860 presidential election, was required, as payment, to walk from Boston to Washington, DC to watch President Lincoln's inauguration. Weston received such notoriety from the feat that he was able to embark on a long and highly lucrative career as an ultra-long-distance walker. Weston, followed by countless copycats, took part in point-to-point challenges against the clock, or against other competitors, between cities such as New York to Philadelphia; Portland, ME to Chicago; and New York to St. Paul, MN. In Europe, the famous London-to-Brighton[2] and Paris-to-Alsace races exist to this day. Of course with all the transit strikes going on over there, walking is probably the only way of getting from city to city most days, perhaps explaining the longevity of these races. ☺

The "walking boom" reached its pinnacle in the decades after the United States Civil War as pedestrianism became the most popular pastime in America, surpassing horse racing and bare-knuckle boxing in popularity throughout the 1870s and early 1880s. In addition to the various city-to-city events, long-distance track races or exhibitions became popular at festivals and fairs, and as the pedestrian boom crested, within just about any indoor space that could hold a track and a paying audience. Although Championship multi-day races like the famed "Astley Belt" and "O'Leary Belt" series were often held on ⅐ or ⅛ mile tracks in huge indoor spaces, walking exhibitions featuring a single walker attempting to cover a set distance in a given time often occurred in much smaller venues such as theaters or roller rinks where hastily erected tracks could be as small as 35 yards, or *50* laps to the mile! During this "Golden Age" walking continued to be an ultra-endurance pursuit, with "short" races lasting a mere 24 hours—a sprint compared to the brutal, and much more popular, six-day ultra-marathon walks. Some of the best-attended six-day races were held at London's Royal Agricultural Hall ("The Aggie") and New York's original

[2] In one form or another… The classic 53-mile London-to-Brighton walking race was held from 1919 to 1984. It was resurrected in 2012 as the "London 2 Brighton Challenge" race. Most still walk, but runners are now permitted to take part.

Madison Square Garden, built by P.T. Barnum in 1874. The venues held 10,000 to 25,000 spectators who would come and go, watching for a few hours at a time, drinking beer and eating sandwiches over the course of the six days. For the time, these were uncharacteristically egalitarian events. While most sportsmen of that era were wealthy white men, pedestrian races attracted African-Americans and women as competitors, and rich and poor alike as spectators.

In those early years, there was no serious attempt made to codify the rules. In "go-as-you-please" pedestrian events, mainly held in England, running was permitted. In "fair-heel-and-toe" events, more popular in the US, participants had to walk, but the definition of what constituted walking was vague. The arbitrary line separating walking from running was left up to the discretion of the judges, leading to more and more controversy as the sport grew in popularity.

Professional walker Charles Westhall complained of the "*inability or want of courage on the part of the judges and referee to stop the man, who, in his eagerness for fame or determination to gain money anyhow, may trespass upon fair walking and run.*"[3] Despite the problems brought on by a lack of clearly defined rules, the vague concept of "fair heel-and-toe," as determined by the appointed judges, continued to define walking throughout the pedestrian era.

While America was caught up in the ultra-long-distance-walking fad, walks of a more spectator-friendly duration were being contested across the pond. In Britain, racewalking (aka race walking) was developing into a bona fide amateur track and field event. A seven-mile walk was included on the program of the first-ever Amateur Athletic Club of England Championships in

The start of the 5th International Astley Belt race at Madison Square Garden, New York City, September 22nd, 1879.

[3] "A Potted History of the Rules of Race Walking" from the website of the Victoria (Australia) Walking Club, https://www.vrwc.org.au/vrwchistrules.shtml

1866, and one or more walking races at distances between two and seven miles have been included in every edition of the championships ever since.

Although pedestrianism's "Golden Age" petered out in the early 1880's (as bicycle-racing, boxing, and baseball captured America's attention, and soccer/football overtook Europe), competitive walking still had enough support in Britain and the United States around the turn of the century for an 880-yard racewalk to be included on the Olympic program at the 1904 Games in St. Louis as part of the "all-rounder" competition—a ten-event precursor to the decathlon. 1,500- and 3,000-meter racewalks were contested at the 1906 "Interim" Games in Athens,[4] and 3,500-meter and ten-mile races were held at the 1908 Olympic Games in London. Since that time, one or more walks have been included in all but one edition of the Olympic Games.

These early Olympic walks continued to be judged by the unwritten principle of "fair heel-and-toe," with judges forming their own opinions concerning a walker's legality—if it looked like walking, it was legal. Beyond these subjective, aesthetically based judgments, there were still no definitive written rules to define legal racewalk technique. It should come as no surprise then, that judging controversies plagued the early Olympic walks. Disqualifications in the 1,500- and 3,000-meter walks at the 1906 Games, and the 3,500-meter and ten-mile walks in 1908 led to protests by the affected athletes. Conditions deteriorated at Stockholm in 1912 as six entrants were disqualified, leaving only four finishers in the 10,000-meter event.

Because of these and other controversies, an international governing body was created to oversee athletics, as track and field and its related disciplines are known outside the United States. The International Amateur Athletic Federation (IAAF—now known as World Athletics) was created in 1912 to govern track and field, long distance running, cross-country running, and racewalking. Despite the placement of IAAF-certified judges, controversy once again erupted over the Olympic walks at Antwerp in 1920. Once again, several walkers in the field were disqualified. On the plus side, this led to the strongest showing by American walkers ever. U.S. athletes finished 3rd, 5th and 8th in the 3,000 meters, and 2nd and 6th in the 10,000 meters. Beaten by the Americans, and fearing removal of the troublesome walks from the Olympics, the British responded in 1922 by drafting the first rules to govern racewalking. The British Road Walking Association provided this first formal definition:

> *"Walking is a progression by steps so taken that the heel of the foremost foot must reach the ground before the toe of the other foot leaves it."*

---

[4] The Olympic Games are held every four years, save for world wars and Covid-19 interruptions. In the early years there was a great deal of debate whether the Olympics should be held in different countries or always in Athens, Greece. A quadrennial international Olympics won out, but as a compromise there was an event held in Athens in 1906 named the "Second International Olympic Games in Athens" by the International Olympic Committee. At the time it was considered an Olympic Games on par with the quadrennial Olympics, but it has since been downgraded and the IOC no longer recognizes the medals as true Olympic medals.

Despite the new definition, controversies continued to dog the walks. At the 1924 Games in Paris, an Austrian was disqualified in an early heat of the 10,000-meter walk but was permitted to race in the finals after a jury of appeals overruled the racewalk judges. Upset by the reversal, the judges resigned and a new panel had to be found before the event could continue. After the Paris debacle, the walks were left off the program of the 1928 Olympics in Amsterdam. Following the Games, the IAAF met in Amsterdam to establish an improved set of rules for competitive walking and the judging of the sport. The wording of the definition of racewalking was simplified to: *"Walking is a progression of steps so taken that unbroken contact with the ground is maintained."* The Amsterdam conclave also eliminated the difficult-to-judge shorter track races. Racewalking returned to its long-distance roots, reappearing at the 1932 Games at Los Angeles as a 50-kilometer (31.1 miles) road walk.

After World War II, the British lobbied the IAAF and the International Olympic Committee (IOC) for an Olympic track walk to provide more exposure for racewalking. A 10k walk was reinstated at the 1948 Games in London as well as at the 1952 Games in Helsinki. The distance was increased to 20 kilometers for the 1956 Olympic Games in Melbourne. The 20k and 50k racewalks have become the standard IAAF distances for men; both events have been included in every Olympic Games since 1956, with the exception of the 1976 Games at Montreal where the 50k was dropped as a consequence of "down-sizing" the Games. 20k and 50k walks are also contested at the World Athletics Championships, the World Athletics Race Walking Team Championships, and area competitions like the Pan American Games, the European Championships, the All-Africa Games and the Asian Games.

Although women's competitive walking was quite popular during the heyday of pedestrianism in the 1870s, there were no Olympic or global championship walks for women until the late 20th century. Women's walking began in earnest at the world level only in 1968, with the inception of an annual 5k "World Meeting." By 1979 the first "Eschborn Cup" 5k for women was held in conjunction with the men's Lugano Cup finals in Eschborn, West Germany. The women's international distance at IAAF/World Athletics events evolved into a 10k, beginning with the 1987 World Championships in Rome, and then, after much lobbying by female walkers and their supporters, to 20 kilometers starting with the 1999 World Championships in Seville, Spain, and the 2000 Olympics in Sydney, Australia. But there still wasn't complete parity between men and women in the walks, as men had the choice of competing in either the 20k or 50k at the world level, while women were only permitted to compete in the shorter event. Finally in 2016 and 2017, after several successful lawsuits, a women's 50-kilometer walk was added to the biennial IAAF/World Athletics Team Championships and then to the World Track & Field Championships.

The International Olympic Committee (IOC) took a bit longer to come around, but with the addition of a women's 10k walk to the Olympic program in 1992, women were finally able to share the same competitive opportunities that men have enjoyed since the turn of the 20th century. Almost. While there is parity between men and women in almost every other Olympic track & field event, women have only been able to compete in the seven-event heptathlon vs. the men's ten-event decathlon, and as of this writing, there is only one Olympic walking event for women vs. two for men. Additionally, in typical patronizing fashion for World Athletics and the IOC, the women's distance was shorter than the men's distances for the first two women's Olympic walks in 1992 and 1996. The women's Olympic distance was finally increased to 20 kilometers for the 2000 Olympic Games.

Women now compete at the 20-kilometer distance at the Olympics, the World Athletics Championships, the World Athletics Team Championships, the Pan American Games, the Commonwealth Games, and at a number of other international competitions. In 2016 World Athletics opened up the 50k to women at the World Team Championships, paving the way for a women's 50k at the World Athletics Championships, and eventually—it is hoped—in the Olympic Games. As of this writing lawsuits are moving through the Court of Arbitration for Sport to get a women's 50-kilometer event added to the Covid-19-delayed Tokyo Olympic program. Stay tuned!

An ugly side note that must be mentioned here is that of doping[5] in racewalking. In a backhanded testament to the extreme athletic demands of competitive walking, the racewalking world became embroiled in a doping scandal leading up to the 2016 Olympics. Several medalists at

Women competing in the 20 kilometer racewalk at the 2016 Rio Olympics

[5] Doping is the use of illegal performance-enhancing drugs by athletes.

prior Olympic and World Championships were suspended retroactively after their urine and blood samples dating back as far as the 2008 Olympics were retested using more advanced testing methods. Alex Schwazer of Italy was banned from the 2012 and 2016 Olympics and stripped of his gold medal from the 2016 World Team Championships, and the entire Russian team was banned from the Rio Olympics after blatant evidence of systemic doping became too obvious to ignore. Tainted medals from suspended athletes were eventually redistributed to the athletes the dopers had beaten in competition. Most notably, Jared Tallent of Australia, a perennial bridesmaid, was upgraded to gold medals from the London Olympics and the 2016 World Team Championships in Taicang, China, but getting a medal delivered in the mail years after the fact is somewhat underwhelming when compared to standing atop the podium in front of your peers and thousands of cheering fans.

Doping not only hurts the very top athletes who are kept off of, or bumped lower down on the medal stand, but also those a rung or two down the ladder who never get the chance to compete at the highest levels because of cheaters ahead of them. Although I feel the worst for Jared, Jefferson Perez, Robert Heffernan, and many others who were repeatedly bumped down or off of podia, I have to wonder whether I would have made the 1996 Olympic Team had entry standards not been so badly skewed by the many dopers in the international ranks ahead of me. The Olympic "A" standard in 1996 was 1:24:00 for 20 kilometers. The time was based on the world top-100 list that was at the time full of dopers. Assuming that a dozen or more cheating Russians (as well as the occasional "other"—Italians, Spaniards, Chinese…) were ahead of me in the world rankings, would the Olympic standard have been more realistic and attainable by a reasonably talented non-doping athlete? (Like me!) Had the standard been just 30 seconds slower, Tim Seaman and I—both under 1:24:30, but not under 1:24:00—would have made the Olympic Team in 1996.[6] Had it been 90 seconds slower (1:25:30) Tim, Curt Clausen and I would have all made the team. How many others were similarly affected? It's impossible to tell, but infuriating to ponder. Oh well, water under the bridge...

Hopefully, with advances in out-of-competition testing and increased scrutiny of rogue national anti-doping agencies (I'm looking at you, Russia!), we'll get to the point where only the fastest "clean" athletes make teams and win medals.

Non-racewalking competitive walking

Outside of Olympic racewalking, competitive walking saw a surge in popularity in the United States during the 1990s and into the '00s. Although walkers had certainly entered local 5ks and other races here and there since at least the 1980s and beyond, the late 1990s saw a boom in walkers competing

---

[6] Come to think of it, the 1:24:29 I walked in 1996 would have broken the world record had I walked that time just 20 years earlier in 1976, and would have won every Olympic 20k until Maurizio Damilano's 1:23:35 in 1980. So there's that. ☺

in half-marathons and marathons. Major marathons such as New York City, Los Angeles, Portland, Honolulu, Mardi Gras (New Orleans) and Walt Disney World have featured judged walking divisions with awards for the top finishers, and nowadays walkers make up an ever-growing percentage of entrants in marathons and half-marathons. Many of these marathon and half-marathon walkers participate with charity fundraising teams such as the Leukemia and Lymphoma Society's "Team in Training," the Crohn's & Colitis Foundation's "Team Challenge," and the United Mitochondrial Disease Foundation's "Team Activate Your Mitochondria."

Nordic walk World Champions, Philip Dunn and Karen Asp, at the Portland Marathon. Photo Credit: Karen Asp

Concurrent with the boom in marathon and half-marathon walking in the late 1990s was the growth of "Nordic walking"—recreational or competitive walking with the aid of cross-country ski-type poles. Although its roots date back to the 1930s in Finland, Nordic walking in the US began to flourish after Tom Rutlin developed his "Exerstriding" program in 1985. Europe's boom came in the late 1990s, with the term "Nordic walking" being coined by Finnish ski manufacturer Exel, creator of the first walking-specific poles for European-technique Nordic walking. The growth in the fitness activity/sport led to the creation of the International Nordic Walking Association in 2000, and in 2006 the Portland Marathon hosted the first World Nordic Marathon Walking Championship, won by three-time Olympic racewalker Philip Dunn, and five-time Nordic walking world champion and world-record holder Karen Asp. 2006 also saw the 24 Hours of Wiesau (Austria) World Nordic Walking Championship. Although not yet as popular in the US as in Europe, Nordic walking continues to grow stateside, and seems to be on the brink of another major boom.

Beyond northern Europe and North America, recognized Nordic walking federations exist in China, Japan, Korea, Australia, New Zealand, India, Israel, and even Iraq! Individual federations hold their own championships, and world records are recognized at five and ten kilometers, ten miles, half-marathon, 20 miles and the marathon. Ultra-endurance Nordic walking records are kept at 50k, 50 miles, 100k, 100 miles and six, 12, 24, and 48 hours.

The "final frontier" for competitive walkers is the "run" portion of triathlons. Although time limits demand a brisk pace in these events, more and more walkers are competing in triathlons without running a step. On a personal note, I would coach one or two triathletes per year at my World Class Racewalking clinics throughout the 1990s and '00s. Now I see one or two triathletes at just about every clinic as more and more multi-sport athletes realize that it's okay to walk rather than run. The story often goes like this: a runner gets injured and resorts to swimming and spin classes to cross-train while recovering from the injury. The injured runner eventually takes out a second mortgage and buys a bike, and after a while a light bulb goes off: "Hey, I'm a runner—an injured runner, but a runner nonetheless!—and now I'm doing all of this swimming and biking. I should do a triathlon!" Before long the runner is injured again, but has already plunked down $750 to enter a triathlon so decides to walk. If this story sounds familiar, you're not alone! Whereas in years past the only walkers you would see in a triathlon were runners who had "hit the wall" or sustained an injury during the marathon portion of an Ironman, now more and more triathletes are walking, by choice, from gun to tape.

The future of competitive walking

Where does competitive walking go from here? Is it gaining or waning in popularity? Those are tricky questions. Competitive *racewalking* at the elite level is both growing, and under threat. A women's 50k walk has been added to the World Athletics Team Championships, and to the World Athletics Championships. In contrast to many Olympic sports, racewalking is practiced globally, with athletes from all six inhabited continents routinely placing in the top ten at the Olympic and World Championships walks. More and more people are taking up racewalking at the recreational level as well, both in the US and abroad. But despite having roots dating back to the 1904 Olympics and (far!) beyond, racewalking seems to be under attack by the IOC, which is trying to downsize athletics and many other sports as it adds new events (think skateboarding, sport climbing, surfing, break-dancing, etc.) The quirky nature of the rules is also problematic, as shorter and shorter attention spans don't allow sufficient time to explain them to the viewing public. Ironically, World Athletics has decided that the solution to the problem is to further complicate the event! They have added a time-penalty "pit lane" or "penalty zone" to many competitions and are experimenting with "shoe alarms" to detect loss of contact. (More on that later.) World Athletics is also floating the idea of shortening the distances of the walks. (Keep in mind that the distances have been lengthened over the past century to make judging easier…) We'll see where all of this upheaval goes, but hopefully the walks will continue to survive as Olympic events just as they have done following the many previous attempts over the decades to remove them from Games.

The future of competitive walking?

Non-racewalking competitive walking (walking in races that don't enforce strict racewalking rules) seems to be growing as well, both in the US and globally. Figures are difficult to come by, but walking is consistently the most popular fitness activity (by far) in the US, according to the Bureau of Labor Statistics.[7] 2016 BLS figures indicate that some 110 million Americans walk regularly for fitness. Certainly not all participate competitively, but in my own experience as a coach and participant in races all over the world, I see a higher and higher percentage of walkers taking part in "running" races.

I'm also seeing many more ultra-runners who walk during part of their 24-hour or six-day events. In the 1980s I taught American Ultra-Running Hall of Famers Donna Hudson and Stu Mittleman to racewalk. They were looking for a way to lose less time during the inevitable walk breaks they would take during six-day runs, and they set American and world records after improving their walking technique. At the time they seemed to be the exception, rather than the rule. But increasingly, I'm seeing more and more ultra-runners at my clinics looking for that edge, and participation in walk-only Centurion races (100-mile/24-hour walks) and other ultra-walking events seems to be experiencing a resurgence. At the extreme end, in 2017 Yolanda Holder became the first walker to complete the Sri Chimnoy Self-Transcendence 3,100-mile "running" race, walking some 60 miles per day for 52 days straight to accomplish the feat. The publicity surrounding Holder's many exploits—and her own engaging personality—can't hurt the popularity of ultra-long-distance walking.

Nordic Walking's popularity, too, seems to be on the rise. According to the International Nordic Walking Federation, the sport is one of the fastest growing health and fitness activities worldwide, with more than 10 million participants in more than 40 countries. More sporting goods manufacturers are introducing walking poles, and sponsorship dollars/euros/yen/yuan/dinars for

[7] Sports and exercise among Americans, https://www.bls.gov/opub/ted/2016/sports-and-exercise-among-americans.htm

events and individual athletes are on the rise. I've noticed a steady increase in the number of Nordic walkers on bike trails that I train on locally, and elsewhere, as I travel around the country/world for my clinics, and have also noticed more and more poles at half-marathons and marathons around the country.

Finally, walking in triathlons is absolutely on the rise, and not just among triathletes too tired to run anymore! Again, I used to see maybe one triathlete per year at my racewalking clinics, and now rarely a clinic goes by that I don't see at least one or two triathletes looking for an edge to improve their walking. Most choose to not run a single step, seeing nothing wrong with walking the entire marathon portion of an Ironman event. It's been a few years since I've participated in a triathlon (I competed in the first-ever St. Croix Triathlon in 1985 and did a number of recreational triathlons as a member or the Hudson Valley [New York] Triathlon Club in the early 2000s), but in recent years as a spectator I've seen a growing number of walk-only triathletes, even in sprint- or Olympic-distance events. Will there be walk-only divisions in triathlons some day? Who knows? But as more and more people walk in triathlons, their leverage to request walk-only divisions of race directors will only grow. What a friend used to say of racewalking holds true for triathlon walking: "We're taking over the world, we just need more of us!" ☺

The history of competitive walking is still being written. You can be a part of that history by lacing up your shoes and getting out there. But first, read on….

CHAPTER 2: WHY WALK?

As outlined in the previous chapter, competitive walking has a long and varied history. Of course the same could be said for cliff diving, elephant polo and competitive hot-dog eating, but I wouldn't necessarily recommend that you engage in those pursuits. (Okay, maybe hotdog eating. I'm a big fan…) ☺ I would, however, recommend competitive walking to just about anybody, especially anyone who is already walking for fitness. And depending on your goals, I would probably even suggest you give racewalking a try, or at least add some elements of racewalking to your current walking technique if your goal is to walk *fast*. (And if you're reading a book titled *The Complete Guide to Competitive Walking*, I'm guessing it is!) ☺

Elephant polo: Hard to believe it's not in the Olympics. ☺ Photo Credit: TTR Weekly

Why walk? If you're into bipedal locomotion, why not just run? Well, if the only criterion is to get from point A to point B as quickly as possible on two feet, then sure, go ahead and run. But there are plenty of reasons why some people—okay, lots of people!—may be better off walking than running. Walking is easier on the joints than running, easier for beginning athletes to take up than running, and with the proper technique—and equipment, if you're a Nordic walker—it can be as physiologically challenging as running. Sure, to some trolls, competitive walking is akin to a contest to see who can whisper the loudest.[8] Inexplicably, it seems to really get under some people's skin that thousands of otherwise healthy, sane and reasonably fit people would want to *walk* competitively. "WHY NOT JUST RUN?!" they silently, or occasionally not so silently, scream. Well, they—we—walk because running simply isn't for everybody. It can be very hard on the body both orthopedically and physiologically. Still, running is a popular fitness pursuit and competitive activity.[9] As popular as running is today, it's hard to imagine that distance runners were once considered weird fanatics before the running boom of the 1970s—and maybe to some people they still are considered weird fanatics. ☺ Fast-forward half a century, and competitive walkers are still considered a little "out there" by some in the general (unfit) public, but we've discovered the great secret that walking is the perfect competitive outlet: it's inexpensive—all you need is a good pair of shoes, and maybe some shorts, and you can get going[10]—it's physically easy for beginners to take up, and it's an activity that most healthy people can continue doing into their golden years.

One of the most popular selling points of walking as a fitness or competitive activity is its low injury rate. Every year 65% of competitive runners sustain significant injuries compared to only 21% of walkers.[11] As happy as you may be with your Obama/Trump/Bidencare policy, wouldn't you rather spend your time on the road rather than in the doctor's office? Even highly competitive walkers and racewalkers sustain far fewer injuries than runners do, mainly because of the greatly reduced impact forces experienced by walkers versus runners. Maintaining one foot in contact with the ground at all times allows walkers to impact the ground with ⅓ of the force that runners do. Since walkers stay so low to the ground, they're much less likely to suffer joint damage, stress fractures and other overuse injuries so common to runners.

Another great thing about walking is that it's a "scalable" activity. There's really no such thing as "training wheels" when you run. Even at slow paces, running requires a lot of energy because you're launching your entire body up into the air with every step. But beginning walkers can work at an extremely low effort level and ramp up from there, all the way up to very high-energy power walking, Nordic walking, or racewalking. One of the things that some injured runners who have become walkers miss is the heart-pounding workout they used to experience as runners. But they don't have to! With some technique modifications, walkers can achieve the same high heart rates that runners do. Even if you never plan to enter a judged racewalking event, by incorporating a few elements of this powerful and efficient technique you'll suddenly be able to get a much better

---

[8] Among other insults, former NBC sportscaster Bob Costas, while introducing the walks at the 2000 Olympics, compared walking races to a contest to see who could whisper the loudest. Racewalkers never let him live it down.

[9] Just not as popular as walking… Over 110 million Americans walk for fitness regularly, compared to fewer than 50 million who run.

[10] If you decide that Nordic walking is your thing, add poles to the equation.

[11] Physical Activity-Related Injuries in Walkers and Runners in the Aerobics Center Longitudinal Study, at https://pubmed.ncbi.nlm.nih.gov/11086751/

workout than you could ever get with "regular" walking, without subjecting yourself to the high risk of injury experienced by runners. Additionally, racewalking speeds can be much faster than what can be achieved with regular walking. For most people, limited free time to walk, not a lack of endurance, is what keeps them from walking more miles. Walking faster will allow you to walk further, and burn many more calories, in a given period of time. As an added bonus, it can boost your heart rate much higher than what you could ever achieve with "regular" walking. Nordic walking, too, can give you a better all-body workout than you may be used to if all you've ever done is amble along at a bird-watching pace without poles.

Don't get me wrong, I love "regular" walking and partake in some post-prandial perambulation—an after-dinner family walk—almost every day. Even walking at a strolling pace is a great calorie-burning exercise that almost anyone can do. But to burn a lot of calories, you need to walk for a long time. (And who has lots of time to exercise?) The low intensity of regular walking makes it a great activity for beginning exercisers, but not for people who are looking for a higher-intensity cardio workout. It's almost impossible for most walkers to get their heart rates up beyond a very light aerobic effort no matter how hard they pump their arms and stomp their feet. Walking is a terrific way to go long distances at a relatively pedestrian pace, but the technique puts a real damper on your high-end speed. If you've ever tried to fitness walk really fast you know what I'm talking about. You have probably discovered that normal walking technique breaks down and becomes pretty awkward once you get beyond a 15- to 12-minutes-per-mile pace. In fact, most people can't walk any faster than that 12-minute-mile pace no matter how hard they try. But you don't have to settle for that rather pedestrian speed limit. By modifying your walking technique, and possibly using some elements of racewalking technique, you can spin your wheels much faster, allowing you to achieve much higher heart rates, and to burn many more calories per hour, than you could ever hope to do with regular walking form. Racewalkers actually burn as many calories as runners, and achieve comparable working heart rates.[12] Nordic walkers, too, can achieve much higher heart rates than their counterparts who walk using "regular" walking technique.

One of the strongest selling points of walking as a fitness or competitive activity is that it can be performed by just about anyone, anywhere. We'll talk about all the many different places you can walk in Chapter 6, but as a walker, you don't need to be tied to a golf course, basketball court, swimming pool or ski slope—or pay for those facilities—as you would have to do to take part in those activities. You can literally just get up, head out the door and walk, no matter where you are. You can walk on hills or level ground, on roads, trails or tracks, in parks or on city sidewalks, or you can even stay indoors and walk on a treadmill, in a shopping mall, or in some other large

[12] Back in the 1980s I was tested along with other members of the US National Race Walk Team and the Mexican National Team at the US Olympic Training Center in Colorado Springs, CO. Nearly every one of us was able to achieve higher maximum heart rates and $\dot{V}O_2$ max values while racewalking than what we maxed out at when running.

enclosed space. Walking is for everybody and anybody, anywhere. The question I posed as the title of this chapter could very well have been "Why *NOT* walk?" But then it would have been a very short chapter!

Why walk? Because you can, and because you should! For your health, and for competition, walking is a great activity for just about anyone. Read on to find out how to get started!

CHAPTER 3: SHOES AND EQUIPMENT

Get two competitive walkers in a room and the conversation will invariably turn to the latest shoes for walking fast. I remember a time when there was pretty much one shoe for running, walking, skipping, jumping, tiddlywinking and alligator wrestling: Converse Chuck Taylors. But that's because I'm old. Today there is a mind-numbing variety of shoes for every possible activity. It just makes sense that golfers, ballerinas, javelin throwers, football players, and runway models would wear different shoes. But why wouldn't all *walkers* be okay using the same shoes? Do walkers *really* need different shoes for strolling vs. hiking vs. racewalking vs. marathon walking vs. Nordic walking? Well, in a word, yes! Not all walkers were created equal. Just as Cinderella's slipper fit only her foot, your shoes may "fit" only one form of walking. Different types of walking really do require different shoe designs and materials. The lightness and flexibility of a racewalking shoe might spell disaster on a tough hike over rough terrain or in an ultra-race. Here's a rundown—er, walk-down—of the things you should look for in your walking shoes (besides your missing socks.)

Casual walking

For casual low-mileage fitness walking, anything goes. Almost. Fitness walkers who aren't planning to cover more than three to five miles at a time are generally pretty safe using just about anything from lightweight running shoes, to cross-trainers, to racewalking shoes, and—for off-road use—

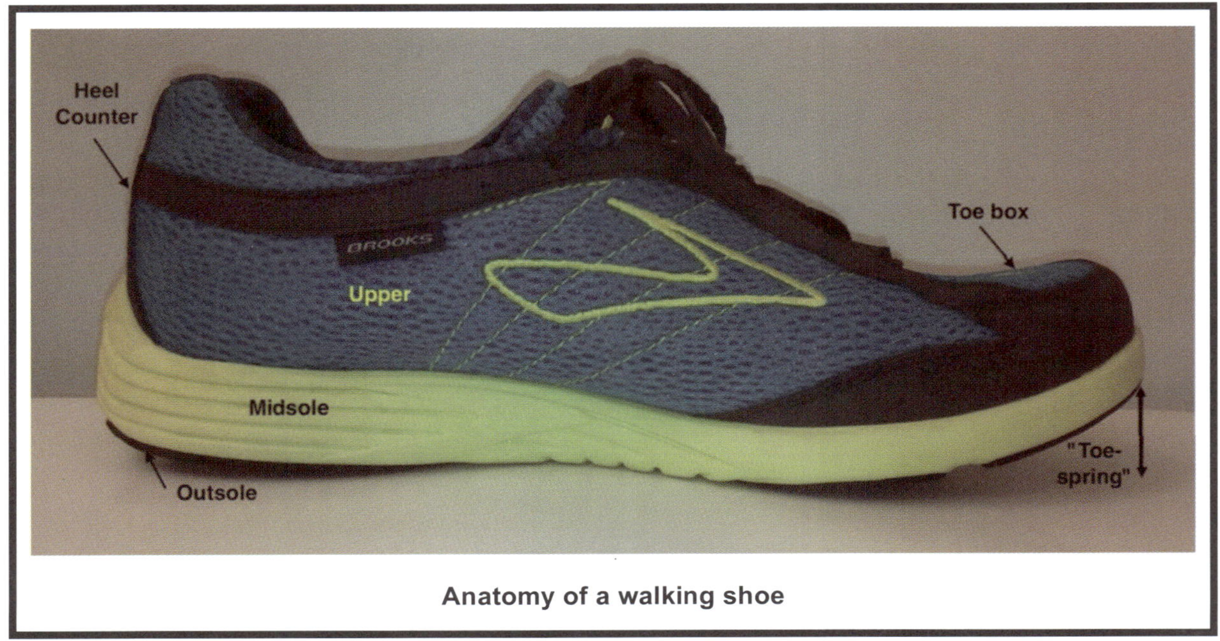

Anatomy of a walking shoe

trail-running shoes. Walkers impact the ground with about one-third of the force of runners, so we don't need excessive cushioning. In fact, too much fluff in the heel can lead to shin pain and other problems. A good rule of big toe (as opposed to thumb) is that any comfortable, supportive running, walking, or racewalking shoe that doesn't give you blisters is probably okay for low-mileage, low-speed casual walking.

Racewalking

Racewalking uses many more muscles and relies on the feet much more than casual walking does. Consequently, the right shoes are critical. Racewalking shoes need to be very flexible to allow the feet to "roll" from heel to toe, and they should have a very low heel to reduce leverage that can cause the feet to slap the ground after heel contact. I also like a high "toe-spring"—the height of the toe of the shoe above the ground. A lot of toe-spring gives the shoes a "rounder" profile, which is well suited to rolling from heel to toe. "Real" racewalking shoes and running "racing flats" or "trainer-racers" are your best bets. About once a decade or so, one of the major shoe companies will try to market an actual racewalking shoe for the US market. In the 1980s it was the Adidas Race Walk and the short-lived Nike El Viento; in the 1990s we had the New Balance 100 and 110; in the 2000s Bart Hersey hand-crafted custom racewalking shoes out of his shop in Maine;[13] and now we have Decathlon's Newfeel RW 900 which are not only terrific shoes, they are very reasonably priced. (You can find them at: www.decathlon.com/collections/race-walking/). Swedish company Salming mainly serves the Europe market, but their shoes are starting to sneak their way into the US and Canada. They sponsor a lot of Europe's top walkers, and even some Americans. On a smaller scale, racewalker and coach Carmen Jackinsky has her own start-up out of Beaverton, Oregon, called "Reshod." Carmen's original business model was to replace the midsole and outsole of your favorite shoes with her own custom midsole/outsole, but now she makes her own shoes for competitive walking and racewalking, with a model for training and another for racing. Check them out at Reshod.com/.

Research and development costs being what they are, a big shoe company has to sell on the order of 5,000 pairs of shoes to break even when they come out with a new model. It's very difficult to sell 5,000 pairs of racewalking shoes because most racewalkers are perfectly happy wearing running racing flats. Consequently, most companies eventually realize they can't make much money on racewalking shoes, so they pull the plug after a year or two. ☹ Adidas has been making racewalking shoes for the European market for decades, and the elite Japanese walkers

---

[13] Bart sold the business to Stephen Keoseian in 2007 and the racewalking shoes were unavailable for a while. Apparently they're back! Hersey's shoes are a bit pricey, but they're specifically handmade for your feet, and they can be resoled several times for somewhat less than the cost of a pair of "off the shelf" shoes. Check out the racewalking section of the Hersey website at: www.herseycustomshoe.com/product-category/race-walking/.

always seem to be supplied with Asics racewalk shoes, so they are out there if you're a resourceful Googler and don't mind paying an arm and a leg for shipping.

Long-distance walking

Most long-distance walkers use everyday walking technique, so anything from lightweight running shoes to racewalking shoes is appropriate for marathon and ultra-marathon training and racing. If you plan on *racewalking* a marathon or longer event, you'll need a good racewalking shoe, or a stable runner's racing flat as described above. Running shoes are available in most athletic shoe stores, but racing flats and racewalking shoes can be more difficult to find. For many years I hosted a frequently updated list of the best shoes for competitive walking on my website, but shoe models change so frequently it always seemed out of date. If you can't find what you're looking for, asking what people are wearing on competitive walking/racewalking message boards and Facebook groups[14] always generates a lot of responses. If you have one, your local running/walking specialty store would be another good source of information on distance walking shoes.

Power walking

Competitive power walkers "run" the gamut from high-speed hikers to actual racewalkers, so shoe needs will vary depending on what technique is used. Those using more "pedestrian" walking technique can usually get by with lighter-weight running training shoes or trainer/racers, while those with technique closer on the spectrum toward racewalking will need running racing flats or actual racewalking shoes.

Nordic walking

Although Decathlon/Newfeel and Inov-8 make sport-specific Nordic walking shoes, most Nordic walkers wear trail running shoes, or just plain old lightweight trainer/racers. Since many races are held off-road, waterproof trail shoes are recommended. In any case, your shoes should be flexible-soled, comfortable, not too heavy, and ideally, waterproof. We'll get to socks later in the chapter, but many Nordic walking instructors recommend waterproof socks, which would obviate the need for waterproof shoes.

Shoe shopping

Picking the right kind of shoe for your form of walking is important, but the fit of the shoe, and how it works with YOUR individual biomechanics, are by far the most critical factors when buying shoes. Don't worry what the Olympic Champion wears, or whether the colors of the shoes match your new walking outfit. The only thing that matters is how the shoes fit on your feet, and fit your

[14] Of course my own "World Class Racewalking" Facebook group at is the best of the bunch! ☺ To join, head to: www.Facebook.com/groups/WorldClassRacewalking/

biomechanics. Shoes that are too tight (or too loose) can cause painful blisters or black toenails, and shoes that aren't designed for your individual needs can lead to ankle, knee or hip injuries. (More on that in Chapter 37!)

Although every foot is different, competitive walkers can be broadly separated into three distinct categories based on how their feet move through the stride cycle. Walkers can be described as:

- **Neutral pronators-** The foot rolls slightly inward as it rolls forward after the heel's initial contact with the ground.
- **Over-pronators-** The foot collapses substantially inward after contacting the ground. Many, although not all, over-pronators have "flat" feet.
- **Supinators-** The foot remains more or less on the outside (lateral) side of the foot from contact to push-off. Also known as "under-pronators," supinators often have high, rigid arches.

Whether you are a pronator, a supinator, or a neutral walker, you can make first contact with the ground in different ways. Most walkers are heel-strikers, though. As the name suggests, heel-strikers contact the ground with the bottom of the heel first, then roll forward toward the ball of the foot and toes before pushing off the ground. Add all of these factors together and shoe selection becomes a bit more complicated than picking a cute shoe that comes in your favorite color.

Ignoring the fact that there are no industry size standards—Nike's size 9 is not the same as Brooks' size 9 or New Balance's size 9—a number of factors can affect the actual size of a shoe, as opposed to the number printed on the box and on the size tag, including the temperature and humidity in the factory where the shoes were made, substitution of different fabrics and threads, individual differences in the way different workers in the factory do their jobs, etc.[15] So it's important that you try on your shoes before buying them, even if you have previously purchased the same brand, model, and size.

Your best bet is to head to a running/walking specialty store rather than a "big box" sporting goods store or online retailer to find your shoes. The best way to find a good pair of walking shoes locally is by Googling "Running shoe store" for your location. (Sorry, despite the fact that many more people walk for fitness than run, there just don't seem to be a whole lot of walking specialty stores out there—yet!) Runner's World online used to have a great store-finder page but it appears they've taken it down.

[15] I once got a pair of shoes in the mail that was *very* tight, even though I had previously worn several pair of the same brand, same model. I imagined a scenario where the factory worker in Vietnam or Indonesia or wherever had a big fight with her husband the night before she made my shoes and she took it out on them, angrily stitching the fabric together way too tightly. ☺

You may be able to find shoes cheaper online, but again, sizing can be highly variable no matter what the number printed on the tag says, so you're better off shopping for shoes in person to ensure a good fit. Wearing the wrong shoes can lead to discomfort and injuries, so let a professional help pick out the right shoes for your form of walking, anatomy, and biomechanics. Some running store employees will assume you're a "dawdler" when you tell them you're a walker. Make sure you get the point across that you're a competitive walker looking for performance shoes or you may get steered to some klunkers that are not appropriate for fast walking. In general, you should select a shoe that is ½ to one full size larger than your street shoe size, but since there are no shoe industry sizing standards, that's a bit of a guess.

If finances allow, it's a good idea to purchase two pairs of shoes and wear them in rotation from workout to workout. It takes about 48 hours for the foam in the shoes' midsoles to fully rebound after being compressed by your footfalls, so if you're walking every day, or nearly so, the midsoles will wear out much faster if you only have one pair to train in. In addition, by wearing different shoes (especially if they are different models/brands) you will strengthen slightly different muscle fibers in your feet and legs through a slightly different range of motion, leaving you less prone to over-use injuries.

Each shoe company (Adidas, Asics, Brooks, New Balance, Nike, Puma, Reebok, Saucony, etc.,) makes versions of three different types of shoes: Cushioned, stability, and motion control. The difference between the categories is the degree of emphasis that each places on biomechanical correction vs. neutrality. The staff at your local running/walking specialty store will be able to help you find which is best for you.

- **Cushioned-** Cushioned shoes are soft and flexible, but provide only minimal biomechanical correction. Cushioned footwear emphasizes enhanced shock dispersion in its midsole and/or outsole, and is designed for supinators.
- **Motion control-** Motion-control shoes are more rigid, straight-lasted shoes with a lot of mid-foot support such as arch supports and dual-density midsoles. These are typically for feet that are very flat or unstable. Over-pronators will tend to wear motion-control shoes.
- **Stability-** These shoes attempt to balance the two approaches to athletic footwear. They have some support or reinforcement, such as a dual-density midsole or some arch support for the mild over-pronator with an arch that has the tendency to compress when bearing weight. Stability shoes are designed for neutral runners and walkers.

Staff in a quality running/walking specialty store will be able to guide you to the right shoes for your needs based on your foot type, body build, goals, experience level, and any biomechanical "quirks" you may have.

Once you've found the perfect shoes, don't go out and walk twenty miles in them on the first day! You'll need to "break them in" a bit, but many people have the wrong idea about what breaking in a new pair of shoes means. With today's high-quality shoes, there shouldn't be a prolonged break-in period. The right shoe should fit comfortably and feel good right out of the box, and depending on how many miles you typically walk every week, they should hold up to several months of training and racing. Typically, training shoes will last for about 500 miles; racing flats somewhat less—about 300-400 miles. In reality, what you need to do is break in your feet (and ankles and knees and hips) to the shoes, not the other way around. If a new pair of shoes is very different from your previous shoes, you will need to strengthen very specific micro-muscle fibers by wearing the shoes a few miles at a time at first, and by being especially careful when doing hills, speed work, or any other intense training in the new shoes.

The cushioning provided by the foam midsole is what provides the most protection, but it can be hard to tell when the midsole of a shoe is shot. The outsoles of most training shoes will long outlive the integrity of the midsole; so don't use the amount of wear on the bottom of the shoe as a guide. Keep track of the mileage you put on your shoes. If you suspect your shoes are past their prime (if the shoes are approaching the 500-mile mark, if you are suddenly feeling some uncharacteristic aches and pains, or if the old shoes are misshapen, or feel hard with very little cushioning or support), bring the old shoes back to the store and compare them to a new pair of the same shoes. If there are pronounced differences between the old shoes and a new pair, it's time to give the dead shoes a rest!

Socks

If you thought picking the right shoes was difficult, you'd better sit down! You may have found the perfect shoes, but they're only as good as the socks you put in them. Make sure you try on new shoes with the socks you'll wear when walking, since socks have a huge influence on the fit of the shoes. Picking the right socks is a bit of a free-for-all. They can be thick or thin; of uniform thickness or padded in certain areas; high, low or in between; single- or double-layered; designed for blister protection, cushioning, support, compression, or all of the above. There are even socks—Inijis—made like gloves for your feet, with separate little pockets for each of your toes. (They kind of freak me out, but you be you, Boo!) Other quality brands include "Balega," "Feetures," "Double Layer," and "Thorlo." All of the major shoe companies make high-quality socks as well.

The one hard and fast rule is that socks should be made of wool (ew!) or a technical moisture-wicking material like "Coolmax" or "Dri-Fit." No cotton! Cotton will absorb perspiration and create friction with the foot, resulting in blisters. Socks should fit snugly so they don't bunch up, which could also cause blisters. I recommend buying socks at your local running/walking specialty store when you try on shoes, and try on a lot of different styles until you find one you can't live without.

Other considerations:

- Be prepared to spend at least 30 minutes trying on shoes.
- Bring your old shoes with you to the store. The wear pattern on your old shoes tells a story about your biomechanics.
- Shop in the late afternoon when your feet are at their largest because your feet will expand during exercise or throughout the day if you are on your feet a lot.
- One foot may be slightly larger than the other, so make sure the salesperson checks the size of both feet. You should be fitted for the larger foot.
- Many running/walking specialty stores will have a treadmill to allow customers to test out the shoes. If not, you should be allowed to walk around the store or on the sidewalk outside of the store. Make sure you do!
- Before you try on any shoes, the salesperson should talk to you about your walking habits and plans in order to guide you to appropriate shoe models.
- No matter what the shoe reviews say, and no matter what the cost, there is never one "Best" shoe out there. The best shoe for you is the shoe that is comfortable and suits your needs.
- If the shoes work for your biomechanics, they fit properly, and they are in your "price-point," then, and only then, are you allowed to pick a pair that matches your walking shorts and top!

Inserts

The "sock liner"—the thin, molded foam insert that comes in your shoe—is probably the cheapest, flimsiest component of your shoe outside of the laces. It offers very little in the way of arch support, pronation control, or impact protection. Most running/walking specialty stores sell higher-quality insoles to replace the flimsy sock-liner. Although probably more important for those silly injury-prone runners than walkers, many walkers do use inserts. If you have shin, knee, or lower back pain when you walk, you might want to consider investing in a pair. Expect to pay between $15 and $50 per pair for your inserts. (The good news is that they will generally last through the life of two to three pairs of walking shoes.)

Orthotics are another option if you have persistent problems that don't clear up with a cheaper insert. Orthotics are custom-made inserts that are molded to your feet by a podiatrist or orthopedist. They can be effective, but at $400 to $600 per pair, I would certainly consider them a last resort only if cheaper, ready-made inserts don't work for you. Incidentally, I've suggested to many walkers who started out as runners that they try walking without their running orthotics.

Many of these converts have found that the lower impact of walking allows them to train and race without the orthotics they couldn't do without as runners.

Clothing

What to wear while walking is difficult to cover in one or two paragraphs. You need to be prepared to train in the sun, rain, heat, cold and even snow, depending on your location and time of year. In addition, men wear different things from women; and there's a huge range in personal preferences. One rule is inviolable, however: Do not train in cotton clothing! As with cotton socks, cotton clothing traps moisture, which can—will!—lead to discomfort and chafing.

In warmer weather, shorts, a sleeveless "singlet" or technical T-shirt made from technical wicking fabrics that pull moisture away from the skin—Coolmax, Thermax and Dry-Fit, for example—and a light-colored hat for sun-protection are your staples. Add a sports bra for women, and sunglasses on sunny days and you're good to go. Alternately, some women prefer walking skirts or "skorts," and Lycra bike-length tights are also popular for both men and women to prevent chafing. If you're not a fan of sunscreen, a lightweight, long-sleeve tech shirt will provide protection from the sun without trapping in too much heat.

Colder weather requires layering, starting with a long-sleeve technical shirt if you don't already wear one in warmer weather. As temperatures fall, add a lightweight vest or jacket made of waterproof material or a technical fabric like Gore-Tex to provide warmth and comfort. Gore-Tex or similar fabrics "breathe," vs. rubberized waterproof jackets that will keep you dry from the outside but will not breathe, causing sweat to collect inside. Technical fabrics cost more, but your comfort is well worth it in the end. An insulating layer between the wicking under-layer and the water/wind-proof outer layer will become necessary as temperatures fall. Fleeces are an excellent choice. Look for long-sleeve shirts and lightweight jackets made of Polartec, Microfleece or Thermafleece.

Do not wear thick sweatshirts or other heavy clothing for training. Several lighter layers will offer more warmth, as well as the option of taking off a layer or two as you warm up during the workout. Layers should include:

- **1st layer-** A close-fitting bottom layer to wick away perspiration;
- **2nd layer-** an insulating layer for cold days that can be removed if you get too warm;
- **3rd layer-** a wind- and waterproof outer layer to protect against the elements. A jacket or vest can be used to protect from wind-chill, rain and/or snow.

A hat or visor can offer both sun and rain protection. In colder temperatures, a winter hat will help to prevent heat loss from the head, but it should be made from fleece or some other technical fabric, which will be lighter and stay drier than cotton or wool. Gloves or mittens are also a must in very cold temperatures. In cold weather, full-length tights or shorter bicycle-length tights are popular choices to keep the legs warm. Looser-fitting "running" pants—there must be a better name!—are another excellent choice for comfort and warmth. Men generally wear full-length pants, while capri-length pants are popular with many women.

Sports bras provide much better support than "fashion" bras, and are made of technical fabrics to wick perspiration away. Most running/walking specialty stores, and many sporting goods stores, will have a large selection of sports bras from which to choose. Try on two or three different bras to ensure a good fit.

Sweatshirts and sweat pants may keep you warm before and after workouts, but don't train in them since they are usually made of cotton, which will not breathe. Bring a change of clothing for after training sessions so you have something dry to change into, even if it's a warm day. It's not uncommon for training groups to enjoy coffee or breakfast together after a workout, and it's easy to get chilled in wet clothing. In any case, dress as if it's 10 to 15 degrees warmer than the actual temperature. If you're comfortably warm at the start of the workout, you'll be roasting a mile or two in. If you do need to take off a layer, long-sleeved sweatshirts or jackets can be easily tied around your waist. Alternately, I like to train on loop courses, so the extra layer can be dropped off at the completion of a short first warm-up loop.

Sunscreen and Body Glide

Although I'm not a fan of slathering goopy stuff on my body, sunscreen is critical to prevent sun-damaged skin, and eventual skin cancers. Dermatologists recommend applying sunscreen an hour before you head outside to allow it to absorb into your skin, and to reapply every hour during your workout. Look for an SPF of at least 30, but beyond that there is little practical difference between a 30, a 50 and a 100+ sunscreen. Nowadays there are of course the traditional lotions, but also gel and even powdered sunscreens. I never thought I would live long enough to worry about skin cancer (my father died of a heart attack at 46) but as I get older and the "age spots" accumulate, I'm getting more diligent. My town has installed free sunscreen dispensers at the beaches where I train, so I don't have the "I forgot my sunscreen" excuse anymore. ☺

Despite my spotty history with sunscreen, I have always been very diligent about lip balm. Without it, the combination of sun damage and dehydration from a long workout in the blazing sun, or alternately, winter windburn, can really shred your lips. As with sunscreen, I try to find sticks with an SPF of 30 or higher and I keep them everywhere—in the car, in gym bags, in my pockets, so I'm always able to find one when I need it.

Body Glide is like an antiperspirant stick that contains moisturizers to protect the skin from chafing. They're popular, and by all accounts they work well, but I'm old... I started training and competing long before Body Glide came out and I discovered early on that if I take a shower before my long workouts and apply hair conditioner to areas susceptible to chafing, then rinse, it prevents chafing. (I know, I'm weird…) But go ahead, do what your normal friends do, use Body Glide. Apparently there's even a version with sunscreen.

So there you have it. Shoes, socks, and some weather-appropriate clothing and you're good to go! One of the great things about training for competitive walking is that you can do it without a great deal of expensive equipment. That said, don't scrimp on what you do need! A few dollars spent today on quality equipment can save you from days off from training and dollars spent on doctors down the road. When you "dress for success," you'll be able to handle anything Mother Nature throws at you!

Now that we've gone over the weather outside, next up: a few words on what's going on *inside* your body when you walk!

CHAPTER 4: BASICS OF ENDURANCE PHYSIOLOGY

The human body is an amazing machine; a collection of extremely efficient physiological systems capable of doing amazing things if properly trained to do them. Our ability to adapt to our environment, and to the stresses we impose upon ourselves through our daily training, are the reasons we're able to transform ourselves from sedentary couch potatoes into competitive endurance athletes. During one of my training camps in Mexico my coach wrote in my training log *para derrotar a tu enemigo, debes conocer a tu enemigo*—"to defeat your enemy, you must know your enemy." Fatigue is the enemy of any endurance athlete. Knowing what causes it, and knowing something about all of these incredible physiological systems will help you to understand why I'll be asking you to do the different kinds of workouts that are laid out in the training schedules in Section III.

Gas, ethanol, diesel, or electric?

Our bodies are a lot like hybrid cars that can run on a number of different fuel systems. But instead of using batteries, gas, or diesel fuel, our bodies create energy through the aerobic (with oxygen) combustion of fats, carbohydrates, and a very small amount of protein when walking slowly; aerobic, plus some anaerobic (without oxygen), combustion of carbohydrates when walking faster; and through the direct utilization of adenosine triphosphate (ATP) and phosphocreatine when sprinting.

Are we Motaurs?

We can derive energy from other sources, including protein, and even alcohol, but their contribution is negligible in all but the most extreme situations. For example, under normal conditions we only get about 5% of our energy from protein. The remaining 95% of our energy comes from a mix of fats and carbohydrates; the percentage of each is determined by the amount of oxygen that we can supply to the muscles, and the muscles' ability to utilize that oxygen. That's not to say protein isn't important! Protein is critical for repairing the daily damage we do to our muscles and other tissues, and also it kick-starts the Krebs cycle, which is the major source of energy in living organisms, from bacteria to baboons—not to mention competitive walkers! Protein, metabolism can rise well beyond the usual ~5% of the "fuel mix" during long races where glycogen (intra-muscular carbohydrate) can become depleted, in which case muscle protein is catabolized for energy—something to be avoided at all cost! To quote Jeff Goldblum in Jurassic Park, "Life, uh, finds a way." Your body will always find a way to get the job done. You *can* finish a marathon without proper training and fueling, but it'll tear your muscles up as ferociously as the T-rex in the movie that ate Gennaro the lawyer while he was cowering on the toilet.

Like the aforementioned hybrid car, our bodies tend to utilize the most efficient system available under the prevailing operating conditions. Since some fuels are more efficient, more plentiful in the body, or more readily utilized than others, our muscles must "decide" which system to emphasize under a variety of different conditions—these conditions primarily being the duration and the pace of the workout or race, but also the internal conditions dictated by the fuels that have been supplied to the body through dietary intake. Want to give a low-carb Keto diet a try? Go ahead, but don't blame me if your calves start to feel like T-rex chew toys eighteen miles into your next marathon...

Athletes undergoing lactate threshold testing at a World Class Racewalking training camp.

Pros and cons

Each of our bodies' energy systems have advantages and disadvantages: Fat is a great fuel source because it's "clean burning,"[16] very energy-dense, and it exists in the body in abundant quantities. But since fat can only be burned in the

[16] Aerobic fat metabolism results in the release of ATP, which ultimately fuels muscle contractions; carbon dioxide, which is exhaled; and water. Carbohydrate metabolism releases the same innocuous byproducts, but also lactic acid.

presence of both oxygen and glycogen, it can only be used effectively as a "low-speed" fuel during easy workouts or long, relatively slow races.

Carbohydrates (aka "carbs") are another great fuel source, but since we can only store a limited supply of them in our bodies, carbs can be depleted within as little as 90 minutes of hard work. Glycolysis, the combustion of carbohydrates for energy, is "bad" for another reason: It's your body's equivalent of a diesel engine—a reliable energy system under a variety of operating conditions, but when oxygen is limited, it's a very "dirty" fuel. Instead of spewing out smog, however, your anaerobic glycolysis "engine" spits out buckets of nasty lactic acid. The faster you walk, the more lactic acid you produce and accumulate in your blood and muscles. Although chemically, lactic acid is really just incompletely burned carbohydrate and is therefore a useful fuel for the muscles, without sufficient oxygen to break it down, lactate slows down the metabolic enzyme activity within the muscles preventing them from contracting rapidly. The higher the lactic acid levels, the harder it is for the muscles to contract. Your *lactate threshold* or *anaerobic threshold* is the highest walking intensity at which your body can still produce energy and muscular contractions aerobically, without accumulating fatiguing levels of lactic acid. Your lactate threshold can be determined by testing in an exercise physiology lab, or with your own portable lactate analyzer if you're a nerd like me. (See Chapter 38 for more on lactate threshold testing.)

It's all about oxygen

Ultimately, the availability of oxygen will dictate how energy is produced, and how "clean" the combustion will be. In any race longer than about 3,000 meters (1.86 miles), most of the energy required to produce muscle contractions will be created aerobically, so the bulk of your training for these races should be easy, aerobic distance work. Too much speed work, or too many hard, rather than easy, miles on the roads will teach the muscles to rely on anaerobic glycolysis, resulting in excess lactate production when racing—not a good scenario. To very much over-simplify things, there are three types of skeletal muscles fibers: Type IA "slow twitch" fibers, Type IIB "fast twitch" fibers, and Type IIA fibers which are more or less hybrid fibers somewhere between fast-twitch and slow-twitch fibers. Type IA slow-twitch fibers are "oxidative" fibers that burn fat, combined with oxygen, to create energy; Type IIB fast-twitch fibers are "glycolytic" fibers that burn glycogen anaerobically to produce energy; and Type IIA fibers can be trained to work like oxidative or glycolytic fibers, depending on how you train, and to some extent, your diet. The name "slow twitch" sounds like a negative, but as an endurance athlete, you want to have lots of slow twitch fibers. That's because slow-twitch fibers burn fat, not carbs, so they don't produce fatiguing lactic acid. These are your endurance fibers. Fast twitch fibers, on the other hand, spit out lactic acid. Yes, they do contract more quickly and more powerfully than slow-twitch fibers, so if you're a 100-meter sprinter or weightlifter you want lots of them. But since they are anaerobic/glycolytic fibers they create lots of lactic acid. Train those convertible Type IIB fibers to work glycolytically rather than oxidatively by doing lots and lots of speed work and not enough mileage, and you'll become a fantastic 400-meter sprint walker. (Too bad 400-meter sprint races for walkers don't exist...)

But back to oxygen... As your walking speed increases, so does your oxygen uptake, or $\dot{V}O_2$ (V is for Volume, O_2 for oxygen, and the little dot over the V means that it's a rate, in this case, per minute). $\dot{V}O_2$max is a measure of the maximum amount of oxygen that your lungs can take in and send to the muscles to be consumed to help produce energy. After using inhaled oxygen to help burn fats and carbohydrates, carbon dioxide is released and exhaled as a by-product. Measuring the ratio of exhaled carbon dioxide to oxygen is the only *direct* way to determine which systems are producing energy, but the equipment is very bulky so the tests can only be performed by doctors or exercise physiologists in a laboratory setting. That involves getting on a treadmill while you're hooked up to what looks like a cross between a welder's helmet and Mom's old Electrolux vacuum cleaner—not the kind of thing you'd want to wear during your next 5k. But there are indirect methods of monitoring your energy consumption, the easiest and most readily available being heart rate monitoring.

The heart of the matter

All that inhaled oxygen has to get to the working muscles somehow, and it does so bonded to hemoglobin in the blood and pumped throughout the body by the heart. As the oxygen demand of the muscles increases, heart rate also increases—in lock-step with the increase in your oxygen consumption. Heart rate, then, is a very reliable—albeit indirect—indicator of oxygen use. That's why the Neanderthals (back in the 1960s and '70s) used to stop to take their pulse during rest breaks in their interval workouts. We'll talk more about heart-rate-based training later, but for now the important thing to remember is that heart rate can tell you which systems are producing energy at any particular pace.

Your lactate threshold, $\dot{V}O_2$ max, and your walking *economy*—the percentage of your $\dot{V}O_2$ max that you can maintain during a workout or race without accumulating exhausting amounts of lactic acid—determine, for the most part, how well you can perform in an endurance event like competitive walking. Luckily, these variables, as well as your overall endurance, can be improved with the right kinds of training.

The lean, mean walkin' machine

Obviously there's a lot going on "inside" when you train or race. The muscles need to have lots of enzymatically active mitochondria and lots of oxygen to turn food into energy aerobically. If they don't get enough oxygen the muscles will have to produce energy anaerobically and they'll become polluted with contraction-inhibiting lactic acid. So the lungs have to be able to draw in lots of oxygen, the heart has to be able to pump that oxygen, bonded to hemoglobin within the blood, throughout the body, and the circulatory system has to have lots of dense capillary beds developed to get that oxygen-rich blood into the working muscles. Finally, the neuromuscular system must be highly coordinated so that you can walk with fast, economical (oxygen-sparing) technique. All of these systems have to be working efficiently for you to be truly "race ready." Hard to believe all that is going on inside your body when "all you're doing" is walking… ☺

The next chapter will discuss proper nutrition to fuel the machine, and Section III will go into great detail on the different kinds of workouts that can be used to train each of your various energy systems, and how to put these workouts together into training schedules appropriate for whichever distance, or combination of distances, you choose to train for.

CHAPTER 5: NUTRITION AND HYDRATION

What to eat and drink before, during, and after walking has a big influence on how you'll perform, both in training and on race day. The specifics of what you should ingest depend on a number of factors. The intensity and duration of the exercise, your body mass, sex, GI tolerance, the weather, your own individual sweat rate, and personal preference all play a role. With so many variables to consider, it can be difficult to figure out the best fueling plan for your individual situation, and it may involve a lot of trial and error. This is not a nutrition book, and every athlete has different needs and preferences,[17] but this chapter should give you a good starting point to help you sort out what to eat and drink to improve your walking performance.

As outlined in the previous chapter, when we walk we burn fuel—for the most part fats and carbohydrates, but also some protein. Fat is a great fuel source. It's very energy-dense—nine calories per gram compared to only four calories per gram for carbs or protein. Fat is also a "clean-burning" fuel source. Metabolizing fat results in the creation of energy (ATP), with water (H_2O), and carbon dioxide (CO_2) as byproducts. Energy is what we're looking for from our food; H_2O is used by the body or exhaled as water vapor; and CO_2 is also exhaled. Therefore, there are no nasty byproducts left hanging around to foul up the works after burning fat as a fuel. The only downside to burning fat is that you need a lot of oxygen to burn it, and oxygen is a limited (and limiting!) resource.

Like fats, carbohydrates are another great fuel source. Carbohydrates aren't as energy-dense as fat, but they are very "versatile." You can burn carbs whether training slow or fast, going long or short. The only problem with carbs is that when you're walking fast, you produce some energy anaerobically (without oxygen), and this results in the production of lactic acid by your fast-twitch muscle fibers. Lactic acid is actually a good fuel source if there's enough oxygen in the body to metabolize it, but if you don't have enough oxygen to break it down, lactic acid builds up in the muscles and inhibits their ability to contract forcefully. So carbs allow you to perform at a high intensity, but you'll eventually fatigue if you haven't trained your body to supply the muscles with sufficient oxygen to burn them aerobically.

Protein normally only supplies about 2-5% of our energy while exercising, but that doesn't mean it isn't important. Protein helps rebuild damaged muscles, ligaments, tendons, blood cells,

[17] For example, throughout most of my career I was *a bit* of a nutritional atheist. I subscribed to Don Kardong's precept that "there's no such thing as a bad carbohydrate" and John L. Parker's mantra: "If the furnace was hot enough, anything would burn, even Big Macs." I'd like to say that at age 55 I've changed, but with four young kids now, Fruit Loops are still on my training table.

and blood vessels caused by training and racing. The use of protein as a fuel source can rise well above 5% when caloric intake isn't sufficient to fuel exercise, but don't let that happen! You need to eat, and eat carbs, to perform. Unless ALL of your training is at a very easy aerobic pace, you'll need to take on a reasonably high level of carbs in order to create energy without relying on protein as a fuel. If you've ever done a long, hard workout or race without taking in enough carbs, and your clothes reeked of ammonia afterward, congratulations! You've experienced *catabolysis*. The human body is a very resourceful machine. If there is no other readily available fuel source, it can use protein for energy. Unfortunately, we don't *store* protein in our bodies; we *make* our bodies out of protein! If you force your body to use protein as a fuel source because you're not taking in enough carbohydrates (I'm looking at you, "keto" diets!) you'll end up breaking down your muscles for energy rather than building them up. At my clinics I talk about a hunter waiting out a snowstorm in a log cabin. It's really cozy inside, so he doesn't want to go out to the woodshed in the middle of the blizzard to get more logs for the fire. He *could* get more wood by staying inside and chopping up the log walls of the cabin for firewood. It'll work—for a while! But eventually he'll have a cabin full of holes that won't keep the cold wind and snow out. The same thing applies to exercising without taking in enough carbs. It'll work. For a while…

Of the three main fuel sources outlined above, carbohydrates are the primary fuel source for endurance athletes. But because glycolysis (the breakdown of carbohydrates for fuel) can result in excess lactate production, and because there is a limit to how much carbohydrate you can ingest and store, you actually want to train your body to burn fat more readily. Your training, especially the long days, will teach your muscles to burn fat preferentially. Burning fat (mainly by the slow-twitch muscle fibers) doesn't result in lactic acid production, and since the human body is really, really good at storing fat(!), you certainly won't run out of it. Conversely, carbohydrates are not very easily stored. Athletes can, under normal circumstances, only store about 2,000 to 2,500 calories worth of carbs, so it's important to eat a relatively high-carb diet, and when training and racing, to supplement with sports drinks, energy gels[18] and other carb sources.

The pace that you walk will dictate what type, and how much, fuel you are burning. At lower intensities your body is very effective at utilizing its plentiful fat stores for fuel. At higher intensities—think 10k race pace or faster—you can't take in enough oxygen to burn much fat for fuel so you'll rely a lot more on carbohydrates. If you are working hard, you'll burn between 600 and 1,200 calories per hour, so if the activity is greater than about 90 minutes in duration, you can run the risk of carbohydrate-depletion. Carb-depletion may also occur if you're not careful about replenishing carbs day to day after each workout.

---

[18] Energy gels are a conveniently packaged source of concentrated carbohydrates about the consistency of honey. They are a great shot of rocket fuel that can really wake up the body and mind if you are getting carb-depleted, but like everything else, you must try them in training first!

Long, easy walks, and later in the season the "not-so-easy" long days, are the best workouts for teaching the muscles to recruit the slow twitch fibers that burn fat rather than carbs. It sounds contradictory, but if you want to walk fast 5ks, 10ks, half-marathons, etc., you need a lot of slow-twitch fibers. But even though you do want to burn fat as a fuel, you don't need to "fat load"! A traditional endurance athlete's diet will supply all the fat you need to get through your everyday training and racing, as long as your total caloric intake is sufficient. Your training, however, is only half of the story! Your diet, too, will have a profound effect on which fuels you burn. When training and racing at relatively low intensities (for example, during activities lasting longer than 90 minutes) ingesting a lower-carb diet, especially just before your long days, can teach your body to burn fat preferentially over carbs. This has the effect of sparing your limited carb stores late in the workout or race. But if you don't take in enough carbs, or train/race at too high of an intensity, you'll crash/bonk your workouts or races. Balance…

This brings us back to catabolysis. I realize ketogenic ("keto") diets are currently popular, and they may work reasonably well for a while if your main goal is weight loss and you're not doing any hard training, but they can be very damaging when you jack up the intensity. That's not to say there's no place in endurance training for keto. When done properly[19] a "cyclic," or better yet, a "targeted" ketogenic diet, can be effective. Ketogenic diets usually allow only 30 to 50 grams of carbs (120 to 200 calories) per day, combined with a high fat intake. The theory behind these diets is that this extremely low carb intake helps you to achieve ketosis, a process where ketones—a byproduct of fat metabolism produced in the liver—become the main source of energy for the body and brain. There are several versions of the keto diet, including:

- **Standard ketogenic diet-** This is an extremely low-carb, moderate-protein, high-fat diet. It typically contains 75% fat, 20% protein and 5% carbs. I would steer clear of a straight keto diet if your goal is improved athletic performance.
- **Cyclical ketogenic diet-** This diet involves periods of higher-carb "refeeds," such as five keto days followed by two high-carb days. Better, but you'll probably only have one or two decent workouts in that five-day period.
- **Targeted ketogenic diet-** This diet allows you to add carbs, usually around periods of intense exercise or workouts. Bingo! But this is basically not a keto diet… ☺ The idea is to go keto when you're doing easy training but then take in carbs before longer and harder workouts.

In short, I'm not *completely* against keto diets, if done properly, especially if your primary goal is short-term weight loss, not athletic performance. Be sure to get in enough carbs whenever you're

[19] Very few people do it properly! ☺

training at intensities higher than an easy recovery pace, though. I do think it's a good thing to teach your body to burn fats more readily, but everything in moderation! Starving yourself, or at least starving yourself of carbs, is not a healthy or sustainable diet regimen for an endurance athlete. The "Supernova" study at the Australian Institute of Sport (AIS) is instructive. Supernova set out to prove that an HFLC—High Fat, Low Carb—diet could make the body much better at burning fat as a fuel. Twenty-six elite racewalkers from around the world took part in a training camp at AIS where for twenty-five days some of the athletes—the control group—trained on a normal athletic (high carb intake) diet while the rest, according to Canadian 50k walker Evan Dunfee, basically "got used to eating sticks of butter." ☺ The study did prove that the "butter eaters" got better at burning fat for fuel, but it also showed that their training and race performance suffered, while the pasta-and-potato-eating control group enjoyed improved performance. It was actually kind of fun to follow the walkers on Twitter and Instagam during the study. It became very apparent which athletes were on the HFLC diet and which were eating carbs, as the carb-starved walkers' posts became progressively more sarcastic and angry over the course of the study! Obviously the choice is yours, but I'm going with pasta, potatoes, and PopTarts!

Fluids

Dehydration can adversely affect muscle strength, endurance and coordination, and can lead to cramps, heat exhaustion and heat stroke. Even a 2-3% loss in body weight due to fluid loss can decrease endurance performance by 20% or more. So how do you know how much to drink when everybody sweats at different rates? There are formulas for determining how much the "average" person should drink on a daily basis and during training—eight ounces every fifteen minutes, for example—but how do you know if you're "average"? You can find out how much fluid you lose during training by performing a "sweat-rate test." Weigh yourself before a workout—for example, a steady one-hour walk on a hot, humid day—then again afterward. The weight loss in ounces will roughly correspond to the amount of sweat lost in fluid ounces during the workout. (Don't forget to account for the weight of anything ingested during the workout. Keep track of how much you drank in ounces, and subtract that out.) One fluid ounce of water actually weighs a bit more than one ounce (1.04 ounces, to be exact), so if you lost a pound during the workout, you've actually only lost about 15.34 fluid ounces of sweat, but again, keep it simple and just round up to sixteen.[20] Try to keep pace with your fluid intake during the workout. It's not necessary to replace every single ounce of fluid lost on the go, but try to not lose more than a pound or two. Losing more than 1% of your body mass in sweat will begin to hurt your performance, which means 1.5 lbs. or

[20] Come to think of it, it's slightly more complicated than that, since sweat is not just water, but water with a small amount of salts, electrolytes, ammonia, urea and even some sugar (glucose). To further complicate matters, the 1.04 ounce figure is assuming a standard temperature of 62 degrees Fahrenheit, but if your sweat is coming out at 62 degrees F, you're probably recently deceased, which would make it exceedingly difficult to perform complicated math problems. Or walk, for that matter.

about 24 fluid ounces for a 150 lb. person. Interestingly, carbohydrate depletion and dehydration are closely linked. Athletes store almost three grams of water with every gram of glycogen in the muscles, so when carbs run low, dehydration isn't far behind.

Electrolytes

Mineral and electrolyte imbalances are another cause of impaired endurance performance. Sodium (Na^+), potassium (K^+), calcium (Ca^{2+}), and magnesium, (Mg^{2+}) are the most important electrolytes to keep your digestive, cardiac, muscular and nervous systems functioning well. Chloride (Cl^-), phosphate (PO_4^{2-}), bicarbonate (HCO_3^-), and sulfate (SO_4^{2-}) play a lesser role, but are still important. Most people are aware that electrolyte imbalances can cause muscle cramps, but other symptoms can include muscle spasms, dizziness, fatigue, nausea, constipation, dark urine, decreased urine output, dry mouth and bad breath, dry skin, muscle weakness, and stiff and achy joints.

Sport drinks and gels

Sports drinks and energy gels are designed to replenish what you lose through metabolism and sweat while exercising. You propel yourself forward with muscle contractions. These muscle contractions burn up your limited carb stores, and while doing so, create lots of heat. To prevent frying your own brain, your body needs a way to dissipate that heat. To do so, the capillaries near the surface of the skin dilate to allow more blood to flow just below the surface of the skin. That blood is cooled by evaporating sweat and then it's pumped to the muscles and other organs to cool them off. Problem is, there's a limited amount of carbohydrate to fuel the muscle contractions, a limited amount of fluids to create the sweat, and a limited amount of electrolytes dissolved in that sweat. All of these limited resources need to be replenished. Ingesting sport drinks is a good way to stave off carbohydrate depletion, electrolyte imbalances, and of course dehydration. The conditions you're training under (heat, humidity), the duration of the workout, your diet, and your own physiology will dictate what kind of supplementation will work best for you. In cooler weather, especially if you're not a heavy sweater, you'll probably gravitate more towards replenishing carbs than fluids and electrolytes. If that's the case, think energy gels or traditional sports drinks. Most of the more common sport drinks (Gatorade Sport, Powerade, etc.) provide about 15 grams of carbohydrate (60 calories) per eight-ounce serving, and most gels contain about 22 to 27 grams of carbs (88-108 calories). If it's hot and humid, especially if you're a heavy sweater, you'll probably need more fluid and electrolyte replacement than carbs. Sport drinks like Nuun focus on electrolytes, not carbs, and only contain one gram of carbs (four calories) per eight-ounce serving. There are also electrolyte tablets (Endurox) that are taken with water if you don't want any carbs/calories at all.

Keep a training/diet log

Keeping a training log in which you record your mileage, paces, heart rates, etc., is critical to help you find out what kinds of workouts you should be doing, but it can be even more important if you have any dietary issues, or need to tweak your fueling/hydration regimen. Science has some of the answers, but everybody is different, so there will always be some trial and error before you'll be able to find out exactly what works best for you. Write down everything you eat and drink the night before, morning of, and during training. Eventually you'll be able to tease out patterns that will elucidate what works, and what foods and drinks may cause problems. I used to write down any big "discoveries" I made during the year by noting these patterns on the last page of my training log, where they were easy to find and refer back to. One of the most important things to track and record is your morning body weight. Noting changes in body weight is a good way to monitor both dehydration and carb depletion. If you wake up three pounds lighter the morning after a long workout, it is not cause for celebration! Most of the weight loss is from water and carb-depletion, not fat loss. Monitor your fluid intake and eat sufficient carbs to ensure you have the fuels you need to get through your workouts.

Important points:

- **Everybody is different!** (Some more different than others...) What may work for other athletes may spell disaster for you. You need to find what works best for your body in training and stick with what works and avoid what doesn't.
- **Mamma was right-** Common sense foods, like plenty of fruits and vegetables, lean meats, and healthy grains, etc., are the way to go. Be sure to steer away from fad diets. You are an endurance athlete! You will not make it through your workouts on low-carb diets. Endurance athletes need carbs!
- **Water is really, really important-** (In moderation...) The human body is about two-thirds water. If you get dehydrated, it won't function properly. Having said that, there's a huge amount of variability in how much fluid different people need. You should aim to finish your workouts close to the same weight as when you started the workout. If you're three pounds lighter after a workout (and didn't use the bathroom), you've lost through sweat almost a quart and a half of water. ("Almost" because you have actually lost a small amount of weight by burning carbs and fat as fuel.)
- **Don't overdo it!** Having said all that, over-hydration is arguably more dangerous than under-hydration. Drinking too much water (weighing more after a workout than before) can cause dilution of your body's sodium, potassium, magnesium, and other electrolyte stores, which, in extreme cases, can cause disorientation, vomiting, and ultimately cerebral edema and death. You have to really go overboard to get this far, like drinking gallons of

water, but every year one or two people die in marathons by drinking literally gallons of water over the course of the race. Moderation...

- **The most important meal of the day...** You should eat a light breakfast two to four hours before training, aiming for a high percentage of carbohydrates and a total of about 100 to 150 calories for each hour of time that the meal takes place before the workout. Huh? If the meal is two hours before the workout or race, aim for 200 to 300 calories, if three hours before, 300-450 calories, if four hours before… what the Hell, why not go for that Big Mac? (Kidding!) (Kind of…) ☺
- **Fuel on the go!** For workouts over 60 to 90 minutes in duration, take in some carbs starting about 30 minutes into the workout. Sports drinks or energy gels are good sources. A good rule of thumb is to ingest approximately 100 calories every 20-30 minutes on the go, but this is a highly individual thing. Although all athletes will burn somewhere around 110 +/- calories per mile, faster walkers and racewalkers will burn considerably more calories per minute because they are completing those miles faster. Walking at 20 minutes/mile will burn about 330 calories per hour; racewalking at ten-minutes/mile about 660 calories per hour; and at eight minutes/mile will burn 880 calories per hour. Therefore, it will be more necessary for faster walkers and racewalkers to replenish carbs than it will be for slower walkers since the slower walkers will be utilizing a higher percentage of fat, and they will be burning these calories at a slower rate than racewalkers. In other words, five miles of walking will burn about as many calories as five miles of racewalking, or even five miles of running,[21] but the runner or racewalker may be finished in 30 to 45 minutes while the slower walker may be out there for 90 minutes or more.
- **Refuel!** Your muscles are able to store energy much more readily immediately following a workout. Ingesting some carbohydrates within 15 minutes of finishing the workout will speed your recovery. Drink a sports drink or eat an energy bar or gel as soon as you're finished, while stretching. Within two hours, eat a more substantial meal with a mix of carbs and protein.
- **Get used to it!** You should use the sports drink of your choice, but that choice should be the same choice as the choice of the race director for your upcoming event. ☺ The same goes for energy gels. You never want to try a new sports drink or gel on race day, so always check the race website for the event's drink and gel sponsors and secure a supply for yourself to test them out in training.

---

[21] This is ignoring basal metabolic rate (BMR), which is actually REALLY important! Sleeping burns about 70 calories per hour, so if you walk *really* slowly—one mile per hour—that 110 calories you burn is only about 40 calories more than you would have burned at rest; at two miles per hour you'll burn about 220 calories per hour, which is 150 more than BMR; at three miles per hour you'll burn about 330 calories, which is 260 more than at rest. Ergo, walking at 1mph only burns about 40 more than BMR, at 2mph each mile burns about 75 more than BMR, at 3mph it's about 87 more, at 4mph it's 93 more, at 5mph it's 98 more and at 6mph it's 99 more.

Things to avoid

No matter what time of day you train, keep these points in mind:

- Avoid overeating shortly before exercising;
- Avoid sugary foods—including gels and overly sweet sport drinks—within one hour of workouts or races to prevent "bonking." (Bonking is an insulin-induced blood sugar crash.) It's okay to start taking these energy sources on the fly, once you're 30 to 45 minutes into the workout, just avoid them in the window between 60 minutes and five minutes before the start of the race or workout;
- Avoid carbonated beverages when exercising since they may cause gas and related discomfort.

Sports nutrition is a huge topic. I have lots of really thick books on my shelf and I've taken semester-long masters-level courses on the subject. With the huge range of individual variation among walkers, and the different requirements for different race distances, everybody has different needs. I can't possibly cover everything in a couple of pages, so consider this chapter a brief introduction. I always found that if I trained a lot I could eat a lot and by doing so I always had enough of what I needed. Now, older and training less, I have to be a bit more careful, but I'm still not one to count calories or get caught up in the latest fad. Eat what makes you happy (in moderation!), stay hydrated, don't drink too much alcohol or eat too much sugar, and everything should work out fine. Of course I'm generalizing.... And of course all bets are off if you've unwisely decided to get into ultra-racing! ☺ I'll cover more on fueling for 100-milers and such in Chapter 22; otherwise, let's move on to where to train!

CHAPTER 6: WHERE TO TRAIN

Most competitive walking races are held on roads or tracks, but some races, especially longer races, are contested as trail races. Whatever the venue, it's important to train on similar surfaces and topography—think hills—to what you'll be traversing during your target competition. Failing to train under similar conditions to what you'll experience on race day can lead to foot and lower leg injuries, and even larger muscle strains in the case of races on hills. Hamstrings, glutes, and hip-flexors, in particular, can be strained when walking uphill, while shins, quadriceps and knees can take a beating on the downhill sections. It's not necessary to train every day on the roads for an upcoming road race or every day on a track for an upcoming track race, but you certainly should try to do the majority of your training on surfaces similar to those on which you will be racing.

Tracks

Tracks are terrific training "safe spaces" for many competitive walkers. In a busy, traffic-filled world, they are quiet oases where you will be surrounded by like-minded individuals without having to worry about being hit by a bus or bicycle while walking. Although asphalt, cinder, and compacted dirt or sand tracks still exist, most modern ovals are made of a forgiving rubber surface. "Tartan" and "Mondo" are the most popular brand names of the rubber surface, so any modern rubber tracks are often referred to generically by these names. The standard distances are 200-meters (approximately ⅛ mile) for most indoor tracks and 400-meters (approximately ¼ mile) for

Tracks are a great option when you're looking for a flat place to train—usually!

most outdoor tracks. Exceptions would be smaller tracks (on the order of 12 to 20 laps to the mile) in some athletic clubs, and as large as 450 meters around in speed-skating ovals (Pettit Ice Center in Milwaukee, Wisconsin, and the Olympic Oval in Kearns, Utah, for example).[22] Tracks are perfect sites for speed workouts where an exact, known distance is desired. 2½ times around lane one on a standard outdoor track is exactly 1,000 meters or one kilometer. English distances are a bit trickier, but due to geometry (the further away from the turn you are the longer you'll have to walk) and since four laps is so close to a mile (one mile is 1,609.3 meters) unless you're very careful to walk on the inside of lane one around the turns, four laps is pretty close to one mile.

Track "intervals" are a great way to work on high-end speed for shorter races (1,500m to 5,000m). Interval sessions are fast workouts broken up by short rest intervals. The duration of the speed repetitions ("reps") and the duration of the rest intervals will vary depending on the distance of the race for which you are training, the phase of training you're in, and your experience level, among other factors. Although intervals are a key component of "sprint" training for 1,500m to 5k walkers, the high-end speed of your reps will trickle down to your workout paces for longer races, so intervals can be a key component of half-marathon and marathon training, as well. By doing short, fast 200m or 400m repetitions with rest breaks of 1:00 to 2:00 minutes you'll improve your speed at the upper end, but that improved speed will boost your longer interval workout paces, like kilometer or mile repeats, making them faster.

A bit about track etiquette... The innermost lane of a track is the accurately measured 400 meters (or 200 meters indoors). If you're doing timed intervals, on most tracks you should be able to do them on the innermost lane. However… Some tracks reserve use of the first lane, and sometimes as many as the first four lanes, for the track team only, to limit wear and tear of the (expensive!) track surface. If that's the case, you may be out of luck, but if such rules aren't posted, and some random runner tries to kick you out of lane one because you're "just a walker," then feel free to stand your ground. If you're NOT doing timed intervals, then courtesy dictates you use the outer lanes for warm-ups, cool-downs, and random easy mileage. The convention for track races is to run or walk in a counter-clockwise direction, so unless posted otherwise, you should walk counter-clockwise, especially on the innermost lanes. Having said that, when you're alone on the track—or at least alone in your lane—it's not a bad idea to switch directions from time to time to prevent overuse injuries, especially on indoor tracks which have tighter turns than larger outdoor tracks. For the same reason, many tracks, especially indoor tracks, will enforce alternating directions (clockwise on even-numbered days and counter-clockwise on odd-numbered days, for example). Always obey these local conventions lest you make me, or your coach, look bad. ☺

---

[22] It's no picnic trying to hold a racewalking clinic on one of these tracks, which I've done several times at both the Pettit Center in Wisconsin and the Olympic Oval in Utah. The skating rinks covering the infield make it impossible to cut across from one side of the track to the other and the high walls of the hockey rink block views, so at both clinics I would keep losing people! In addition, the extra-large track size means it takes a lot longer for people to make their way around. It's definitely worth the trouble though, to be protected from the elements year-round! ☺

Roads/bike paths:

I've always been a stickler for accuracy on my training courses. For years I've owned a surveyor's wheel and have measured and marked courses anywhere that I've lived for more than a week or two. There are orange dots and cryptic markings on roads, in parks, and on bike paths in probably half the states in the US attributable to me, my wheel, and my marking-paint can. Things have gotten easier with the advent of mapping programs and apps like the mapmywalk.com site and app, usatf.org/routes, and the Charity Miles app, as well as the now ubiquitous watches with GPS capability and/or connectivity to inertial sensor "shoe pods" that measure speed and distance. Now walkers can go just about anywhere and know to a high degree of accuracy their walking speed and distance covered.

For my own purposes (and yes, I agree that there is something wrong with me...) the portable units have historically not been accurate enough. 99% accurate, to me, means 1% inaccurate, or up to ten meters off, plus or minus, per kilometer, or 52.8 feet per mile. I pride myself on being able to walk blind within two seconds per kilometer of my desired pace. That means my own internal sense of pace has always been more accurate than that of my GPS, so I was never very happy with the results when using one. Things have gotten MUCH better over the years. Measurements on my wrist-worn GPS/heart monitor (I use a Polar Vantage M), mapping web sites, and my old measuring wheel, are now all within a meter or two per kilometer or 99.8% accurate or better.

For courses that I'll be using repeatedly over time, I'll rough out the course on Mapmywalk.com or usatf.org/routes using their aerial maps. The programs have street map, topographic map, terrain view, satellite view and hybrid features. I use the hybrid view, which superimposes street names on top of a satellite view. The detail is fine enough so that individual trees, driveways, fire hydrants, and other landmarks can be identified on the map and then located on the course itself. With map in hand I can then go out with my trusty spray paint and mark my kilometers. (Oh... Hmm... This may be illegal where you live, so of course I'm not suggesting you do the same. Although it has been my experience that if you go out with a reflective vest and a hard hat—even if it's a Fisher Price hard hat you've borrowed from your six-year-old—you can get away with just about anything.) ☺ I'll use these courses when I need a very accurate loop course where a second or two per kilometer is a big deal (to me... Again, I'm a little picky about accuracy...). For very long workouts where I don't want to be chained to a loop course, I'll just head out with my wrist-worn GPS and go. After years of training almost exclusively on measured loop courses, being able to walk anywhere I want, and still have a reasonably accurate idea of how far and fast I'm going, is a real treat. One caveat about wrist-worn GPS monitors: Although they are accurate when recording times per kilometer or per mile, they are not very accurate on the fly, so take the instantaneous pace readings with a grain of salt.

I tend to seek out and do a lot of my training on flat courses because most of my racewalking races are held on flat loop courses, but if I have a marathon coming up on a hilly course I'll try to pick locations that match the race's topography as closely as possible. Part of your pre-race reconnaissance should always include heading to the race web site to look at the course map and elevation profile[23] and then lay out topographically similar training courses.

Treadmills

Sure, training on a treadmill violates the train-under-conditions-that-match-your-upcoming-race principle—unless your next race is being held on a treadmill, of course—but treadmills do have their place. On very hot, humid days it can be very difficult to do long, hard workouts outside. Same story for heavy rain or snow. Treadmills are also great if you live in a very flat area (think south Florida) and don't have access to "real" hills.[24] The incline feature on the treadmill can help you to acclimate to hills if you have a hilly race coming up. Finally, now that I have kids, I frequently need to train on the treadmill to have access to childcare. (Free childcare at the gym beats the heck out of $15/hour for a babysitter!) If you're similarly encumbered (I mean blessed!), treadmill training may be a good option for you.

Although to some degree walking is walking is walking, there are differences between walking outdoors and walking on a moving rubber belt. First and foremost, you need to be careful about introducing a treadmill to your routine if you've never used one before. The first time getting on a moving belt can be hazardous—search on YouTube for "treadmill fails" for proof. But even ignoring the risk of tripping and face-planting on a moving belt, the minor differences in the range of motion and the way your muscles work when walking outdoors versus walking on the treadmill can lead to injuries. Your technique is changed just enough to strain some muscles, ligaments and tendons, and possibly adversely affect the legality of your technique if you're a racewalker. The change in surface from rubber belt to asphalt or concrete outdoors when you race can also lead to injuries during the race if all of your training leading up to it was on the more forgiving rubber belt.

Another issue many people have is the real or perceived speed difference between walking on the treadmill and walking outdoors. Psychological issues have a big effect on how you feel in any workout or race. I don't *hate* the treadmill, but I very much prefer to walk outdoors. When I do train inside it can feel more physically demanding than walking at the same pace outside. If I'm able to do two hours at 'X' pace outdoors I may be really straining after only an hour indoors. It's probably mostly psychological, but there are some very real physical differences. There's no wind resistance on the treadmill, but also no cooling effect from the wind, which could make things more difficult. If you're in an enclosed space or in a gym with other walkers and runners throwing

---

[23] A caveat about elevation profiles: Race directors can choose whatever vertical vs. horizontal scale they want. If they want to promote a "flat, fast course"—and they ALWAYS do!—they can use a big vertical scale so the mountains look like molehills. Always check the vertical scale numbers on the left-hand side of the elevation chart.

[24] Although… South Florida and other flat areas do have arched bridges and parking garages with several-story-high ramps upon which you can do hill work.

off 98.6-degree+ heat, plus treadmill motors also throwing off heat, it can get pretty uncomfortable, temperature-wise. Finally, you can't always trust the accuracy of the pace on the treadmill display. It might be right on, or maybe you're actually walking 30 seconds per mile faster than the treadmill display says you're going.[25]

To help with the drudgery of walking in place, a lot of people listen to music or watch television while on the treadmill. My gym's treadmills are hooked up to the Internet, so I like to pass the time by watching YouTube videos of Olympic and World Championship walking competitions. It really helps to make the time go by as well as being a great way to visualize great walking technique.

Whether you train on the roads trails, track or treadmill, staying safe is paramount. Safety is a very broad topic, which deserves its own chapter, so on to Chapter 7!

---

[25] I'm the proud owner of a Shimpo hand-held tachometer that can gauge the speed of a treadmill belt with mind-blowing accuracy. (Once again, yes, I am a nerd…) I use it to verify the speed of my home treadmill as well as those at my gym. But really, who *doesn't* do that? ☺

CHAPTER 7: SAFETY

Although walking is one of the safest fitness or sporting activities around, anything can become dangerous if not done properly or in an unsafe location. The most common threats to life and limb can be broadly placed into three categories: The weather, animals, and the most dangerous animals… people.

The weather

As adaptable as humans are, we actually have a very limited safe operating temperature range. If our core temperature rises very far above or falls below the normal range of 36.5 to 37.5 °C (97.7 to 99.5 °F), very bad things can happen. Optimal temperature while exercising is 37.5 °C or 99.5 °F, and our bodies are very well designed to maintain that temperature under normal conditions. But walking in high heat and humidity, especially when combined with dehydration, can cause the body's cooling system to break down, resulting in *hyperthermia.* At the other end of the spectrum is *hypothermia*, which occurs when body temperature falls below 35 °C (95 °F). Few have the luxury of walking any time of day, but if you are able to, walking early in the morning or later in the day during the summer, and at mid-day in winter, can help you to avoid weather-related problems. Doing some reconnaissance at weather.com, the local news, or other weather resources, can help you to find the best time of day to train.

Hot weather walking tips

Here are some tips for "keeping your cool" when training outside during the summer months:

- Wear light-colored, wicking, breathable clothing. Technical fibers are best, but whatever you do, avoid cotton, which retains moisture. Short sleeves or no sleeves are best unless… Some walkers don't like sunscreen and prefer to cover up with a lightweight long-sleeve tech shirt and wide-brimmed hat to block UV rays. My good friend Jonathan Matthews competed on several international teams for the US and raced in several Olympic Trials wearing just such a get-up. Another exception would be when acclimating for a warm-weather race. I like to overdress for a couple of weeks leading into warm-weather races when the conditions at home are cooler than what I'm expecting on race day. Strange looks aside, wearing a winter hat, gloves, and a sweat jacket while training can quickly get your body used to what it will experience on race day. Don't overdo it though, and never when it's warmer than about 28 °C (82.4 °F).

- Drink! Sweating keeps your body cool, but it can cause you to lose about eight ounces of fluid for every fifteen minutes of fast walking. And once you become dehydrated you'll stop sweating, making it very difficult to cool yourself. Pre-hydrating with eight to sixteen ounces of fluid ten to fifteen minutes prior to training or racing, and drinking fluids every 20 to 30 minutes during, will help to prevent dehydration. To determine if you're hydrating properly, do a sweat-rate test as outlined in Chapter 5. It's okay to lose a pound or two during a long hot workout, but any more than that and your walking performance will suffer, putting you at risk of sustaining a heat injury. Indications of dehydration are: a persistent elevated pulse after finishing your walk, and dark yellow urine. Thirst is not an adequate indicator of dehydration, so drink early and often. Having said that, don't overdo it! Water intoxication is real, and dangerous. Hyponatremia and hypokalemia[26] (low blood sodium and potassium) caused by drinking too much plain water without electrolytes can cause dizziness, nausea, headaches, and in extreme cases, death. Sports drinks, especially lower-carb, higher electrolyte sports drinks (Nuun, for example), are the best way to stay hydrated without risking hyponatremia and/or hypokalemia.
- Lay out loop courses that allow you to drink frequently. If the thought of repeated loops isn't appealing, plan your route in a way that allows you to refill water bottles or use drinking fountains.
- Carry identification, and tell someone where you are training and how long you expect to be gone. Consider purchasing a Road ID—a bracelet containing your name, contact information and medical alerts. Road IDs are popular enough with walkers and runners, that most EMTs and even other walkers/runners/bikers would know to check for one if they were they ever to find you in an incommunicative state. Head to www.RoadID.com to order one.
- Although there's no definitive cut-off temperature or heat index (combination of heat and humidity) that would preclude training outside, do be very careful venturing out when both temperature and humidity are high. Sweat can't evaporate whenever humidity is high, and evaporative cooling is what cools the skin and the blood beneath it. If sweat doesn't evaporate, all you're doing is covering your body with salty, 100 °F fluid, which is less than helpful.
- Train in the shade whenever possible.
- If you become dizzy, nauseous, have the chills, or stop sweating, STOP YOUR WORKOUT! Find shade, sit down, and drink. If you don't feel better, seek medical

[26] If you thought "that's Greek to me!" the first time you saw sodium and potassium on a periodic table, you need to brush up on your ancient languages. Natrium and kalium are actually the Latin, not Greek, words for sodium (Na) and potassium (K). The prefixes "hypo" and "hyper" ("below" and "over") and the suffix "emia" (referring to the blood), are Greek. Hyponatremia and hypokalemia, then, mean low blood sodium and potassium, respectively.

attention. Heatstroke occurs when the body fails to regulate its own temperature, so the core temperature continues to rise. Symptoms of heatstroke include mental changes (such as: confusion, delirium, or unconsciousness) and skin that is red, hot, and dry, even under the armpits. Heatstroke is a life-threatening medical emergency, requiring immediate medical intervention.

Speaking of heat… If walking in 95 °F heat can fry your brain, imagine what 50,000°F will do! That's the temperature of a typical lightning strike, which is about five times as hot as the surface of the sun. On average about 50 Americans per year die from lightning strikes. If skies look threatening, especially if you hear thunder, seek shelter immediately.

- If possible, get to lower elevation.
- Never lie flat on the ground. The best position to be in is crouched down with both feet on the ground and close together.
- Never shelter under an isolated tree, cliff or rocky overhang.
- Immediately get away from any body of water.
- Stay away from objects that conduct electricity (metal fences, power lines, windmills, etc.)
- If you're with a group, spread out, keeping at least twenty feet between members.

In some parts of the world, thunderstorms can be harbingers of tornadoes. If you're in an area with warning sirens heed them immediately. If you aren't, but see or hear the following:

- A dark, often greenish, sky;
- a wall of clouds or an approaching cloud of debris;
- large hail often in the absence of rain;
- a sudden stillness (before a tornado strikes, the wind may die down and the air may become very still);
- an approaching cloud of debris, even if a funnel is not visible;
- a loud roar similar to a freight train,

seek shelter in a sturdy building, if possible. If not, lie flat and face down on low ground, protecting the back of your head with your arms. Stay far away from trees, cars, and anything else that could fall, or be blown into/onto you.

Cold weather walking tips

On the flip side to training in hot weather, training in cold weather has its own hazards. Even temperatures as high as 50 degrees or more can be dangerous if you're underdressed or walking in wind and rain, so you need to be prepared for hypothermia at almost any time of the year. Here are some helpful cold-weather walking tips:

- Dress in layers. It's okay to be a little cold at the start of a workout. Within a few minutes you should warm up to a comfortable temperature. A good rule of thumb is to dress for a temperature about ten to fifteen degrees warmer than the actual temperature. If the temperature is 40 degrees, dress as if it's 50 or 55 degrees. If you dress to be comfortable in 40-degree weather you'll be overheating within a few minutes.
- If it's windy, try to plan routes that will take you into the wind at the start of the workout, so that you'll have the wind at your back at the end when you're more tired and less able to maintain your body temperature.
- Winter means fewer daylight hours. Wear bright-colored, reflective clothing or a reflective vest, so drivers can see you. Bonus points for a headlamp or flashing lights. I don't have a particular favorite brand. A quick Google search will bring up lots of choices in the $15 to $25 range.
- Avoid walking on snowy or icy roads. Not only are you at risk of slipping and falling, drivers will have more trouble stopping, or reliably steering around you.
- Consider wearing traction devices on your shoes when walking in snow or on ice. Yaktrax are the industry leader.
- Keep a change of dry clothes and a blanket in the car for emergency situations.
- Stay alert and aware of changing weather conditions. Oncoming storms can quickly drop the temperature, putting you at risk for hypothermia or frostbite if you're caught wearing the wrong clothes. (As they say in Sweden "there's no such thing as bad weather, just bad clothing.") I'll always remember an impromptu eight-mile hike at Glacier National Park in Montana. It was a beautiful August morning, so I rolled out of my tent and just headed out on a trail, dressed for sunny, 68-degree weather. About five miles into the hike, the wind picked up, dark clouds rolled in, and before long I was caught in a torrential downpour. Within 30 minutes the temperature dropped into the low 50s. I eventually emerged onto a park road and was able to flag down a passing pick-up truck. Sure, the driver was probably a serial killer, but he did offer to take me back to my campsite. Soaking wet from the rain, I was thinking the wind-chill in the back of the pick-up was about the worst thing I had ever experienced, but that was before golf ball-sized hail started… Long story short, be prepared for anything!
- Know where to find shelter on your route if the weather gets really bad.

- Don't ignore shivering. It is an important first sign that the body is losing heat, and you may be in danger of hypothermia.

Animals

Ask most walkers what animal they fear most when out for a walk, and "Man's Best Friend" (ironically) would probably be the top answer. But danger more often lurks in smaller packages. I've been hospitalized by bee stings, slogged through nearly two years of fatigue and other symptoms brought on by Lyme disease transmitted by ticks, and although, even with all my travels, I've never contracted malaria myself, a number of athletes I've coached have been profoundly affected by the mosquito-borne disease, which kills 750,000 to 1,000,000 people per year, worldwide.

The author, walking with 'gators. Just don't.

Photo credit: Carolyn Kealty

Threats vary regionally, but it's important to be aware of, and be able to identify, your local poisonous spiders, scorpions, snakes, and other creepy-crawlies, avoid them, and know what to do if you're bitten, stung, or swallowed by one of them. Wear bug spray to ward off bees as well as mosquitoes and other pests, and if you know you're allergic to bee stings, carry an EpiPen. When trail walking, stay in the center of the trail and try to avoid brushing up against foliage, which could allow a tick to hitch a ride (and could also result in a nasty case of poison ivy/oak/etc.) If larger fauna are common in your area be prepared for an encounter. You may be thinking bears, mountain lions or alligators, which occur in some parts of the country, but deer, cows, and horses are much more common and kill far more people per year.[27]

---

[27] Admittedly, most of the 120 or so US deaths per year caused by deer are through car-deer collisions, but dozens of people are gored by antlers or kicked by hooves, sometimes fatally. About 20 to 25 people per year are killed by cows, and about the same number are killed each year by horses.

But back to dogs… Rather than reinvent the wheel, I'll take the liberty here of lifting the following from an old article I wrote shortly after being chased by some deranged fleabag while out for a workout:

Canine confrontations

Nothing puts a damper on a good workout like losing a leg to a pit bull. But although common sense can prevent most attacks, dogs are unnatural creatures—we've selectively in-bred them to the point of comical excess. (Ever seen a Chihuahua try to "get friendly" with a Great Dane's hind leg?) So they're apt to behave in somewhat bizarre and unpredictable ways. In any case, there are a few things you should definitely NOT do when confronted by a Kamikaze canine charging at you like Dennis Rodman on a bender. Among these:

- **Don't pay attention to anything the owner says or does**! This is between you and the crazed beast—the dog, that is. I once lost a good-sized chunk of hip flesh to a German shepherd whose owner assured me that "Princess" wouldn't bite—that she was just "playing." Playing, in this case, meaning locking onto a terrified twelve-year-old's hip and shaking vigorously until beaten off with a flurry of fists, feet, elbows and knees. It may be embarrassing for you to beat a dog senseless while the owner stands by with mouth agape, but Zen-like focus on the task at hand has kept me bite-free ever since.
- **Never "play dead" or turn your back on a dog-** Unlike bears, which will just swat you around a bit like the animated versions do in the old Bugs Bunny cartoons, the typical genetically scrambled mutt will only become confused by such behaviors and mistake you for a giant, cowering salami.
- **Never try to outrun the dog-** I'll put my money on a blind, three-legged Pekinese against Usain Bolt every time. ANY dog can outrun ANY human any day of the week. Research has shown that to 43% of unchained dogs, a brightly-colored pair of rapidly departing walking shorts is indistinguishable from a rapidly departing Frisbee, and will elicit an identical "Jump and Chomp" response; 34% will mistake you for a flying two-legged salami, while the remaining 23% will be asleep on the porch—no doubt dreaming about chewing on your leg like an old soup bone.

I could probably go on forever here: Never go walking with your cat on a leash; never use Alpo in the place of Body Glide as a pre-workout lubricant; never exercise with pork chops in your pockets... But it's probably more beneficial for most people to know what they *should* do if they're ever confronted by that deranged Doberman down the block. Now don't quote me on this stuff. I'm not getting paid for this, and I'm not an AKC-certified dog wrangler (although I did stay at a Holiday Inn Express last night). But the following are some things that have worked for me in the past—proven strategies that may help you to remain bipedal for many years to come... Probably... Well, maybe... If you're really lucky... And you don't go anywhere near the house at the end of my street where the two Satanic Labradors live—the ones that ate the Amazon driver last week…

1. **Be the Top Dog-** When a Menacing Mongrel comes bolting at you with fur and fangs flying, run directly at the dog, yelling maniacally and waving your arms like Jack Nicholson escaping from a straitjacket. These belligerent beasts are used to being the aggressors. When they see that you are bigger, louder and more serious than they are, they'll usually back down. (Amazing but true: We've so screwed up dogs' natural instincts that they actually take Jack Nicholson seriously.)
2. **Every man for himself-** If and only if you're with training partners, use them as human shields/sacrificial lambs and run like Gilligan when his pants catch on fire at the end of the "Attacked by the Head-Hunters" episode. Your mantra should be, "I don't have to outrun the dog, I just have to outrun my friends."
3. **Smash 'em!-** If you have enough time, grab a good Goliath-slaying-sized rock or a hefty stick, and try your best to merge it at high velocity with the dog's frontal lobe, where the "kill" impulse originates. It's amazing how quickly this will communicate the message that you do not wish to become his rawhide chew toy at any time during this particular workout. Even if you miss (and you're really lucky) you may be able to trigger the bonehead's human-induced "fetch" response, instantly transforming the evil cur into a tail-wagging, spit-slobbering Pavlovian marshmallow.
4. **Try "The Poitras"-** I wouldn't recommend it, but if you think you have The Gift you may want to try the "Poitras." I was training with Canadian Olympic racewalker Tina Poitras and two of my US team training partners one day long ago, when we were suddenly charged by an enraged Rottweiler. I was ready to employ strategy #1, Ernesto[28] looked like he was going for #3, while Wolfgang looked like a deer caught in the headlights, ready to try the Wet-My-Pants-and-Hope-the-Doggie-Stops-to-Sniff-the-Puddle Method. Tina, instead, simply held out her hand and began cooing "Good boy! What a good doggie you are!" in her adorable French-Canadian accent. Amazing stuff at work here, folks. The brute instantly stopped to let himself be scratched and stroked while we stood and watched in amazement. Even Wolfgang was ready to roll onto his back for a good belly rub.
5. **Pepper spray-** Finally, as a last resort, mace the little &@$+@&% to Kingdom Come. It didn't work for the Amazon guy, but then again, he had his hands full at the time with those 20 lb. boxes from the Salami of the Month Club...

[28] Some names have been changed to protect the easily embarrassed.

People

Okay, with that bit of levity out of the way, a more serious note. Over the course of some 40+ years as a competitive endurance athlete I've had hypothermia, frostbite, and heatstroke, bee stings, and dog bites, but by far my biggest fear is… People. People in cars, people on bikes, pant-less people lurking in the bushes, people throwing beer cans and batteries at my head. People. On the one hand, I've always been a reasonably fit white male in a country where such attributes provide relative safety. On the other hand, high-speed racewalking tends to put a target on your back for—at the very least—verbal abuse. (Not everywhere, just in areas where verbally abusive middle-school-age boys tend to congregate.) Even so, I've been able to train more or less unmolested most of the time all over the US, and in travels all over the world. Not so for many women, unfortunately. I only rarely hear verbal abuse from passing cars[29] and have only once had a troglodyte get out of his pick-up truck and threaten me with bodily harm, but tragically that's often not the case for women walking alone.

General walking safety

Even post-#MeToo, I'm not overly optimistic that things will get better any time soon for women walking alone, so until men get their collective act together, here are some general walking safety tips (for both men and women) modified from RRCA guidelines:

- DON'T WEAR EARBUDS! I've coached a lot of competitive walkers and runners and I realize a lot of them like to listen to music while training. Please don't! Being aware of your surroundings is critical to staying safe when training outdoors. Earbuds/headphones not only make it difficult to hear cars, animals, or people coming from behind, they also distract your attention, making you less responsive to these threats.
- Always walk facing traffic. Not only can you see cars coming, it also enables you to determine whether the driver is paying attention to the road and you, or his/her cellphone.
- Look both ways before crossing. Make eye contact to confirm that the driver of a car acknowledges your right-of-way before crossing in front of the vehicle.
- Cross at intersections, and obey traffic signals.
- Wear a Road ID, or some other form of identification, or at the very least, write your name, phone number, and blood type on the inside (medial) sole of your walking shoe. Include any medical information.

[29] Kids who yell out of car windows don't seem to be aware of the Doppler effect. The speed of a car relative to your walking speed increases the frequency of the sound waves as the car approaches you and decreases their frequency as the car speeds off. When the kids start yelling, it takes a moment for you to figure out what you're hearing since the pitch is off, then as soon as your brain kicks in and processes that the sound is human speech, the car departs and the waves are slowed down, or in the non-PC physics term, they're *retarded*. No matter how witty the yelling kids think they are, what you hear always sounds, well…

- Always stay alert and aware of what's going on around you. The more aware you are, the less vulnerable you are.
- Carry a charged cell phone.
- Trust your intuition about a person or an area. React on your intuition and avoid a person or situation if you're unsure. If something tells you a situation is not right, it probably isn't.
- Walk in familiar areas if possible, but alter or vary your walking routes and times so you're not a predictable "target." In unfamiliar areas, such as while traveling, contact a local walking or running club or running/walking specialty store. Know where open businesses or stores are located in case of an emergency.
- Walk with a human or canine partner.
- Write down or leave word of the route of your walk. Tell friends and family of your favorite routes.
- Avoid unpopulated areas, deserted streets, and overgrown trails. Avoid unlit areas, especially at night. Stay clear of parked cars or bushes.
- Ignore verbal harassment and do not verbally harass others. Use discretion in acknowledging strangers. Look directly at others and be observant, but keep your distance and keep moving.
- Wear reflective clothing or shoes if you must walk before dawn or after dark. Avoid walking on the street when it is dark.
- Practice memorizing license plates or identifying characteristics of strangers.
- Carry a whistle.
- Get training in self-defense.
- When using multi-use trails, follow the "rules of the road." If you alter your direction, look over your shoulder before crossing the trail to avoid a potential collision with an oncoming cyclist or passing runner.
- CALL THE POLICE IMMEDIATELY if something happens to you or someone else, or you notice anyone out of the ordinary. It is important to report incidents immediately

All in all, walking is one of the safest activities around, but it's a crazy world out there. As I can attest, getting hit by a car while training is no fun. Not for the person getting hit, anyway. I've only ever been hit by a car once while training, but unfortunately it was while I was with a group of half a dozen other maladjusted elite racewalkers who laughed their butts off as the old lady who hit me kept on driving her big ol' Mercedes at about 12 miles per hour with me on her hood. She could barely see over the steering wheel, let alone over my body on the hood of her car, yet she kept on going like nothing had happened. I eventually rolled off, taking one of her windshield wipers with me. I kept that thing for years as a souvenir. In any case, be careful out there, ok?

SECTION II: TECHNIQUE

As noted previously, walking is a great way to travel very long distances on foot if you're not overly concerned with how long it takes you to get there. The problem with "regular" walking though, is what if you *are* concerned with how long it takes? What if you're a *competitive* walker? Clearly regular walking is not the fastest way to get from point A to point B. For very long races (think 24 hours) high-end speed isn't really an issue, but for shorter races (50k and under!) the 4- to 5mph speed limit of regular walking technique can be a real impediment to walking a fast mile, 5k or half-marathon. This section will introduce you to some strategies for walking faster. Elements of Olympic racewalking technique will be introduced, but fear not, I'm not (necessarily!) trying to turn you in to a racewalker. However… even if you don't ever plan to compete in judged, Olympic-style races, adopting some of the elements of racewalking technique that allow the pros to walk mile after mile at speeds approaching ten miles per hour, can give just about anyone a big boost in their walking speed! And if Nordic walking is your thing, you'll learn tips from the pros that will make you speedier and more fluid while walking with poles. Want to walk faster? Read on!

CHAPTER 8: THE EVOLUTION OF COMPETITIVE WALKING TECHNIQUE

Competitive walking technique has undergone a dramatic evolution from its early pedestrian roots to the remarkably fast, fluid athleticism practiced today by Olympic racewalkers, and high-level Nordic walkers. The men's world record for the 20k racewalk held by Yusuke Suzuki of Japan stands at a mind-boggling 1:16:36 (one hour, sixteen minutes and thirty-six seconds). That works out to 6:10 *per mile* for 12.42 miles. Liu Hong of China has the women's world record of 1:24:38 for 20k, which is under 6:50 per mile. Nordic walkers, too, reach impressive speeds. Jor Hakkinen of Finland has walked 21:09 for 5k and 44:20 for 10k. That's 6:49 and 7:08 per mile, respectively. These walkers are obviously superbly conditioned athletes, but technique is a major part of the equation as well.

Before competitive walking rules were codified, athletes pushed their own individual interpretations of "fair heel-and-toe" ambulation to the edge of the rather arbitrary limits set by walking officials. Some took advantage of the rules vacuum and shuffled or "creeped" their way to fast times and victories. In 1862, professional pedestrian Charles Westhall, frustrated by the lack of concrete rules in competitive walking, described his idea of the model walker:

> *"To be a good and fair walker, the attitude should be upright or nearly so, with the shoulders well back, and the arms when in motion held well up in a bent position, and at every stride swinging with the movement of the legs well across the chest, which should be well thrown out. The loins should be slack to give plenty of freedom to the hips, and the leg perfectly straight, thrown out from the hip boldly and directly in front of the body, and allowed to reach the ground with the heel being decidedly the first portion of the foot to meet it. The movement of the arms will keep the balance of the body and bring the other leg from the ground."*

(I've actually tried this, to great comic effect—at least I made myself laugh out loud. There's just something about slack-loined walking that puts a big smile on my face.) But I digress… By 1874, English authorities were reaching consensus on what constituted fair walking, defining a fair heel-and-toe gait as:

> *"One foot always on the ground, and the heel always touching the ground first, the body kept strictly upright and the knee joints kept as rigid as possible. The toe of the hindmost leg must not leave the ground before the heel of the leg striding forwards has been placed upon the ground."*

In 1900 Australia adopted perhaps the first formal rules governing competitive walking:

- *"That a racing walker must have contact with the ground with one foot during a stride, and with both feet at the end of a stride.*
- *That the heel of the front foot must touch the ground before the back foot leaves it.*
- *That as the heel of the front foot touches the ground the leg must not be bent, its knee must be locked.*
- *That the body and head must be kept upright."*[30]

It was a great step forward, but the Australian rules were not adopted universally until decades later. The 1913 IAAF rule book simply stated *"Each judge of walking shall have the power to disqualify a competitor when walking unfairly, who shall give to the competitor two cautions, on the third, disqualification."* Finally, in 1928 the IAAF published its first formal definition of competitive walking: *"Walking is progression by steps so taken that unbroken contact with the ground is maintained,"* which was modified in 1949 to:

> *"Walking is progression by steps so taken that unbroken contact with the ground is maintained. At each step, the advancing foot of the walker must make contact with the ground before the rear foot leaves the ground."*

In 1956 the IAAF codified what most competitive walkers were already doing by adding the "straightened leg" rule, effectively creating modern racewalking: *"During the period of each step in which a foot is on the ground, the leg shall be straightened at least for a moment."* This was further modified in 1972 to dictate exactly *when* the leg must be straightened:

> *"Walking is progression by steps so taken that unbroken contact with the ground is maintained. At each step, the advancing foot of the walker must make contact with the ground before the rear foot leaves the ground. During the period of each step when a foot is on the ground, the leg must be straightened (i.e. not bent at the knee) at least for one moment, and in particular, the supporting leg must be straight in the vertical upright position."*

Finally, the present World Athletics definition, since 1996, reads:

---

[30] A Potted History of the Rules of Racewalking. http://www.vrwc.org.au/vrwchistrules.shtml accessed 11/14/2017.

"Race Walking is a progression of steps so taken that the walker makes contact with the ground, so that no visible (to the human eye) loss of contact occurs. The advancing leg shall be straightened (i.e. not bent at the knee) from the moment of first contact with the ground until the vertical upright position."

These rules, particularly since 1956, describe competitive *racewalking*. But competitive walking is more than just racewalking. It has branched out over the years into at least three distinct styles: racewalking, power walking, and Nordic walking, all of which are governed by their own sets of rules. As the rules for each style have developed, walking techniques have evolved to allow athletes to walk as quickly as possible within the constraints of these rules. In particular, modern racewalk technique and the rules that govern the sport/athletics event have evolved in response to one another over time. As the athletes have gotten faster, the rules have been revised to bar innovations that would have taken the technique beyond its original concept as race *walking*. The compromise is a system that permits athletes to push themselves to their physiological limits without gaining unfair mechanical advantage due to sketchy technique. Solid, legal technique allows the best athletes to walk as fast as their fitness will allow them to go without having to slow down for fear of disqualification.

Despite any public relations problems that racewalking may have, the rules are really quite simple and can be described in two sentences. Not so with Nordic walking and power walking. Without the clear-cut simplicity of the straightened-leg rule, it becomes much more difficult to differentiate high-speed power walking or Nordic walking from running. I like to ask the participants at my clinics for their definitions of regular walking, and then ask how they would define running. With that settled, I try to tease out how the words they use to describe running differ from their definitions of walking. I have yet to receive a satisfactory response! Clearly there are many walkers out there who are legitimately walking according to the opinion of Olympic-level judges, and yet these walkers are off the ground for up to ten percent of each stride. Conversely, there are plenty of slow runners who never leave the ground, but who are clearly running—or at least attempting to run, anyway. Ground contact, then, is not the defining characteristic differentiating walking from running.

Just as racewalking has, Nordic walking and power walking have codified their rules over the years—just not in the simple two sentences that define racewalking. Nordic walking is governed by a number of different organizations, so the rules can vary from competition to competition, but all are similar to the International Nordic Walking Association (INWA) rules:

- *Ensure that the arms and legs move alternately in a natural manner.*
- *Ensure that at no point both feet or both poles are off the ground at the same time. Running is forbidden.* [Ed.: But what is "running"?!]
- *Ensure the poles contact the ground at the same time as the opposite heel.*

- *Ensure the poles must be placed on the side of the distance and longitudinal area between the toes of the front foot and the heel of the rear foot with the exception of ascending or descending steep rises or steps.* [Ed.: Huh?]
- *Ensure that the center of gravity is not abnormally lowered.*
- *Ensure that there is an active push through the poles in order to propel the body forward. When pushing through the pole there should be arm extension and the hand should at the minimum reach the bodyline but ideally pass the bodyline backwards.*
- *Ensure that the leading hand holding the grip of the pole is to pass the body line when placing the pole in front.*
- *Ensure that the poles are gripped when placing them on the ground and actively released when pushing with open hand at the back.*
- *Ensure that non-use of the poles by any participant is only allowed at the drinking stations according to the specific course rules.*
- *Ensure that the participants wear the straps of the poles correctly.*
- *Ensure that the participants must wear the race number correctly.*
- *Ensure that the participant is not allowed to block the path of other participants.*

Power walking's rules also run more than a page, but that seems to be what is required when there is not a straightened leg to differentiate walking from running. It may sound like I'm knocking on power walking… I'm not! Power walking is a great sport, and certainly easier to master for most people than racewalking. But I've seen what can happen in local running races with walk divisions when there is no clearly defined dividing line between walking and running. Post-race "'You were running!' 'No, YOU were running!'" squabbles ensue, race directors get caught in the middle, and they decide to never hold a walking race or put a walking division into their running races ever again. Hence the very long list of rules for power walking competitions. Without further ado, the U.S. Power Walking Association's rules:

- *One foot must be on the ground at all times. Loss of contact with the ground may result in a red card issued by a judge or monitor. Continued violation can result in disqualification.*
- *Each advancing foot-strike must be heel-to-toe at all times. Striking with the toe or ball of the advancing foot is considered running, and may result in a red card issued by a judge or monitor. Continued violation can result in disqualification.*
- *Creeping, where the advancing leg is stretched forward beyond a normal walk form, and the knee is bent into a running form, may result in a red card issued by a judge or monitor. Continued violation can result in disqualification.*

- *A slightly bent knee is the accepted form; however, a bent knee in a running or jogging form may result in a red card issued by a judge or monitor. Continued violation can result in disqualification.* [Ed.: Where is the line between "slightly bent" and "bent"?]
- *Running or jogging mode is forbidden, and may result in a red card issued by a judge or monitor. Continued violation can result in disqualification.* [Ed.: What is "running"?]
- *Any violation of the above rules in the last 100 meters, as determined by a single judge or monitor, is cause for immediate disqualification.*
- *The advancing leg as it moves forward, and when the heel strikes the ground, does not have to be completely locked as it passes under the body, as it does in Race Walking. A soft knee is acceptable; however, an overly excessive bent knee that is deemed to be in a creeping or running shuffle is not acceptable, and may result in a red card issued by a judge or monitor. Continued violation can result in disqualification.*
- *Unsportsmanlike conduct can result in disqualification by the judges, monitors or race official.*
- *People requiring a cane as an aid will be allowed to compete, but walking sticks or walkers are not allowed.*
- *Disqualification will result when an athlete is judged to be in violation of the above rules in three separate instances by three separate officials or monitors, or by the race director, during the course of the competition.*
- *Each athlete is responsible for counting his or her own laps, even if lap counters are provided.*
- *Rules are strictly enforced to maintain the integrity of the sport.*

Not exactly the paragon of simplicity, now is it? ☺ While power walking's rules may be lacking in brevity, the technique itself, being more akin to "regular" walking, is certainly easier to understand and master than racewalking or Nordic walking. The simplicity of the technique (in contrast to the rules governing it) is why power walking has been quickly gaining in popularity in the US and beyond, especially among older participants who may have difficulty with the knee-straightening of racewalking or the pole action of Nordic walking.

As racewalking's rules have changed over time, and as Nordic walking and power walking's rules have been codified, the styles used by individual athletes have evolved to allow them to race as quickly as possible within the constraints of these rules. Let's look at some of the modern modifications of walking technique, beginning with racewalking:

The rushin' Russians and magnificent Mexicans

According to former Australian National Racewalk Coach Harry Summers, the 1956 Olympic Games represented one of the major milestones in the development of modern walking technique. Soviet coaches, the first to seriously scrutinize the efficiency—or more to the point, the inefficiency—of the walking gait, advised their athletes to start the stride cycle by landing with the heel of the lead foot as close to the body as possible. The faster cadence rates generated with the new technique enabled Soviet athletes to sweep all three medals in the 20-kilometer event and to take the silver in the 50k in Melbourne. Some judges had trouble accepting the new "quick-stepping" technique, but the Russians were walking according to the rules as written, so the judges eventually adapted.

The emergence of elite Mexican walkers on the international scene—beginning with José Pedraza's Olympic silver medal in 1968—represented another quantum leap in both walking technique and speed. Mexican National Coaches Alfonso Marquéz and Jerzy Hausleber built upon the Soviet technique, but with the superior flexibility of the Mexican athletes, were able to develop a technique that maximized stride frequency *and* effective posterior (behind the body) stride length. The result was a continuous string of successes including numerous Olympic and world championship medals, and a number of world records.

The champion Chinese

Beginning in the mid-1980s the Chinese have been climbing to the top of the world rankings by carrying the "quick-stepping" technique to its extreme. Whereas the Mexicans have walked with a pronounced front-to-back hip drive, the Chinese have maximized their stride frequency by all but

Chinese women, led by Liu Hong, swept the top three places at the 2019 World Athletics Championships 20 kilometer racewalk.

eliminating pelvic rotation. The unconventional technique led to disqualifications for several of the Chinese walkers at the 1987 IAAF World Cup and a number of subsequent international competitions but, as in the past, the judges and athletes have reached agreement on the limits of fair, legal technique and the Chinese have enjoyed considerable success at the world level ever since. The 1995 IAAF World Cup in Beijing was something of a coming out party for China as Chinese athletes swept the women's 20k, and the men's 20k and 50k races. The 1996 Olympics were a bit of a speed bump, as four of the eight Chinese walkers entered were disqualified, but by 1997 the walkers and judges once again found common ground. Every Chinese walker passed muster at the World Championships that summer, where four Chinese walkers placed in the top 10 in their events. Chinese walkers also held the world records in the men's and women's 20k racewalks throughout the mid- to late-1990s.

In the early 2000s Russia's Olimpiada Ivanova used her take on the Chinese style to great effect, establishing world records and winning a treasure trove of Olympic and World Championship medals. The Chinese innovation seems to have gained near universal acceptance, as the majority of the world's best female walkers now use varying degrees of the "quick-step" technique internationally—a significant outlier being another Russian, Olga Kaniskina, who ruled women's racewalking in the 20-aughts, winning the 2007 IAAF World Championships, 2008 IAAF World Cup and the Olympics, and taking Olympic silver in 2012 using a style reminiscent of the Mexicans, with lots of hip action and posterior stride length.

The straight-on-contact rule

A technique innovation that World Athletics judges have not accepted in international racewalking competitions is a bent knee when the heel first contacts the ground. During the 1980s walkers began experimenting with a "soft knee" on contact. This allowed for maximum stride frequency, especially in taller, longer-legged athletes. Some coaches have suggested the technique was also beneficial in relieving shin pain. Daniel Plaza of Spain survived the scrutiny of the judges and won the Barcelona Olympic 20k walking with a bent knee on contact, but there's a very fine line between landing with a bent knee and straightening as the body passes over it, and a "late lock"—straightening the knee *after* the body has passed over it—or perhaps not straightening at all. Athletes of all abilities who used this technique were failing to achieve full straightening as the leg passed through the vertical support phase. The IAAF responded to the problem by requiring a straightened leg *"from the moment of first contact with the ground until in the vertical upright position."* The rule change was not without controversy. Some walkers—especially older walkers—many of whom did not have any trouble under the old rules, were disqualified in races under the modified rule—in many cases through no fault of their own. In some languages the knee had to be "straightened" but in others it had to be "straight." As coach and IAAF/WA judge Gary Westerfield explained, "racewalkers are not stick figures." Walkers have calves and knees and quads, so even when a leg is straightened, or in biomechanical terms, "fully extended," it is not necessarily "straight." Some judges may not have fully understood the biomechanics of racewalking—especially given the poor wording of the new rule in some languages—so they red-carded athletes who may have been walking perfectly legally. This was certainly unfortunate, but eventually rulebooks were re-translated, and most judges caught up. I believe the rule change renewed the integrity of the sport. Bent-knee-on-contact racewalking never looked right to me, and I've always taught my walkers to use a straight-on-contact landing. I believe it's more efficient, as well as better looking. As always, the athletes and judges found an equilibrium point, and the sport "marched on."

The knee-drivers

Over the past few years some of the top walkers in the world have gravitated toward a style with considerably less emphasis on a long rearward stride and more emphasis on a powerful, punching knee drive to advance the body forward. 2019 World Championships 20-kilometer bronze medalist, Perseus Karlström of Sweden, and one-mile and 3,000m world record-holder, Tom Bosworth of Great Britain, are fine examples of the technique. When I was at the peak of my athletic career I would get compliments on my technique from judges and others, but occasionally I would hear grousing from "old timers" who were elite walkers during the 1960s and 1970s, expressing their disdain for the "new" technique. I laughed it off as "Grumpy Old Man-ism," recognizing that *their* technique was probably criticized by *their* predecessors who were competing in the 1940s and '50s. Not wanting to be a Grumpy Old Man myself, I had to catch myself when I first started analyzing the technique of some of the newest generation of walkers, because it is a bit different from what I was used to, but it works, and in my view it does conform to both the letter and the spirit of the rules. It requires more from the judges, however, because there's a bit of an optical illusion created when there is such a short rearward stride. With a shorter single-support phase after the leg passes through the vertical position, the knee can appear to be bent when it is actually fully straightened, but if the judges are up to the task, this new technique could lead to some very fast times for racewalkers in the future. In addition to Karlström's World Championships bronze medal, he also won the 2019 IAAF Race Walking Challenge, and of course Bosworth holds both sprint world records, so the knee-drivers are being given the green light by international judges, even when racing at the highest speeds. Both men are among my picks to top the podium in the 20k at the Tokyo Olympics—if and whenever they are held.

Power walking

Competing in running races with monitored walking divisions has always been problematic. Without the straight-knee rule of racewalking there is a very fuzzy line between walking and running. Ground-contact is presumed by many to be the defining line between the two, but as pointed out previously, many racewalkers have short "flight phases" in which they are momentarily airborne, while many slow runners fail to ever come off the ground. That being the case, how do we distinguish between power walking and running? To paraphrase U.S. Supreme Court Justice Potter Stewart, "I can't define power walking, but I know it when I see it." In my mind there's too much subjectivity in this kind of judging, but this is where we are now—essentially right back to where we were in the 1870s. The solution is judges' education, and at the highest level (National Senior Games, the Huntsman Games, etc.) the judging is actually quite good. As long as the walkers and judges understand where the line is between walking and running, power walking will continue to grow.

There are still variations in the rules from event to event, but by way of example, the current power walking rules at the Huntsman Games are:

> *1. One foot must be on the ground at all times. Running, deemed to be when both feet are off of the ground, is forbidden and is cause for disqualification.*
>
> *2. Each foot-strike must be heel to toe at all times. "Creeping," wherein the lead toe strikes prior to the heel, is forbidden and is cause for disqualification.*
>
> *3. A slightly bent knee is the accepted form in power walking compared to Technical Race Walking, where the lead leg must remain straight from heel-strike until the knee passes under the body.*

Once again, there is a degree of subjectivity when it comes to differentiating between "bent" and "slightly bent" knees, and whether running really is defined solely by ground contact, but I'll let that point go. For now. ☺

Nordic walkers at the start of the 2017 Nordic Walking World Cup in Yixing, China.

Nordic walking

Nordic walking is walking with poles. In 1991 I first met and raced against eventual four-time Olympic gold medalist Robert Korzeniowski at the World University Games in Sheffield, England. On the starting line of our race I asked Robert what time he was hoping to walk. He said, "Of course I will win. The only question is: how fast does second-place want to push me?"[31] Special K has never lacked confidence... Later, while preparing for the 1996 Olympic Trials I trained for two years under Coach Bohdan Bulakowski, and with 50k racewalk Olympian Andrzej Chylinski, both from Warsaw. But none of these guys is the kind of Pole we're talking about here. ☺ Booming in popularity in recent years, Nordic walking is walking with specially modified *ski* poles. The sport can trace its roots back to the 1930s and '40s as Finnish cross-country skiers power-walked with poles as off-season training for their winter sport. In 1966 physical education instructor Leena Jääskeläinen introduced walking with ski poles to her classes in Helsinki, and in 1979 cross-country ski coach Mauri Repo expanded the popularity of the nascent activity within Finland when he published a popular handbook of off-season cross-country ski training techniques, including walking with poles.

Meanwhile, in the United States, Nordic skier and coach Tom Rutlin created an exercise program in 1985 that used walking poles. Rutlin, who called his creation "Exerstriding," was the first to design poles specifically made for walking. In 1997, Finnish company Exel Oy began producing their own poles, called "Nordic Walkers," officially coining the universally recognized name for the activity. (In these early days, Nordic walking was not yet a competitive sport.) Aki Karihtala, then a Senior Vice President at Exel, founded the International Nordic Walking Association (INWA) in 2000 as a way to popularize Nordic walking—of course more Nordic walkers means more pole sales, but the INWA offers a lot to Nordic walkers. INWA develops educational programs and coach/instructor networks, and also hosts World Cup events. Karihtala is currently the President of the INWA.

Based in Vantaa, Finland, the rather defensively named "Original World Nordic Walking Federation" has a creation story centered around a Finnish article written and originally published only in the Finnish language, in 1997. The article by Marko Kantaneva describes *"sauvakävely,"* or "pole walking," retroactively translated in subsequent reprints as "Nordic walking" beginning in 1999—two years *after* Exel coined the term. At no point does the article mention Nordic walking in the context of competition, describing it only as a fitness activity. The article is also by no means a quantum leap forward in the evolution of Nordic walking technique, since very little constructive technique advice is provided. According to Kantaneva, *"Practice has shown that there is no reason to pay*

[31] I also asked Korzeniowski if he knew Andrzej Chylinski, who had moved from Warsaw to the US earlier that year. Korzeniowski replied, "Pffft! Chylinski! He is an amateur!" Andjrzej went on the make the US Olympic Team in 1996.

too much attention to technical details because sauvakävely *movements are very natural. Actually the same as at age 6 months when you last crawled on the floor."* If I took the same approach to racewalking technique, this would be a very thin book. ☺

In 2000, American adventure racer Dan Barret created the FitTrek technique (or more accurately, series of techniques). Barrett proposed four different Nordic walking techniques, the Full Power, Standard Power, Fast Power, and Speed techniques. The Speed technique is Barrett's most enduring contribution to competitive Nordic walking. The FitTrek speed technique reduces the degree of arm movement and propulsion with the poles, but the increased cadence rate results in higher speeds than the other techniques. At press time, Barrett's FitTrek website seems to be out of commission, but you can learn about his various techniques here: www.wr-nw.com/fittrek.html/.

With Barrett's speedier technique spreading around the world, Nordic walking was ready to become a bona fide competitive sport. The Portland Marathon caught the wave, becoming the first organization to host a Nordic walking world championship, presenting the World Nordic Walking Marathon Championship in October of 2006. Portland continued to host the Nordic Walking World Marathon Championship until 2011. In 2012 Portland hosted what they claimed to be the first World Half-Marathon Nordic Walking Championship. Four years earlier, and across the pond, the Austrian Nordic Walking Association organized what they called the Nordic Walking World Half-Marathon Championship in 2008

INWA claims to be the global governing body for the sport of competitive Nordic Walking. They conduct two world cup events per year, and a world championship every three years. Information on these events, the rules, and the history of Nordic Walking can be found on its website at: www.inwa-nordicwalking.com/. INWA, however, has competition for the title of global governing body. World Ranking-Nordic Walking (WR-NW) has a strong claim to the title of global clearinghouse for Nordic Walking on the web, overseeing competitions and records sub-categorized under the INWA, Exerstrider, and FitTrek techniques. Add to the mix the World Original Nordic Walking Federation, which promotes its own coaching certification program, and you have the makings of a confusing power struggle for world Nordic walking domination. Thankfully, yet another organization has swooped in to sort it all out. The World Nordic Walking Federation was formed in 2011 to unify the various organizations under one global governing body. Um… they're still working on that... ☺

Now that we know something about how the various forms of competitive walking got here, the next chapter will further discuss the rules currently governing racewalking, power walking and Nordic walking.

CHAPTER 9: MORE ON THE RULES

The previous chapter dug into the evolution of competitive walking technique. You may have noticed that there was a whole lot of verbiage about the rules. Why? Why not just "go-as-you-please" as competitive pedestrians did back in the 1870s? Well, back then walkers were covering such long distances that "the experts" didn't feel that running gave much of an advantage. Sure, a runner could beat a walker over 100 meters or a mile, or even a marathon, but when distances stretch to 100 miles or six days, the advantage diminishes. Without our modern shoes and training methods, improperly trained runners were usually hobbled by injuries within a few hours. Walkers almost always did beat runners in six-day races initially. American heel-and-toe walker Daniel O'Leary beat all comers, including runners, at the first two Astley Belt Championship races in March and September of 1878. As prize purses grew, however, so too did the motivation to gain any advantage to win. When runners began to beat the best walkers in "go-as-you-please" races—British "go-as-you-please" pedestrian Charles Rowell mixed running and walking to finally beat O'Leary at the 3rd Astley Belt race in March of 1879—"fair heel-and-toe" technique became the standard in most races, especially in the United States.[32] If only it were that easy… Even though "fair-heel-and-toe" races were strictly walk-only, controversies erupted from time to time due to the imprecise definition of what walking actually was, so more objective rules had to be codified, and over time, amended, as walking technique evolved.

Competitive walking has basically been an arms race (or maybe a legs race?) between athletes wanting to go as fast as possible under the constraints of the existing rules, and officials and governing bodies modifying those rules to rein in athletes who perhaps pushed the envelope a bit too far. The rules ensured fair competition while allowing competitors to push themselves to their physical limits. Nobody likes to get beaten by a cheater. The rules ensure a more-or-less level playing field so the fittest athlete wins, or at least has the best chance of winning.

Terminology

When a power walker or racewalker fails to maintain visible contact with the ground, the infraction is called "loss of contact," or more colloquially, "lifting." If a walker doesn't straighten his or her knees properly, particularly in a racewalking race, he or she is charged with a "bent knee" (aka, "creeping") violation. In racewalking races and some higher-level power walking races, if any of the six to nine judges on the course believe you're in danger of violating one of the rules, they'll usually show you a paddle with a ~ sign for lifting or a > sign for bent knee—although they are not

[32] Go-as-you-please races continued to be the standard in the United Kingdom.

required to do so. This is called a "caution." Each judge can give you only one caution for each violation per race.

Cautions don't count against you; they can be seen as friendly advice from the judge that you're borderline but not yet walking illegally. If, however, a judge feels that you're definitely in violation of the rules he or she will give you a "proposal for disqualification" or "red card," either with or without first showing you a caution paddle. If you receive three red cards from three different judges, you'll be asked to withdraw from the race by the chief judge, or in major events like the Olympics, World Championships, and the US Junior and Open Championships, sent to the "penalty zone" to sit out a time penalty. If you receive a fourth red card after the time penalty, you'll be pulled from the race. This is called a "disqualification," a "DQ," or occasionally a "Dairy Queen." Learn these terms. Throwing them about fluently will make you very popular at pre-race pasta parties. ☺ In many local races (running races with walking divisions, for example) judging is less strict. Even if you are disqualified, the judges don't pull you out of the race. You will be allowed to finish, but you will be recorded in the running division results rather than the walking division.

Are racewalkers "cheaters?"

Every four years the general public rediscovers racewalking—and not in a good way! The Olympic racewalks get a miniscule amount of television coverage, and the talking heads use that quadrennial

Racewalkers being closely judged at the 1912 Olympic 10,000m walk.

opportunity to breathlessly reveal that—OMG!—the walkers aren't maintaining contact with the ground! Athletics and running internet message boards and groups are flooded with comments about racewalkers "cheating" and there are calls for the walks to be removed from the Olympics. Every. Four. Years.

The misconceptions that outsiders have about what racewalking is and what it is not has a lot to do with the ongoing controversies that plague the event. It's simple these days for someone with an iPhone camera to "catch" a racewalker off the ground for twenty milliseconds (20 thousandths of a second) per stride—probably about as easy as it is to "catch" a basketball player traveling, or a butterfly swimmer doing whatever the Hell it is that a butterflyer isn't supposed to be doing in the pool. But the rules don't say walkers can't be off the ground *at all*; the rules say walkers can't be off the ground an *excessive* amount—excessive meaning any longer than what can be detected by the unaided human eye.

The media love to show photographs of racewalkers off the ground—"cheating," according to the press. The ironic thing is that lifting is not per se beneficial to the walker. A bit of simple high school physics, if I may: A body can only accelerate while there is a positive force acting upon it. Once you leave contact with the ground, gravity and wind/air resistance are the only forces acting on you, so you begin to decelerate—you begin to slow down. Having a strong, propulsive push from behind with the rear foot is great, but the longer it takes the front heel to make contact with the ground after the rear foot leaves the ground, the longer it will take before the next propulsive push. So that "flight phase"—the time when both feet are off the ground—can help a little, but there's definitely a limit to how much. The added stride length contributed by the flight phase can contribute to forward speed, but only if it comes without excessive reduction in stride frequency, and that's very difficult to master. Lifting, then, is inefficient racewalking. So to call a lifting racewalker a cheater is a bit like calling a runner dragging an "illegal" parachute behind himself a cheater.

Finally, to "cheat" at something, you need to be aware that you're doing it. But a very short flight phase, or loss of contact, is impossible for a racewalker to feel. Walkers can only begin to feel flight phases if they last more than about 40 milliseconds, which is conveniently about the threshold beyond which a judge can begin to see it happening with the unaided eye. So if a racewalker is caught on film walking with a very short flight phase, but he can't feel it, the judges can't see it, and he's not benefiting from it, is it really cheating? No. No, it is not. But try telling that to the haters on LetsRun.com…

Different strokes

Whenever I walk in road races, one or more of the runners I beat will ask me, "What's the point? Don't you ever just want to break into a run? It's faster..." to which I'll respond, "Don't you ever just want to break into a car and drive? It's faster..." Nobody ever said walking was the fastest way to get from point A to point B. But neither is running. Swimming the butterfly is not the fastest way to get across a pool, but nobody asks Michael Phelps why he doesn't just break into the crawl when he's doing the butterfly or the breast stroke—they're different but equally valid swimming strokes governed and judged by different rules. Walking is a different and equally valid athletics/track and field event governed by different rules from the open running events. Just as in swimming, in athletics/track and field there are different strokes for different folks.

Just for kicks, next time you're at a track meet ask the hurdlers why they don't just go *around* the barriers or the discus throwers or shot-putters why they don't throw a Frisbee or a baseball. (After all, it'll go a lot farther...) Why do people think walkers are so odd?

Changes in the wind?

Despite the fact that a "flight phase" shorter in duration than that which can be detected by the unaided human eye is perfectly legal, it does pose a public relations problem. The IAAF changed the women's international distance from 10k to 20k in 1999 hoping to slow women down, figuring the longer distance would reduce the number of photographs of them seemingly violating the rules appearing in the press. All that did was allow women to walk incredibly fast in front of those cameras for twice as long. ☺ World Athletics has also—once again—floated the idea of "shoe alarms,"[33] as well as other rule changes, including the introduction of the ill-conceived (in my opinion…) penalty zone. Shoe alarms would feature a pressure-sensitive insole that athletes at the highest level (at the Olympic and World Championships) would wear in their shoes to detect losses of contact with the ground. There are so many flaws in the technology and the underlying philosophy that the idea is bound to fail, but World Athletics seems Hell-bent on introducing them. In early 2019 the World Athletics Race Walk Committee voted to require them beginning in 2021. And then after a trial run (or walk?) decided, just as they did several times before, that the idea wasn't going to work. Wash, rinse, repeat... The penalty zone, another absurd idea, was introduced in 2014. The idea, initially, was to reduce the number of disqualifications of youth athletes by imposing a time penalty when an athlete received a third red card. Instead of disqualifying the athlete, he or she is sent into a designated penalty zone to wait out a time penalty. It's a well-meaning idea, but it further complicates an event that is already confusing to the general public, and in the vast majority of cases, if an athlete is walking poorly enough to get three red cards, he or she will probably end up with a fourth and get pulled out of the race eventually anyway. Unfortunately, what should have been limited to youth competitions was moved up the food chain to the World Team Championships in 2018, the World Championships in 2019, and will ultimately be used at the Tokyo Olympics, if and whenever they eventually occur. Ugh.

---

[33] The IAAF/World Athletics floats this horrible, unworkable idea about every ten years. It gets shot down, forgotten, then reintroduced again ten years later. Wash, rinse, repeat… Somebody in power must be in a position to make a lot of money from the technology, otherwise the idea would never see the light of day.

Another attempt by World Athletics to shoot itself in the foot has been the decision to reduce the historic Olympic distances of 20k and 50k down to 10k, and 30- or 35k.[34] One thing racewalking has going for it is that it is the longest footrace in the Olympics—a grueling event five miles longer than the marathon. Now they want to take that away. The reduction of the 20k back down to a 10k again—a walk distance not seen in the Olympics since 1952—will make it that much harder for walkers sprinting at six-minutes-flat per mile to stay grounded.

Keeping in mind that all of these changes stem from the public relations problem that racewalking is too complicated for the general public to understand—"Why not just run?" "If they're supposed to keep one foot one the ground at all times, why are there so many photos and slow-motion videos of walkers off the ground?" These innovations only serve to make this beautiful athletics event more and more complicated, and by shortening the distances, even more difficult to judge. It boggles the mind and breaks my heart… I believe all of these knee-jerk reactions stem from the same ignorance of the rules by the media and unenlightened spectators who see our event as some kind of farce. The athletes themselves realize that some walkers have a momentary 20- to 40-millisecond flight phase during their stride, but very few are overly concerned about it. It's an accepted part of the event.

Putting detractors in the media aside, if you're a racewalker, your job is simply to walk as quickly as possible with one foot on the ground at all times (as judged by the unaided human eye), while straightening the leg from the point of heel contact to the vertical support phase. All we have to do now is figure out how to accomplish that. Stick around: The following chapters will show you how to racewalk, power walk, and Nordic walk *really* fast while playing by the rules! But first, a little bit more on the rules of Nordic walking.

Nordic walking

With at least four different Nordic walking techniques, there doesn't seem to be universal agreement on the rules when it comes to competition. In most cases the rules are pretty vague, allowing whichever technique the walker chooses. The Portland Marathon's Nordic walking page suggests that:

> *"There is but one simple requirement: the participant is asked to adopt a Nordic Walking style where the pole tips are planted somewhere behind a line extending from the leading hand plumb to the ground. Apart from this, there is NO control over the style actually adopted; we call upon your sense of fairness and personal integrity!"*

Similarly, the INWA defines that:

[34] This after increasing the women's distance from10k to 20k in 1999 to make judging the events easier. SMH…

"Nordic walking is a form of physical activity, where the active use of a pair of specially designed Nordic Walking poles are added to regular natural walking. However, the characteristics of natural, biomechanically correct walking and appropriate posture are maintained in all aspects. It also means that the arm movements of the correct NW technique respect the range of movement of natural walking."

Without consistent, clearly defined rules, it would seem that the best course of action would be to develop a Nordic walking technique that's fast, comfortable, and doesn't lead to injuries. We'll get into that more in Chapter 14. But before we go there, let's get back to square one, and first figure out how to power walk faster!

CHAPTER 10: IMPROVING "REGULAR" OR POWER WALKING TECHNIQUE

My father, rest his soul, grew up in the Bronx, New York City. He never learned to drive as a teenager, so when he got married and moved out to the 'burbs he had to teach himself. Which he did; just not very well. ☺ When I was a kid I would lean over the back of his seat watching and asking questions, which you could do back then in the days when seatbelts were either non-existent, or merely a suggestion. When it came time for me to learn to drive, I was surprised to discover that you're *not* actually supposed to drive with both feet on the pedals like my dad did, which, in a nutshell, is the perfect metaphor for "regular" walking. When bio-mechanists describe human motion, they begin with walking. Walking, they'll say, is a series of pendulums in motion, or that walking is a repeated loss and recovery of balance. I vividly remember when each of my four kids learned to walk, all at around ten months of age. (Part good genes, part good coaching, I say!) When they took their first tentative steps, the loss of balance was quite evident; the recovery, not so much! As we get older we get much better at that recovery part.

Competitors in the 2015 Huntsman World Senior Games 3,000m power walk.

Photo Credit: Bonnie Parrish-Kell

But that's not always a good thing. That recovery of balance is essentially your body putting the brakes on forward motion—much like driving with one foot on the gas and one the brake. As I wrote in Section I, regular walking is perfect for traversing very long distances at a slow pace. But as competitive walkers, we're all about traversing those distances *fast!*, not slowly. And that's not easy to do when you're constantly slamming on the brakes.

Impeded by this braking effect, most people have a hard time walking much faster than about four miles per hour, or a 15-minutes-per-mile pace, even if said people are in very good shape. Some very fit people can even get down to 12-minute miles, or even into the tens, but that's a rarity. Again, walking is great for going slowly for long distances, but its mechanical limitations make it less than ideal for sprinting.

So what do we do about that? How do we walk fast without putting on the brakes with every step? Simple. (Physics *is* simple, right?) ☺ It all comes down to those pendulums. The longer a pendulum is, the longer its *period*. The period is the amount of time it takes for a pendulum—in this case, your leg—to swing out and back. If you're just passively waiting for your leg to swing forward, you're really limiting yourself. The average human leg is about 45% of a person's height, so the average 5'10" (178cm) male—me ☺—has a leg length of about 80cm. I'll spare you the calculations, but an 80cm pendulum has a period of almost 1.8 seconds, so a passively swinging leg would move at about 33 strides (66 steps) per minute—and that's not taking into account the braking effect. These are all rough figures, but considering that a "brisk" walk is said to be 100 steps per minute, a "vigorous" walk about 130 steps per minute, and Olympic racewalkers routinely spin their wheels at 210 to 220 steps per minute or more, 66 steps per minute is downright pedestrian. Clearly, simple gravitational acceleration is not enough. Competitive walkers need to make some dynamic modifications to their normal walking gait if they ever hope to achieve speeds beyond three to four miles per hour.

If we can somehow shorten our pendulums, we should be able to walk a lot faster. But how do we shorten our God-given pendulums without resorting to a bone saw and many boxes of Band-Aids? Simple: Just bend them! If you've spent any time watching people walk, you'll notice that a good percentage of them swing their arms fully extended. Straight arms are long pendulums. By simply bending your elbows at about 90 degrees, give or take, you effectively shorten the pendulums and your arms will swing much faster. Same thing with your legs. If you bend your knee as the leg is swinging forward, the leg will swing forward much faster. But even if you succeed in shortening and speeding up the pendulum by bending the knee as the leg swings forward, why wait for it to *passively* swing forward? By making the motion more active by *driving* the knee forward rather than just allowing it to passively swing forward, you'll generate a faster, more powerful stride.

We'll talk about Olympic-style racewalking in more detail in the next chapter, but suffice to say adding some elements of racewalking technique to your "normal" walking can speed up your walking considerably. Essentially there are three simple elements that you should consider: bending your elbows at about 90 degrees to shorten those pendulums; actively using your feet when you walk; and taking shorter faster strides rather than long slow ones.

Bend your elbows

Generally speaking, whatever the arms do, the legs will follow. You'll be able to quicken your cadence by simply bending your elbows to roughly 90-degree angles. The exact angle will depend on your body proportions and what you're trying to accomplish. A slightly tighter angle—85 degrees?—will help you to achieve a very fast step rate for shorter, faster races, or if you're a tall, long-legged person looking to break out of your natural long, slow stride. A slightly more open angle—95 degrees?—will help to produce more power from the hips for longer races, or to help you open up your stride if you have shorter legs or tight hips. Whichever elbow angle you settle on, focus on driving the elbows back powerfully, keeping the arms swing relatively short in front. Again, the legs will do what the arms do, so a long arm swing to the front will lead to over-striding.

Use your feet

Fast, efficient competitive walking technique starts with the feet. Most regular walkers do very little with their feet, other than pick them up and plop them down. But actively using the feet can add to both stride length and stride frequency. The feet initiate the knee drive that provides most of the forward propulsion of the body. The feet also set the body up for an efficient transfer of energy from the body to the ground, providing even more forward propulsion. Fitness walkers tend to not use the feet very much, instead relying on the hips, and a simple pendulum motion of the leg, to swing it forward. Racewalkers speed up the forward drive of the thigh by bending the knee at about 90 degrees to shorten the pendulum. Although using the hip-flexors to drive the thigh forward will eventually unlock the knee behind the body, using the feet to unlock the knee results in a much faster forward drive of the knee. The effect is similar to what happens when someone knocks an unsuspecting person behind the knee, causing the knee to unlock and the "victim" to collapse to the ground (if done properly!) In both cases, the knee unlocks and the thigh moves forward quite suddenly. Not such a good thing when you're the one getting the legs knocked out from under you, but a very good thing for a walker looking for a source of speed and power!

In addition to initiating a strong forward knee drive, using the feet effectively behind the body also helps to push the whole body forward at the end of the stride. Biomechanists describe the single-support phase of the walking motion as that of an "inverted pendulum." As the straightened leg pivots over the ankle, the body starts to fall forward. Many walkers instinctively catch themselves with the advancing foot to keep from falling on their faces. That reflex can save you a lot on dental work, but doing so halts the stride prematurely, limiting stride length and forward speed. Allowing the body to fall a little bit further forward by rolling all the way to the tips of the toes and pointing the toes behind the body by plantar-flexing the foot, allows for a much longer and more powerful stride without limiting stride frequency. So using the feet provides quickness by unhinging the knee more quickly, and also adds to stride length. Since forward speed is a product of stride length x stride frequency, using your feet when you walk is a double-whammy!

Quick-steps

Repeating myself, your forward speed as a walker is a product of your stride length times your stride frequency [Speed = SL x SF]. To walk faster, it would make sense to take longer, faster strides. The problem, however, is that the two work against each other. Take very long strides, and your stride frequency/cadence invariably drops off; take very quick steps, and your stride length tends to diminish. The solution is to pick a comfortable stride length, and then spin your wheels as quickly as possible.

As mentioned previously, a normal brisk walk starts at about 100 steps per minute. If your goal is to walk faster, you'll have to jack that up. Taking quicker steps may result in a somewhat shorter stride, but by adhering to the previous two suggestions—bending your elbows and driving them back vigorously, and using your feet, you'll be able to take quicker steps without losing much in the way of stride length.

I'm such a nerd that I actually did a study in grad school comparing the increase in stride length vs. the increase in stride frequency as walking speed increases. (Brian Hanley at Leeds Metropolitan University in the UK, arguably the world's biggest racewalk nerd—even more so than me—did a similar, albeit better funded study in 2019.)[35] I found that as walking speed increases, ⅔ of that increase in speed comes from increased cadence rate while only ⅓ comes from increased stride length. In other words, to increase speed 25% (from 15-minute miles to 12-minute miles) most people will see, on average, an increase in stride frequency of about 16.67%, but will only see an increase in stride length of about 8.33%. Let's assume a walker has an initial stride length of two yards, or 72 inches, and is moving at fifteen minutes per mile = 4mph = 7,040 yards/hour. 7,040 yards/hour divided by 60 minutes = 58.66 steps per minute, or, dividing by two, 29.33 strides per minute. (Remember that a stride is two complete steps, for example from right foot heel strike to the next right foot heel strike.) That 16.67% increase in stride frequency means going from 29.33 strides per minute to 34.2 strides per minute. At the same time, stride length will increase only about 8.33%, or from 72 inches to 76.8 inches. Could you increase speed by just increasing stride length, or by increasing stride length more than stride frequency? Sure! But doing so will quickly lead to over-striding and marked inefficiency.

I could geek out some more and go on all day about this stuff, but I know you want to get on to the juicy bits about improving racewalking technique, so let's head there. ☺

---

[35] Hanley, Brian. (2019). Using Biomechanics to Improve Race Walking Performances, Coaching and Judging. University of Huddersfield Sport, Exercise and Nutrition Seminar Series, DOI:10.13140/RG.2.2.13622.24646.

CHAPTER 11: RACEWALKING TECHNIQUE

Racewalking is a technique that allows the best Olympic-level practitioners to blitz a mile in just over 5½ minutes and a marathon in less than three hours by maximizing the efficiency of the natural walking gait. As outlined previously, there are specific rules that racewalkers must follow in judged racewalking events. Form follows function, to quote 19th century architect Louis Sullivan. Racewalk form has evolved over the past one and one-half centuries as athletes have tried to walk as fast as possible while adhering to the rules in place at the time.

Most regular walkers take progressively longer strides as they try to increase their speed (Figure 1A). But racewalkers have learned that taking long anterior strides (the part of the stride in front of the body) is terribly inefficient. As your heel strikes the ground in front of your body, leverage causes your foot to flatten out prematurely if your strides are too long. That flat foot out in front of the body acts like a brake, slowing your forward momentum in the same way that landing flat-footed when cutting from side to side while playing tennis or basketball suddenly puts the brakes on your momentum. Pushing your whole body up and over that long front leg and flattened foot wastes a lot of energy. Racewalkers take much shorter anterior strides, so they roll very easily over their front feet and legs (Figure 1B). To further increase speed, a racewalker tries to maximize both stride frequency and stride length. The secret is to maximize stride length *behind* the body. That way the long stride doesn't get in the way of a fast cadence rate. One of the keys to increasing both stride length and foot speed is to use the arms effectively. Walking with your arms swinging fully extended, like two long pendulums, causes a very long, but slow stride. By bending your elbows to about 90 degrees you'll walk with much faster, more powerful strides.

The rule requiring the leg to be straightened as the heel touches the ground, forces racewalkers to use their legs as levers, rather than using them like springs, as runners do. The straightened leg makes racewalking somewhat less efficient than running, but the leverage created by that straightened leg makes racewalking much more powerful and much faster than regular walking. Admittedly, it also makes racewalking somewhat challenging for many people to pick up without some effort.[36] But if that weren't the case, this book would be unnecessary, and I would probably have been sitting in a cubicle for the past thirty years counting widgets for a living instead of traveling all over the world teaching people how to walk! ☺ In any case, let's look at how we can modify regular walking technique into the athletic wonder that is racewalking!

---

[36] Kids, on the other hand, more often than not, just "get it" right off the bat. Whenever I walk by a group of two or more middle school students* they'll invariably entertain each other by mimicking my technique, and most of the time they're actually pretty good.

* It's *always* the middle-schoolers. ☺

Figure 1.

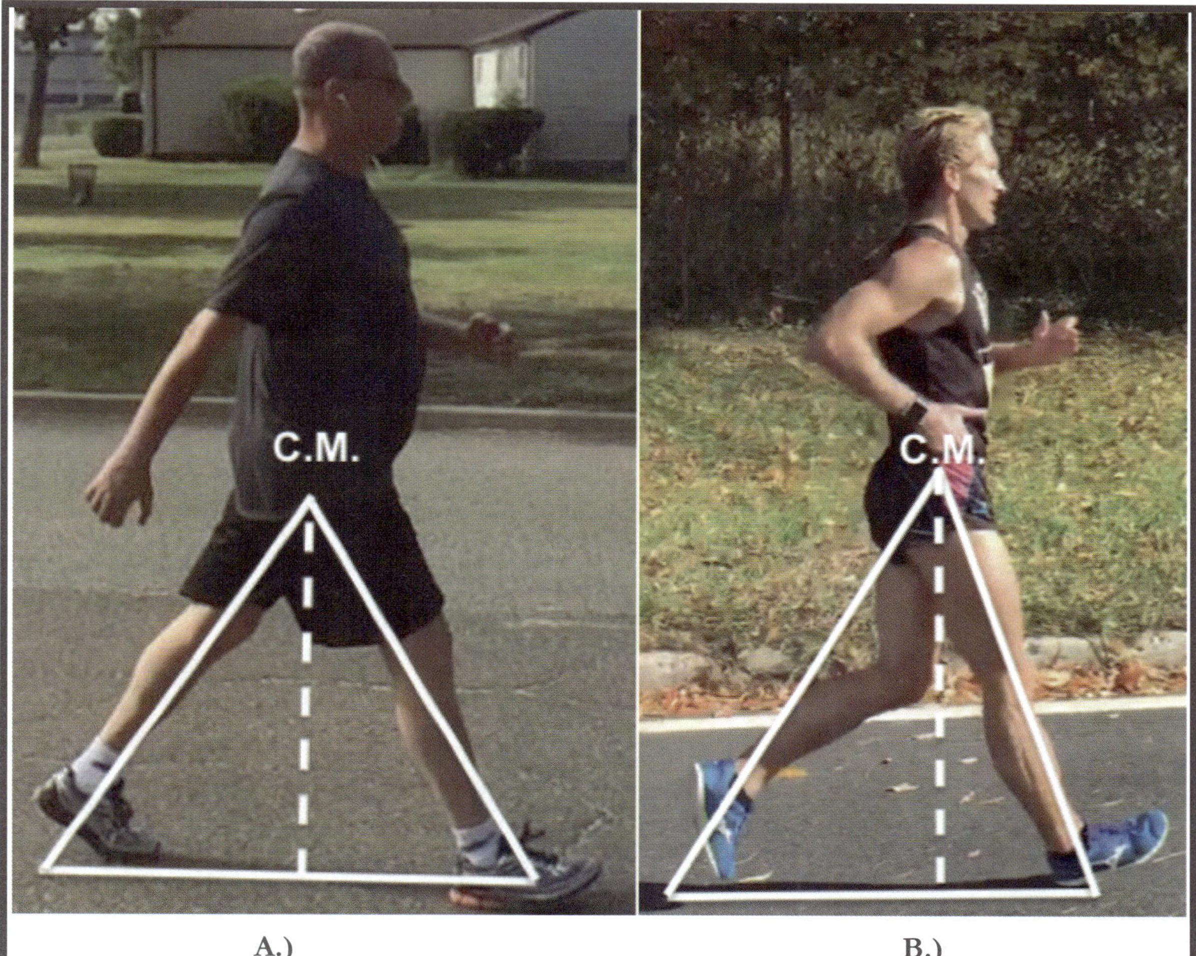

A.) B.)

Photo **A.)** shows an inefficient, overstriding walker whose heel lands far in front of a vertical line dropped down from the center of mass **(C.M.)** . The heel strikes the ground at a very sharp angle, which causes the foot to "flatten out" just after heel contact. A flat foot in front of the body puts the brakes on forward momentum. Photo **B.)** shows the heel landing very close to **C.M.**, and the front leg almost vertical, making it much easier to vault over the leg. Since the heel contacts the ground at a much lower angle there is less force acting to flatten out the foot, allowing a smooth "rolling" motion to occur. At heel contact, Walker **B.)** has about 70% of the stride pushing from behind the body, and only 30% in front compared to Walker **A.)**'s inefficient 50/50 proportion. Walker **A.)** also walks with the arms fully extended, while Walker **B.)** bends the elbows. Bending the elbows helps Walker **B.)** to achieve shorter, faster, more powerful strides.

Knee-pumping and Frankenstein walking

The value of an efficient walking stride can't be overstated, but reading about walking efficiently and doing it are two entirely different things. So how do you learn to take those quick, efficient strides? To get an idea of what racewalking feels like, simply stand in place with your feet together and your arms held by your sides with the elbows bent at 90 degrees. Now pump your knees forward and back while keeping your weight on your heels and your feet flat on the ground. Each time you pull your knee back, your leg will straighten under your body just as it will when you're racewalking. Focus on what it feels like when you pull the thigh back. You throw the thigh forward every day when you walk, run, climb stairs, ride a bicycle, etc. Pulling the thigh all the way back until the knee fully straightens is probably something you only do when you're bored, shifting your weight from side to side, waiting in line at the bank. (Do people wait in line at the bank anymore?) But instead of shifting your weight and straightening one leg, then the other, three to four times per minute, now you need to do it three to four times *per second.* At this point all you need to do is add some stride length by stepping forward a bit each time you pump your knees forward. Just be sure to land on your heels. If you land too flat-footed your knees will probably bend when your foot hits the ground. Concentrate on taking short, quick steps rather than long, slow ones. If you do that, you'll have an easier time keeping your knees straight, and you'll expend much less energy. As you get stronger, your stride should get longer. Try to make sure the extra stride length is behind your body, though. Keep it short up front.

Most people can pick up the technique the way I just outlined it, but if you feel you're not getting the hang of the straightened knee, you may have to try "Frankenstein walking"[37] until you get your knees sorted out. Start out by walking on your heels with your toes held up. Take short steps and maintain good posture. (Full disclosure: You will look ridiculous.) ☺ After you get the hang of that, allow your foot to flatten out as your body passes over it, but keep walking with stiff legs. Continue landing on your heels, and then keep your weight on your heels as long as you're able to throughout the stride. (At the last instant you'll roll forward from the heels to the toes to push off of the back foot.) Now just take quicker and quicker steps, pumping your arms to dictate the cadence of your feet and legs. Your knees will start to bend as you step forward, but that's okay. Just make sure you continue landing on your heel so the knee stays straight when that leg is supporting the body. Once you've gotten the feel of Frankenstein-walking with straight knees, you can gradually make it feel more like racewalking by bending the advancing knee more and more as

[37] I don't know that Mary Shelley, author of *Frankenstein, or The Modern Prometheus* had any connection to competitive walking, but a gentleman by the name of Abraham Stoker most certainly did. Sickly and bed-ridden since birth, Stoker suddenly began to thrive at age seven. To develop his new-found strength, doctors suggested he walk as much as possible. And walk he did! By 17, Stoker had grown into a 6' 2" giant, who began winning awards as a champion racewalker in his first year at Trinity College Dublin. He was never beaten in a race. Stoker retained his passion for walking throughout his life, serving as a racewalk judge, including at the first Irish National Championships in 1873. Later, during a long-distance walk in the countryside surrounding Aberdeen, Scotland, he stumbled upon Cruden Bay, the gloomy fishing village where in 1895 he wrote *Dracula*, published two years later under the name "Bram Stoker." The rest, as they say, is literary history.

it drives forward. Walking on a very gradual (three to five percent grade) hill, starting out using either the knee pumps or the Frankenstein walk, will make it even easier to pick up the technique. Once you have it, you can get faster by pumping your arms and driving your knees more vigorously to give yourself a longer, more powerful stride. With the basic technique locked in, the next step is to refine individual elements. Let's take a look at each of these components of racewalking technique, from the ground up:

Spin your wheels

You may have to sacrifice stride length a bit at first to master the straight knee and to achieve a high cadence rate. Not a problem! Efficient racewalking is a lot like "spinning" in a high gear on a bicycle: With a shorter stride it's much easier to achieve a high stride frequency. In the end, you'll wind up moving forward faster and with less effort even with the slightly shorter stride. And added speed isn't the only benefit of limiting your stride length in front of your body: Long, slow strides aren't just inefficient, they also increase your air time, so shortening your stride length in front isn't just faster, it's actually more legal. Research has shown that in world-class racewalkers heel strike occurs at a point no more than thirty to forty centimeters in front of the center of mass, and Chinese women—some of the fastest walkers in the world—achieve heel-strike distances of just ten centimeters.[38] The incredible cadence rates these athletes generate enable them to cover 20 kilometers at better than seven-minutes per mile. Want to walk faster? Get those heels down quickly and close to the body!

Counting your strides every once in a while is a good way to make sure your new, quicker technique isn't getting sloppy. Count every other footfall for 15 seconds, and then multiply by eight to determine your step rate per minute. There's no "right answer" but a stride count over 160 is a pretty good clip. A good racewalker will be closer to 180 or more. If you fall toward—or below—the low end of the range, work on shortening and quickening your stride. Counting your strides, or at least being aware of the sound of your footfalls, will not only help your technique, it can also help you to gauge your walking pace. After putting in many mile of training you'll begin to learn the "feel" of your various training paces, from your easiest recovery day pace to race pace and beyond.

Use your feet

The first "step" to taking quicker steps is to simply do it: Just take quicker steps! But *actively* using the feet while racewalking is the next, critical step. The feet are the only parts of your body that are ever in contact with the ground when you racewalk. An obvious point perhaps, but one that's often overlooked. The feet need to be a very active part of the racewalking motion. But as mentioned above, the first thing to remember is to keep them out of your way. The foot should roll like a

[38] Brian Hanley's 2014 Leeds Metropolitan University PhD thesis is a terrific distillation of racewalking biomechanics research over the past quarter century.

wheel or a rocking chair rocker from heel to toe as the body pivots over the lead leg. If the muscles of the foot and lower leg are weak, the force of the ground acting on the heel will cause the foot to flatten out. If the foot flattens out prematurely, it will be in the way, hindering forward motion and causing an inefficient, slow, percussive, "stumpy" stride. Overstriding will cause an even more pronounced flattening, since the heel strikes the ground at a sharper angle. Big, heavy, inflexible, "klunky" shoes will exacerbate flattening of the lead foot, barring a smooth rolling motion.

Keeping your feet out of the way at the front of the stride is critical, but it's equally important to actively use them for propulsion and stride lengthening at the back of the stride. Forward propulsion comes from pushing the rear foot back against the ground, which creates leverage that help to vault your body forward. Keeping the rear foot on the ground as long as possible, pushing through the ball of the foot and rolling all the way up to the tip of the toes at push-off will maximize this leverage. Another advantage to using the feet is that the flick off the back foot at the end of the stride also helps to unlock the straightened knee, which helps to drive the advancing leg forward. I do a drill at my clinics where I have everybody stand on one foot with the knee locked, and the other foot barely touching the ground. When everyone is ready I'll tell them to very suddenly shift the body weight from the heel and arch of the foot up to the tip of the toes. When doing so, the knee suddenly unlocks as if someone kicked them in the back of the knee, as described in the previous chapter. The same thing happens when you use your feet when racewalking: the feet initiate the stride, helping to unlock the knee and start driving it forward, creating the momentum that helps to propel the whole body forward.

To get the right asymmetrical look of a racewalker, with a long stride behind the body and a shorter stride to the front (Figure 1B)—and to maximize cadence rate—your feet must be very active, rolling smoothly from the heel all the way to the toes with each stride. Failing to use the feet properly will result in a "stumpy" technique and difficulty generating sufficient forward propulsion and speed.

Weakness and inflexibility hinder effective use of the feet and ankles, but strength and flexibility can be improved. One of the best ways of doing so is by racewalking while wearing a wet vest or other flotation device in a swimming pool. The resistance of the water forces the foot to open and close in relation to the shin. Even better, *don't* use the flotation vest, instead using your feet like paddles to keep yourself afloat. Calf raises and "Theraband" exercises can also be used to strengthen the feet, shins and ankles (see chapter 35).

Toe the line

Each foot should fall more or less along the same imaginary line as the one before to limit lateral motion of the body ("wiggling") and to maximize effective stride length. If possible, the toes should be pointed forward rather than angled out. Some athletes walk with the toes pointed out to the sides as much as 30 degrees. Doing so cuts stride length by as much as two inches per stride with no gain in power. Two inches per stride x 200 strides per minute = 400 inches (33 feet, 4 inches) per minute. Over the course of a 10k race that's more than two minutes! Minor technique changes can make a very big difference in race times without requiring you to train any harder.

Figure 2.

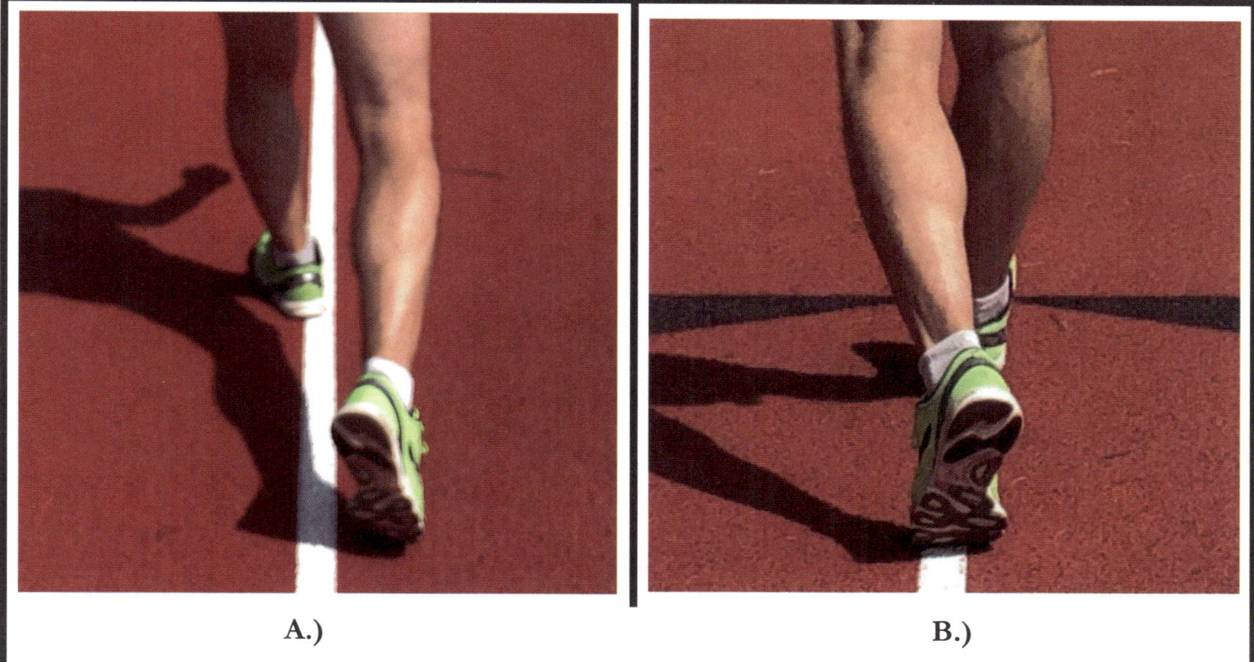

A.) **B.)**

Walker **A.)** walks inefficiently, with the feet landing on either side of an imaginary line. Walker **B.)** walks efficiently, using the hips so that one foot falls directly in front of the other along the line, maximizing effective stride length and limiting side-to-side motion of the body's center of mass.

Use both the "driving" and "vaulting" phases of your stride

Keeping out of your own way and generating some propulsion with your feet is a good start, but now you have to generate some real power to propel yourself forward. There are two ways to do this, and you should take advantage of them both: They are the "driving" and "vaulting" components of your stride. The two phases proceed concurrently: As one leg creates momentum by driving forward, the other leg pushes back against the ground, launching the body forward by way of a powerful vaulting effect. Biomechanists refer to the driving component of your stride as the "swing" phase, but this, to me, indicates a passive movement. The knee should drive forward aggressively, as opposed to the leg passively swinging forward as it does during the normal walking gait. You may also hear the vaulting phase of your stride called the "stance" phase. This, too, connotes passivity. Alternately, the stance phase is sometimes called the "propulsive" phase. Certainly better, but this is also a bit of a misnomer, since the legs provide forward propulsion during both phases of the stride cycle, albeit in different ways. In my mind, driving and vaulting more accurately describe how the legs generate force throughout the racewalking stride cycle.

<u>The driving phase-</u> The driving phase begins with the body in the double-support phase, balanced on the heel of the front foot and the toe of the back foot (Figure 3A). The knee of the rear leg then punches forward after the toe of the back foot pushes off the ground. More simple physics: When you take a 25 or 35 pound object—your leg—and throw it forward, the momentum of the accelerating mass will cause your body to pivot over the planted foot, carrying your body forward. This pivoting is best seen in Figures 3B-D. As the left leg drives forward, the body pivots over the right leg. Many beginning racewalkers think the rules say you can't bend your knees. Not true! You can, you should, and you have to bend your knees—but only as the leg is moving forward. The advancing leg should drive forward much like a runner's leg, only lower to the ground. The knee should punch forward vigorously, bending to about 90 degrees shortly after the foot pushes-off (Figures 3C). Think about your arm swing: You bend your elbows 90-degrees angles to create a shorter, faster pendulum. You should bend your knees to about 90 degrees for the same reason: to maximize the speed and power of the advancing leg.

Continue driving the knee forward until you feel your body beginning to fall forward, pivoting over the ankle joint of the planted foot. *Before* face-planting, ☺ use your glutes and hamstring

Figure 3.

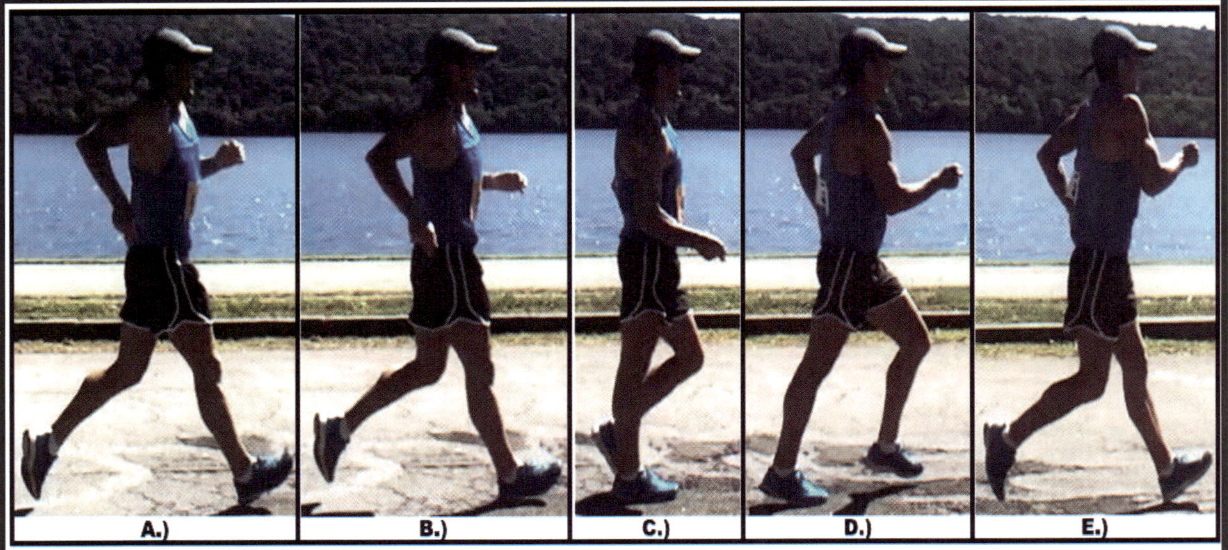

This walker[39] demonstrates excellent racewalking technique. The stride sequence begins at the double-support phase **A.)** with the rear foot pushing off at about a 135-degree angle in relation to the shin. Notice how close to the body the front heel has landed. After the rear foot pushes off, the knee punches forward, bent at a 90-degree angle, initiating the driving phase of the stride **B.)**, with the advancing foot sweeping through very low to the ground **B.)** through **D.)**. Notice the support leg (the right leg) beginning to push back, creating a "vaulting" effect **D.)** concurrent with the "driving" of the left leg. As the thigh of the advancing leg begins to pull back **E.)**, the lower leg swings open and the knee straightens. After the right heel contacts the ground, the left knee will punch forward to begin the next stride.

---

[39] James Rendón of Colombia, in the later stages of his South American record-setting 50k racewalk at Valley Cottage, New York, concurrent with the US 30k Championships. I was the race director (and photographer...)

muscles to pull the thigh back, planting the heel on the ground close to the body just as the knee is straightening (Figure 3E).

You shouldn't be trying to straighten the knee by contracting the quadriceps muscles; the quads should be relaxed. Momentum is what straightens the knee. After the thigh changes direction from forward to rearward motion, the momentum of the lower leg continuing to move forward while the thigh is pulling back straightens the knee automatically. Just relax and let it happen. Have you ever opened a switchblade?[40] You flick your wrist, and then suddenly stop or change the direction of that flicking motion—the blade opens up as it continues moving in the same direction, straightening just as your leg does as the thigh changes direction. The more sudden that change in direction, the more firmly the knee will straighten.

One caveat: When driving the knee forward, avoid a high knee lift. You always want your energy to be moving forward toward the finish line, not up. Bringing the knees high is very inefficient and is a flashing red light to a racewalk judge. If you punch the knee through low and vigorously, the advancing leg should come through with the foot sweeping very low to the ground (see figure 3B-D). If you get the timing right, your heel should make contact with the ground very close to the body just as the leg straightens. It's fast, efficient, and when you get it right, wow, does it feel cool!

One more "minor" technique change that could make a big difference is a kick of the lower leg just before heel contact. When I was training for the 1996 Olympic Trials I had the opportunity to

Figure 4.

This walker demonstrates poor technique. He leans forward, overstrides, "lifts", and his feet are inactive.

---

[40] No? Neither have I, but I did have one of those cool switchblade combs in junior high school. Back when I had hair.

work with the coaches of some of the top walkers in China.[41] I had just walked my fastest 20k ever and was preparing to race another 20k in Békéscsaba Hungary in a few weeks. While slamming through some 400-meter reps with 1995 World Cup Champion Li Zewen, during a rest interval I asked the coaches if they had noticed anything that I could do to improve my technique. The coaches conferred, then ran their conclusions through Sonny, their translator who had mastered at least several dozen words in English. ☺ The conclusion: I had a "razy rower reg," which I myself translated to a "lazy lower leg." In the previous chapter I pointed out that racewalkers take many of the passive motions of regular walking and make them more active. Apparently my arms and knees were driving well, my feet were active, but my lower legs were *passively* swinging forward rather than actively contributing to my forward momentum. I took their advice, added a bit of lower leg kick just before heel contact, practiced for the next two weeks, and wound up taking two minutes off of my best 20k time, bringing it down to 1:24:29, just 30 seconds off of the automatic Olympic qualifying standard. Sometimes it's the little things…

Coach Dave blitzing 400-meter repeats with 1995 World Cup 20k Champion, Li Zewen Photo credit: Mo Roberts

The vaulting phase- The vaulting phase begins as soon as the heel contacts the ground in front of the body. As the bent knee of one leg drives forward, the body passes over the other leg—the straightened "support leg." This is where racewalking differs considerably from running—or regular walking, for that matter. When a runner's foot is on the ground directly under the body, the knee is bent with the leg "cocked" and ready to spring the body forward. Racewalkers, on the other

[41] As a reward for winning all three races at the 1995 World Cup in Beijing, each of the champion athletes was gifted by the Chinese Athletics Federation with a trip to Atlanta, along with their coaches, to view the 1996 Olympic walks course. I became their babysitter for their trip. I had a previously scheduled clinic in Miami so I convinced them to come with me. Instead of flying I rented a 15-passenger van and we drove down from LaGrange, Ga. It's a funny story involving high-speed mall-walking, topless beaches, forcible ejection from my favorite all-you-can-eat sushi place, Karaoke, Gatorland, and "up-trousers." You can find it on my website at https://racewalking.org/pdfs/Other%20Articles/Fun/china.pdf/.

hand, keep the knee of the support leg straightened during the single-support phase, using the leg as a lever to vault the body forward, rather than using the springing action of a runner's leg. It's a different way of propelling the body forward, but a very effective one once you get the hang of it!

The key to an effective vaulting phase is to maximize the leverage launching the body forward. More high school physics: The longer a lever is, the more force it will generate. After the body's center of mass passes over the planted foot, the calf muscles contract, plantar-flexing the ankle (pointing the toe behind the body, as seen in Figures 3B and E). Rolling off the toe in this manner is one way to lengthen the lever. Using your hips more effectively is another way to create a longer, more powerful lever. Instead of walking with just your feet and legs, imagine that your leg doesn't start at the hips, but starts all the way up toward the base of your rib cage. Using the hips and the strong oblique muscles along both sides of your abdomen will, in effect, create a longer leg, which will act as a longer lever to vault your body forward. Not only will using your hips properly generate more propulsive force, you will also increase your "effective stride length"—the part of your stride that extends behind your body, helping to vault your body forward.

Even without actively using your abdominal oblique muscles to create more leverage and open up your stride, a "blocking" effect acting on the hips will open them up automatically if you roll off the toes properly. As one side of the hip is anchored by the support leg, the opposite side of the hip swings forward like a gate, pulled forward by the driving knee of the other leg. Proper hip action extends your effective stride length and also helps to align the feet on a line, one in front of the other, as in Figure 5B. The result is more power, and more of that power moving in the right direction—forward toward the finish line instead of sashaying from side to side.

As you may have inferred by now, the hips are very important in racewalking. Forward

Figure 5.

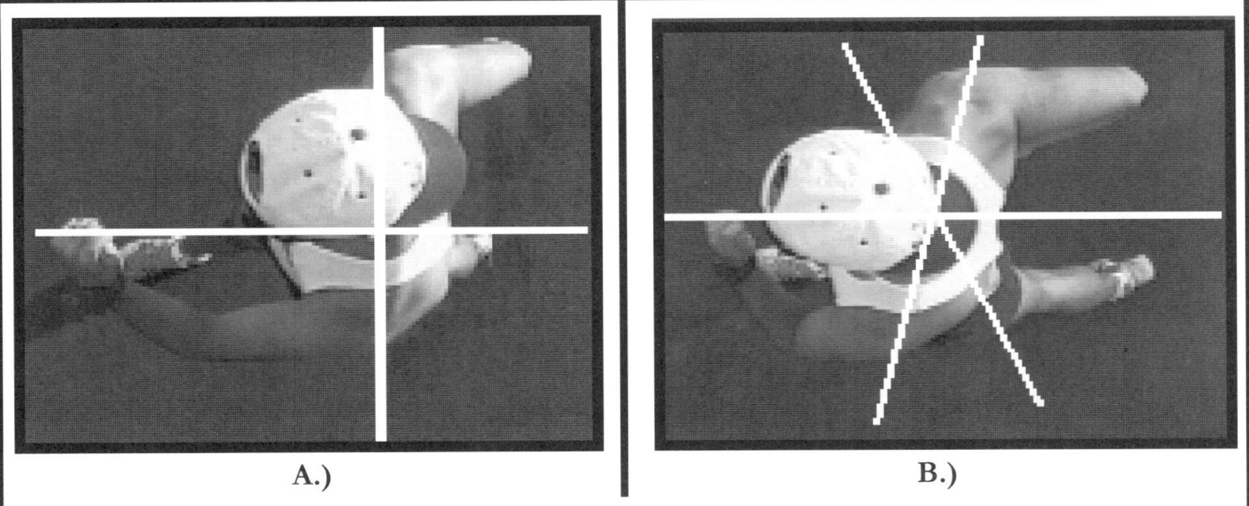

Walker **A.)** is not using his hips effectively; overall stride length is limited, effective (behind the body) stride length is relatively short, and the feet are not in line. Walker **B.)** uses his hips, creating a longer overall stride length, a long stride behind the body, and in-line foot placement.

propulsion is achieved by pushing the ground behind you with the rear leg, while the advancing leg punches forward with a low but vigorous knee drive. A strong front-to-back hip action will facilitate both the vaulting and driving phases of the stride. Concentrate on this front and back action rather than a side-to-side hip "sashay." Additionally, a certain amount of "hip drop" should occur naturally after push-off: As the rear leg comes forward, and the foot loses contact with the ground, the hip is no longer supported so it drops slightly, pulled down by the weight of the advancing leg. The benefit of waking with some hip drop is that with it, the foot can glide forward very close to the ground even with the knee bent at 90-degrees as it drives forward. The "skimming" low foot looks great to judges, and the 90-degree knee bend contributes to a very powerful knee drive

Maintain erect posture

Posture, posture, posture! Weak abs and tight lower-back muscles can cause "slouchy" walking technique. Bending at the waist, or leaning forward excessively while racewalking, artificially forces the lead leg to extend too far out in front of the body. The long anterior stride seen in forward-leaning racewalkers causes a tooth-jarring braking effect as they land onto their straightened legs like Frankenstein's monster lurching around the laboratory. Some misguided souls theorize that gravity will pull the body forward, but even if gravity did somehow help to pull Frankenstein's racewalking monster forward—and when I studied physics, gravity pulled all the apples, bullets, and cannon balls down, not forward—the braking force of this percussive, stiff-legged landing prevents a smooth transition into the next stride. I could never understand why the villagers always ran away from poor Frank. Sure, a forward leaning, overstriding monster coming after you is scary to look at, but with that inefficient technique, he sure couldn't have walked very fast!

So leaning from the waist is ugly and slow, but it's also very hard on the body—on the lower back in particular. Try balancing a broom handle vertically on the palm of your hand. It feels very light when it's standing vertically, doesn't it? Now try holding the broom parallel to the ground by the end of the handle. It feels much heavier. Even holding the broom five to eight degrees beyond vertical is more difficult than holding it upright. The same thing happens when you try to lean forward when you walk or racewalk. And your torso, supported by your poor lower back muscles, ligaments and tendons, is a whole lot heavier than any broom handle. I could blather on all day here, but I'll stop now if you promise to straighten up and fly right. I don't want to be a pain in the neck...

Relax your neck and shoulders

Speaking of necks, walking with your head down can cause tension in the neck and shoulders that can be transferred to the rest of the body. If possible, focus your eyes on a point on the horizon. If you have to, keep your head level but your eyes down to keep from tripping, kicking road kill, etc., but try to look at least 15 to 20 meters down the road. Wearing a hat with a brim or visor causes many athletes to walk with their eyes and head down, so either turn the hat backwards, or simply remind yourself to look ahead while wearing a brimmed hat. Keep your shoulders relaxed and as low as possible. Obviously you could just tell yourself to keep your shoulders down throughout your walk, but instead, I tell myself to scrape the ground with my elbows when swinging my arms forward to help keep my shoulders down. Obviously the elbows don't actually touch the ground, but the motion helps to keep my chronically tight shoulders down and relaxed.

The amount of torso rotation depends a lot on an individual athlete's anatomy. Perhaps counter-intuitively, the torso and the hips will rotate in opposite directions, working in concert to help power the legs. In general, athletes with the most torso rotation have the least pelvic rotation and vice-versa. Brian Hanley's studies[42] have shown that among elite 50k men, 20k men, 20k women and U20 (under age 20) 10k male and female racewalkers, 50k men have the most pelvic rotation and the least torso rotation, while 20k women and 10k U20 women have the most torso rotation and the least pelvic rotation. It has always been drilled into my head by coaches that pelvic rotation helps add to stride length—and it does. But *excessive* pelvic rotation slows down a walker's cadence, at least partially negating any benefit gained from the added stride length. So, as with most elements of a walker's technique, there's a cost/benefit calculation to be made. In the case of a 95lb. elite female racewalker with a very narrow pelvis, lots of pelvic rotation has relatively little impact on stride length, and for a woman with relatively little upper body mass, there's not much downside in terms of energy cost, to increased torso rotation. The torso makes up about 40% of a person's body mass, or in the case of the 95lb. female 20k walker, about 38lbs. Compare that to a 175lb. male 50k walker, whose torso weighs about 70lbs. In his case, too much torso rotation can be detrimental, and the additional pelvic rotation will probably contribute more benefit in terms of added stride length than it would for a tiny woman. It is probably also likely that the male 50k walker is not as flexible as the 95lb. female 20k walker, so it may be more difficult for him to gain additional stride length via other means, such as superior ankle-flexion or hip-flexor extension. In any case, whether to use more or less pelvic rotation vs. torso rotation depends upon individual anatomy, flexibility and other factors.

Arm yourself

A racewalker's legs follow the lead of the arms. A powerful rearward arm drive helps to propel pelvic rotation without the wasted energy that comes as a result of excessive torso rotation. It's important to make sure that the arm drive is an *effective* arm drive, though. "Chicken-winging" your

---

[42] Brian has a great presentation (slide show) synthesizing much of this research here: https://www.researchgate.net/publication/329275753_Kinematics_of_Elite_Race_Walking/.

Two racewalkers demonstrating powerful rearward arm drive and low, close to the body, arm swing to the front.

elbows out to the sides will cause an energy-wasting side-to-side hip wiggle, while excessive forward "uppercut punches" will alternately raise and drop your center of mass, adding an inefficient and DQ-drawing "hoppiness" to your stride. And extending the arm swing too far forward will almost always result in overstriding. At most, your hands should swing forward to a point in front of the breastbone, then swing back vigorously to at least the level of your hip socket. Your hands should be relaxed—no clenched fists—and your arms should move freely as if they were pendulums hung from the shoulders. The forearms should be held at about 90 degrees relative to the upper arm, but this will vary plus or minus a few degrees, depending on the distance of the race and personal preference. The most important thing is to keep the neck and shoulders relaxed even though the arms are driving back powerfully.

If you happen to be a beginning, or even intermediate racewalker, please skip ahead to the next paragraph. I'll wait… Some weather we've been having, huh? Never seen anything like it… Ok, they're gone! If you're a very experienced racewalker, you can get even more out of your arms by not just driving them back, but also punching them forward, lo and powerfully. The forward punch helps to provide a little bit of extra momentum to the body, and helps kick the lower leg out as I described earlier in the chapter. The forward punch is designed to add inches to your "flight phase" if you have one. It's a little tricky to get it just right and it only works if you do get it just right, but it's worth the effort if you can get it. If you *don't* get it just right it can lead to a lot of disqualifications, so be careful! Internationally, Robert Korzeniowski was a great model of this technique, as was Tim Seaman in the US, but like Babe Ruth's home run to strike out ratio, both Robert and Tim suffered some big high-profile DQ's to go with their many successes.

Relax your head—inside

I've said a lot about the action of various body parts, but fast, efficient racewalking doesn't really begin with the feet—it begins with the mind. Relaxation is one of the real keys to walking fast, and relaxed technique begins with a relaxed mind. Due to the limitations imposed by the rules, the energy costs of inefficient racewalking accumulate much more quickly than in running. What does that mean? You can fake it to some degree in running, but you'll fatigue and slow down much more quickly when racewalking with inefficient technique, and tension can lead to inefficient technique.

It's very important to continually remind yourself to relax—especially during stressful races or workouts. You don't need to clench your teeth and fists to walk fast. Tightness in the jaw and upper body will be referred to the lower extremities, shortening your effective stride length. Similarly, attempting to "power" yourself forward by driving your hands and arms too far out in front of your body, will lead to tight shoulders, costly overstriding, and likely, illegal lifting. Don't force things—just relax and let it flow.

Symmetry

If only we lived in a world without muscle strength and flexibility imbalances, leg-length discrepancies, scoliosis, etc… But we don't. Very few walkers, even at the highest levels, are completely symmetrical from one side of the body to the other. Differences in muscle strength, range-of-motion, and mechanics between sides of the body are extremely common and don't necessarily lead to an increased likelihood of injuries or disqualifications.[43] Of course flexibility is very important for racewalkers, and we should all strive to improve, or at least maintain, flexibility in our ankles, hip-flexors, quadriceps, hamstrings, lower back, and around the knees, in particular, but you don't need to achieve perfect mirror-image balance to racewalk well, even at a very high level. I've been a student of walking and running technique for as long as I can remember, and I've always been intrigued that some of the best endurance athletes in the world do not have perfect mechanics. I recall being intrigued by Long Island, New York, "Hometown Hero" marathon runner Pat Peterson who was a three-time top-five New York City Marathon finisher and who briefly held the American marathon record in the late-1980s. Peterson was as well known for "his unorthodox running form of flailing arms and swaying shoulders"[44] as he was for his running prowess. I'll keep myself out of trouble by not naming names, but there have been many top walkers over the years who have not been blessed with picture-perfect, symmetrical walking style. That's not to say that technical perfection isn't something to strive for. It is. But not having perfect form *today* doesn't mean that you shouldn't train hard, racewalk in public, or enter races. If everybody waited until they had perfect, and perfectly symmetrical, form before testing themselves in competition, we would have no elite walkers! To quote Osgood Fielding III in *Some Like it Hot,* or, if you prefer, Hanna Montana/Miley Cyrus: Nobody's perfect!

---

[43] Tucker, Catherine B., and Hanley, Brian. (2020). "Increases in speed do not change gait symmetry or variability in world-class race walkers." https://www.tandfonline.com/doi/abs/10.1080/02640414.2020.1798730/.

[44] And that was from a flattering article in his hometown "Long Island Newsday" newspaper! ☺

Technique vs. style

Although used interchangeably by some authors, the terms "technique" and "style" are really not synonymous. Technique refers to racewalking under the constraints of the rules: Everyone who walks with continuous visible ground contact and straightens the supporting leg with each step is exhibiting racewalk technique. Each of these individuals, however, has their own "style." A walker's style is the sum total of all individual variations in arm carriage, body posture, hip drive, etc., and is largely influenced by morphology (muscle strengths and weaknesses, degree of flexibility, relative limb lengths, etc.), but also personal preferences.

The rules of racewalking make no mention of aesthetics. Many top racewalkers cruise by with extremely fluid styles that may or may not technically allow them to maintain contact with the ground at all times. Other walkers may be less efficient, exhibiting herky-jerky styles that attract the unwanted attention of judges. These less efficient athletes may actually be more "grounded" and letter-of-the-law legal than more fluid athletes who often float above the ground for several milliseconds per stride. Even so, "klunky" walkers are often disqualified by judges for lifting, while smoother, but "liftier," walkers get by. Is this fair? Maybe not, but it is the reality of the sport. Not only is a smooth walking style faster, more efficient, and less likely to cause injuries, it also gives the appearance of legality whether the "beautiful" walkers are actually on the ground at all times or not.

And one more thing...

While we're on the subject of terminology, you may have noticed that I refer to racewalk, racewalker, racewalking, etc., as one word. Many dictionaries, spell-check programs, and newspaper editors, still don't recognize the term racewalk, and refer to us as inconsequential race walkers race walking that goofy race walk thing. Spacewalk has been considered a "real" word for years and racewalkers have been doing their thing for a whole lot longer than astronauts have been doing theirs. The only way to make the change is to use the one-word terms without fail in all publications, and even in personal correspondence. Funk & Wagnalls will eventually get around to recognizing us. I'm proud to say that my local hometown newspaper (The New York Times) has been using one word for *racewalking* and *racewalker* since at least the turn of the millennium.[45] Little steps…

[45] In the body of the articles, anyway. About half the time racewalking is mentioned in the headline, the Times still edits the word to race walking, yet uses racewalking throughout the body of the article. Sigh…

CHAPTER 12: HOW DO YOU LEARN A NEW TECHNIQUE?

Unlike runners, walkers have technical limitations imposed upon them by rules—whatever those rules may be. Whether it's power walking, racewalking or Nordic walking, the requirement to have one foot at least appear to be in contact with the ground at all times puts an upper limit on stride length and that, in turn, puts a limit on speed. To learn the technique and to achieve a fast, efficient style, a high degree of neuromuscular coordination is required. Fortunately, such coordination is trainable if you're willing to put in the time needed to "rewire" your neuromuscular system. When learning any new technique via the printed page, photo sequences and diagrams are great, but to be honest, I prefer live lessons whenever possible. As a coach, I realize there are different learning styles, so when I'm teaching at one of my clinics or camps, or during private sessions, I try to mix it up, using a combination of teaching methods. Over time I've gravitated toward the following sequence, which aligns very closely with what I learned much later in an academic setting.[46] This is the sequence that I use:

- **Verbal instructions-** First I'll talk about the history of competitive walking, the development of the rules, technical requirements, and what the various body parts do.
- **Demonstrations-** After describing the technique I'll do "live" demonstrations using myself or a proficient participant as a model.
- **Mimicry-** Next up I'll have the athletes mimic the technique while I record them.
- **Video review-** We'll then look at and analyze video of elite walkers and the video of the participants, noting the differences, and any progress made during the "mimicry" phase.
- **Repetition-** Finally, I'll have the participants walk again (and again, and again!) working on making the changes I pointed out during the video review.

Verbal instructions

Whichever form of walking you're hoping to learn, it's important to know the rules and technical requirements before getting started. I think verbal instructions are helpful in that regard for anyone learning a new technique, but especially for technically oriented people. (I'm looking at you, engineers!) ☺ I like to give a (probably overly) detailed explanation of the rules and then describe

[46] There's a very good overview of the skill-learning process in: Yarrow, K., Brown, P., & Krakauer, J. W. (2009). "Inside the brain of an elite athlete: The neural processes that support high achievement in sports." *Nature Reviews Neuroscience,* 10, 585-596. doi:10.1038/nrn2672.

what the feet, the knees, the hips, the shoulders, the arms, etc., should be doing. Breaking the technique down body part by body part helps give a deeper understanding of where and how power is generated when walking, and how focusing on these areas can considerably improve a walker's technique.

Demonstrations

Being a visual learner myself, I think having a good model to demonstrate proper walking technique is critical. I like to demonstrate both good and bad form myself, but when I have a talented walker with me, it can be very useful to have him or her walk while I narrate, pointing out what each of the body parts is doing. My assistant or I will demonstrate technique from both sides, from the front, and the back, to best show every aspect of the technique, from foot action and alignment, knee-straightening, pelvic and torso rotation, arms, shoulders, posture, etc.

Mimicry

As I noted earlier, if you've ever power walked or racewalked past a herd of adolescents, you've probably noticed them imitating you after you went by. They probably exaggerated the arms and hips a bit, but they usually get it pretty darned close. For some reason, adults tend to over-analyze things instead of "just doing it." According to former Soviet National Racewalking Team coach Anatoliy Fruktov, mimicry is by far the most effective way for athletes to learn proper technique. As described above, Fruktov suggests coaches introduce new athletes to the sport by explaining the major points of walking mechanics, then demonstrating the technique themselves, or by showing slow-motion and actual-speed films of top athletes. Fruktov advises that the coach repeat the demonstration several times at normal speed as well as at a deliberately slow pace. The new walkers should then imitate the demonstrated technique at various paces over distances of 50 to 60 meters. After the athletes try the new technique a few times the coach will comment on the positives, then point out what still needs further refinement: the ankles, knees, arms, hips or whatever. I spend a lot of time at my clinics having my walkers mimic my technique, or that of my assistant, if I have one. I always video before and after shots of each participant, which tees-up the next method:

Video analysis

Any time that I have any of my clinic participants walking, I'm recording. After years of coaching walkers, I've become very good at picking out most technique flaws at a glance. But every once in a while I'll get stumped. Something won't look quite right in somebody's technique, but no matter how many times he or she walks by I won't be able to figure out exactly what's causing the problem. After a few seconds of watching a frame-by-frame video, though, I'll usually be able to figure it out. From the athlete's perspective, video affords an opportunity to see the differences between their present technique and that of more advanced or elite walkers, and to get immediate visual feedback after adopting the new techniques. It is an invaluable tool and should be used whenever possible as an adjunct to the three methods described previously. I used to rely on very expensive video cameras with freeze-frame and slow-motion capabilities at my clinics, but I had a persistent bad habit of dropping them and breaking them. I finally realized that my iPhone has everything I need to shoot and replay videos in high definition, forwards, backwards, in slow-motion, and frame-by-frame. Coach's Eye, and similar apps and programs, allow users to superimpose video of the athlete onto video of another (presumably, elite) athlete, or a previous video of the same athlete. These apps allow instant comparisons, making it easier to point out to the athlete—or yourself, if self-coached—any corrections that need to be made.

Repetition

According to Malcolm Gladwell, writing in *Outliers: The Story of Success*, it takes 10,000 hours of repetition to achieve mastery in any given field. Although I don't completely buy into such a broad statement, it is true that repetition is the way to permanently lock in technique changes. Howard Null, my favorite sport psychologist, explained to me that learning a new technique happens in the cerebrum. It's conscious thought, he used to tell me. But to lock in the changes where they become automatic, those conscious thoughts have to be moved into the cerebellum where motor learning and "muscle memory" occur. Once there, the thoughts become subconscious. In everyday terms, it's like riding a bicycle. You never forget how to walk properly once you've written the motions into your muscle memory by repeating them again and again and again.

Returning specifically to racewalking for a minute, the technique is its own unique form of locomotion but it is in some ways a cross between walking and running, which draws from elements of both. Accordingly, I've been able to teach walkers and runners how to racewalk using templates already familiar to them: a walking template and a running template.

The walking template

According to former British National walking coach Julian Hopkins, racewalking technique is merely an extension of ordinary walking and should be taught as such. To some extent this is true, but today's racewalking technique is so far removed from its pedestrian roots that—excluding absolute beginners—this may not be the most effective approach. Still, a walking template may be of some use to beginning athletes who are having difficulty learning racewalk technique by other means. Hopkins suggests a four-stage approach beginning with walking at a brisk but comfortable pace, making certain that continuous contact is maintained, then progressing through the stages by adding on various elements of the racewalking gait: the bent elbows, hip drive, ankle flexion and in-line foot placement. This method can turn into a laborious process, but it's sometimes effective when other methods fail, and the walker is patient enough to spend the time mastering each step. I use a variation where I concentrate mostly on the feet, having athletes first walk on their heels with their knees straight for several yards. Then I'll have them walk on their heels again, this time allowing the toes to drop as the body passes over the foot. Finally, the walkers do more of the same, with extra emphasis on rolling all the way to the tip of the toes as the leg passes behind the body, and gradually increasing speed as they head down the track. During the whole process the arms are bent at 90 degrees. If everything works, we usually get a fair approximation of racewalking before too long. As the walkers get faster it becomes impossible to keep the legs stiff as they advance forward. As the thigh is thrown forward, the knee starts to bend, which is fine, and something I'll have the new racewalkers emphasize as they get faster. Once they have achieved some minimum approximation of racewalking, there will invariably still be some flaws that will have to be ironed out. At this point I usually switch to a part-by-part approach to correct these deficiencies. I'll explain and show the athlete what still needs more work, be it more hip drive, better toe-off, or a more relaxed posture.

The running template

Former Australian national coach Harry Summers suggests using a running template to teach new racewalkers, especially if they are coming to racewalking from a running background. Athletes are asked to run for a short while, and then change over to a straight-legged landing. In "Placement of the Lead Foot in Racewalking," Summers explains, "it is advisable to use a role model in the teaching of this technique. After observing the action, the walker is asked to jog along at a pace of approximately five minutes per kilometer [8:00 minutes per mile] and gradually change to a straight-leg landing. Faults are then corrected. Experience has shown that an explanation alone is not satisfactory, as the action is too fast for the neuromuscular coordination. Faster results can be obtained with the jogging-straight leg method [than by other means]." The running template method works best with established, well-coordinated athletes who are attempting to make the transition from running to racewalking. I've found that non-runners with less developed body awareness never seem to get the knee-straightening part figured out when using this method.

Train Your Brain

Anyone who has ever watched a basketball game knows pretty much how to throw a free throw—you stand at the line, hold the ball in one hand, and "push" the ball toward the basket. Same thing with throwing darts: Stand behind the line and toss the thing at the target. Most people even have a pretty good idea how to hit a baseball, juggle live kittens, or ride a unicycle on a tightrope. Intellectually *knowing how* to do these activities isn't the problem; the trouble lies in actually *doing them*. Michael Jordan wasn't born with the ability to shoot free throws—and he *definitely* wasn't born with the ability to hit a baseball![47] He had to miss a lot of baskets (and fastballs) before these actions became reflexive for him. Once you have *cerebrally* learned how to racewalk by working with your coach and have seen yourself on video, you have to repeat the motion many times before it moves back into the cerebellum and becomes part of your *muscle memory*. Technique drills can help to lock in specific parts of the walking motion, whether you're a power walker, racewalker, or Nordic walker. On top of that, it takes a lot of actual time-on-your-feet walking to ingrain efficient, legal technique. The good news is that once it's etched into your muscle memory, you don't have to think about it very much after that. By training with good technique every day, you'll "re-wire" your neuromuscular system so that you'll never have to worry about anything during races other than pushing your body to its absolute limit.

Drill Baby, drill!

Over the years I've had the great fortune to be able to train with walkers, and under coaches, from Mexico, the UK, Sweden, Poland, China, South Africa, Ireland, etc., etc., etc. I've learned a lot about their different training programs, but interestingly enough, many of the technique drills they use have been more or less universal. For the most part, *everybody* does the same drills, no matter where they're from! I think most of the drills were created by, or were at least passed down by, the great Mexican-by-way-of-Poland coach, Jerzey Hausleber. For decades, beginning with the 1968 Olympics, "The Professor" and his athletes were responsible for more Olympic medals for Mexico than all other Mexican athletes from all other sports combined. I never trained directly under Hausleber, but I did spend a month training with Seoul Olympic 50k silver medalist and three-time World Cup Champion Carlos Mercenario, at the CDOM—the Mexican Olympic Training Center—leading up to the 1996 US Olympic Trials. Carlos was at that point working with World Cup, Pan Am Games, and three-time Pan Am Cup Champion Martin Bermudez, and Dr. Sergio Granados Diaz, but he had spent most of his career under Hausleber. On a typical day, Hausleber would be on the track coaching '96 Olympic bronze medalist and, at the time, 20,000m world record holder Bernardo Segura, and the rest of his athletes; coach Miguel Rodriguez would be with '97 20k World Champion Daniel García and the rest of his own stable of walkers at the other end of the track; Carlos, Shadat Mendoza, and I would be doing easy laps of the CDOM's perimeter recovering from a speed session in the morning; while Hausleber's son was out at Tepotzotlan or Desierto de Los Leones coaching his own group of athletes. Although they were all members of the Mexican National Team, and were training out of the same training center loosely overseen by Hausleber, they were functioning like different teams competing against each other, which made

[47] I never got to see Jordan play basketball, but I did get to see him play minor league baseball—badly—with the Birmingham Barons in 1994. The Barons were in town to play Knoxville the same weekend that I was competing at the USATF Championships at the University of Tennessee. We went to the game the evening before our race on the track the next day. I was in third place through 18k, behind Olympians Alan James and Andrzej Chylinski, but puked several times over the last 2k and finished 5th. Still, I'm pretty sure I had a better performance than MJ. ☺

for a very competitive environment. Come to think of it, when I trained with some of the best Chinese walkers earlier in 1996, they all had their own individual coaches as well. So much for the need for one national coach, with one national program… Where I'm heading is they all used the same warm-up and technique drills, which were the same drills I've seen athletes from around the globe doing while warming up for races throughout my career, and to this day you can find many of the same drills posted on Facebook/Instagram/YouTube by racewalking coaches and athletes from here, there, and everywhere. I have my own YouTube video with many of the same drills at youtu.be/4xkeZhbxsiA and I also have a downloadable .pdf posted on my website at: racewalking.org/pdfs/Other%20Articles/dynamic-flexibility-drills.pdf but you've got this book in your hands now, so I might as well put some of them here, too:

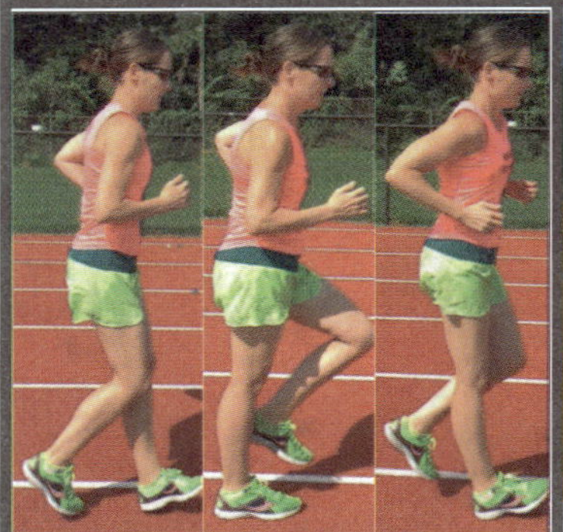

Quick steps: Just like it sounds. Racewalk or walk with very short, quick steps. Your heel should land just in front of the toes of the foot of the support leg. Even regular walkers will often straighten the knees when taking such short, fast strides.

Cross-overs: Racewalk on a line, exaggerating pelvic rotation and arm drive so that the heel-plant crosses over to the other side of the line rather than having the heels line up one in front of the other. Cross-overs help to develop pelvic rotation and more efficient foot placement.

Long arms: Racewalk with arms straight, palms facing back. Push off the tips of the toes to accentuate the back part of your stride. The long-arms drill helps to teach toe push-off, opens up the hips, and stretches the groin.

Heel walk: Walk on your heels with your toes up, first pointing straight ahead, then toes in, then toes out. Once your shins start to hurt, take ten more steps!

Toe walk: The same as the heel walk, but this time do all three variations while walking on your tippy toes.

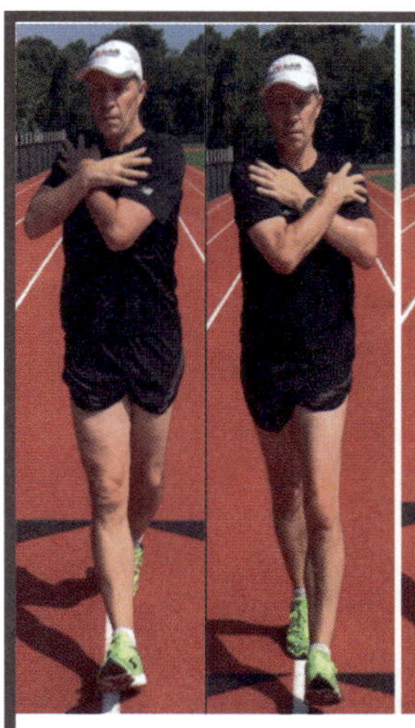

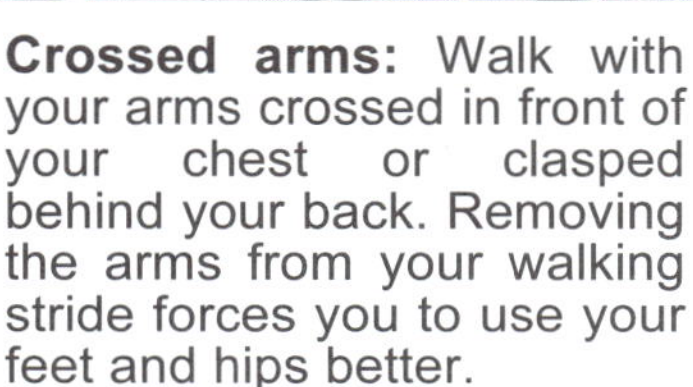

Crossed arms: Walk with your arms crossed in front of your chest or clasped behind your back. Removing the arms from your walking stride forces you to use your feet and hips better.

Backing up the kayak: Walk with your fingertips on your shoulders, elbows out to the sides. While walking, transcribe a circle with each elbow like you're backing up in a kayak. Dipping the shoulders and rotating the torso help to develop hip drop and pelvic rotation.

Frankenstein/sleep walker: Walk or racewalk with both arms extended out in front of your body with one hand clasping the opposite thumb. This drill helps to reinforce the push off the back toe and a bit of a "lean from the ankles."

Rocking the baby: Clasp your hands together. Walk or racewalk while accentuating a strong rearward elbow drive to one side, with a normal arm swing on the other side. The strong rearward arm drive accentuates the forward thrust of the leg on the same side. Driving the elbows back to both sides is another variation.

Pop-ups: Clasp your hands and walk, accentuating the drive back from the elbow on alternate sides with each step. On each third step, pop up, fully flexing the ankle and pushing through the toe with a straight leg. Upon landing, take three more steps and repeat, popping up on the other side. Pop-ups strengthen the calves and help to develop a powerful push-off of the rear foot.

Knee pumps: While holding on to a fence or other sturdy support and keeping the back straight, extend the legs far behind the body keeping your weight on the balls of your feet. Pump your knees vigorously while rolling up to the toes. While doing so, pull the other thigh back so the knee fully straightens behind the body.

Figure-eights: Walk quickly, with very short strides in a tight figure-eight pattern around a cone or other real or imaginary object. The figure-eight drill can help to develop a quicker turn-over (cadence) rate, a feel for landing on the outside part of the sole of your foot, and teaches tight-turning ability, including leaning in to the turns for races with tight single-cone turn-arounds. You don't necessarily need to use cones, but having an actual object to navigate around helps you to learn how tightly you need to make your turns while still maintaining good technique.

Caveats

Although I've said a lot here about refining your walking technique, be very careful when making any dramatic changes. All walkers are individuals with unique underlying biomechanical "quirks." Strength, flexibility, and morphological imbalances may lead to technique flaws, but it's not always wise to tinker with them. There's probably plenty of room for improvement, but your body will normally tend toward its most efficient state. If you're disqualified frequently, injury-prone, or if there's clearly something in your style that's keeping you from fulfilling your potential, it may be worthwhile to make some changes. Just make sure you fully understand the nature of the underlying problem before trying to monkey with your style, which may stem from something that cannot be easily fixed (scoliosis, fused discs, leg-length discrepancies, etc.).

A good coach can absolutely help you decide what in your technique should and what should not be altered, and if something isn't working for you, help you to make those changes. On the other hand, a well-meaning but inexperienced coach may try to convince you to change something that should not necessarily be messed with. In any case, if you do decide that you're in need of a technique tune-up, make one change at a time and phase it in gradually to give your body a chance to adapt. Drastic changes to the biomechanics your body has grown accustomed to could lead to injuries—or worse yet: disqualifications!

At the outset it's more important to lock in the new technique than it is to walk fast. Be patient: You may actually have to slow down for a while to give your body a chance to adapt. It's a good idea to avoid races and hard speed workouts for the first four to six weeks after making a change to keep yourself from reverting back to your old habits or getting injured. Once you lock in the new changes, you'll easily be able to get back to—and exceed—your old training and racing paces.

If you're already a fit athlete, but are just now learning how to racewalk or Nordic walk, be especially careful. You'll definitely have the cardiovascular tools to walk fast, but your walking-specific muscles, tendons and ligaments will not be fully developed. Avoid the temptation to enter races for at least the first six or eight weeks, or you'll end up like a golf cart fitted out with a rocket engine: It'll go *really* fast—until the contraption rattles itself apart and winds up in the scrap heap—or the sports-med. doctor's office…

CHAPTER 13: COMMON TECHNIQUE PROBLEMS AND HOW TO FIX THEM

The following are a number of common technique problems that I frequently encounter when working with walkers and racewalkers at my clinics and camps. These technique flaws can lead to disqualification in races or, worse yet, slowness! The solutions are things I've found to be effective for eliminating these nasty habits.

Problem 1: Flat or slapping feet

Cause: Weak shins, bad shoes, and/or overstriding.

How you know you have it: You hear a loud slapping sound as your foot flattens prematurely in front of your body when you walk; shin pain; "bent-knee" calls in judged races, since the flattened foot causes a lot of force to be transferred to the knee as the body advances over it.

Solution:

- Avoid wearing "fat" shoes. Wear "real" racewalking shoes or running racing flats with a low heel to reduce the amount of leverage acting upon the foot.
- Stretch your calves. Tight calves cause the feet to plantar-flex, which causes flat-footed landings.
- Do the heel-walking drill shown in Chapter 12. Walk on your heels with straight knees to strengthen the shin muscles, then walk on the outsides of the feet to work the peroneus muscles on the outside of the lower leg. Continue for about 30 seconds, then stretch and repeat several times.
- Perform toe raises for shin strength. Stand with your heels on the edge of a step with the front ¾ of the foot hanging over the edge. Slowly dip your feet down, then all the way up. Repeat until fatigue forces you to stop—then do five more! Stretch your shins, then repeat several times.
- Do elastic band exercises (described in chapter 35) to strengthen your shins.

Problem 2: Overstriding

Cause: Erroneously thinking that long strides must be faster than short ones. Walkers with a fitness walking background often fall into this trap.

How you know you have it: You walk with a very percussive stride; shin pain; "creeping"; inability to generate speed for even short distances; lifting and/or bent knee calls in races; people say, "Hey, look at the guy over there over-striding." ☺

Solution:

- Awareness often helps. Simply shorten your stride in front of your body when walking/racewalking.
- Perform the "quick-step" and "figure-eight" drills (Chapter 12) to develop a short, quick cadence.
- Shorten your arm stroke. A short fast arm swing = a short fast leg swing.

Problem 3: "Robot legs"

Cause: Believing you can't bend your knees when racewalking. Wrong! You can and should bend your knees to about 90-degrees as the leg drives forward. The leg only has to be straightened from the point of heel-contact, until the body passes over it.

How you know you have it: The advancing leg comes through too straight; people tell you that you look like a robot or tin soldier when you walk; creeping, possibly; you scuff your feet on the ground as they come forward; also, you're probably slow, and you have no hip drive.

Solution:

- Just do it: Bend the knee more—up to 90 degrees—as the leg drives forward.
- Think about "leading with your knees," driving them low and vigorously with each stride.
- Imagine "punching" a target with your knees. To keep that knee drive very fast and powerful, put a face on the target: your mother-in-law, the prom date who stood you up in high school, a politician who shall remain nameless. (You know who I'm talking about.) Whatever it takes.
- Get to the weight room. Do squats, lunges and other hip flexor-strengthening exercises.

Problem 4: Bent knees ("creeping")

Cause: Various. Overstriding, weak shins, insufficient knee-bend during the driving phase.

How you know you have it: Creeping calls and DQ's in races; if you're a racewalker, people say you're fitness walking; people mistake you for Groucho Marx. For many people, this is the #1 problem—I put it after overstriding and weak feet and shins in the order here because these are the primary causes of creeping.

Solution:

- Shorten your stride in front of your body. Quickstep drills will help.
- Bend your knees *more* during the driving phase to generate more lower-leg speed. More lower leg speed will help to straighten the leg before the heel makes contact with the ground.
- Walk hill repeats up a gradual incline. Hills force you to take a shorter stride in front, and the extra push from behind needed to overcome gravity helps to straighten the knee.
- Stretch and strengthen the hamstrings, quadriceps and calves.

- Do not use running for cross-training.
- Maintain good posture. Bending at the waist shifts the center of mass forward, over the knee, which may cause it to "collapse" upon heel contact.

Problem 5: "Dead" ankles

Cause: Weak/inflexible ankles and feet; over-reliance on the driving phase of your stride rather than utilizing both the driving and vaulting phases.

How you know you have it: Your foot makes a 90-degree angle throughout the entire stride cycle (the foot angle never "opens up" in relation to the shin.) You have a short stride behind your body. Your head bobs up and down when you walk. Your walking action is not "smooth." You don't feel like you're "rolling" forward on your foot from heel to toe.

Solution:

- Awareness of the problem often helps. Simply focus on rolling up onto the toes more at toe-off. I like to do a "shopping cart drill" while at the supermarket. While pushing the cart and walking normally I'll accentuate my roll from heel to toe. You'll really be able to feel the more powerful push-off you get when using your feet vs. not using them.
- Another great drill is to walk VERY slowly (2mph or slower) on a treadmill while supporting much of your body weight with straight arms on the handrails of the treadmill and consciously rolling from heel to toe with your feet. (Special "footnote" to my Mesa, AZ clinic hostess, Lauri Berger, the creator of this drill.)
- I do a similar drill when "aqua walking" in the pool. I don't wear a flotation vest. Instead, I use my feet like paddles to keep myself afloat.
- Racewalk slowly up a gradual incline to strengthen the ankles and calves. Somewhat faster hill repeats may be used to develop an explosive toe-off.
- Perform calf raises. Stand on the edge of a step with the back ¾ of the foot hanging off the step. Slowly dip the feet down, then all the way up. Repeat until you're tired. (Then do ten more!) ☺
- Use toe-grip exercises to strengthen the bottoms of your feet. Repeatedly pick up a towel or other soft object with your foot by curling your toes around it.
- Perform specific range-of-motion exercises with an elastic band or tubing to isolate weak areas of the feet and ankles. Simply loop a heavy elastic band (Theraband, surgical tubing, bungee cord, etc.) around the foot and work the muscles against the resistance provided by the elastic.

Problem 6: No pelvic rotation

Cause: Tightness, lack of "body awareness."

How you know you have it: People tell you that you don't use your hips; you have a short stride behind your body and a hard, percussive landing upon heel contact.

Solution:

- Stand in place in front of a mirror and practice rotating the hips from front to back in synch with an effective arm stroke.
- Practice the long-arms drill (Chapter 12).
- Use better foot action, especially a better roll forward onto the toes before push-off. Keep the rear foot on the ground longer to force the hips to swing open.
- Drive the advancing knee through more powerfully, making sure that the knee is bent to about 90 degrees. The momentum of the thigh advancing forward will help you to rotate the pelvis forward as the leg advances.
- Swing your arms closer to the centerline of the body, or even a bit more, if you tend to swing them too straight front to back.
- Don't be afraid of falling on your face! A lot of walkers cut their strides short, failing to follow through with enough knee drive as soon as they start to feel their body starting to fall forward. Driving the knee just a bit further forward will allow the hip to rotate through a full range of motion.

Problem 7: Excessive "forward lean"

Cause: Many walkers who lean forward excessively while walking do so because they've been coached to walk that way. Overstriding walkers often lean forward to help move the center of mass forward to get over the overstriding lead leg.

How you know you have it: You notice a very percussive front foot landing at heel contact ("Frankenstein walking"); people say you lean forward or bend at the waist; lower-back pain during or after walking.

Solution:

- Straighten up! Try to walk with a more upright posture. You don't want to lean *back,* but you should definitely ignore any demonic voices in your head telling you to lean forward while walking.
- Pretend someone is pulling you up by your hair while you're walking, or just think about "walking tall."
- Watch other athletes racewalking with a pronounced forward lean. You'll be so horrified you'll never do it again!
- Don't overstride. Overstriding forces walkers to find ways of moving their centers of mass forward (usually by bending forward at the waist) to try to get their bodies over the overstriding lead leg. Don't!

Problem 8: High knee lift

Cause: Driving the knees too far up rather than forward; often seen in former runners, or walkers who have been coached to "prance" like a horse.

How you know you have it: You get DQ's for lifting in races. People say you look "prancy" or "runny."

Solution:

- Forget the horse image, if you've been told to prance like a horse.
- Concentrate on driving your knees forward rather than up—aim for a "target" at knee-level.
- Keep your feet very low to the ground as they come forward.

Problem 9: Chicken-winging

Cause: Your arms cross your body too much, causing the elbows to poke out to the sides with each arm stroke.

How you know you have it: By looking down at your arms while walking it should be easy to notice that your arm action is more side-to-side than front-to-back. All your competitors have bruised ribs from being banged by your elbows in races.

Solution:

- Practice walking in place in front of a mirror, possibly while holding small, 3 to 5 lb. hand weights. Watch to see that your elbows remain tucked in. Continue for ten minutes at a time, at least three days per week until the motion becomes very natural.
- Imagine that you're walking in a narrow tunnel. If you don't keep your elbows tucked in they'll bang against the walls.

Final Thoughts

Although each walker will develop his or her own individual style, we should all strive to eliminate anything that doesn't move us toward the finish line efficiently. Imagine carrying a heavy box. Keeping it steady and close to your body is much easier than swinging it to the left and right, or lifting it up and down as you carry it. The same principle applies to your walking: If your elbows are chicken-winging out to the sides, if you're toeing in or out, if your hips are sashaying from side to side, or if your center of mass is bobbing up and down, you're expending a lot of energy in the wrong directions.

Every element of your technique should be compact, efficient, and heading you toward the finish line, not the sidelines. It may take some time to lock in these changes, but be patient. Once good technique is ingrained, it will always be there for you when you need it. If you have to slow down a bit at first, by all means, do. It will pay off in the end with faster times and fewer injuries and disqualifications.

CHAPTER 14: NORDIC WALKING

Because it evolved more or less independently on two different continents, there are to this day two distinct versions of Nordic walking, the American "Exerstrider" technique developed by Tom Rutlin, and the European "Nordic walking" technique developed in Finland by physical education instructor Leena Jääskeläinen. Both techniques began as ways to add an upper-body component to fitness walking, but while Rutlin continues to promote Exerstriding as a fitness activity, not a sport, the European technique is absolutely viewed as a competitive activity, having transitioned from its birth as a group fitness activity for kids, to a summer cross-training activity for Nordic skiers, to its current incarnation as a competitive sport in its own right. Perhaps due to the different origin stories and philosophies of their creators, the two techniques employ somewhat different types of poles, so that would be a logical place to start the discussion about the differences between the two techniques.

Poles apart

The main difference between European Nordic walking poles and Exerstrider poles is that Nordic walking poles have a strap, an attached glove, or a fingerless glove ("demi-glove"), while Exerstrider poles have a handgrip with a flared bottom, and no strap or glove/demi-glove. In the Exerstriding technique, the pole is extended forward and planted while the arm is extended in the "handshake" position. The pole is then pushed firmly against the ground while the walker steps forward. The flared bottom of the handgrip allows maximum pressure to be placed on the pole during the push, giving the upper body an excellent workout. The pole is gripped firmly throughout the stride cycle.

The European technique is designed to mimic Nordic (cross-country) skiing, which requires a substantial range-of-motion of the arms. The arm passes behind the torso and the grip of the pole is released at the end of the swing—hence the need for the pole to have a strap. The long range of motion of the arms facilitates hip rotation and a correspondingly long stride, and also requires a longer pole. European poles are manufactured by established Nordic skiing brands such as Exel, Gabel, Leki, Komperdell and Swix, while Exerstriding poles, designed to keep the stride as similar to the normal walking gait as possible, are made by Rutlin's own Exerstrider brand as well as the Fittrek and Urban Poling brands.

Single-piece poles are sturdier and lighter than adjustable poles, but must be fitted to the individual. Poles should be between 68% and 70% of the user's height, so a 5 ft. 4 in. woman (64 inches) would look for a 45" or 46" pole. Two-piece, telescoping poles are not quite as stiff or sturdy, but are more convenient for traveling, as are three-piece collapsible poles. Telescoping poles are adjustable for walkers of various heights. All poles have a metal point that can be used on grass or packed dirt, and attachable rubber "boots" or "paws" for use on asphalt or concrete.

Technique

Since this book is about competitive, not fitness, walking, I'll focus more on the European technique, rather than the more fitness-oriented Exerstriding technique. Even though the European technique is based on a cross-country skiing model, not a walking model, and you may or may not be a cross-country skier, don't overthink it! The rhythm of your arms and legs is similar to what you've been doing your entire life; it's just vigorous walking assisted by poles. Your stride length is determined by the range-of-motion of your arms: The longer the pole thrust, the more powerful your hip action, and the longer your stride.

Start by holding the poles lightly, with the tips on the ground behind you. The poles should be held at a 45-degree angle. Walk with the poles opposing the motion of your legs. As the left arm pushes back, the left leg moves forward, and vice versa. Every step should begin with the heel touching the ground and the foot rolling forward to the ball and toe area, where you will push off to propel yourself forward. Once your arms and legs feel coordinated, grip the poles again and plant them between the heel of the front foot and the toe of the back foot, then push them back against the ground instead of dragging them. Continue planting the poles at the same 45-degree angle behind yourself, with your elbows close to your body and your arms straight and relaxed. The hands should grip the pole firmly every time it hits the ground, but once the pole is drawn back behind the body, the grip is released at the end of the arm swing, being held to the hand only by the strap or glove/demi-glove. As the arms continue to move the poles, the torso and hips will rotate in opposite directions, similar to the racewalking motion.

Dos and don'ts

Do keep the poles close to your body, lean slightly forward, and remember to open and close the hands with each step. Wendy Bumgardner, Walking Editor of the VeryWellFit website adds:

- Keep the shoulders down and relaxed;
- Take longer strides than normal;
- Do not allow both feet or both poles to be off the ground at the same time;
- Roll the foot from the heel to the ball with each step;
- Swing the poles forward with long arms and a loosely gripped and guiding hand;
- Plant the poles between the front and back foot;
- Push the pole as far back as possible, the arm straightening to form a continuous line [from] the fully extended arm [through the pole], the hand opening off the grip by the end of the arm swing;

- The palm of the hand is open and fingers are stretched out at the release position;
- The poles contact the ground at the same time as the opposite heel.

Don't plant the poles too far from the body. Also:

- Don't walk with your hands closed at all times through the stride cycle. Release at the rear of the stride to allow proper blood circulation;
- Don't walk with your hands held open throughout the stride cycle. Doing so reduces the power of your poling;
- Don't move the arm and leg on the same side in tandem.

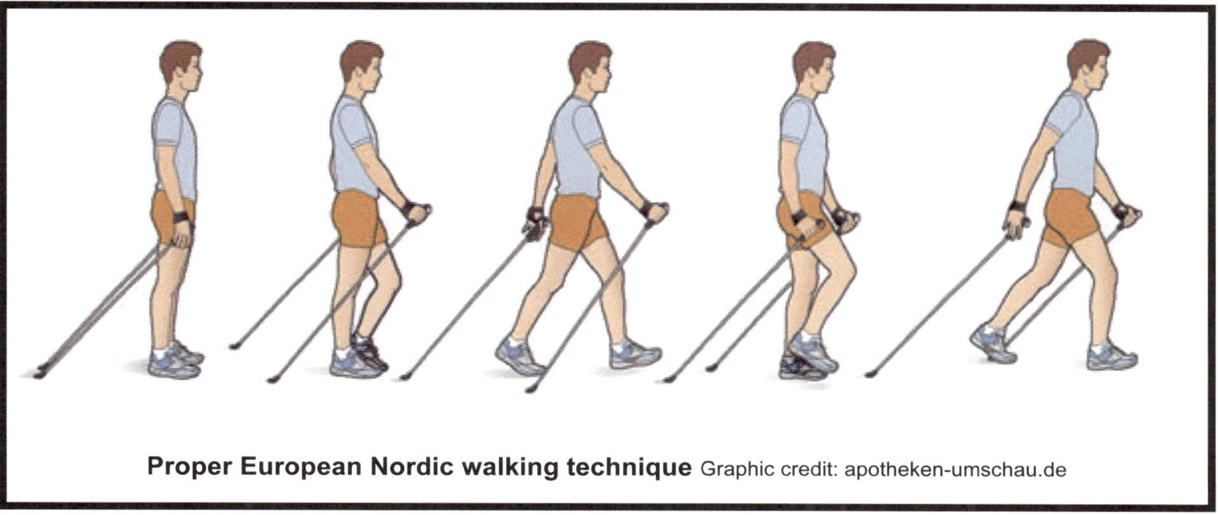

Proper European Nordic walking technique Graphic credit: apotheken-umschau.de

Double-poling

Double-poling does not refer to Al Capone's maxim[48] to "vote early and often!" It refers to pushing with both poles at the same time while Nordic walking. The technique is commonly used by cross-country skiers, especially when going downhill, or as a break from the basic "classic" or "skating" techniques. In double-poling while Nordic walking, both arms are brought forward together and you take two, or sometimes three, steps before the next poling action. It's an intense upper body workout, so try it in short bursts at first. As good as double-poling is as a workout, it's not permissible in most racing situations since both poles are lifted off the ground at the same time in contradiction of the rules as outlined in Chapter 8. Double-poling can be very helpful when walking down very steep hills. Ordinarily when walking downhill the pole tips stay behind you as in the basic Nordic Walking technique. But there will come a point where a hill is so steep that it

[48]The phrase actually has much earlier origins, going back at least as far as New York's corrupt Tammany Hall political machine of the late 1850s. Sorry, Al, there's a reason Chicago is called the Second City. ☺

becomes difficult to keep the pole tips behind you. On such occasions plant the pole tips in front, using the double poling action.

For further information on Nordic walking, including lessons, competitions, or local clubs, head to the American Nordic Walking Association web site at: www.americannordicwalking.com or the International Nordic Walking Federation web site at: www.inwa-nordicwalking.com.

CHAPTER 15: ULTRA-WALKING

IN the running community, anything longer than a 26.2-mile marathon is designated an "ultra" marathon. The bar is a somewhat higher in the walking world. The 50-kilometer (31.1 miles) walk has been a standard Olympic event in athletics/track & field since 1932. Many walkers, then, consider anything longer than 50k to be an ultra—50 miles, 100k, 100 miles, 12 hours, 24 hours and six days being the most commonly contested ultra distances.

A goal for many ultra walkers is to complete 100 miles in less than 24 hours. Doing so earns the walker the coveted designation as a "Centurion." There are seven Centurion clubs worldwide, and walking a Century under the auspices of each of the clubs is a "bucket list" goal for some ultra-walkers. Rudy Schoors and Caroline Mestdagh of Belgium, Justin and Sharon Scholz of Australia, Marco Bloemerts of the Netherlands, and Rob Robertson of Oklahoma, USA, have walked 100 miles in under 24 hours in the United States, the United Kingdom, on continental Europe, in South Africa, Australia, and New Zealand. Their "White Whale" is Malaysia. (The Malaysian club has been inactive since 2007.) Jill Green of Great Britain has walked all of the above *and* Malaysia, except… she has not completed a century on the African continent. No man has become a member of all seven clubs. No *man*. But of course a member of the stronger sex has! Legendary British endurance walker (and runner) Sandra Brown has, to date, walked (or run) 178 100-milers in under 24 hours. Of course only her walking exploits count for Centurion qualification, but she has walked at least one (and in most cases many, many more!) Centuries in each of the seven clubs' jurisdictions; the only *human* to have done so. But how do we differentiate between Brown's walking and running accomplishments? What constitutes "walking" in a Century race?

Many nineteenth-century pedestrian races, especially in Britain, were "go-as-you-please" affairs. In the early years of the Pedestrian Era, most competitors walked, but they were permitted to jog to loosen up their legs if they needed to. And in later years, athletes trained themselves to run more and more over the course of the 24-hours or six days of the competition. "Centurion" and other ultra-walking races today, however, are judged, walk-only events. Not as strictly judged as high-level racewalking competitions, but judged nonetheless. In track and short loop (1-kilometer to 1-mile) races, the accepted practice is that a single judge circles the course in the opposite direction of the athletes, watching to ensure that contestants are walking, not running. Essentially, the judge or judges, watch for the first rule of racewalking—that continuous contact with the ground is maintained—but they do not enforce the rule that the knee must be fully straightened. Without the straightened-knee rule, distinguishing between walking and running becomes trickier, and to some extent the "if-it-looks-like-walking-(or racewalking)-it's-walking" rule applies.

Without question, if the goal is to walk fast, racewalking is faster in the short run than garden-variety "pedestrian" walking. But complete straightening of the knees can take a toll after many hours of legal racewalking, as I found out in my first (failed) Century attempt. My goal was to become only the third American to walk 100 miles in less than 19 hours. I was able to cover 40- and even 50-mile workouts in training at well under that pace, and assumed I would be able to do the same for the entire distance. Hubris... On race day the backs of my knees were achy after 40 miles of racewalking, and about 55 miles in, my overworked hip-flexors seized up. Lesson learned... If the rules don't require a fully straightened knee, don't fully straighten your knees!

The trick with walking ultra-marathons is to find a reasonably fast technique that's also comfortable enough to be sustainable for many hours, or days, or weeks of walking. As described in Chapter 10, a modification of racewalking technique, using short, fast strides, active feet, and vigorous arm strokes, but without worrying about fully straightening the knees, will allow you to go both fast *and* far. And if you want to go *really* fast, keep in mind that if you're one of the lucky ultra-walkers who has good walking technique *and* who has also mastered racewalking technique, you have two gears available instead of just one when racing. By using racewalking form when you can, mixed with frequent regular walking breaks, you'll be able to walk very fast with a reduced chance of sustaining the kind of injury that ended my Centurion attempt. (You heard it here first... I'm going to make it next time!) ☺

One of the best technicians among multi-day walkers is Yolanda Holder. Yolanda is a legend in long-distance walking circles. She's also a legend at walking *in* circles for very long distances! Holder

Yolanda Holder completing her historic 3,100-mile walk. Photo credit: Sri Chinmoy Ultra Photo

is the first African American Woman, and second African American, Centurion,[49] and the oldest person (age 61) to walk 100 miles under 24 hours (23:52:17). She's a two-time Guinness World Record holder for "Most Marathons Completed in a Calendar Year," finishing 106 marathons/ultras in 2010 and breaking her own record in 2012, finishing a staggering 120 marathons and ultras. Yolanda is the first American woman and first African American to run or walk over 100 marathons in a calendar year and the first woman in the world to ever do it twice. Yolanda has completed six six-day races with a personal best of 413 miles. That total beat Amy Howard's world record of 409 miles set in May of 1880. (No, that's not a typo.) ☺ What's more amazing is that Holder set her record at the age of 61! (Amy Howard was 23 when she set her record.) Yolanda is also the women's ten-day walk world record holder with a best of 622 miles, but in my eyes her most amazing—and likely never-to-be-topped—accomplishment was her world record as the first walker to ever complete the Sri Chinmoy Self Transcendence 3,100-Mile Race in Queens, NY, under the 52-day time limit, finishing in 51 days, 17 hours and 13 seconds in the 2017 edition of the race. I'm sure there are accomplishments I'm leaving out, but I'm really trying to keep this book under 400 pages… ☺

Yolanda's advice, with respect to technique in ultra-races is to mix it up—and smile! ☺ Yolanda says: "When I am racing 100 milers and six-day races, I combine power walking and racing walking techniques. I use the heel-toe movement, 90-degree pumping arms and shorter steps for speed. I also add smiling and having fun. These two skills are the key elements to power/racewalking ultra marathons & multi-day races."[50]

So there you have it! If Yolanda says it, who am I to argue? ☺ Now that we've covered technique, it's time to move on to training. Let's go!

---

[49] The legendary ultra-walker Alan Price was the first. Alan was a reasonably good 10- and 20-kilometer walker, with whom I had the pleasure of racing and socializing quite a bit in the 1980s and early '90s. Alan didn't take the shorter races very seriously—he almost always showed up late, often missing the start, but he was never late to the finish line of a 100-miler! Alan walked two-dozen sub-24-hour 100 milers, and is the 2nd fastest American ever at the distance with his 18:46:13. Only Larry Young, 2-time Olympic Bronze medalist, has gone faster. Alan, who passed away in 2015, still holds the American 24-hour record of 118 miles 316 yards.

[50] I can verify that! ☺ Yolanda walked the open 50k race held alongside the US Olympic 50k Trials in January of 2020 and I was energized every time we passed each other going the other direction on the 50-lap 1-kilometer loop course. She had a smile on her face every step of the way!)

SECTION III: TRAINING FOR SPECIFIC CHALLENGES

Section III is all about training for specific race distances. A good walker is a good walker is a good walker, but training for a 1,500m or 1-mile competition is quite different from training for a marathon or 50k. The schedules that follow will prepare you for individual races like a 5k or half-marathon, or combined events like the 1,500m/5k double at the National Senior Games or the Disney Marathon's "Goofy Challenge" involving a half-marathon one day and a full marathon the next.

Every walker is different, obviously. We all have different bodies, differing propensity for injuries, different amounts of time to train during the day, etc., so no schedule will be perfect for every walker. Use these schedules as a basic foundation, but modify to your own needs with consultation with your coach. For self-coached athletes, make modifications based on lessons learned from your training log. (You DO keep a training log, don't you?!) Over time you will find what mix of walk training, cross training, and rest works best for your body.

With that in mind, it's very difficult to write training schedules for a broad audience. (I didn't even bother putting training schedules in *The Complete Guide to Racewalking,* believing that my choices were all, or nothing. I chose nothing, rather than try to tackle the monumental task of writing schedules for every possible racing scenario. In this book I've gone with the "all" option!) Even so, it's impossible to write a 5k schedule that will work for everyone, let alone schedules for everything from 1,500 meters to six days, plus combined events, for power walkers, racewalkers and Nordic walkers of all ability levels. One thing that makes the task easier is using the great equalizer: heart rate. Different types of workouts are done at different intensities. Easy days are easy, tempo days are hard, intervals are fast, and usually based on your current or goal race pace, long slow distance is—you guessed it!—slow. But one walker's "slow" is another walker's "impossible." How do you know how hard to go? Well, you need some measure of intensity. There was a lot of information about lactate threshold and $\dot{V}O_2$ max in Chapter 4, and these are both very good measures of training intensity in the right hands, but they are not easily accessible to most people. There are about a dozen other ways to measure intensity, but there are three or four that are both reasonably precise and accessible to most walkers: Perceived exertion, pace, and heart rate, plus cadence, if you don't mind doing a little math in your head, or have the focus to count to 150 to 200 or more within the span of sixty seconds. Perceived exertion is simply how hard you feel you're working. The more experienced you get the more accurate your sense of pace and exertion will become. It's not a great tool for beginners, though, because for the first few months—or years—*everything* seems hard!

Pace is probably a more meaningful measure of intensity because it relates to the most important variable in competitive walking: your speed! What really matters is how fast you can go, because speed is what wins races. I use your target race pace, or your current pace for other distances—like using 5k race pace as the target for short intervals when training for a 20k or half-marathon, for example, as the goal for a lot of the workouts in the schedules. Training based on your 5k or 10k race pace is a tangible measure that makes it a little easier to write, or follow, training schedules. I can tell you to walk ten miles at 90 seconds to two minutes per mile slower than your 5k race pace, and you know exactly what to do. The problem comes when externalities affect your ability to walk at the prescribed pace. What if it's hot and humid, or you had a bad night's sleep, or you've been sick, or you're hung over? (Or all of the above…) How do you adjust your pace? It's hard to say, and certainly hard to write those variables into a training schedule months or years before you're going to use it. That's where heart rate comes in. Using heart rate equalizes a lot of these externalities. 80% of maximum heart rate is 80% of maximum heart rate whether it's cool and dry or hot and humid, whether you're tired or well rested. You'll end up going slower on a hot, humid day when you're tired, but the effort will still be an 80% effort. Heart rate factors in those externalities.

For heart rate, or more precisely, percentage of maximum heart rate, to be effective as a training tool you need to first know what constitutes a maximum effort. In other words, to know how hard a 75%, 80%, or 90% effort is, you need to first be able to quantify what a 100% effort is. So to use a heart rate monitor as a tool you need to first come up with a way of finding or estimating maximum heart rate—the highest number of beats per minute your heart can achieve at an all-out, gut-busting maximum intensity effort. Since most people won't ever work this hard unless being chased by a hungry grizzly bear, finding true maximum heart rate can be tricky—and mathematical formulas do not work. At my clinics I tell my participants that using formulas like [220-age = max heart rate] is akin to me going to a shoe store and asking for a size nine because that's what the "average" American male wears, or because I found a formula that says 67 – age = shoe size. (I'm 55½ and I wear size 11.5.) 67 – 55.5 = 11.5. IT WORKS! For me. Today. But it probably doesn't work for everyone, and it's not even going to work for me next year. (Unless my feet suddenly get a lot bigger.) 220-age is a bogus formula with a long history. Basically a cardiologist and an exercise physiologist were at a conference and the cardiologist wanted a number to point to telling him when a patient should get off of the treadmill during a stress test. He had a very small population of patients. Cardiac patients. The physiologist crunched some numbers and came up with something like 220 – age for maximum heart rate for that small population. Of cardiac patients... (A much older, and arguably more accurate—or more accurately, less inaccurate—formula was presented in 1938, which is 212 - .77 * (age). There's also the Ball State formula 214 - .8 * (age), and the Miller formula, 217 - .85 * (age), among others, and all of these formulas have a female version (226 – age = max HR, etc.) But they're ALL wrong! Or at least wildly inaccurate. (+/- 20 beats per minute.) The problem is, you simply can't tell anything about one person based on a population average. Especially when that average was derived from the wrong population (cardiac patients instead of athletes). Nor can you say much of anything with any confidence when dealing with a small population size. And that small, non-representative population? They weren't even tested for maximum heart rate! The numbers were actually *peak* heart rates for treadmill tests, not necessarily *maximum* heart rates. Lots of people get freaked out by treadmills, so they get off way before they've hit their true maximum heart rates. They just want the test to be done, so they stop. Anyway, this is getting long-winded. Formulas don't work. Do something to find your actual maximum heart rate if you want to use it to guide your training. One way to find your actual maximum heart rate is to do a series of three 400-meter intervals with one-minute rest breaks, the first two at a very hard, but not all-out effort, and the third one just about all-out, saving just enough to be able to really blast the last 50 meters. This is a really hard, but accurate way to get maximum heart rate. For runners. ☺ It's also possible for racewalkers with very good technique who are able to get up to 100% of maximum heart rate when racewalking. Unfortunately, due to the mechanical limitations of normal walking, most people can't get to maximum heart rate when walking. An easier way, which is more likely to work for most walkers, is to get up to a sub-maximum effort and extrapolate from there. Most people are able to get to about 90 to 92% of maximum heart rate during a hard 30-minute effort, so for a lot of racewalkers, a 5k race can be used as a test. Average heart rate during the race should come pretty close to 90% of maximum. Alternately, a spot check of heart rate at about the two-mile mark should be pretty close to 94% of maximum heart rate. Dividing by .9, or .94, respectively, will give a pretty reliable estimate of maximum heart rate. Or, if you're so inclined, we do a sub-maximal interval test to derive maximum heart rate at all of my clinics.[51] Just sayin'…

Once you have an actual or estimated maximum heart rate value, you can go about determining heart rate intensity zones for different types of workouts. These are as follows:

- **Recovery-** One of the most commons training errors is overdoing it on easy days. Your body actually gets weaker and less fit after hard workouts; the adaptation to training takes place after recovery from the hard efforts. Pushing too hard on the easy days doesn't allow for full recovery from the hard efforts, so the quality of your training will suffer on subsequent hard days. Heart rate should be 60 to 75% of maximum on recovery days.
- **General Endurance-** The long day is designed to improve cardiovascular endurance. Endurance sports are all about getting as much oxygen to the working muscles as possible, and these workouts are the best sessions for improving your "plumbing." They increase the number of capillaries (tiny blood vessels) that supply each working muscle fiber with

[51] Details and clinic dates are at https://racewalking.org/clinic-dates.html

oxygenated blood, and they increase the number of red blood cells, and the amount of oxygen-carrying hemoglobin in the blood. Muscle and joint strength is also improved. General endurance workouts should be done at about 65 to 75% of maximum heart rate.

- **Long sub-threshold and tempo training-** These workouts are the most race-specific workouts for longer races. They are hard efforts that approach race distance, approaching race intensity. For 5k to 10k training these are the traditional 20- to 45-minute tempo workouts at or near lactate threshold pace or heart rate. When training for longer races (half-marathon and marathon) these are long (nine- to 15-mile) workouts at anywhere from 15 to 30 seconds per mile slower than race pace all the way up to race pace and faster if the distance is significantly shorter than race distance (e.g., when walking a hard 15-miler at marathon race pace), or when done as long intervals, such as 3 x 5k at 20k pace for 20k/half-marathon training. Heart rates will range from 80 to 90% of maximum. These workouts should be used sparingly, only in the weeks leading up to important races.
- **Lactate threshold intervals-** These are medium-range (800-meter to 2k) intervals at or very near 5k to 10k race pace, which corresponds closely to lactate threshold pace. Threshold training causes the metabolic enzymes in the muscles to get more "bang" out of the oxygen and fuel (fats and carbohydrates) that is supplied to them. High intra-muscular levels of lactic acid foul up the metabolic enzymes, causing the muscles to lose power and contract more slowly. (If you've ever started out too fast in a 5k race and felt like you were walking through Jell-O after that first three or four minutes of sprinting, you know very well the feeling of high lactate levels!) Lactate threshold training allows you to go faster without producing high levels of lactate, and allows you to keep going fast even if you do wind up with relatively high lactate levels. For 5k to half-marathon training, intervals should be done at current race pace. The total volume of the intervals should add up to close to the race duration, broken down into three to eight intervals. Examples include 6 x 800 meters for 5k training, 5 x 1 mile for 10k training, and 8 x 2k for 20k/half-marathon training. Heart rates should range from 85 to 92% of maximum.
- **$\dot{V}O_2$ max intervals-** Having a high $\dot{V}O_2$ max means a high volume (V) of precious oxygen (O_2) gets to the working muscles. Since $\dot{V}O_2$ max is measured in milliliters of oxygen per kilogram of body mass per minute, it can be improved by losing some of that body mass (fat) through regular endurance training. But quicker gains can be achieved through high-end interval training, which improves your ability to take in and process more oxygen. 400-meter to 1-mile intervals with long recoveries (rests intervals should equal the duration of the work interval) at 95 to 98% of maximum heart rate are typical $\dot{V}O_2$ max interval workouts. Volume should be low, for example, 3 x 1 mile or 10 x 400 meters.
- **Economy intervals-** Economy intervals are very short, very fast, reps designed to boost your body's ability to use oxygen efficiently by improving your high-speed racing technique.

Since the reps are so short (in general, 15 to 45 seconds in duration) heart rate doesn't have a chance to rise to much more than 80 to 85% of maximum, even though the pace is nearly all-out. Accordingly, heart rate isn't used to gauge the intensity of economy intervals. They should simply be walked at a very fast pace, but with perfect, relaxed technique.

The final, readily available method with which to gauge walking intensity is cadence. As mentioned in Chapter 10, stride length is somewhat fixed in walkers by the requirement to keep one foot on the ground at all times, so much of your increase in speed has to come from increasing stride frequency. By counting your steps you can get a pretty good handle on how hard you are working. The numbers are highly variable between individuals, so it's not a useful measure when writing training schedules, but it is a useful variable to keep track of while training for your own purposes. My Polar Vantage M counts steps for me, so I don't have to do it in my head anymore.

Whichever method you use to measure the intensity of your training, the devil, of course, is in the details. Deciding the appropriate mix of hard and recovery workouts for your level, and for your chosen race distance, takes some work, but knowing that you're training at the right intensity each day will go a long way towards helping you to achieve your goals. As a competitive athlete, you may be tempted to overdo it occasionally. *Overtraining* can lead to injuries, a weakened immune system, and sluggish training. It's always better to go into a race marginally undertrained than over trained. Steady improvements in fitness come from allowing your body to adapt to reasonable stresses. Consistent, intelligent training leads to success; overstress with insufficient recovery does nothing but make you tired. Here are some common warning signs that you may overtraining:

- Sudden unexplained weight loss;
- Recurrent headaches;
- Personality changes like irritability or lack of enthusiasm;
- Heavy legs or sore muscles;
- Changes in sleep habits or insomnia;
- Loss of appetite or excessive thirst;
- Diarrhea;
- Diminished sex drive;
- Swollen glands;
- Worsening allergies;
- Persistent colds, flu, or respiratory infections;
- An unusually high morning pulse rate.

Heart rate, in fact, may be the best early warning sign of overtraining. By monitoring your heart rate in the morning and during workouts, you may pick up on some of the early warning signs of overtraining. If any of the following occur, overtraining can be headed off by simply taking a day or two off from training or continuing training at a reduced workload, staying well hydrated, eating more carbs, and getting more sleep:

- Increase in morning resting heart rate of more than five beats per minute;
- Abnormal rise in heart rate after standing, for example, heart rate rising more than 20 beats per minute, 20 seconds after standing up;
- Abnormal rise in heart rate during and after a standard workout;
- Slower recovery in heart rate after exertion.

A heart rate monitor is a very accurate and sensitive tool that can give you early warning signs that you're pushing too hard long before you've reached a state of full-blown overtraining. It's up to you to cut your training back to prevent a state of chronic fatigue. Don't ignore the warning signs. It's always better to err on the side of doing too little rather than doing too much and "crashing."

Due to space limitations, the schedules contain abbreviations for many of the workouts. To make sense of my shorthand, please refer to Appendix I for Training Schedule Definitions, but here are a few of them: The base-training schedules will start with a lot of easy base mileage. Easy means easy! The workouts should be done at a comfortable "conversational" pace, meaning you should be able to carry on a conversation with a training partner without getting out of breath. Later in the base-training schedules you'll find workouts to help you make the transition from base training to more intense speed work. "Fartlek" is a Swedish word for "speed play." It means shifting gears constantly during the workout.[52] For example, starting at a moderate pace for a few minutes, picking up to race pace for several minutes, then backing down to moderate pace again, repeated throughout the workout. Closer to your races, especially for races from 10k to the marathon, you'll learn to love "tempo" workouts. Tempo workouts can come in the form of "steady-state" tempo workouts or "progressions." Steady-state tempos are walks done at a steady, fast pace, while progressions are workouts where you'll start at a moderate pace, then build faster and faster throughout the workout. Training for any distance will involve at least some interval workouts. As described in Chapter 6, interval workouts are periods of fast training interspersed with rest intervals. Interval workouts/reps differ from fartleks in that the work and rest intervals are of a set duration, where fartleks are unstructured workouts with many random changes in pace.

---

[52] Unless... In their books, Jeff Salvage and Tim Seaman refer to interval workouts with moving recoveries as fartleks. The workouts they lay out, such as 8 x 1000m/500m (1,000m fast followed by 500m moderate, repeated eight times) are excellent workouts, and there probably should be a more succinct word or phrase to describe them than "intervals with moving recoveries," but they definitely are not fartleks because the work and rest intervals are not random—the defining characteristic of a fartlek.

Hill repeats are reps done up a moderately steep (5 to 8% grade) hill, with easy recoveries accomplished by simply walking slowly back down to the bottom, repeat, repeat, repeat. Nothing builds walking strength better than hill repeats, and they are also great for improving technique as they force a shorter, quicker anterior stride, a strong push-off with the feet, an explosive knee-drive, and a powerful arm swing. As you grow stronger, your technique and speed will both improve. Hills, then, are a great transition workout between base training and speed work, and most of the schedules to follow include a hill-training phase. I'm a big believer in hill training and have sought out hilly training courses throughout my career. One of my favorites for repeats has always been a 400m hill on Landing Road from the Hudson River to the firehouse above Rockland Lake, NY. The road is closed to traffic and rises from the river up to the top of the Palisade—a 50m climb over 400 meters. That's a 12.5% grade, on average, but it starts nearly flat, rises quickly to a steady 8- to 10% grade, then has several brutal 16% grade sections, before flattening out again near the top. It's a perfect hill!

When I recommend hills to my clinic groups, someone will always protest that he or she doesn't have hills near their home. Nonsense! *Everybody* has hills within a reasonable distance of where they live. If you don't have actual *topographic* hills in your neighborhood, get creative! I've coached athletes in South Florida who did their hill training on bridges and highway onramps, and one in New Orleans who did his hill training on parking garage ramps. And if that doesn't work for you, of course most treadmills have incline functions. There is always a way—find it!

A final note: I think in kilometers, not miles. Most of our races as walkers are in kilometers: 1,500m, 5k, 10k, 20k, 50k, etc. Even the odd-distance marathon and half-marathon are odd distances in both systems (26 miles, 385yds., vs. 42.195 kilometers). So a lot of the training schedules, especially on track days, have workouts written in meters or kilometers. But not always… ☺ Most US-based competitive walkers who race in running road races with—or without—walk divisions, rather than track or metric loop-course racewalk races, are so used to thinking in miles rather than kilometers that I've given up the fight. For most of the schedules I use miles for the long days. It may be discombobulating at first, but it's not a bad idea to be fluent in both "languages." One mile is a bit over 1.5 kilometers. (One mile is 1,609.3 meters or 1.6093k); 5k is 3.1 miles; 8k is just short of 5 miles (4.96); 10k is 6.2 miles; 16k is just short of ten miles (9.92); and 32k is close to 20 miles (19.84). So if a workout calls for you to do 16k and you're more fluent in miles, by all means, go ahead and do ten miles, or vice versa. Now on to the schedules!

CHAPTER 16: BASIC TRAINING

The schedules in the following chapters run from sixteen to twenty-four weeks. In many cases, they can be considered the *final* sixteen to twenty-four weeks of training because most competitive walkers train in one form or another year-round. "Periodization" means breaking the year up into different periods where the focus of training shifts from base-building, to a pre-competition phase, to the competition season, and finally to a post-season "active rest" phase. The training schedules in the subsequent chapters all include short base-building phases, but for best results each schedule should be preceded by a several-months-long base-building phase.

All training is cumulative. Everything you've done—or not done—over the past five, ten, twenty—or in my case forty—years contributes to your current fitness. But the type of training you do, how often you race, layoffs you take due to injuries, etc., also contribute to or detract from your fitness. Your base-training phase is a way to top off the tank every year to get yourself ready for the hard training that will get you ready for your big race, races, or racing seasons.

Walkers hill training together at my February, 2020 World Class Racewalking clinic in Campbell, CA.

That being said, periodization can mean different things to different people. In Chapter 31 I quote 2013 50k world champion Robert Heffernan. Robbie, following the lead of his coach, four-time Olympic and three-time world champion, Robert Korzeniowski, did his best to put all of his eggs into one big peak every few years, taking breaks and cranking out miles at lower intensity during down times. Other walkers—myself included—prefer to be "up" year-round. I've won a lot of off-season and early-season races during my career, and made lots of early season Pan-Am Cup and World Cup teams, but was, unfortunately, rarely a world-beater when it really mattered—at the Olympic or World Championships Trials in late June or early July. Sweden's Perseus Karlström is a better model, managing to win the 2019 World Athletics Grand Prix as well as the European Championships 20k by being ready to race well from February through May, but also still being in great shape in August when he took home the bronze medal from the World Athletics Championships in Doha, Qatar, racing under very hot conditions. Of course the Tokyo Olympics and the 2020 World Athletics Grand Prix were cancelled due to Covid-19, but Perseus won every race he could find, including the Swedish 10,000m and 20,000m Championships, and what are usually big international 20k events in Alytus, Lithuania, and Podebrady, Czech Republic. I asked Perseus how he manages to be ready to take on the world's best walkers at any time of year, every year:

Perseus Karlström celebrating his 2019 World Athletics World Championships 20k bronze medal.

Photo credit: World Athletics

"I would say the way to stay race-ready year-round is simply a matter of consistency. Not necessarily training hard all year around, but never getting detrained and out of shape. Most people take really long breaks and in that break many go full stop, and put on weight. Then when starting again, being unfit and 5 kilograms overweight... But I maintain my fitness while having my breaks. For example in 2018 I had my longest continuous break: 28 days, but I maintained fitness playing/running with my dog. Five days after getting back to training I was repping 1ks under four minutes. I would say at worst, I'm maybe 96% of full fitness, so doing 1:21 [for 20 kilometers] *instead of doing 1:18. So basically this: never get unfit! It takes longer to build fitness again, and from an injury perspective, you have to hold back and take a longer time before getting back to a full training load. It's a good strategy and the best one for gradually improving, I would*

say. You don't lose a couple of months getting back to the same level you were; you can continue building and improving pretty much straight away."

So there you have it, different strokes for different folks. If your goal is to be really ready for one big race every couple of years, like the Olympics or a masters (over age 35) world championship, you'll want to use a long, low intensity base-training phase; if, on the other hand, you want to have fun and be reasonably race-ready year-round to smoke the competition all season long at your local grand prix race series or at masters national championships throughout the year, you should keep your rest phase to a minimum and do some sort of speed work year round. The downside to that approach is there's never a sustained period of time to recover from injuries and no mental break from training. But if you're not injured very often and you really love to train, walking year-round may be a better option for you. Even if that is your plan, though, you will still need to spend some time putting in the base miles before moving on to the specific training schedules in subsequent chapters.

What follows are appropriate base-training schedules for beginning, intermediate and advanced walkers training for various race distances. Because these are general schedules, they are appropriate for walkers using power walking, racewalking, or Nordic walking technique. You should modify them to reflect your own training preferences and racing goals based on your own experience and/or in consultation with your coach. So without further ado, the base training schedules:

Beginner Base-Training for Events Up to Half-Marathon							
Week	**Monday**	**Tuesday**	**Wednesday**	**Thursday**	**Friday**	**Saturday**	**Sunday**
1	Off or easy cross-train	Easy 20 minutes	Off or easy cross-train	Easy 20 minutes	Off or easy cross-train	Easy 20 minutes	Easy 25 minutes
2	Off or easy cross-train	Easy 25 mins.	Off or easy cross-train	Easy 25 mins.	Off or easy cross-train	Easy 25 mins.	Easy 30 mins.
3	Off or easy cross-train	Easy 30 mins.	Off or easy cross-train	Easy 30 mins.	Off or easy cross-train	Easy 30 mins.	Easy 35 mins.
4	Off or easy cross-train	Easy 35 mins.	Easy 30 mins.	Easy 30 mins.	Off or easy cross-train	Easy 30 mins.	Easy 40 mins.
5	Off or easy cross-train	Easy 40 mins.	Moderate 30 mins.	Easy 35 mins.	Off or easy cross-train	Moderate 30 mins.	Easy 45 mins.
6	Off or easy cross-train	Easy 45 mins.	Moderate 30 mins.	Easy 40 mins.	Off or easy cross-train	Moderate 30 mins.	Easy 50 mins.
7	Off or easy cross-train	45-minute fartlek	Moderate 30 mins.	Easy 45 mins.	Off or easy cross-train	Moderate 30 mins.	Easy 60 mins.
8	Off or easy cross-train	30-minute fartlek	Moderate 30 mins.	Easy 30 mins.	Off or easy cross-train	Moderate 30 mins.	Easy 45 mins.
9	Off or easy cross-train	45-minute fartlek	Moderate 30 mins.	45-minute fartlek	Off or easy cross-train	Moderate 30 mins.	Easy 4 miles (or 6k)
10	Off or easy cross-train	45-minute fartlek	Moderate 30 mins.	45-minute fartlek	Off or easy cross-train	Moderate 30 mins.	Easy 4.5 miles (or 7k)
11	Off or easy cross-train	45-minute fartlek	Moderate 30 mins.	45-minute fartlek	Off or easy cross-train	Moderate 30 mins.	Easy 5 miles (or 8k)
12	Off or easy cross-train	30-minute fartlek	Moderate 30 mins.	30-minute fartlek	Off or easy cross-train	Moderate 30 mins.	Easy 5 miles (or 8k)

The Beginner Base-Training Schedule for Events Up to Half-Marathon presupposes… nothing! It's a beginner's schedule early in the season, so you don't need any prior competitive walking experience to get started and succeed in completing this schedule. Off or easy cross training days can be complete days off, or if you would rather stay active, try something else you like to do, whether it's a spin or group-fitness class, yoga class, or a solo activity you enjoy like swimming, cycling, or—in season—cross-country skiing or snow-shoeing; easy days are truly easy walks; moderate days should get you breathing more heavily; Tuesday and Thursday fartleks are completely unstructured speed work. Walk at an easy to moderate pace, then pick it up for a "quickish" sprint for anywhere from fifteen seconds to a minute or so, then back it down to the easy to moderate pace for a while, then repeat, repeat, repeat. Just like a 19th-Century pedestrian, go as you please! Finally, the mile and kilometer distances on the weekend are not precise conversions (6k is actually closer to 3¾ miles than 4 miles), but I like to stick to round figures whenever possible. This is a pretty reasonable build-up for most people, but be sure to look for any of the signs of overtraining that were outlined in the introduction to this section!

Intermediate Base-Training for Events Up to Half-Marathon							
Week	**Monday**	**Tuesday**	**Wednesday**	**Thursday**	**Friday**	**Saturday**	**Sunday**
1	Off or easy cross-train	Easy 30 mins.	Moderate 30 mins.	Easy 30 mins.	Off or easy cross-train	Moderate 30 mins.	Easy 45 mins.
2	Off or easy cross-train	Easy 35 mins.	Moderate 30 mins.	Easy 35 mins.	Off or easy cross-train	Moderate 30 mins.	Easy 50 mins.
3	Off or easy cross-train	Easy 40 mins.	Moderate 30 mins.	Easy 40 mins.	Off or easy cross-train	Moderate 30 mins.	Easy 55 mins.
4	Off or easy cross-train	Easy 45 mins.	Moderate 30 mins.	Easy 45 mins.	Off or easy cross-train	Moderate 30 mins.	Easy 60 mins.
5	Off or easy cross-train	45-minute fartlek	Moderate 30 mins.	Easy 45 mins.	Off or easy cross-train	Moderate 35 mins.	Easy 4 miles (or 6k)
6	Off or easy cross-train	45-minute fartlek	Moderate 30 mins.	Easy 45 mins.	Off or easy cross-train	Moderate 40 mins.	Easy 5 miles (or 8k)
7	Off or easy cross-train	45-minute fartlek	Moderate 30 mins.	Easy 45 mins.	Off or easy cross-train	Moderate 45 mins.	Easy 5.5 miles (or 9k)
8	Off or easy cross-train	30-minute fartlek	Moderate 30 mins.	Easy 30 mins.	Off or easy cross-train	Moderate 30 mins.	Easy 5 miles (or 8k)
9	Off or easy cross-train	50-minute fartlek	Moderate 30 mins.	50-minute fartlek	Off or easy cross-train	Moderate 50 mins.	Easy 6 miles (or 10k)
10	Off or easy cross-train	55-minute fartlek	Moderate 30 mins.	55-minute fartlek	Off or easy cross-train	Moderate 55 mins.	Easy 7 miles (or 11k)
11	Off or easy cross-train	60-minute fartlek	Moderate 30 mins.	60-minute fartlek	Off or easy cross-train	Moderate 60 mins.	Easy 8 miles (or 13k)
12	Off or easy cross-train	45-minute fartlek	Moderate 30 mins.	45-minute fartlek	Off or easy cross-train	Moderate 45 mins.	Easy 6 miles (or 10k)

The Intermediate Base-Training Schedule for Events Up to Half-Marathon assumes you are currently able to walk up to an hour several days per week, and that you participate in the occasional 5k or 10k race. You will probably walk more days per week than on the Beginner schedule, rather than taking off or cross training on those days, but if you ever start to feel run down, take the day off before you wear yourself out. The base-training phase is all about building up, not breaking down!

Advanced Base-Training for Events Up to Half-Marathon

Week	Monday	Tuesday	Wednesday	Thursday	Friday	Saturday	Sunday
1	Off or easy cross-train	Easy 45 mins.	Moderate 45 mins.	Easy 45 mins.	Easy 5 miles (or 8k)	Moderate 45 mins.	Easy 8 miles (or 13k)
2	Off or easy cross-train	Easy 50 mins.	Moderate 50 mins.	Easy 50 mins.	Easy 5 miles (or 8k)	Moderate 50 mins.	Easy 9 miles (or 15k)
3	Off or easy cross-train	Easy 60 mins.	Moderate 60 mins.	Easy 60 mins.	Easy 5 miles (or 8k)	Moderate 60 mins.	Easy 10 miles (or 16k)
4	Off or easy cross-train	Easy 45 mins.	Moderate 45 mins.	Easy 45 mins.	Easy 5 miles (or 8k)	Moderate 45 mins.	Easy 8 miles (or 13k)
5	Off or easy cross-train	60-minute fartlek	Moderate 60 mins.	60-minute fartlek	Easy 5 miles (or 8k)	Moderate 60 mins.	Easy 10 miles (or 16k)
6	Off or easy cross-train	60-minute fartlek	Moderate 60 mins.	60-minute fartlek	Easy 5 miles (or 8k)	Moderate 60 mins.	Easy 10 miles (or 16k)
7	Off or easy cross-train	60-minute fartlek	Moderate 60 mins.	60-minute fartlek	Easy 5 miles (or 8k)	Moderate 60 mins.	Easy 10 miles (or 16k)
8	Off or easy cross-train	45-minute fartlek	Moderate 45 mins.	45-minute fartlek	Easy 5 miles (or 8k)	Moderate 45 mins.	Easy 8 miles (or 13k)
9	Off or easy cross-train	60-minute fartlek	Moderate 60 mins.	60-minute fartlek	Easy 5 miles (or 8k)	Moderate 60 mins.	Easy 10 miles (or 16k)
10	Off or easy cross-train	60-minute fartlek	Moderate 60 mins.	60-minute fartlek	Easy 5 miles (or 8k)	Moderate 60 mins.	Easy 10 miles (or 16k)
11	Off or easy cross-train	60-minute fartlek	Moderate 60 mins.	60-minute fartlek	Easy 5 miles (or 8k)	Moderate 60 mins.	Easy 10 miles (or 16k)
12	Off or easy cross-train	45-minute fartlek	Moderate 45 mins.	45-minute fartlek	Easy 5 miles (or 8k)	Moderate 45 mins.	Easy 8 miles (or 13k)

The Advanced Base-Training Schedule for Events Up to Half-Marathon is for experienced long-distance walkers who frequently race ten kilometers and longer, including half-marathons or even full marathons, and thus should be ready to jump right into longer workouts from day one. Walkers on this schedule should also be comfortable with speed and tempo training, but are not planning to do races longer than half-marathon in the near future.

Beginner Base-Training for Events Beyond Half-Marathon							
Week	**Monday**	**Tuesday**	**Wednesday**	**Thursday**	**Friday**	**Saturday**	**Sunday**
1	Off or easy cross-train	Easy 20 mins.	Off or easy cross-train	Easy 20 mins.	Off or easy cross-train	Easy 20 mins.	Easy 25 mins.
2	Off or easy cross-train	Easy 25 mins.	Off or easy cross-train	Easy 25 mins.	Off or easy cross-train	Easy 25 mins.	Easy 30 mins.
3	Off or easy cross-train	Easy 30 mins.	Off or easy cross-train	Easy 30 mins.	Off or easy cross-train	Easy 30 mins.	Easy 35 mins.
4	Off or easy cross-train	Easy 35 mins.	Easy 30 mins.	Easy 35 mins.	Off or easy cross-train	Easy 30 mins.	Easy 40 mins.
5	Off or easy cross-train	Easy 40 mins.	Moderate 30 mins.	Easy 40 mins.	Off or easy cross-train	Moderate 35 mins.	Easy 45 mins.
6	Off or easy cross-train	Easy 45 mins.	Moderate 35 mins.	Easy 45 mins.	Off or easy cross-train	Moderate 40 mins.	Easy 50 mins.
7	Off or easy cross-train	Easy 45 mins.	Moderate 40 mins.	Easy 45 mins.	Off or easy cross-train	Moderate 45 mins.	Easy 55 mins.
8	Off or easy cross-train	Easy 30 mins.	Moderate 30 mins.	Easy 30 mins.	Off or easy cross-train	Moderate 30 mins.	Easy 45 mins.
9	Off or easy cross-train	Easy 45 mins.	Moderate 40 mins.	Easy 45 mins.	Off or easy cross-train	Moderate 45 mins.	Easy 4 miles (or 6k)
10	Off or easy cross-train	Easy 45 mins.	Moderate 45 mins.	Easy 45 mins.	Off or easy cross-train	Moderate 45 mins.	Easy 4.5 miles (or 7k)
11	Off or easy cross-train	Easy 45 mins.	Moderate 45 mins.	Easy 45 mins.	Off or easy cross-train	Moderate 45 mins.	Easy 5 miles (or 8k)
12	Off or easy cross-train	Easy 30 mins.	Moderate 45 mins.	Easy 30 mins.	Off or easy cross-train	Moderate 30 mins.	Easy 6 miles (or 10k)
13	Off or easy cross-train	45-minute fartlek	Moderate 60 mins.	45-minute fartlek	Off or easy cross-train	Moderate 45 mins.	Easy 6.5 miles (or 10.5k)
14	Off or easy cross-train	50-minute fartlek	Moderate 60 mins.	50-minute fartlek	Off or easy cross-train	Moderate 45 mins.	Easy 7 miles (or 11k)
15	Off or easy cross-train	60-minute fartlek	Moderate 60 mins.	60-minute fartlek	Off or easy cross-train	Moderate 45 mins.	(Easy 8 miles (or 13k)
16	Off or easy cross-train	45-minute fartlek	Moderate 45 mins.	45-minute fartlek	Off or easy cross-train	Moderate 30 mins.	Easy 6 miles (or 10k)

The Beginner Base-Training Schedule for Events Beyond Half-Marathon is for relative beginners who want to jump right into longer-distance races. I highly recommend training for and racing 5k, 10k, and half-marathon races for at least two years before jumping into a marathon or longer, but nobody ever listens… ☺ If you are a beginner and have your heart set on doing a marathon or other long event, this base-training schedule will lay the foundation for the beginner training schedules for any of those events.

Intermediate Base-Training for Events Beyond Half-Marathon							
Week	**Monday**	**Tuesday**	**Wednesday**	**Thursday**	**Friday**	**Saturday**	**Sunday**
1	Off or easy cross-train	Easy 30 mins.	Moderate 30 mins.	Easy 30 mins.	Off or easy cross-train	Moderate 30 mins.	Easy 60 mins.
2	Off or easy cross-train	Easy 35 mins.	Moderate 30 mins.	Easy 35 mins.	Off or easy cross-train	Moderate 30 mins.	Easy 4 miles (or 6k)
3	Off or easy cross-train	Easy 40 mins.	Moderate 30 mins.	Easy 40 mins.	Off or easy cross-train	Moderate 30 mins.	Easy 4.5 miles (or 7k)
4	Off or easy cross-train	Easy 45 mins.	Moderate 30 mins.	Easy 45 mins.	Off or easy cross-train	Moderate 30 mins.	Easy 5 miles (or 8k)
5	Off or easy cross-train	45-minute fartlek	Moderate 30 mins.	Easy 45 mins.	Off or easy cross-train	Moderate 35 mins.	Easy 5.5 miles (or 9k)
6	Off or easy cross-train	45-minute fartlek	Moderate 30 mins.	Easy 45 mins.	Off or easy cross-train	Moderate 40 mins.	Easy 6 miles (or 10k)
7	Off or easy cross-train	45-minute fartlek	Moderate 30 mins.	Easy 45 mins.	Off or easy cross-train	Moderate 45 mins.	Easy 7 miles (or 11k)
8	Off or easy cross-train	30-minute fartlek	Moderate 30 mins.	Easy 30 mins.	Off or easy cross-train	Moderate 30 mins.	Easy 5 miles (or 8k)
9	Off or easy cross-train	50-minute fartlek	Moderate 30 mins.	50-minute fartlek	Off or easy cross-train	Moderate 50 mins.	Easy 7.5 miles (or 12k)
10	Off or easy cross-train	55-minute fartlek	Moderate 30 mins.	55-minute fartlek	Off or easy cross-train	Moderate 55 mins.	Easy 8 miles (or 13k)
11	Off or easy cross-train	60-minute fartlek	Moderate 30 mins.	60-minute fartlek	Off or easy cross-train	Moderate 60 mins.	Easy 9 miles (or 15k)
12	Off or easy cross-train	45-minute fartlek	Moderate 30 mins.	45-minute fartlek	Off or easy cross-train	Moderate 45 mins.	Easy 6 miles (or 10k)
13	Off or easy cross-train	45-minute fartlek	Mod. 30 mins.	45-minute fartlek	Off or easy cross-train	Mod. 30 mins.	Easy 10 miles (or 16k)
14	Off or easy cross-train	45-minute fartlek	Mod. 30 mins.	45-minute fartlek	Off or easy cross-train	Mod. 30 mins.	Easy 11 miles (or 17k)
15	Off or easy cross-train	45-minute fartlek	Mod. 30 mins.	45-minute fartlek	Off or easy cross-train	Mod. 30 mins.	Easy 12 miles (or 19k)
16	Off or easy cross-train	45-minute fartlek	Mod. 30 mins.	45-minute fartlek	Off or easy cross-train	Mod. 30 mins.	Easy 8 miles (or 13k)

The Intermediate Base-Training Schedule for Events Beyond Half-Marathon assumes you have been training for and racing in 5k to half-marathon events for at least two years and are currently able to walk up to an hour several days per week.

Advanced Base-Training for Events Beyond Half-Marathon							
Week	**Monday**	**Tuesday**	**Wednesday**	**Thursday**	**Friday**	**Saturday**	**Sunday**
1	Off or easy cross-train	8k fartlek	Easy 6 miles/10k	Moderate 5 miles/8k	Easy 6 miles/10k	Moderate 5 miles/8k	Easy 10 miles (or 16k)
2	Off or easy cross-train	8k fartlek	Easy 6 miles/10k	Moderate 5 miles/8k	Easy 6 miles/10k	Moderate 5 miles/8k	Easy 11 miles (or 17k)
3	Off or easy cross-train	8k fartlek	Easy 6 miles/10k	Moderate 5 miles/8k	Easy 6 miles/10k	Moderate 5 miles/8k	Easy 12 miles (or 19k)
4	Off or easy cross-train	8k fartlek	Easy 6 miles/10k	Moderate 5 miles/8k	Easy 6 miles/10k	Moderate 5 miles/8k	Easy 10 miles (or 13k)
5	Off or easy cross-train	10-min. warm-up, drills, then 8 x 200m @ 5k race pace w/ 200m breaks	Easy 6 miles/10k	Moderate 5 miles/8k	Easy 6 miles/10k	Moderate 5 miles/8k	Easy 12 miles (or 19k)
6	Off or easy cross-train	10-min. warm-up, drills, then 8 x 400m @ 10k race pace w/ 200m breaks	Easy 6 miles/10k	Moderate 5 miles/8k	Easy 6 miles/10k	Moderate 5 miles/8k	Easy 13 miles (or 21k)
7	Off or easy cross-train	“” 10 x 200m @ 5k race pace w/ 200m breaks	Easy 6 miles/10k	Moderate 5 miles/8k	Easy 6 miles/10k	Moderate 5 miles/8k	Easy 14 miles (or 22k)
8	Off or easy cross-train	“” 10 x 400m @ 10k race pace w/ 200m breaks	Easy 6 miles/10k	Moderate 5 miles/8k	Easy 6 miles/10k	Moderate 5 miles/8k	Easy 12 miles (or 19k)
9	Off or easy cross-train	“”12 x 200m @ 5k race pace w/ 200m breaks	Easy 6 miles/10k	Moderate 5 miles/8k	Easy 6 miles/10k	Moderate 5 miles/8k	Easy 15 miles (or 24k)
10	Off or easy cross-train	“”12 x 400m @ 10k race pace w/ 200m breaks	Easy 6 miles/10k	Moderate 5 miles/8k	Easy 6 miles/10k	Moderate 5 miles/8k	Easy 15 miles (or 24k)
11	Off or easy cross-train	“”14 x 200m @ 5k race pace w/ 200m breaks	Easy 6 miles/10k	Moderate 5 miles/8k	Easy 6 miles/10k	Moderate 5 miles/8k	Easy 15 miles (or 24k)
12	Off or easy cross-train	“” 12 x 400m @ 10k race pace w/ 200m breaks	Easy 6 miles/ 10k	Moderate 5 miles/8k	Easy 6 miles/10k	Moderate 5 miles/8k	Easy 12 miles (or 24k)
13	Off or easy cross-train	“”16 x 200m @ 5k race pace w/ 200m breaks	Easy 6 miles/ 10k	Moderate 5 miles/8k	Easy 6 miles/10k	Moderate 5 miles/8k	Easy 15 miles (or 24k)
14	Off or easy cross-train	“” 12 x 400m @ 10k race pace w/ 200m breaks	Easy 6 miles/ 10k	Moderate 5 miles/8k	Easy 6 miles/10k	Moderate 5 miles/8k	Easy 15 miles (or 24k)
15	Off or easy cross-train	“”16 x 200m @ 5k race pace w/ 200m breaks	Easy 6 miles/ 10k	Moderate 5 miles/8k	Easy 6 miles/10k	Moderate 5 miles/8k	Easy 15 miles (or 24k)
16	Off or easy cross-train	“”12 x 400m @ 10k race pace w/ 200m breaks	Easy 6 miles/ 10k	Moderate 5 miles/8k	Easy 6 miles/10k	Moderate 5 miles/8k	Easy 12 miles (or 24k)

The Advanced Base-Training Schedule for Events Beyond Half-Marathon is for experienced long-distance walkers training for an upcoming marathon, 50k or other long-distance event. The assumption is that a +/- 20k long day is a walk in the park. ☺ Many running marathon training schedules have no speed work in the base phase, but I believe that the high cadence rate of competitive walking, especially racewalking, requires some form of speed work year-round.

CHAPTER 17: THE SPRINTS: 1,500 METERS TO 5 KILOMETERS

Competitive walking has historically been, at its heart, a long-distance pursuit. Yet sprint walks of 1,500 meters and 3,000 meters were the first stand-alone walks to be added to the Olympic program, appearing at the 1906 Games in Athens, Greece. Sprints are very popular today among youth and senior power walkers and racewalkers. 1,500-meters, 1,600-meters and 1-mile are the most commonly contested distances for youth and high school racewalkers, and for Senior Olympics (over age 50) participants who compete at these distances in both racewalking and power walking. 3,000 meters (1.86 miles) is the standard indoor racewalking distance for both elite and masters walkers, while 5,000m (3.1 miles) is the most popular distance for running races with competitive walk divisions. 5k is also a world record-eligible distance in Nordic walking.

The sprints present unique challenges for walkers. Physiologically, the shorter distances should allow a walker to go at much faster paces than he or she can go in longer events, but the mechanical limitation of standard walking technique prevents many competitors from maximizing that potential. Well-developed racewalking or Nordic walking technique allows walkers to go *very* fast! Racewalking world records for men are 5:31 for the mile and 18:05 for 5,000m,[53] while the men's Nordic walking world record for 5,000m stands at 21:09. Obviously speedy technique is critical, but to hit anywhere near these kinds of times, walkers must train for speed. Having said that, even walks as short as 1,500 meters and 1 mile are technically not sprints in the physiological sense of the word since they last several minutes rather than a few or a few dozen seconds. Accordingly, "sprint" walkers will have to do some endurance training, but will also hone top-end speed via short economy intervals in the 50-meter to 200-meter range. One of my favorites for beginners is "turns & straights." This is a classic economy interval workout where you'll walk easy (but with great technique!) on the turns of a high school or college track, then blast the straightaways. You'll also need to improve your lactate threshold with intervals in the 300m to 500m range when training for 1,500m and 1-mile races; 500m to 800m intervals for 3,000m races; and 800m to 1,600m intervals for 5k training. Short (four kilometers to four miles) tempo and progression workouts are also helpful when prepping for 5k/5,000m competitions.

The pages to follow will plot out the final sixteen weeks of training to prepare for 1,500m/1,600m/1-mile; 3,000m/2 miles; and 5,000m/5k races, after the base-training in Chapter 16 has been completed. Although warming up completely, including doing five or ten minutes of

[53] The women's racewalking world records are 6:16 for the mile and 19:46 for 5k.

the dynamic flexibility drills described in Chapter 34, is a good idea before any workout, doing so before undertaking the speed work necessary for sprint racing is critical to avoid injuries. Don't even think about skipping your warm-up before doing fast intervals, and don't try to max out your speed initially. Walk fast, but not all-out, until you've successfully completed several of these workouts without undue soreness or tightness the next day. If you do wind up "tweaking" something during or after a speed workout (or any workout!) take a few days or a week of easy walking before attempting to go fast again, no matter what the schedule says.

Schedules for 1,500m, 1,600m and 1-mile are combined. The distances are so similar that the training for each race is nearly indistinguishable. The same thing goes for the 3,000m/2 miles (3,218m) distances. 5,000m and 5k *are* the same distance—3.1 miles. So obviously that training will be the same, other than the venue: You should train on the track at least a few days per week for an upcoming 5,000m track race, and on the road for a road 5k. The reason some races are measured in meters and the other in kilometers has its roots in track & field tradition and terminology. By convention, all track races are measured in meters, while all road events are measured in kilometers. Separate national and world records are kept for track vs. road events, so there are male and female world records for the 5,000m (track) racewalks, and different male and female records for the 5k (road) walks. The same conventions apply for power walking and Nordic walking. With that bit of trivia out of the way, on to the schedules!

Beginner 1,500m/1,600m/1-Mile Training Schedule

Week	Mon.	Tues.	Wed.	Thurs.	Fri.	Sat.	Sun.
1	Off or easy XT	45-minute fartlek	Moderate 30-mins.	45-minute fartlek	Off or easy XT	Moderate 30-mins.	Easy 6 miles (or 10k)
2	Off or easy XT	10-min. warm-up, drills, then 8 x 30 sec. hill reps	Mod. 30 mins.	45-minute fartlek	Off or easy XT	Mod. 30 mins.	Easy 6 miles (or 10k)
3	Off or easy XT	10-min. warm-up, drills, then 8 x 1:00 min. hill reps.	Mod. 30 mins.	45-minute fartlek	Off or easy XT	Mod. 30 mins.	Easy 6 miles (or 10k)
4	Off or easy XT	10-min. warm-up, drills, then 8 x 1:30 hill reps.	Mod. 30 mins.	45-minute fartlek	Off or easy XT	Mod. 30 mins.	Easy 6 miles (or 10k)
5	Off or easy XT	“” 8 x 2:00 min. hill reps.	Mod. 30 mins.	45-minute fartlek	Off or easy XT	Mod. 30 mins.	Easy 6 miles (or 10k)
6	Off or easy XT	Track. 10 min. w/up then 8 laps of Turns & Straights	Mod. 30 mins.	45-minute fartlek	Off or easy XT	Mod. 30 mins.	Easy 6 miles (or 10k)
7	Off or easy XT	Track. 10 min. w/up then 10 laps of T&S.	Mod. 30 mins.	10-min. warm-up, drills, then 5 x 300m @ race pace, w/ 200m breaks.	Off or easy XT	Mod. 30 mins.	Easy 6 miles (or 10k)
8	Off or easy XT	Track. 10 min. w/up then 12 laps of T&S.	Mod. 30 mins.	“” 6 x 300m @ race pace w/ 400m breaks.	Off or easy XT	Mod. 30 mins.	Easy 6 miles (or 10k)
9	Off or easy XT	“” 12 x 200m fast w/200m breaks	Mod. 30 mins.	“” 5 x 400m w/ 400m easy walk breaks.	Off or easy XT	Mod. 30 mins.	Easy 6 miles (or 10k)
10	Off or easy XT	“” 12 x 400m @ goal race pace, w/ 200m breaks.	Mod. 30 mins.	“”4 x 500m w/ 400m easy walk breaks.	Off or easy XT	Mod. 30 mins.	Easy 6 miles (or 10k)
11	Off or easy XT	“” 12 x 200m fast w/200m breaks	Mod. 30 mins.	“”6 x 400m w/ 400m easy walk breaks.	Off or easy XT	Mod. 30 mins.	Easy 6 miles (or 10k)
12	Off or easy XT	“” 6 x 400m w/ 200m breaks.	Mod. 30 mins.	“”5 x 500m w/ 400m easy walk breaks.	Off or easy XT	Mod. 30 mins.	Easy 6 miles (or 10k)
13	Off or easy XT	“” 12 x 200m fast w/200m breaks	Mod. 30 mins.	“” 1 x 800m; 2 x 400m @ 1,600m pace; 1 x 200m fast! All w/ 200m breaks.	Off or easy XT	Mod. 30 mins.	Easy 6 miles (or 10k)
14	Off or easy XT	“” 12 x 400m w/ 200m breaks.	Mod. 30 mins.	6 x 400m w/ 400m easy walk breaks.	Off or easy XT	Mod. 30 mins.	Easy 6 miles (or 10k)
15	Off or easy XT	“” 10 x 400m w/ 200m breaks.	Mod. 30 mins.	“” 1 x 800m; 2 x 400m @ 1,600m pace; 1 x 200m fast! All w/ 200m breaks.	Off or easy XT	Mod. 30 mins.	Easy 5 miles (or 8k)
16	Off or easy XT	Easy 30 mins.	Off	“” 4 x 30 seconds sprints, cool down, then stretch.	**RACE!**	Off or EZ 30-mins.	Easy 5 miles (or 8k)

The goal race day here on the 1,500m/1,600m/1-mile schedule—and for the beginner and advanced 3,000m schedules—is Friday, because most high school meets are held on weekdays, and the Senior Games 1,500m walk, and the Masters Indoor 3,000m, are held on Fridays. If your race is on a different day, for example the Junior Olympics 3,000m walks are usually held on a Sunday, shift the last week or two to reflect your actual race day. I have already done this for the Intermediate 3,000m schedule. All my abbreviations are in the index, but as seen above, XT = cross-train and EZ = easy.

Intermediate 1,500m/1,600m/1-Mile Training Schedule

Week	Mon.	Tues.	Wed.	Thurs.	Fri.	Sat.	Sun.
1	Off or easy XT	45-minute fartlek	Moderate 30-mins.	45-minute fartlek	Easy 30 mins. or XT	Moderat e 30-mins.	Easy 6 miles (or 10k)
2	Off or easy XT	10-min. warm-up, drills, then 8 x 30 sec. hill reps.	Mod. 30 mins.	45-minute fartlek	Easy 30 mins. or XT	Mod. 30 mins.	Easy 6 miles (or 10k)
3	Off or easy XT	10-min. warm-up, drills, then 8 x 1:00 min. hill reps.	Mod. 40 mins.	45-minute fartlek	Easy 30 mins. or XT	Mod. 40 mins.	Easy 6 miles (or 10k)
4	Off or easy XT	10-min. warm-up, drills, then 8 x 1:30 hill reps.	Mod. 45 mins.	45-minute fartlek	Easy 30 mins. or XT	Mod. 45 mins.	Easy 6 miles (or 10k)
5	Off or easy XT	"" then 8 x 2:00 min. hill reps.	Mod. 45 mins.	45-minute fartlek	Easy 30 mins. or XT	Mod. 45 mins.	Easy 8 miles (or 13k)
6	Off or easy XT	"" 3 x {100m/200m/300m} w/ 100m breaks	Mod. 45 mins.	45-minute fartlek	Easy 30 mins. or XT	Mod. 45 mins.	Easy 8 miles (or 13k)
7	Off or easy XT	"" 8 x 200m fast w/200m breaks	Mod. 45 mins.	10-min. warm-up, drills, then 5 x 300m @ race pace, w/ 200m breaks.	Easy 30 mins. or XT	Mod. 45 mins.	Easy 8 miles (or 13k)
8	Off or easy XT	"" 4 x {100m/200m/300m} w/ 100m breaks	Mod. 45 mins.	"" 6 x 300m @ race pace w/ 400m breaks.	Easy 30 mins. or XT	Mod. 45 mins.	Easy 6 miles (or 10k)
9	Off or easy XT	"" 10 x 200m fast w/200m breaks	Mod. 45 mins.	"" 5 x 400m w/ 400m easy walk breaks.	Easy 45 mins. or XT	Mod. 45 mins.	Easy 8 miles (or 13k)
10	Off or easy XT	"" 4 x {100m/200m/300m} w/ 100m breaks	Mod. 45 mins.	""4 x 500m w/ 400m easy walk breaks.	Easy 45 mins. or XT	Mod. 45 mins.	Easy 8 miles (or 13k)
11	Off or easy XT	"" 10 x 200m fast w/200m breaks	Mod. 45 mins.	""6 x 400m w/ 400m easy walk breaks.	Easy 45 mins. or XT	Mod. 45 mins.	Easy 8 miles (or 13k)
12	Off or easy XT	"" 4 x {100m/200m/300m} w/ 100m breaks	Mod. 45 mins.	""5 x 500m w/ 400m easy walk breaks.	Easy 45 mins. or XT	Mod. 45 mins.	Easy 6 miles (or 10k)
13	Off or easy XT	"" 12 x 200m fast w/200m breaks	Mod. 45 mins.	"" 1 x 800m; 2 x 400m @ 1,600m pace; 1 x 200m fast! All w/ 200m breaks.	Easy 45 mins. or XT	Mod. 45 mins.	Easy 8 miles (or 13k)
14	Off or easy XT	"" 4 x {100m/200m/300m} w/ 100m breaks	Mod. 45 mins.	6 x 400m w/ 400m easy walk breaks.	Easy 45 mins. or XT	Mod. 45 mins.	Easy 8 miles (or 13k)
15	Off or easy XT	"" 8 x 200m fast w/200m breaks	Mod. 45 mins.	"" 1 x 800m; 2 x 400m @ 1,600m pace; 1 x 200m fast! All w/ 200m breaks.	Easy 30 mins. or XT	Mod. 45 mins.	Easy 5 miles (or 8k)
16	Off or easy XT	20-minute fartlek	Off	"" 4 x 30 seconds sprints, cool down, then stretch.	**RACE!!!**	Off or EZ 30-mins.	Easy 5 miles (or 8k)

Advanced 1,500m/1,600m/1-Mile Training Schedule							
Week	**Mon.**	**Tues.**	**Wed.**	**Thurs.**	**Fri.**	**Sat.**	**Sun.**
1	Off or easy XT	45-minute fartlek	Easy 10k	45-minute fartlek	Easy 10k or cross-train	Moderate 8k	Easy 10 miles (or 16k)
2	Off or easy XT	10-min. warm-up, drills, then 8 x 30 sec. hill reps.	Easy 10k	45-minute fartlek	Easy 10k or cross-train	Moderate 8k	Easy 10 miles (or 16k)
3	Off or easy XT	10-min. warm-up, drills, then 8 x 1:00 min. hill reps.	Easy 10k	45-minute fartlek	Easy 10k or cross-train	Moderate 8k	Easy 10 miles (or 16k)
4	Off or easy XT	10-min. warm-up, drills, then 8 x 1:30 hill reps.	Easy 10k	45-minute fartlek	Easy 10k or cross-train	Moderate 8k	Easy 8 miles (or 13k)
5	Off or easy XT	"" then 8 x 2:00 min. hill reps.	Easy 10k	45-minute fartlek	Easy 10k or cross-train	Moderate 8k	Easy 10 miles (or 16k)
6	Off or easy XT	"" 3 x {100m/200m/300m} w/ 100m breaks	Easy 10k	45-minute fartlek	Easy 10k or cross-train	Moderate 8k	Easy 10 miles (or 16k)
7	Off or easy XT	"" 8 x 200m fast w/200m breaks	Easy 10k	10-min. warm-up, drills, then 5 x 300m @ race pace, w/ 200m breaks.	Easy 10k or cross-train	Moderate 8k	Easy 10 miles (or 16k)
8	Off or easy XT	"" 4 x {100m/200m/300m} w/ 100m breaks	Easy 10k	"" 6 x 300m @ race pace w/ 400m breaks.	Easy 10k or cross-train	Moderate 8k	Easy 8 miles (or 13k)
9	Off or easy XT	"" 10 x 200m fast w/200m breaks	Easy 10k	"" 5 x 400m w/ 400m easy walk breaks.	Easy 10k or cross-train	Moderate 8k	Easy 10 miles (or 16k)
10	Off or easy XT	"" 4 x {100m/200m/300m} w/ 100m breaks	Easy 10k	""4 x 500m w/ 400m easy walk breaks.	Easy 10k or cross-train	Moderate 8k	Easy 10 miles (or 16k)
11	Off or easy XT	"" 10 x 200m fast w/200m breaks	Easy 10k	""6 x 400m w/ 400m easy walk breaks.	Easy 10k or cross-train	Moderate 8k	Easy 10 miles (or 16k)
12	Off or easy XT	"" 4 x {100m/200m/300m} w/ 100m breaks	Easy 10k	""5 x 500m w/ 400m easy walk breaks.	Easy 10k or cross-train	Moderate 8k	Easy 8 miles (or 13k)
13	Off or easy XT	"" 12 x 200m fast w/200m breaks	Easy 10k	"" 1 x 800m; 2 x 400m @ 1,600m pace; 1 x 200m fast! All w/ 200m breaks.	Easy 10k or cross-train	Moderate 8k	Easy 10 miles (or 16k)
14	Off or easy XT	"" 4 x {100m/200m/300m} w/ 100m breaks	Easy 10k	"" 6 x 400m w/ 400m easy walk breaks.	Easy 10k or cross-train	Moderate 8k	Easy 10 miles (or 16k)
15	Off or easy XT	"" 8 x 200m fast w/200m breaks	Easy 10k	"" 1 x 800m; 2 x 400m @ 1,600m pace; 1 x 200m fast! All w/ 200m breaks.	Easy 10k or cross-train	Moderate 8k	Easy 8 miles (or 13k)
16	Off or easy XT	20-minute fartlek	Easy 8k	Off or easy 8k	"" 4 x 30 seconds sprints, cool down, then stretch.	**RACE!!!**	Easy 6 miles (or 10k)

Beginners 3,000m Training Schedule

Week	Mon.	Tues.	Wed.	Thurs.	Fri.	Sat.	Sun.
1	Off or easy cross-train	45-minute fartlek	Moderate 30 mins.	45-minute fartlek	Off or easy cross-train	Moderate 30 mins.	Easy 6-mile (or 10k)
2	Off or easy cross-train	10-min. warm-up, drills, then 8 x 30 sec. hill reps	Mod. 30-mins.	45-minute fartlek	Off or easy cross-train	Mod. 30-mins.	Easy 6 miles (or 10k)
3	Off or easy cross-train	10-min. warm-up, drills, then 8 x 1:00 min. hill reps.	Mod. 30-mins.	45-minute fartlek	Off or easy cross-train	Mod. 30-mins.	Easy 6 miles (or 10k)
4	Off or easy cross-train	10-min. warm-up, drills, then 8 x 1:30 min. hill reps.	Mod. 30-mins.	30-minute fartlek	Off or easy cross-train	Mod. 30-mins.	Easy 4 miles (or 6.5k)
5	Off or easy cross-train	"" 8 x 2:00 min. hill reps.	Mod. 30-mins.	"" 6 x 400m @ 3,000m race pace, w/ 200m easy breaks.	Off or easy cross-train	Mod. 30-mins.	Easy 6 miles (or 10k)
6	Off or easy cross-train	Track. 10 min. w/up then 8 laps of Turns & Straights	Mod. 30-mins.	""6 x 500m @ race pace, w/ 300m easy breaks.	Off or easy cross-train	Mod. 30-mins.	Easy 6 miles (or 10k)
7	Off or easy cross-train	Track. 10 min. w/up then 10 laps of T&S.	Mod. 30-mins.	10-min. warm-up, drills, then 20-minute hard progression.	Off or easy cross-train	Mod. 30-mins.	Easy 5 miles (or 8k)
8	Off or easy cross-train	Track. 10 min. w/up then 8 laps of T&S.	Mod. 30-mins.	""4 x 500m @ current race pace, w/ 300m easy breaks.	Off or easy cross-train	Mod. 30-mins.	Easy 6 miles (or 10k)
9	Off or easy cross-train	"" 12 x 200m fast w/200m breaks	Mod. 30-mins.	10-min. warm-up, drills, then 20-minute tempo—steady, hard effort.	Off or easy cross-train	Mod. 30-mins.	Easy 6 miles (or 10k)
10	Off or easy cross-train	"" 12 x 400m @ goal race pace, w/ 200m breaks.	Mod. 30-mins.	""6 x 500m @ current race pace, w/ 300m easy breaks.	Off or easy cross-train	Mod. 30-mins.	Easy 6 miles (or 10k)
11	Off or easy cross-train	"" 12 x 200m fast w/200m breaks	Mod. 30-mins.	""4k/2.5-mile progression.	Off or easy cross-train	Mod. 30-mins.	Easy 6 miles (or 10k)
12	Off or easy cross-train	"" 6 x 400m w/ 200m breaks.	Mod. 30-mins.	""4 x 500m @ current race pace, w/ 300m easy breaks.	Off or easy cross-train	Mod. 30-mins.	Easy 5 miles (or 8k)
13	Off or easy cross-train	"" 6 x 200m fast w/200m breaks	Easy. 20-mins.	**3,000m time-trial!**	Off or easy cross-train	Mod. 30-mins.	Easy 6 miles (or 10k)
14	Off or easy cross-train	"" 12 x 400m w/ 200m breaks.	Mod. 30-mins.	""6 x 500m @ current race pace, w/ 300m easy breaks.	Off or easy cross-train	Mod. 30-mins.	Easy 6 miles (or 10k)
15	Off or easy cross-train	"" 10 x 400m w/ 200m breaks.	Mod. 30-mins.	"" 1,600m; 800; 400m @ 3,000m pace, then 200m fast! w/ 200m breaks.	Off or easy cross-train	Mod. 30-mins.	Easy 5-mile (or 8k)
16	Off or easy cross-train	Easy 30 mins.	Off	10-min. warm-up, then 4 x 30 sec. sprints, cool down, then stretch.	**RACE!!!**	Off or easy 30-mins.	Easy 6-mile (or 10k)

Intermediate 3,000m Training Schedule

Week	Mon.	Tues.	Wed.	Thurs.	Fri.	Sat.	Sun.
1	Off or easy cross-train	45-minute fartlek	Moderate 30 mins.	45-minute fartlek	Easy 30 mins. or XT	Moderate 30 mins.	Easy 6-mile (or 10k)
2	Off or easy cross-train	10-min. warm-up, drills, then 8 x 1:00 min. hill reps.	Mod. 30 mins.	45-minute fartlek	Easy 30 mins. or XT	Mod. 30 mins.	Easy 6 miles (or 10k)
3	Off or easy cross-train	10-min. warm-up, drills, then 8 x 1:30 min. hill reps.	Mod. 30 mins.	45-minute fartlek	Easy 30 mins. or XT	Mod. 30 mins.	Easy 6 miles (or 10k)
4	Off or easy cross-train	"" then 3 x {100m/200m/300 m} w/ 100m breaks	Mod. 30 mins.	45-minute fartlek	Easy 30 mins. or XT	Mod. 30 mins.	Easy 5 miles (or 8k)
5	Off or easy cross-train	"" 8 x 200m fast w/200m breaks	Mod. 30 mins.	10-min. warm-up, drills, then 6 x 400m @ 3,000m race pace, w/ 200m easy breaks.	Easy 30 mins. or XT	Mod. 30 mins.	Easy 6 miles (or 10k)
6	Off or easy cross-train	"" 4 x {100m/200m/300 m} w/ 100m breaks	Mod. 30 mins.	""6 x 500m @ race pace, w/ 300m easy breaks.	Easy 30 mins. or XT	Mod. 30 mins.	Easy 7 miles (or 11.5k)
7	Off or easy cross-train	"" 10 x 200m fast w/200m breaks	Mod. 30 mins.	"" 20-minute hard progression.	Easy 30 mins. or XT	Mod. 30 mins.	Easy 8 miles (or 13k))
8	Off or easy cross-train	"" 3 x {100m/200m/300 m} w/ 100m breaks	Mod. 30 mins.	""4 x 500m @ current race pace, w/ 300m easy breaks.	Easy 30 mins. or XT	Mod. 30 mins.	Easy 5 miles (or 8k)
9	Off or easy cross-train	"" 10 x 200m fast w/200m breaks	Mod. 30 mins.	"" 20-minute tempo—steady, hard effort.	Easy 45 mins. or XT	Mod. 30 mins.	Easy 8 miles (or 13k)
10	Off or easy cross-train	"" 4 x {100m/200m/300 m} w/ 100m breaks	Mod. 30 mins.	""6 x 500m @ current race pace, w/ 300m easy breaks.	Easy 45 mins. or XT	Mod. 30 mins.	Easy 8 miles (or 13k)
11	Off or easy cross-train	"" 12 x 200m fast w/200m breaks	Mod. 30 mins.	""4k/2.5-mile progression.	Easy 45 mins. or XT	Mod. 30 mins.	Easy 8 miles (or 13k)
12	Off or easy cross-train	"" 3 x {100m/200m/300 m} w/ 100m breaks	Mod. 30 mins.	""4 x 500m @ current race pace, w/ 300m easy breaks.	Easy 45 mins. or XT	Mod. 30 mins.	Easy 6 miles (or 10k)
13	Off or easy cross-train	"" 6 x 200m fast w/200m breaks	"" 4 x 30 sec. sprints, cool down, then stretch.	**3,000m time-trial!**	Easy 45 mins. or XT	Mod. 30 mins.	Easy 8 miles (or 13k)
14	Off or easy cross-train	"" 4 x {100m/200m/300 m} w/ 100m breaks	Mod. 30 mins.	""6 x 500m @ current race pace, w/ 300m easy breaks.	Easy 45 mins. or XT	Mod. 30 mins.	Easy 8 miles (or 13k)
15	Off or easy cross-train	"" 8 x 200m fast w/200m breaks	Mod. 30 mins.	"" 1,600m; 800; 400m @ 3,000m pace, then 200m fast! w/ 200m breaks.	Easy 30 mins. or XT	Mod. 30 mins.	Easy 5-mile (or 8k)
16	Off	20-minute fartlek	Mod. 20 mins.	""2 x 500m @ current race pace, w/ 300m easy breaks.	Off!	10-min. warm-up, then 4 x 30 sec. sprints, cool down, then stretch.	**RACE!!!**

Advanced 3,000m Training Schedule

Week	Mon.	Tues.	Wed.	Thurs.	Fri.	Sat.	Sun.
1	Off or easy cross-train	45-minute fartlek	Moderate 8k	45-minute fartlek	Easy 10k or cross-train	Moderate 8k	Easy 10 miles (or 16k)
2	Off or easy cross-train	10-min. warm-up, drills, then 8 x 1:00 min. hill reps.	Moderate 8k	60-minute fartlek	Easy 10k or cross-train	Moderate 8k	Easy 10 miles (or 16k)
3	Off or easy cross-train	"" 8 x 1:30 min. hill reps.	Moderate 8k	60-minute fartlek	Easy 10k or cross-train	Moderate 8k	Easy 10 miles (or 16k)
4	Off or easy cross-train	"" then 3 x {100m/200m/300m} w/ 100m breaks	Moderate 8k	45-minute fartlek	Easy 10k or cross-train	Moderate 8k	Easy 8 miles (or 13k)
5	Off or easy cross-train	"" 8 x 200m fast w/200m breaks	Moderate 8k	"" 6 x 400m @ 3,000m race pace, w/ 200m easy breaks.	Easy 10k or cross-train	Moderate 8k	Easy 10 miles (or 16k)
6	Off or easy cross-train	"" 4 x {100m/200m/300m} w/ 100m breaks	Moderate 8k	""6 x 500m @ race pace, w/ 300m easy breaks.	Easy 10k or cross-train	Moderate 8k	Easy 10 miles (or 16k)
7	Off or easy cross-train	"" 10 x 200m fast w/200m breaks	Moderate 8k	10-min. warm-up, drills, then 20-minute hard progression.	Easy 10k or cross-train	Moderate 8k	Easy 10 miles (or 16k)
8	Off or easy cross-train	"" 3 x {100m/200m/300m} w/ 100m breaks	Moderate 8k	""5 x 500m @ current race pace, w/ 300m easy breaks.	Easy 10k or cross-train	Moderate 8k	Easy 8 miles (or 13k)
9	Off or easy cross-train	"" 10 x 200m fast w/200m breaks	Moderate 8k	10-min. warm-up, drills, then 20-minute tempo—steady, hard effort.	Easy 10k or cross-train	Moderate 8k	Easy 10 miles (or 16k)
10	Off or easy cross-train	"" 4 x {100m/200m/300m} w/ 100m breaks	Moderate 8k	""6 x 500m @ current race pace, w/ 300m easy breaks.	Easy 10k or cross-train	Moderate 8k	Easy 10 miles (or 16k)
11	Off or easy cross-train	"" 12 x 200m fast w/200m breaks	Moderate 8k	""4k/2.5-mile progression.	Easy 10k or cross-train	Moderate 8k	Easy 10 miles (or 16k)
12	Off or easy cross-train	"" 3 x {100m/200m/300m} w/ 100m breaks	Moderate 8k	""5 x 500m @ current race pace, w/ 300m easy breaks.	Easy 10k or cross-train	Moderate 8k	Easy 8 miles (or 13k)
13	Off or easy cross-train	"" 6 x 200m fast w/200m breaks	"" 4 x 30 sec. sprints, cool down, then stretch.	**3,000m time-trial!**	Easy 10k or cross-train	Moderate 8k	Easy 10 miles (or 16k)
14	Off or easy cross-train	"" 4 x {100m/200m/300m} w/ 100m breaks	Moderate 8k	""6 x 500m @ current race pace, w/ 300m easy breaks.	Easy 10k or cross-train	Moderate 8k	Easy 10 miles (or 16k)
15	Off or easy cross-train	"" 8 x 200m fast w/200m breaks	Moderate 8k	"" 1,600m; 800; 400m @ 3,000m pace, then 200m fast! w/ 200m breaks.	Easy 10k or cross-train	Moderate 8k	Easy 8 miles (or 13k)
16	Off or easy cross-train	20-minute fartlek	Off	"" 4 x 30 sec. sprints, cool down, then stretch.	**RACE!!!**	Off or easy 30-mins.	Easy 6 miles (or 10k)

Beginners 5,000m/5k Training Schedule							
Week	**Mon.**	**Tues.**	**Wed.**	**Thurs.**	**Fri.**	**Sat.**	**Sun.**
1	Off or easy cross-train	45-minute fartlek	Easy 30 mins.	45-minute fartlek	Off or easy cross-train	Moderate 30 mins.	Easy 6 miles (or 10k)
2	Off or easy cross-train	45-minute fartlek	Easy 35 mins.	45-minute fartlek	Off or easy cross-train	Moderate 35 mins.	Easy 6 miles (or 10k)
3	Off or easy cross-train	10-min. warm-up, drills, then 8 x 30 sec. hill reps.	Easy 40 mins.	45-minute fartlek	Off or easy cross-train	Mod. 40 mins.	Easy 6 miles (or 10k)
4	Off or easy cross-train	10-min. warm-up, drills, then 8 x 1:00 min. hill reps.	Easy 30 mins.	10-min. warm-up, drills, then 30-min. progression	Off or easy cross-train	Mod. 45 mins.	Easy 4 miles (or 6.5k)
5	Off or easy cross-train	10-min. warm-up, drills, then 8 x 1:30 min. hill reps.	Easy 45 mins.	"" 30-minute tempo—steady, hard effort.	Off or easy cross-train	Mod. 45 mins.	Easy 6 miles (or 10k)
6	Off or easy cross-train	"" 8 x 2:00 min. hill reps.	Easy 45 mins.	"" 30-min. progression.	Off or easy cross-train	Mod. 45 mins.	Easy 6 miles (or 10k)
7	Off or easy cross-train	Track. 10 min. w/up then 8 laps of Turns & Straights.	Easy 45 mins.	"" 4 x 800m @ current → goal 5k pace w/ easy 400m breaks.	Off or easy cross-train	Mod. 45 mins.	Easy 6 miles (or 10k)
8	Off or easy cross-train	Track. 10 min. w/up then 10 laps of T&S.	Easy 30 mins.	"" 30-minute tempo—steady, hard effort.	Off or easy cross-train	Mod. 45 mins.	Easy 5 miles (or 8k)
9	Off or easy cross-train	Track. 10 min. w/up then 12 laps of T&S.	Easy 45 mins.	"" 4 x 1,000m @ current → goal 5k pace w/ easy 400m breaks.	Off or easy cross-train	Mod. 45 mins.	Easy 6 miles (or 10k)
10	Off or easy cross-train	"" 8 x 200m fast w/200m breaks	Easy 45 mins.	"" 6k progression.	Off or easy cross-train	Mod. 45 mins.	Easy 6 miles (or 10k)
11	Off or easy cross-train	"" 6 x 400m @ goal race pace, w/ 200m breaks.	Easy 45 mins.	"" 3 x 1,600m @ current → goal 5k pace w/ easy 400m breaks.	Off or easy cross-train	Mod. 45 mins.	Easy 5 miles (or 8k)
12	Off	"" 8 x 200m fast w/200m breaks	Easy 20 mins.	**"" 5k time-trial!!**	Off or easy cross-train	Mod. 45 mins.	Easy 6 miles (or 10k)
13	Off or easy cross-train	"" 8 x 400m w/ 200m breaks.	Easy 45 mins.	"" 5 x 1,000m @ current → goal 5k pace w/ easy 400m breaks.	Off or easy cross-train	Mod. 45 mins.	Easy 6 miles (or 10k)
14	Off or easy cross-train	"" 12 x 200m fast w/200m breaks	Easy 45 mins.	"" 30-min. progression.	Off or easy cross-train	Mod. 45 mins.	Easy 6 miles (or 10k)
15	Off or easy cross-train	"" 6 x 400m w/ 200m breaks.	Easy 45 mins.	"" 3k tempo; 2k @ current 5k pace; 1k @ goal pace w/ easy 400m breaks.	Off or easy cross-train	Mod. 30 mins.	Easy 4 miles (or 7k)
16	Off or easy cross-train	Easy 30 mins.	10 min. warm-up, then 3 x 500m @ 5k pace w/ 1:00 breaks.	Off	10-min. w/ up, then 4 x 30 sec. sprints, cool dn., stretch.	**RACE!!!**	Easy 5 miles (or 8k)

The Beginners 5,000m/5k Training Schedule is for any beginning walker who has successfully completed the Beginner Base-Training for Events Up to Half-Marathon schedule.

Intermediate 5,000m/5k Training Schedule							
Week	**Mon.**	**Tues.**	**Wed.**	**Thurs.**	**Fri.**	**Sat.**	**Sun.**
1	Off or easy cross-train	45-minute fartlek	Moderate 30 mins.	45-minute fartlek	Easy 3 miles or cross-train	Moderate 30 min.	Easy 7 miles (or 11k)
2	Off or easy cross-train	10-min. warm-up, drills, then 8 x 1:00 min. hill reps.	Moderate 35 mins.	45-minute fartlek	Easy 3 miles or cross-train	Moderate 35 mins.	Easy 7.5 miles (or 12k)
3	Off or easy cross-train	10-min. warm-up, drills, then 8 x 1:30 min. hill reps.	Moderate 40 mins.	45-minute fartlek	Easy 3 miles or cross-train	Mod. 40-min.	Easy 8 miles (or 13k)
4	Off or easy cross-train	"" 8 x 2:00 min. hill reps.	Moderate 45 mins.	10-min. warm-up, drills, then 30-min. progression	Easy 3 miles or cross-train	Mod. 45 mins.	Easy 6 miles (or 10k)
5	Off or easy cross-train	"" 10 x 200m fast w/200m breaks	Moderate 45 mins.	"" 30-minute tempo—steady, hard effort.	Easy 3 miles or cross-train	Mod. 45 mins.	Easy 9 miles (or 14k)
6	Off or easy cross-train	"" 8 x 400m @ 5,000m race pace, w/ 200m breaks.	Moderate 45 mins.	"" 30-min. progression.	Easy 3 miles or cross-train	Mod. 45 mins.	Easy 9.5 miles (or 15k)
7	Off or easy cross-train	"" 4 x {100m/200m/300} m w/ 100m breaks	Moderate 45 mins.	"" 4 x 800m @ current → goal 5k pace w/ easy 400m breaks.	Easy 3 miles or cross-train	Mod. 45 mins.	Easy 10 miles (or 16k)
8	Off or easy cross-train	"" 12 x 200m fast w/200m breaks	Moderate 45 mins.	"" 30-minute tempo—steady, hard effort.	Easy 3 miles or cross-train	Mod. 45 mins.	Easy 8 miles (or 13k)
9	Off or easy cross-train	"" 10 x 400m w/ 200m breaks.	Moderate 45 mins.	"" 4 x 1,000m @ current → goal 5k pace w/ easy 400m breaks.	Easy 3 miles or cross-train	Mod. 45 mins.	Easy 10 miles (or 16k)
10	Off or easy cross-train	"" 4 x {100m/200m/300} m w/ 100m breaks	Moderate 45 mins.	"" 6k progression.	Easy 3 miles or cross-train	Mod. 45 mins.	Easy 10 miles (or 16k)
11	Off or easy cross-train	"" 12 x 200m fast w/200m breaks	Moderate 45 mins.	"" 3 x 1,600m @ current → goal 5k pace w/ easy 400m breaks.	Easy 3 miles or cross-train	Mod. 45 mins.	Easy 10 miles (or 16k)
12	Off	"" 6 x 400m w/ 200m breaks.	Easy 30 mins.	**"" 5k time-trial!!**	Easy 3 miles or cross-train	Mod. 45 mins.	Easy 8 miles (or 13k)
13	Off or easy cross-train	"" 4 x {100m/200m/300} m w/ 100m breaks	Moderate 45 mins.	"" 3 x 2,000m @ current → goal 5k pace w/ easy 400m breaks.	Easy 3 miles or cross-train	Mod. 45 mins.	Easy 10 miles (or 16k)
14	Off or easy cross-train	"" 12 x 200m fast w/200m breaks	Moderate 45 mins.	"" 30-min. progression.	Easy 3 miles or cross-train	Mod. 45 mins.	Easy 10 miles (or 16k)
15	Off or easy cross-train	"" 10 x 400m w/ 200m breaks.	Moderate 45 mins.	"" 3k tempo; 2k @ current 5k pace; 1k @ goal pace w/ easy 400m breaks.	Easy 3 miles or cross-train	Mod. 45 mins.	Easy 8 miles (or 13k)
16	Off or easy cross-train	Easy 30 mins.	10 min. warm-up, then 3 x 500m @ 5k pace w/ 1:00 breaks.	Off	10-min. w/ up, then 4 x 30 sec. sprints, cool dn., then stretch	**RACE!!!**	Easy 6 miles (or 10k)

The Intermediate 5,000m/5k Training Schedule is for walkers who can handle a 6-mile/10k long day—building to ten miles—as well as a healthy amount of economy and threshold speed work.

Advanced 5,000m/5k Training Schedule

Week	Mon.	Tues.	Wed.	Thurs.	Fri.	Sat.	Sun.
1	Off or easy cross-train	45-minute fartlek	Easy 60 mins.	45-minute fartlek	Easy 5 miles/8k or cross-train	Easy 60 mins.	Easy 10 miles (or 16k)
2	Off or easy cross-train	10-min. warm-up, drills, then 8 x 1:00 min. hill reps.	Moderate 60 mins.	50-minute fartlek	Easy 5 miles/8k or cross-train	Moderat e 60 mins.	Easy 10 miles (or 16k)
3	Off or easy cross-train	“” 8 x 1:30 min. hill reps.	Mod. 60 mins.	60-minute fartlek	Easy 5 miles/8k or cross-train	Mod. 60 mins.	Easy 10 miles (or 16k)
4	Off or easy cross-train	“” 8 x 2:00 min. hill reps.	Mod. 60 mins.	10-min. warm-up, drills, then 30-min. progression	Easy 5 miles/8k or cross-train	Mod. 45 mins.	Easy 8 miles (or 13k)
5	Off or easy cross-train	“” 10 x 200m fast w/200m breaks	Mod. 60 mins.	“” 30-minute tempo—steady, hard effort.	Easy 5 miles/8k or cross-train	Mod. 60 mins.	Easy 10 miles (or 16k)
6	Off or easy cross-train	“” 8 x 400m @ 5,000m race pace, w/ 200m breaks.	Mod. 60 mins.	“” 30-min. progression.	Easy 5 miles/8k or cross-train	Mod. 60 mins.	Easy 11 miles (or 17.5k)
7	Off or easy cross-train	“” 4 x {100m/200m/300m} w/ 100m breaks	Mod. 60 mins.	“” 4 x 800m @ current → goal 5k pace w/ easy 400m breaks.	Easy 5 miles/8k or cross-train	Mod. 60 mins.	Easy 12 miles (or 19k)
8	Off or easy cross-train	“” 10 x 200m fast w/200m breaks	Mod. 60 mins.	“” 30-minute tempo—steady, hard effort.	Easy 5 miles/8k or cross-train	Mod. 45 mins.	Easy 8 miles (or 13k)
9	Off or easy cross-train	“” 10 x 400m w/ 200m breaks.	Mod. 60 mins.	“” 4 x 1,000m @ current → goal 5k pace w/ easy 400m breaks.	Easy 5 miles/8k or cross-train	Mod. 60 mins.	Easy 12 miles (or 19k)
10	Off or easy cross-train	“” 4 x {100m/200m/300m} w/ 100m breaks	Mod. 60 mins.	“” 6k progression.	Easy 5 miles/8k or cross-train	Mod. 60 mins.	Easy 12 miles (or 19k)
11	Off or easy cross-train	“” 12 x 200m fast w/200m breaks	Mod. 60 mins.	“” 3 x 1,600m @ current → goal 5k pace w/ easy 400m breaks.	Easy 5 miles/8k or cross-train	Mod. 60 mins.	Easy 8 miles (or 13k)
12	Off	“” 6 x 400m w/ 200m breaks.	“” 4 x 30 sec. sprints, cool dn., then stretch	**“” 5k time-trial!!**	Easy 5 miles/8k or cross-train	Mod. 45 mins.	Easy 10 miles (or 16k)
13	Off or easy cross-train	“” 4 x {100m/200m/300m} w/ 100m breaks	Mod. 60 mins.	“” 3 x 2,000m @ current → goal 5k pace w/ easy 400m breaks.	Easy 5 miles/8k or cross-train	Mod. 60 mins.	Easy 11 miles (or 17.5k)
14	Off or easy cross-train	“” 12 x 200m fast w/200m breaks	Mod. 60 mins.	“” 30-min. progression.	Easy 5 miles/8k or cross-train	Mod. 60 mins.	Easy 12 miles (or 19k)
15	Off or easy cross-train	“” 10 x 400m w/ 200m breaks.	Mod. 60 mins.	“” 3k tempo; 2k @ current 5k pace; 1k @ goal pace w/ easy 400m breaks	Easy 5 miles/8k or cross-train	Mod. 60 mins.	Easy 8 miles (or 13k)
16	Off or easy cross-train	Easy 30 mins.	“” 3 x 500m @ 5k pace w/ 1:00 breaks	Off	“” 4 x 30 sec. sprints, cool dn., then stretch	**RACE!!**	Easy 6 miles (or 10k)

CHAPTER 18: MIDDLE DISTANCES: 8K – 10 MILES

Although 5k is the most commonly contested road race distance, the "middle distances" are popular with walkers looking for more of an endurance challenge without stepping all the way up to 20 kilometers or a half-marathon. This range was always a bit of a sweet spot for me. I was an ok, but not stellar, "sprinter" having come oh so close, but never breaking, six minutes for the mile and 20:00 for 5k—generally regarded as the thresholds to the "Über-Elite" level[54]—and never making an Olympic Team in the 20k. But I did manage to win five 10k, two "1-hour,"[55] and two 15k US racewalking championships, often taking down some of the best 20k walkers in the US. I even held the American record for the 1-hour briefly in the early 1990s.

In addition to the aforementioned US championships, eight kilometers (4.97 miles) and 5 miles are common Turkey Trot and St. Patrick's Day road race distances for walkers. The 8k Shamrock Shuffle in mid-March is the season-opening road race in Chicago, attracting some 20,000 participants every year, including many walkers. The Virginia Beach Shamrock 8k is another very popular road race for walkers, while Detroit's enthusiastic walking community looks forward to the Crim Festival of Races 5- and 10-mile races in August. 10k is a much more commonly contested distance for walkers, being a standard for (non-competitive) "volkssport" walks, Nordic walking races, and racewalks, including at the US and World Masters Championships. The New Albany 10k in New Albany, Ohio in September is a huge walk-only event which draws some of the top racewalkers in the US.

1989 US 10k Championship. I'm #108. I won in 1988 and 1991 (and 1994 and 1995 and 2016!) but could only manage 3rd on this day.
Photo credit: Don Lawrence

[54] 6:00.72 for the mile and 20:06 for 5k. So close! ☺

[55] The US 1-Hour Championship involves walking as fast as you can on a track for exactly one hour. The winner is the walker who goes the farthest in that hour.

One of the few 12k races on the planet, the Bay-to-Breakers 12k is one of the largest, oldest, and craziest road races in the US. Some 60,000 participants, wearing costumes—or nothing other than shoes—have been traversing the city of San Francisco, from San Francisco Bay to the Pacific Ocean at Ocean Beach, annually since 1912. 12k is an oddball distance but worth training for if you ever have the chance to walk in this iconic event.

15k (9.3 miles) is another rarely contested distance, but it is a record-eligible and national championship event in US racewalking. Ten miles seems like it would be a popular race distance, but 10-milers are few and far between—except around Washington, DC! The Army 10-Miler, the Cherry Blossom 10-Miler, and the Georgetown 10-Miler are all popular events for walkers. A bit further out is the Annapolis 10-Miler, on one of the most beautiful race courses anywhere, which has been held annually since 1976. (I raced the 5th annual Annapolis 10-Miler in 1981!) Finally, the Crim 10-Miler in Flint, Michigan, and the Blessing of the Fleet in Narragansett, Rhode Island, offer walking awards. Nordic walkers have more choices than race- and power walkers do, as ten miles is a world record eligible distance.

Middle-distance races can be great tools for marathon training as well, since walking at the relatively fast, sustained pace of a 10-kilometer or 10-mile race not only improves fitness, it makes marathon pace seem that much easier. The following sixteen-week schedules for beginning, intermediate, and advanced walkers can be used to train for "middle distance" races from 8k to ten miles.

Beginner's 8k/5-Mile Training Schedule							
Week	**Mon.**	**Tues.**	**Wed.**	**Thurs.**	**Fri.**	**Sat.**	**Sun.**
1	Off or easy cross-train	45-minute fartlek	Easy 30 mins.	45-minute fartlek	Off or easy cross-train	Moderate 30-min.	Easy 6 miles (or 10k)
2	Off or easy cross-train	10-min. warm-up, drills, then 8 x 1:00 min. hill reps.	Easy 35 mins.	50-minute fartlek	Off or easy cross-train	Moderate 35 mins.	Easy 6.5 miles (or 11k)
3	Off or easy cross-train	10-min. warm-up, drills, then 8 x 1:30 hill reps.	Easy 40 mins.	60-minute fartlek	Off or easy cross-train	Mod. 40-min.	Easy 7 miles (or 12k)
4	Off or easy cross-train	"" 8 x 2:00 min. hill reps.	Easy 45 mins.	10-min. warm-up, drills, then 40-min. progression	Off or easy cross-train	Mod. 45 mins.	Easy 6 miles (or 10k)
5	Off or easy cross-train	Track. 10 min. w/up, drills, then 8 laps of Turns & Straights.	Easy 45 mins.	45-minute tempo—steady, hard effort.	Off or easy cross-train	Mod. 45 mins.	Easy 8 miles (or 13k)
6	Off or easy cross-train	"" 10 laps of T&S.	Easy 45 mins.	45-min. progression.	Off or easy cross-train	Mod. 45 mins.	Easy 8 miles (or 13k)
7	Off or easy cross-train	"" 12 laps of T&S.	Easy 45 mins.	45-minute tempo	Off or easy cross-train	Mod. 45 mins.	Easy 8 miles (or 13k)
8	Off or easy cross-train	"" 10 x 200m fast w/200m breaks	Easy 45 mins.	45-min. progression.	Off or easy cross-train	Mod. 45 mins.	Easy 6 miles (or 10k)
9	Off or easy cross-train	"" 10 x 400m @ goal race pace, w/ 200m breaks.	Easy 45 mins.	"" 6 x 1k @ current → goal 8k pace w/ easy 400m breaks.	Off or easy cross-train	Mod. 45 mins.	Easy 8 miles (or 13k)
10	Off or easy cross-train	"" 12 x 200m fast w/200m breaks	Easy 45 mins.	45-min. progression.	Off or easy cross-train	Mod. 45 mins.	Easy 8 miles (or 13k)
11	Off or easy cross-train	"" 12 x 400m @ goal race pace, w/ 200m breaks.	Easy 45 mins.	"" 4 x 1,600m @ current → goal 8k pace w/ easy 400m breaks.	Off or easy cross-train	Mod. 45 mins.	Easy 8 miles (or 13k)
12	Off	"" 8 x 200m fast w/200m breaks	Easy 30 mins.	**"" 8k time-trial!!**	Off or easy cross-train	Mod. 45 mins.	Easy 6 miles (or 10k)
13	Off or easy cross-train	"" 6 x 400m w/ 200m breaks.	Easy 45 mins.	"" 3 x 2K @ current → goal 8k pace w/ easy 400m breaks.	Off or easy cross-train	Mod. 45 mins.	Easy 8 miles (or 13k)
14	Off or easy cross-train	"" 12 x 200m fast w/200m breaks	Easy 45 mins.	45-min. progression.	Off or easy cross-train	Mod. 45 mins.	Easy 8 miles (or 13k)
15	Off or easy cross-train	"" 10 x 400m w/ 200m breaks.	Easy 45 mins.	45 mins. tempo	Off or easy cross-train	Mod. 30-min.	Easy 5 miles (or 8
16	Off or easy cross-train	Easy 30 mins.	10 min. warm-up, then 3 x 1K @ 8k pace w/ 1:00 breaks.	Off	10-min. w/ up, then 4 x 30 sec. sprints, cool dn., then stretch.	**RACE!!!**	Easy 5 miles (or 8k)

The Beginner's 8k/5-Mile Training Schedule is for any beginning middle-distance walker who has successfully completed the Beginner Base-Training for Events Up to Half-Marathon schedule.

Intermediate 8k/5-Mile Training Schedule

Week	Mon.	Tues.	Wed.	Thurs.	Fri.	Sat.	Sun.
1	Off or easy cross-train	45-minute fartlek	Moderate 30 mins.	45-minute fartlek	Off or easy cross-train	Moderate 30-min.	Easy 7 miles (or 11k)
2	Off or easy cross-train	10-min. warm-up, drills, then 8 x 1:00 min. hill reps.	Moderate 35 mins.	45-minute fartlek	Off or easy cross-train	Moderate 35 mins.	Easy 7.5 miles (or 12k)
3	Off or easy cross-train	10-min. warm-up, drills, then 8 x 1:30 hill reps.	Moderate 40 mins.	45-minute fartlek	Off or easy cross-train	Mod. 40-min.	Easy 8 miles (or 13k)
4	Off or easy cross-train	"" 8 x 2:00 min. hill reps.	Moderate 45 mins.	10-min. warm-up, drills, then 40-min. progression	Off or easy cross-train	Mod. 45 mins.	Easy 6 miles (or 10k)
5	Off or easy cross-train	"" 10 x 200m fast w/200m breaks	Moderate 45 mins.	"" 45-minute tempo—steady, hard effort.	Off or easy cross-train	Mod. 5 miles/8k	Easy 9 miles (or 14k)
6	Off or easy cross-train	"" 8 x 400m @ 5,000m race pace, w/ 200m breaks.	Moderate 45 mins.	"" 45-min. progression.	Off or easy cross-train	Mod. 5 miles/8k	Easy 9.5 miles (or 15k)
7	Off or easy cross-train	"" 4 x {100m/200m/300} m w/ 100m breaks	Moderate 45 mins.	"" 6 x 1k @ current → goal 8k pace w/ easy 400m breaks.	Off or easy cross-train	Mod. 5 miles/8k	Easy 10 miles (or 16k)
8	Off or easy cross-train	"" 12 x 200m fast w/200m breaks	Moderate 45 mins.	"" 45-minute tempo—steady, hard effort.	Off or easy cross-train	Mod. 5 miles/8k	Easy 8 miles (or 13k)
9	Off or easy cross-train	"" 10 x 400m w/ 200m breaks.	Moderate 45 mins.	"" 4 x 1,600m @ current → goal 8k pace w/ easy 400m breaks.	Off or easy cross-train	Mod. 5 miles/8k	Easy 10 miles (or 16k)
10	Off or easy cross-train	"" 4 x {100m/200m/300} m w/ 100m breaks	Moderate 45 mins.	"" 8k progression.	Off or easy cross-train	Mod. 5 miles/8k	Easy 10 miles (or 16k)
11	Off or easy cross-train	"" 12 x 200m fast w/200m breaks	Moderate 45 mins.	"" 4 x 2k @ current → goal 8k pace w/ easy 400m breaks.	Off or easy cross-train	Mod. 5 miles/8k	Easy 10 miles (or 16k)
12	Off	"" 6 x 400m w/ 200m breaks.	Easy 30 mins.	**"" 8k time-trial!!**	Off or easy cross-train	Mod. 5 miles/8k	Easy 8 miles (or 13k)
13	Off or easy cross-train	"" 4 x {100m/200m/300} m w/ 100m breaks	Moderate 45 mins.	"" 4 x 2K @ current → goal 8k pace w/ easy 400m breaks.	Off or easy cross-train	Mod. 5 miles/8k	Easy 10 miles (or 16k)
14	Off or easy cross-train	"" 12 x 200m fast w/200m breaks	Moderate 45 mins.	"" 45-min. progression.	Off or easy cross-train	Mod. 5 miles/8k	Easy 10 miles (or 16k)
15	Off or easy cross-train	"" 10 x 400m w/ 200m breaks.	Moderate 45 mins.	"" 4k tempo; 3k @ current 8k pace; 1k @ goal pace w/ easy 3:00 min. breaks.	Off or easy cross-train	Mod. 3 miles/5k	Easy 6 miles (or 13k)
16	Off or easy cross-train	Easy 30 mins.	"" 3 x 1K @ 8k pace w/ 1:00 breaks.	Off	"" 4 x 30 sec. sprints, cool dn., then stretch	Wm. up then 4 x 30 sec. sprints, cool dn., stretch.	Easy 6 miles (or 10k)

The Intermediate 8k/5-Mile Training Schedule is for walkers who can handle an 8-mile/13k long day—building to ten miles—as well as a healthy amount of economy and threshold speed work.

Advanced 8k/5-Mile Training Schedule							
Week	**Mon.**	**Tues.**	**Wed.**	**Thurs.**	**Fri.**	**Sat.**	**Sun.**
1	Off or easy cross-train	45-minute fartlek	Moderate 45 mins.	45-minute fartlek	Easy 60 mins.	Mod. 45 mins.	Easy 10 miles (or 16k)
2	Off or easy cross-train	10-min. warm-up, drills, then 8 x 1:00 min. hill reps.	Mod. 60 mins.	50-minute fartlek	Easy 60 mins.	Mod. 60 mins.	Easy 11 miles (or 17.5k)
3	Off or easy cross-train	10-min. warm-up, drills, then 8 x 1:30 hill reps.	Mod. 60 mins.	60-minute fartlek	Easy 60 mins.	Mod. 6 miles/10k	Easy 12 miles (or 19k)
4	Off or easy cross-train	"" 8 x 2:00 min. hill reps.	Mod. 60 mins.	10-min. warm-up, drills, then 40-min. progression	Easy 60 mins.	Mod. 6 miles/10k	Easy 8 miles (or 13k)
5	Off or easy cross-train	"" 10 x 200m fast w/200m breaks	Moderate 45 mins.	"" 45-minute tempo—steady, hard effort.	Easy 60 mins.	Mod. 6 miles/10k	Easy 12 miles (or 19k)
6	Off or easy cross-train	"" 8 x 400m @ 5,000m race pace, w/ 200m breaks.	Mod. 60 mins.	"" 60-min. progression.	Easy 60 mins.	Mod. 6 miles/10k	Easy 12 miles (or 19k)
7	Off or easy cross-train	"" 4 x {100m/200m/300} m w/ 100m breaks	Mod. 60 mins.	"" 6 x 1k @ current → goal 8k pace w/ easy 400m breaks.	Easy 60 mins.	Mod. 6 miles/10k	Easy 12 miles (or 19k)
8	Off or easy cross-train	"" 12 x 200m fast w/200m breaks	Mod. 60 mins.	"" 60-minute tempo—steady, hard effort.	Easy 60 mins.	Mod. 6 miles/10k	Easy 10 miles (or 16k)
9	Off or easy cross-train	"" 10 x 400m w/ 200m breaks.	Mod. 60 mins.	"" 5 x 1,600m @ current → goal 8k pace w/ easy 400m breaks.	Easy 60 mins.	Mod. 6 miles/10k	Easy 12 miles (or 19k)
10	Off or easy cross-train	"" 4 x {100m/200m/300} m w/ 100m breaks	Mod. 60 mins.	"" 8k progression.	Easy 60 mins.	Mod. 6 miles/10k	Easy 12 miles (or 19k)
11	Off or easy cross-train	"" 12 x 200m fast w/200m breaks	Mod. 60 mins.	"" 4 x 2k @ current → goal 8k pace w/ easy 400m breaks.	Easy 60 mins.	Mod. 6 miles/10k	Easy 12 miles (or 19k)
12	Off	"" 6 x 400m w/ 200m breaks.	Easy 30 mins.	**"" 8k time-trial!!**	Easy 60 mins.	Mod. 6 miles/10k	Easy 10 miles (or 16k)
13	Off or easy cross-train	"" 4 x {100m/200m/300} m w/ 100m breaks	Mod. 60 mins.	"" 4k tempo; 3k @ current 8k pace; 1k @ goal pace w/ easy 3:00 min. breaks.	Easy 60 mins.	Mod. 6 miles/10k	Easy 12 miles (or 19k)
14	Off or easy cross-train	"" 12 x 200m fast w/200m breaks	Mod. 60 mins.	10k progression.	Easy 60 mins.	Mod. 6 miles/10k	Easy 12 miles (or 19k)
15	Off or easy cross-train	"" 10 x 400m w/ 200m breaks.	Mod. 60 mins.	"" 8 x 1k @ current → goal 8k pace w/ easy 400m breaks.	Easy 60 mins.	Mod. 3 miles/5k	Easy 8 miles (or 13k)
16	Off or easy cross-train	Easy 30 mins.	"" 3 x 1K @ 8k pace w/ 1:00 breaks.	Off	10-min. w/ up, then 4 x 30 sec. sprints, cool dn., then stretch	**RACE!!!**	Easy 6 miles (or 10k)

The Advanced 8k/5-Mile Training Schedule is for walkers who can handle a 10-mile/16k long day—building to 12 miles—as well as a healthy amount of economy and threshold speed work.

Beginners 10k Training Schedule							
Week	**Mon.**	**Tues.**	**Wed.**	**Thurs.**	**Fri.**	**Sat.**	**Sun.**
1	Off or easy cross-train	45-minute fartlek	Easy 30 mins.	45-minute fartlek	Off or easy cross-train	Moderate 30-min.	Easy 6 miles (or 10k)
2	Off or easy cross-train	10-min. warm-up, drills, then 8 x 1:00 min. hill reps.	Easy 35 mins.	50-minute fartlek	Off or easy cross-train	Moderate 35 mins.	Easy 6.5 miles (or 11k)
3	Off or easy cross-train	10-min. warm-up, drills, then 8 x 1:30 hill reps.	Easy 40 mins.	60-minute fartlek	Off or easy cross-train	Mod. 40-min.	Easy 7 miles (or 12k)
4	Off or easy cross-train	"" 8 x 2:00 min. hill reps.	Easy 45 mins.	60 mins. progression	Off or easy cross-train	Mod. 45 mins.	Easy 6 miles (or 10k)
5	Off or easy cross-train	Track. 10 min. w/up, drills, then 8 laps of Turns & Straights.	Easy 45 mins.	60-minute tempo—steady, hard effort.	Off or easy cross-train	Mod. 45 mins.	Easy 7.5 miles (or 12k)
6	Off or easy cross-train	"" 10 laps of T&S.	Easy 45 mins.	60 mins. progression	Off or easy cross-train	Mod. 45 mins.	Easy 8 miles (or 13k)
7	Off or easy cross-train	"" then 12 laps of T&S.	Easy 45 mins.	60-minute tempo—steady, hard effort.	Off or easy cross-train	Mod. 45 mins.	Easy 8 miles (or 13k)
8	Off or easy cross-train	"" 10 x 200m fast w/200m breaks	Easy 45 mins.	60 min. progression	Off or easy cross-train	Mod. 45 mins.	Easy 6 miles (or 10k)
9	Off or easy cross-train	"" 10 x 400m @ goal race pace, w/ 200m breaks.	Easy 45 mins.	"" 6 x 1k @ current → goal 10k pace w/ easy 400m breaks.	Off or easy cross-train	Mod. 45 mins.	Easy 8 miles (or 13k)
10	Off or easy cross-train	"" 12 x 200m fast w/200m breaks	Easy 45 mins.	60-min. progression	Off or easy cross-train	Mod. 45 mins.	Easy 8 miles (or 13k)
11	Off or easy cross-train	"" 12 x 400m @ goal race pace, w/ 200m breaks.	Easy 45 mins.	"" 5 x 1,600m @ current → goal 10k pace w/ easy 400m breaks.	Off or easy cross-train	Mod. 45 mins.	Easy 8 miles (or 13k)
12	Off	"" 8 x 200m fast w/200m breaks	Easy 20 mins.	**"" 10k time-trial!!**	Off or easy cross-train	Mod. 45 mins.	Easy 6 miles (or 10k)
13	Off or easy cross-train	"" 6 x 400m w/ 200m breaks.	Easy 45 mins.	"" 4 x 2K @ current → goal 10k pace w/ easy 400m breaks.	Off or easy cross-train	Mod. 45 mins.	Easy 8 miles (or 13k)
14	Off or easy cross-train	"" 12 x 200m fast w/200m breaks	Easy 45 mins.	60-min. progression	Off or easy cross-train	Mod. 45 mins.	Easy 8 miles (or 13k)
15	Off or easy cross-train	"" 10 x 400m w/ 200m breaks.	Easy 45 mins.	45-minute tempo	Off or easy cross-train	Mod. 30-min.	Easy 5 miles (or 8k)
16	Off or easy cross-train	10 min. warm-up, then 3 x 1K @ 10k pace w/ 1:00 breaks.	Easy 30 mins.	"" 6 x 400m @ 10k pace w/ 200m breaks.	Off	Wm. up then 4 x 30 sec. sprints, cool dn., stretch.	**RACE!!!**

The Beginners 10k Training Schedule is for any beginning walker who has successfully completed the Beginner Base-Training for Events Up to Half-Marathon schedule. I put the race on Sunday because the New Albany Classic—the biggest walk-only 10k in the US—is held on Sunday, as are the US Open and Masters Championships, but the U20 Championship is held on Saturday, as are many local races, especially in the southern US. Switch up the final week's training accordingly.

Intermediate 10k Training Schedule							
Week	**Mon.**	**Tues.**	**Wed.**	**Thurs.**	**Fri.**	**Sat.**	**Sun.**
1	Off or easy cross-train	45-minute fartlek	Moderate 30 mins.	45-minute fartlek	Off or easy cross-train	Moderate 30-min.	Easy 7 miles (or 11k)
2	Off or easy cross-train	10-min. warm-up, drills, then 8 x 1:00 min. hill reps.	Moderate 35 mins.	45-minute fartlek	Off or easy cross-train	Moderate 35 mins.	Easy 7.5 miles (or 12k)
3	Off or easy cross-train	10-min. warm-up, drills, then 8 x 1:30 min. hill reps.	Moderate 40 mins.	45-minute fartlek	Off or easy cross-train	Mod. 40-min.	Easy 8 miles (or 13k)
4	Off or easy cross-train	"" 8 x 2:00 min. hill reps.	Moderate 45 mins.	10-min. warm-up, drills, then 40-min. progression	Off or easy cross-train	Mod. 45 mins.	Easy 6 miles (or 10k)
5	Off or easy cross-train	"" 10 x 200m fast w/200m breaks	Moderate 45 mins.	"" 45-minute tempo—steady, hard effort.	Off or easy cross-train	Mod. 5 miles/8k	Easy 9 miles (or 14k)
6	Off or easy cross-train	"" 8 x 400m @ 5,000m race pace, w/ 200m breaks.	Moderate 45 mins.	"" 50-min. progression.	Off or easy cross-train	Mod. 5 miles/8k	Easy 9.5 miles (or 15k)
7	Off or easy cross-train	"" 4 x {100m/200m/300} m w/ 100m breaks	Moderate 45 mins.	"" 4 x 1,600m @ current → goal 10k pace w/ easy 400m breaks.	Off or easy cross-train	Mod. 5 miles/8k	Easy 10 miles (or 16k)
8	Off or easy cross-train	"" 12 x 200m fast w/200m breaks	Moderate 45 mins.	"" 10k tempo	Off or easy cross-train	Mod. 5 miles/8k	Easy 8 miles (or 13k)
9	Off or easy cross-train	"" 10 x 400m w/ 200m breaks.	Moderate 45 mins.	"" 5 x 1,600m @ current → goal 10k pace w/ easy 400m breaks.	Off or easy cross-train	Mod. 5 miles/8k	Easy 10 miles (or 16k)
10	Off or easy cross-train	"" 4 x {100m/200m/300} m w/ 100m breaks	Moderate 45 mins.	10k progression	Off or easy cross-train	Mod. 5 miles/8k	Easy 10 miles (or 16k)
11	Off or easy cross-train	"" 6 x 200m fast w/200m breaks	Easy 30 mins.	"" 6 x 1,600m @ current → goal 10k pace w/ easy 400m breaks.	Off or easy cross-train	Mod. 5 miles/8k	Easy 10 miles (or 16k)
12	Off	"" 6 x 400m w/ 200m breaks.	Easy 30 mins.	**"" 10k time-trial!!**	Off or easy cross-train	Mod. 5 miles/8k	Easy 8 miles (or 13k)
13	Off or easy cross-train	"" 4 x {100m/200m/300} m w/ 100m breaks	Moderate 45 mins.	"" 5 x 2K @ current → goal 10k pace w/ easy 400m breaks.	Off or easy cross-train	Mod. 5 miles/8k	Easy 10 miles (or 16k)
14	Off or easy cross-train	"" 12 x 200m fast w/200m breaks	Moderate 45 mins.	10k progression	Off or easy cross-train	Mod. 5 miles/8k	Easy 10 miles (or 16k)
15	Off or easy cross-train	"" 10 x 400m w/ 200m breaks.	Moderate 45 mins.	"" 5k tempo; 3k @ current 10k pace; 1k @ goal pace w/ easy 3:00 min. breaks.	Off or easy cross-train	Mod. 3 miles/5k	Easy 6 miles (or 13k)
16	Off or easy cross-train	10 min. warm-up, then 3 x 1K @ 10k pace w/ 1:00 breaks.	Easy 30 mins.	"" 6 x 400m @ 10k pace w/ 200m breaks.	Off	Wm. up then 4 x 30 sec. sprints, cool dn., stretch.	**RACE!!!**

The Intermediate 10k Training Schedule is for walkers who can handle an eight-mile/13k long day—building to ten miles—as well as a healthy amount of economy and threshold speed work.

Advanced 10k Training Schedule

Week	Mon.	Tues.	Wed.	Thurs.	Fri.	Sat.	Sun.
1	Off or easy cross-train	45-minute fartlek	Moderate 45 mins.	45-minute fartlek	Easy 60 mins.	Mod. 45 mins.	Easy 10 miles (or 16k)
2	Off or easy cross-train	10-min. warm-up, drills, then 8 x 1:00 min. hill reps.	Mod. 60 mins.	50-minute fartlek	Easy 60 mins.	Mod. 60 mins.	Easy 11 miles (or 17.5k)
3	Off or easy cross-train	10-min. warm-up, drills, then 8 x 1:30 min. hill reps.	Mod. 60 mins.	60-minute fartlek	Easy 60 mins.	Mod. 60 mins.	Easy 12 miles (or 19k)
4	Off or easy cross-train	“” 8 x 2:00 min. hill reps.	Mod. 60 mins.	10-min. warm-up, drills, then 40-min. progression	Easy 60 mins.	Mod. 60 mins.	Easy 8 miles (or 13k)
5	Off or easy cross-train	“” 10 x 200m fast w/200m breaks	Moderate 45 mins.	“” 45-minute tempo—steady, hard effort.	Easy 60 mins.	Mod. 6 miles/10k	Easy 12 miles (or 19k)
6	Off or easy cross-train	“” 8 x 400m @ 5,000m race pace, w/ 200m breaks.	Mod. 60 mins.	“” 60-min. progression.	Easy 60 mins.	Mod. 6 miles/10k	Easy 12 miles (or 19k)
7	Off or easy cross-train	“” 4 x {100m/200m/300m} w/ 100m breaks	Mod. 60 mins.	“” 8 x 1k @ current → goal 8k pace w/ easy 400m breaks.	Easy 60 mins.	Mod. 6 miles/10k	Easy 12 miles (or 19k)
8	Off or easy cross-train	“” 12 x 200m fast w/200m breaks	Mod. 60 mins.	“” 60-minute tempo—steady, hard effort.	Easy 60 mins.	Mod. 6 miles/10k	Easy 10 miles (or 16k)
9	Off or easy cross-train	“” 10 x 400m w/ 200m breaks.	Mod. 60 mins.	“” 5 x 1,600m @ current → goal 10k pace w/ easy 400m breaks.	Easy 60 mins.	Mod. 6 miles/10k	Easy 12 miles (or 19k)
10	Off or easy cross-train	“” 4 x {100m/200m/300m} w/ 100m breaks	Mod. 60 mins.	“” 8k progression.	Easy 60 mins.	Mod. 6 miles/10k	Easy 12 miles (or 19k)
11	Off or easy cross-train	“” 12 x 200m fast w/200m breaks	Mod. 60 mins.	“” 5 x 2k @ current → goal 10k pace w/ easy 400m breaks.	Easy 60 mins.	Mod. 6 miles/10k	Easy 12 miles (or 19k)
12	Off	“” 6 x 400m w/ 200m breaks.	Easy 30 mins.	**“” 10k time-trial!!**	Easy 60 mins.	Mod. 6 miles/10k	Easy 10 miles (or 16k)
13	Off or easy cross-train	“” 4 x {100m/200m/300m} w/ 100m breaks	Mod. 60 mins.	“” 5k tempo; 3k @ current 10k pace; 1k @ goal pace w/ easy 3:00 min. breaks.	Easy 60 mins.	Mod. 6 miles/10k	Easy 12 miles (or 19k)
14	Off or easy cross-train	“” 12 x 200m fast w/200m breaks	Mod. 60 mins.	“” 60-min. progression.	Easy 60 mins.	Mod. 6 miles/10k	Easy 12 miles (or 19k)
15	Off or easy cross-train	“” 10 x 400m w/ 200m breaks.	Mod. 60 mins.	“” 8 x 1k @ goal 10k pace w/ easy 400m breaks.	Easy 60 mins.	Mod. 3 miles/5k	Easy 8 miles (or 13k)
16	Off or easy cross-train	10 min. warm-up, then 3 x 1K @ 10k pace w/ 1:00 breaks.	Easy 30 mins.	“” 6 x 400m @ 10k pace w/ 200m breaks.	Off	Wm. up then 4 x 30 sec. sprints, cool dn., stretch.	**RACE!!!**

The Advanced 10k Training Schedule is for walkers who can handle a 10-mile/16k long day—building to 12 miles—as well as a healthy amount of economy and threshold speed work.

Intermediate 15k/10-Mile Training Schedule							
Week	**Mon.**	**Tues.**	**Wed.**	**Thurs.**	**Fri.**	**Sat.**	**Sun.**
1	Off or easy cross-train	45-minute fartlek	Moderate 30-min.	45-minute fartlek	Off or easy cross-train	Moderate 30-min.	Easy 7 miles (or 11k)
2	Off or easy cross-train	10-min. warm-up, drills, then 8 x 1:00 min. hill reps.	Moderate 40 mins.	50-minute fartlek	Off or easy cross-train	Moderate 40 mins.	Easy 7.5 miles (or 12k)
3	Off or easy cross-train	10-min. warm-up, drills, then 8 x 1:30 min. hill reps.	Mod. 50-min.	60-minute fartlek	Off or easy cross-train	Mod. 50-min.	Easy 8 miles (or 13k)
4	Off or easy cross-train	“” 8 x 2:00 min. hill reps.	Mod. 60 mins.	10-min. warm-up, drills, then 45 mins. progression	Off or easy cross-train	Mod. 60 mins.	Easy 6 miles (or 10k)
5	Off or easy cross-train	“” 10 x 200m fast w/200m breaks	Mod. 5 miles/8k	“” 45-minute tempo—steady, hard effort.	Off or easy cross-train	Mod. 5 miles/8k	Easy 9 miles (or 14k)
6	Off or easy cross-train	“” 8 x 400m @ 5,000m race pace, w/ 200m breaks.	Mod. 5 miles/8k	“” 50-min. progression.	Off or easy cross-train	Mod. 5 miles/8k	Easy 9.5 miles (or 15k)
7	Off or easy cross-train	“” 4 x {100m/200m/300m} w/ 100m breaks	Mod. 5 miles/8k	“” 8 x 1k @ current → goal 15k/10 mile pace w/ easy 400m breaks.	Off or easy cross-train	Mod. 5 miles/8k	Easy 10 miles (or 16k)
8	Off or easy cross-train	“” 12 x 200m fast w/200m breaks	Mod. 5 miles/8k	“” 10k tempo	Off or easy cross-train	Mod. 5 miles/8k	Easy 8 miles (or 13k)
9	Off or easy cross-train	“” 10 x 400m w/ 200m breaks.	Mod. 5 miles/8k	“” 6 x 1,600m @ current → goal 15k/10 mile pace w/ easy 400m breaks.	Off or easy cross-train	Mod. 5 miles/8k	Easy 11 miles (or 19k)
10	Off or easy cross-train	“” 4 x {100m/200m/300m} w/ 100m breaks	Mod. 5 miles/8k	12k progression	Off or easy cross-train	Mod. 5 miles/8k	Easy 12 miles (or 19k)
11	Off or easy cross-train	“” 6 x 200m fast w/200m breaks	Mod. 5 miles/8k	“” 5 x 2k @ current → goal 15k/10 mile pace w/ easy 400m breaks.	Off or easy cross-train	Mod. 5 miles/8k	Easy 12 miles (or 19k)
12	Off	“” 6 x 400m w/ 200m breaks.	Mod. 5 miles/8k	**“” 12k time-trial!!**	Off or easy cross-train	Mod. 5 miles/8k	Easy 10 miles (or 16k)
13	Off or easy cross-train	“” 4 x {100m/200m/300m} w/ 100m breaks	Mod. 5 miles/8k	“” 6 x 2k @ current → goal 15k/10 mile pace w/ easy 400m breaks.	Off or easy cross-train	Mod. 5 miles/8k	Easy 12 miles (or 19k)
14	Off or easy cross-train	“” 12 x 200m fast w/200m breaks	Mod. 5 miles/8k	12k progression	Off or easy cross-train	Mod. 5 miles/8k	Easy 12 miles (or 19k)
15	Off or easy cross-train	“” 10 x 400m w/ 200m breaks.	Mod. 5 miles/8k	“” 8k tempo; 4k @ current 15k/10-mile pace; 2k @ goal pace w/ easy 4:00 min. breaks.	Off or easy cross-train	Mod. 3 miles/5k	Easy 8 miles (or 13k)
16	Off or easy cross-train	10 min. warm-up, then 3 x 1 mile @ 15k/10-mile race pace w/ 1:00 breaks.	30 mins.	Off	10-min. w/ up, then 4 x 30 sec. sprints, cool dn., then stretch	**RACE!!!**	Easy 6-mile (or 10k) hike

The Intermediate 10-Mile Training Schedule is for walkers who can handle an 8-mile/13k long day—building to twelve miles—as well as a healthy amount of economy and threshold speed work. I've put race day on Saturday because the Crim 10-Miler is on Saturday. If you're training for the US 15k Championships or the British 10-Mile Championships shift the last week to a day later.

Advanced 15k/10-Mile Training Schedule							
Week	**Mon.**	**Tues.**	**Wed.**	**Thurs.**	**Fri.**	**Sat.**	**Sun.**
1	Off or easy cross-train	45-minute fartlek	Easy 15k	45-minute fartlek	Easy 15k	Mod. 45 mins.	Easy 8 miles (or 11k)
2	Off or easy cross-train	10-min. warm-up, drills, then 8 x 1:00 min. hill reps.	Easy 15k	50-minute fartlek	Easy 15k	Mod. 60 mins.	Easy 10 miles (or 16k)
3	Off or easy cross-train	10-min. warm-up, drills, then 8 x 1:30 min. hill reps.	Easy 15k	60-minute fartlek	Easy 15k	Mod. 60 mins.	Easy 11 miles (or 17.5k)
4	Off or easy cross-train	"" 8 x 2:00 min. hill reps.	Easy 15k	10-min. warm-up, drills, then 45 mins. progression	Easy 15k	Mod. 60 mins.	Easy 12 miles (or 19k)
5	Off or easy cross-train	"" 10 x 200m fast w/200m breaks	Easy 15k	"" 45-minute tempo—steady, hard effort.	Easy 15k	Mod. 6 miles/10k	Easy 9 miles (or 14k)
6	Off or easy cross-train	"" 8 x 400m @ 5,000m race pace, w/ 200m breaks.	Easy 15k	"" 50-min. progression.	Easy 15k	Mod. 6 miles/10k	Easy 13 miles (or 21k)
7	Off or easy cross-train	"" 4 x {100m/200m/300} m w/ 100m breaks	Easy 15k	"" 8 x 1k @ current → goal 15k/10 mile pace w/ easy 400m breaks.	Easy 15k	Mod. 6 miles/10k	Easy 14 miles (or 22.5k)
8	Off or easy cross-train	"" 12 x 200m fast w/200m breaks	Easy 15k	"" 10k tempo	Easy 15k	Mod. 6 miles/10k	Easy 15 miles (or 24k)
9	Off or easy cross-train	"" 10 x 400m w/ 200m breaks.	Easy 15k	"" 6 x 1,600m @ current → goal 15k/10 mile pace w/ easy 400m breaks.	Easy 15k	Mod. 6 miles/10k	Easy 10 miles (or 16k)
10	Off or easy cross-train	"" 4 x {100m/200m/300} m w/ 100m breaks	Easy 15k	12k progression	Easy 15k	Mod. 6 miles/10k	Easy 25k (15.5 miles)
11	Off or easy cross-train	"" 6 x 200m fast w/200m breaks	Easy 15k	"" 5 x 2k @ current → goal 15k/10 mile pace w/ easy 400m breaks.	Easy 15k	Mod. 6 miles/10k	Easy 25k (15.5 miles)
12	Off	"" 6 x 400m w/ 200m breaks.	Easy 15k	**"" 15k time-trial!!**	Easy 15k	Mod. 6 miles/10k	Easy 25k (15.5 miles)
13	Off or easy cross-train	"" 4 x {100m/200m/300} m w/ 100m breaks	Easy 15k	"" 6 x 2k @ current → goal 15k/10 mile pace w/ easy 400m breaks.	Easy 15k	Mod. 6 miles/10k	Easy 20k (12.4 miles)
14	Off or easy cross-train	"" 12 x 200m fast w/200m breaks	Easy 15k	12k progression	Easy 15k	Mod. 6 miles/10k	Easy 25k (15.5 miles)
15	Off or easy cross-train	"" 10 x 400m w/ 200m breaks.	Easy 15k	"" 3 x 5k @ current 15k/10-mile pace w/ easy 5:00 min. breaks.	Easy 15k	Mod. 3 miles/5k	Easy 8 miles (or 13k)
16	Off or easy cross-train	"" 3 x 1 mile or 2 x 2.5k @ 15k/10-mile race pace w/ 1:00 breaks.	Easy 30 mins.	"" 2 x 1k @ current → goal 15k/10 mile pace w/ easy 400m break.	Off	Wm. up then 4 x 30 sec. sprints, cool dn., stretch.	**RACE!!!**

The Advanced 15k/10-Mile Training Schedule is designed for walkers training for events like the US Open and Masters 15k Racewalk Championship or Nordic Walking 10-Mile Championships.

CHAPTER 19: "SPEED-ENDURANCE" RACING: 20K – 25K

The 20k (12.4 miles) and half-marathon (13.1 miles) distances are significant to both racewalkers and non-racewalking competitive walkers. 20 kilometers has been one of the two Olympic distances for men since 1956 and the Olympic distance for women since 2000; the half-marathon has been the fastest-growing road race distance in the US since 2008. A lot of walkers like the distance because it's a big challenge, but it doesn't take the same time commitment as a full marathon. The half-marathon is also a popular and record-eligible distance for Nordic walkers.

Some notable half-marathons for walkers include the We Walk! Half-Marathon in Minneapolis, MN, which welcomes and awards walkers of all stripes from racewalkers to power walkers to Nordic walkers; the Portland (Oregon) Half-Marathon offers walk awards in several categories and boasts an 8-hour time limit; the Parkersburg (West Virginia) Half-Marathon has a tight, for some walkers, 3½-hour time limit, but offers 3-deep walk awards for the open winners, as well as in 5-year age groups; the Seacoast Half in Portsmouth, NH has walk awards and regularly attracts some of the top walkers in the US and even Europe—the men's course record of 1:32:31(!) is held by 2016 Olympian Adrian Blocki of Poland; and the D&L Half-Marathon in Northhampton, PA has walk awards and a generous 4½-hour time limit. The Avenue of the Giants Half-Marathon in Arcata, California, does not offer walk awards, but the 6-hour time limit is very walker-friendly, and the course, among 300 ft.-tall old-growth giant redwoods, can't be beat.

25k (15.5 miles) races are a rarity, but the Larry Fuselier 25k on the Lake Pontchartrain Levee in Metairie, Louisiana, is an iconic event that I've raced several times. As with most (all?) New Orleans Track Club races, there are awards for the top walkers. Due to the dearth of 25k racing opportunities, I've only included one 25k training schedule, laid out as an intermediate plan, but easily modifiable for beginners or advanced walkers.

20k/half-marathon schedules for all levels are included since these are classic, and frequently contested distances. For beginners, much of the training involves building weekly and long-day mileage in order to simply get the body ready to cover the distance. The plan is to get a beginning walker to the point where he or she is able to complete one or two ten-mile walks. If you can do that, you will be able to get through a 20k or half-marathon—guaranteed! I have coached literally thousands of beginning half-marathoners and 20k walkers over the years, and I can literally count on one hand the athletes who were not able to complete their events—the guy with the stress-fracture who never should have started the race in the first place; the girl racing in the middle of a

Crohn's disease "flare" who also should not have started; a woman who *I* pulled from a half-marathon when it was clear she was suffering from heat-stroke; and one guy with really, really bad blisters. That's it. The rest of my athletes on the beginner program—literally 99.9%[56]—have completed their events.

The intermediate schedule is for walkers who are experienced at 5k and 10k racing, and so are reasonably expected to be accustomed to some speed and tempo training, and for whom an eight- or ten-mile long day at the beginning of the training schedule is by no means a daunting prospect. The advanced schedule is for truly advanced walkers training for national or international competitions, whether at the open or masters level. I've included an "elite" 20k schedule for illustrative purposes only, detailing my training before the 1996 Olympic Trials when I was at my peak. Instead of showing what I *should have* done, the schedule shows what I *did* do, to demonstrate that consistent training over several years, not necessarily perfect training in the final months, is the key to success. Although I suppose one could argue that I would have sustained my peak longer and would have done better at the Olympic Trials had I not endured so many setbacks that season. Who knows? ☺ Onward!

[56] My own record is 99.9%, but "system-wide" when overseeing other coaches as National Coach for the Crohn's & Colitis Foundation's "Team Challenge," our completion rate for both runners and walkers was 99.7% over the twelve years I was overseeing the program. Many thousands of walkers and runners went through the program and I can enumerate by name nearly every one of our non-finishers because there were so few, and their reasons for dropping out of their half-marathons (and marathons) were almost always somewhat unusual.

Beginner's 20k/Half-Marathon Training Schedule							
Week	**Mon.**	**Tues.**	**Wed.**	**Thurs.**	**Fri.**	**Sat.**	**Sun.**
1	Off or easy cross-train	45-minute fartlek	Easy 30 mins.	45-minute fartlek	Off or easy cross-train	Moderate 30 mins.	Easy 6 miles (or 10k)
2	Off or easy cross-train	45-minute fartlek	Easy 35 mins.	50-minute fartlek	Off or easy cross-train	Moderate 35 mins.	Easy 7 miles (or 11k)
3	Off or easy cross-train	10-min. warm-up, drills, then 8 x 30 sec. hill reps.	Easy 40 mins.	60-minute fartlek	Off or easy cross-train	Mod. 40-min.	Easy 8 miles (or 13k)
4	Off	10-min. warm-up, drills, then 6 x 1:00 min. hill reps.	Easy 30 mins.	Easy 3 miles/5k	Off or easy cross-train	Mod. 30 mins.	Easy 5 miles (or 8k)
5	Off or easy cross-train	10-min. warm-up, drills, then 8 x 1:30 hill reps.	Easy 45 mins.	5 miles/8k progression	Off or easy cross-train	Mod. 45 mins.	"Not so easy" 5 miles/8k
6	Off or easy cross-train	"" 8 x 2:00 min. hill reps.	Easy 45 mins.	5 miles/8k tempo	Off or easy cross-train	Mod. 45 mins.	Easy 8 miles (or 13k)
7	Off or easy cross-train	Track. 10 min. w/up then 8 laps of Turns & Straights.	Easy 45 mins.	5 miles/8k progression	Off or easy cross-train	Mod. 45 mins.	"Not so easy" 6 miles/10k
8	Off or easy cross-train	Track. 10 min. w/up then 10 laps of T&S.	Easy 30 mins.	Easy 5 miles/8k	Off or easy cross-train	Easy 30 mins.	Easy 7 miles (or 11k)
9	Off or easy cross-train	Track. 10 min. w/up then 10 laps of T&S.	Easy 45 mins.	5 miles/8k progression	Off or easy cross-train	Mod. 45 mins.	"Not so easy" 6 miles/10k
10	Off or easy cross-train	"" 8 x 200m fast w/200m breaks	Easy 45 mins.	5 miles/8k tempo	Off or easy cross-train	Mod. 45 mins.	Easy 9 miles (or 15k)
11	Off or easy cross-train	"" 6 x 400m @ goal race pace, w/ 200m breaks.	Easy 45 mins.	5 miles/8k progression	Off or easy cross-train	Mod. 45 mins.	"Not so easy" 6 miles/10k
12	Off	"" 10 x 200m fast w/200m breaks	Easy 30 mins.	Easy 5 miles/8k	Off or easy cross-train	Easy 30 mins.	Easy 8 miles (or 13k)
13	Off or easy cross-train	"" 6 x 400m w/ 200m breaks.	Easy 30 mins.	**10k time-trial!**	Off or easy cross-train	Mod. 45 mins.	"Not so easy" 8 miles/13k
14	Off or easy cross-train	"" 12 x 200m fast w/200m breaks	Easy 45 mins.	5 miles/8k tempo	Off or easy cross-train	Mod. 45 mins.	Easy 10 miles (or 16k)
15	Off or easy cross-train	"" 6 x 400m w/ 200m breaks.	Easy 45 mins.	5 miles/8k progression	Off or easy cross-train	Mod. 30-min.	6 miles, with 3 easy, 3 at race pace.
16	Off or easy cross-train	Easy 30 mins.	Easy 30 mins.	"" 6 x 400m @ 20k/half-mar. pace w/ 200m breaks.	Off!	Wm. up then 4 x 30 sec. sprints, cool dn., stretch.	**RACE!!**

The Beginner's 20k/Half-Marathon Training Schedule is for beginners hoping to complete their first half-marathon or 20k with little prior racing experience. The goal is to build up to a couple of 10-mile/16k walks a few weeks before your event. If you can do that, I've found that you have a +/- 99.7% chance of completing your race ! (And if for some reason you don't get to ten miles/16k in training, if the mind is ready, the body will follow!) ☺

Intermediate 20k/Half-Marathon Training Schedule

Week	Mon.	Tues.	Wed.	Thurs.	Fri.	Sat.	Sun.
1	Off or easy cross-train	45-minute fartlek	Moderate 30 mins.	45-minute fartlek	Off or easy cross-train	Moderate 45 mins.	Easy 8 miles (or 13k)
2	Off or easy cross-train	45-minute fartlek	Easy 4-5 miles/5-8k	50-minute progression	Off or easy cross-train	Mod. 50 min.	Easy 9 miles (or 15k)
3	Off or easy cross-train	10-min. warm-up, drills, then 8 x 30 sec. hill reps.	Easy 4-5 miles/6-8k	50 minute tempo	Off or easy cross-train	Easy 60 min.	"Not so easy" 6 miles/10k
4	Off or easy cross-train	10-min. warm-up, drills, then 8 x 1:00 min. hill reps.	Easy 4-5 miles/6-8k	60-minute progression	Off or easy cross-train	Mod. 60 min.	Easy 8 miles (or 13k)
5	Off or easy cross-train	10-min. warm-up, drills, then 8 x 1:30 min. hill reps.	Easy 4-5 miles/6-8k	60-minute tempo	Off or easy cross-train	Easy 60 min.	"Not so easy" 6 miles/10k
6	Off or easy cross-train	"" 8 x 2:00 min. hill reps.	Easy 5 miles/8k	5-mile/8k progression	Off or easy cross-train	Mod. 60 min.	Easy 9 miles (or 15k)
7	Off or easy cross-train	Track. 10 min. w/up then 8 laps of Turns & Straights.	Easy 5 miles/8k	5-mile/8k tempo	Off or easy cross-train	Mod. 60 min.	Easy 10 miles (or 16k)
8	Off or easy cross-train	Track. 10 min. w/up then 10 laps of T&S.	Easy 5 miles/8k	5-mile/8k progression	Off or easy cross-train	Easy 60 min.	"Not so easy" 8 miles/13k
9	Off or easy cross-train	Track. 10 min. w/up then 12 laps of T&S.	Easy 5 miles/8k	5-mile/8k tempo	Off or easy cross-train	Mod. 60 min.	Easy 11 miles (or 17k)
10	Off or easy cross-train	"" 8 x 200m fast w/200m breaks	Easy 5 miles/8k	5 x 1 mile @ 10k pace w/ 3:00 rests.	Off or easy cross-train	Mod. 60 min.	Easy 12 miles (or 19k)
11	Off or easy cross-train	"" 6 x 400m @ goal race pace, w/ 200m breaks.	Easy 5 miles/8k	5-mile/8k tempo	Off or easy cross-train	Easy 60 min.	"Not so easy" 9 miles/15k
12	Off or easy cross-train	"" 10 x 200m fast w/200m breaks	Easy 5 miles/8k	5 x 1 mile @ 10k pace w/ 3:00 rests.	Off or easy cross-train	Mod. 60 min.	Easy 9 miles (or 15k)
13	Off or easy cross-train	"" 6 x 400m w/ 200m breaks.	Easy 30 mins.	**12k time-trial!**	Off or easy cross-train	Mod. 60 min.	Easy 13 miles (or 21k)
14	Off or easy cross-train	"" 12 x 200m fast w/200m breaks	Easy 5 miles/8k	5 x 1 mile @ 10k pace w/ 3:00 rests.	Off or easy cross-train	Easy 60 min.	"Not so easy" 10 miles/16k
15	Off or easy cross-train	"" 6 x 400m w/ 200m breaks.	Easy 5 miles/8k	5-mile/8k tempo	Off or easy cross-train	Easy 30 minute	6 miles with 3 easy, 3 at half-marathon pace
16	Off or easy cross-train	Easy 30 mins.	Easy 3 miles/5k	15-minute progression down to 20k/ half-mar. pace	Off!	Wm. up then 4 x 30 sec. sprints, cool dn., stretch.	**RACE!!!**

Advanced 20k/Half-Marathon Training Schedule

Week	Mon.	Tues.	Wed.	Thurs.	Fri.	Sat.	Sun.
1	Off or easy cross-train	45-minute fartlek	Easy 5 miles/8k	45-minute fartlek	Easy 5 miles/8k	Moderate 45 mins.	Easy 11 mi. (or 17.5k)
2	Off or easy cross-train	45-minute fartlek	Easy 5 miles/8k	50-minute fartlek	Easy 5 miles/8k	Mod. 50 min.	Easy 12 mi. (or 19k)
3	Off or easy cross-train	10-min. warm-up, drills, then 8 x 30 sec. hill reps.	Easy 10k/ 6.2 miles	60-minute fartlek	Easy 10k/ 6.2 miles	Easy 60 min.	Easy 10 mi. (or 16k)
4	Off or easy cross-train	10-min. warm-up, drills, then 8 x 1:00 min. hill reps.	Easy 10k/ 6.2 miles	Warm-up, drills, then 8 x 1k @ 20k/half-mar. pace w/ 200m breaks	Easy 10k/ 6.2 miles	Mod. 60 min.	Easy 13 mi. (or 21k)
5	Off or easy cross-train	"" drills, then 8 x 1:30 min. hill reps.	Easy 10k/ 6.2 miles	10k progression	Easy 10k/ 6.2 miles	Mod. 6 miles/10k	Easy 14 mi. (or 22.5k)
6	Off or easy cross-train	"" 8 x 2:00 min. hill reps.	Easy 10k/ 6.2 miles	"" 6 x 1 mile @ goal pace w/ 200m breaks	Easy 10k/ 6.2 miles	Mod. 6 miles/10k	Easy 15 mi. (or 24k)
7	Off or easy cross-train	Wm-up, drills, then 4 x {100m/200m/300m} w/ 100m breaks	Easy 10k/ 6.2 miles	10k tempo	Easy 10k/ 6.2 miles	Easy 6 miles/10k	"Not so easy" 20k (12.4 mi.)
8	Off or easy cross-train	"" 20 x 200m w/ 200m breaks	Easy 10k/ 6.2 miles	""5 x 2k @ goal pace w/ 500m mod. Breaks	Easy 10k/ 6.2 miles	Mod. 6 miles/10k	Easy 15.5 mi. (25k)
9	Off or easy cross-train	"" 12 x 400m w/ 200m breaks	Easy 10k/ 6.2 miles	12k progression	Easy 10k/ 6.2 miles	Easy 6 miles/10k	"Not so easy" 20k (12.4 mi.)
10	Off or easy cross-train	"" 4 x {100m/200m/300m} w/ 100m breaks	Easy 10k/ 6.2 miles	""4 x 2.5k @ 20k/half-mar. pace w/ 500m mod. Breaks	Easy 10k/ 6.2 miles	Mod. 6 miles/10k	Easy 25k (15.5 miles)
11	Off or easy cross-train	"" 20 x 200m w/ 200m breaks	Easy 10k/ 6.2 miles	10k tempo	Easy 10k/ 6.2 miles	Easy 6 miles/10k	"Not so easy" 20k (12.4 mi.)
12	Off or easy cross-train	"" 15 x 400m w/ 200m breaks	Easy 10k/ 6.2 miles	4 x 3k @ 20k/half-mar. pace w/ 500m mod.—breaks	Easy 10k/ 6.2 miles	Mod. 6 miles/10k	Easy 25k (15.5 miles)
13	Off or easy cross-train	"" 3 x {100m/200m/300m} w/ 100m breaks	Easy 30 mins.	**15k time-trial!**	Easy 10k/ 6.2 miles	Easy 6 miles/10k	"Not so easy" 20k (12.4 mi.)
14	Off or easy cross-train	"" 20 x 200m w/ 200m breaks	Easy 10k/ 6.2 miles	8 x 1k @ 20k/half-mar. pace w/ 500m mod. Breaks	Easy 10k/ 6.2 miles	Mod. 6 miles/10k	Easy 25k (15.5 miles)
15	Off or easy cross-train	"" 16 x 400m w/ 200m breaks	Easy 10k/ 6.2 miles	5-mile/8k tempo	Easy 10k/ 6.2 miles	Easy 5 miles/8k	6 miles-3 easy, 3 @ 20k/half-mar. pace
16	Off	"" 3 x 1k @ 20k/half-mar. pace w/ 1:00 rests.	Easy 8k/ 5 miles	"" 8 x 400m @ 20k/half-mar. race pace w/ 100m breaks,	Off!	Wm./up, 4 x 30 sec. fast, cool dn., stretch.	**RACE!!!**

Since 20k is an Olympic distance, I've included an elite schedule following this advanced schedule. The advanced schedule is for very experienced walkers headed to the National or World Masters 20k, for example. If you have the time and energy, bump up the easy W and F 10ks to 15k. The "elite" schedule is my own build-up to my 20k PR in 1996. It shows that things don't have to go 100% perfectly for you to have a good race—just keep plugging away! This should give a rough idea of that it takes to qualify for the Olympic Trials, and/or make international teams in the 20k.

Elite 20k Training Schedule – The build-up to my 1:24:29 20k PR

Week	Mon.	Tues.	Wed.	Thurs.	Fri.	Sat.	Sun.
1 (110 km week)	Off (Christmas)	AM: Easy 15k PM: 2k w/ up, 12 x 200m hill reps. 2km cool dn.	20k @ 1:42:22 (5:07/km)	Easy 20km	2k warm-up, then 8 x 1-mile @ 8:02 → 6:51 w/ 3:00 breaks.	2k warm-up, then raced **The Wall 30k in New Orleans in 2:34** (5:08/km)	Off (Felt crappy. Might have had a beer or six after the race.)
2 (40km week)	Easy 10k	2k w/up, 12 x 200m @ :48 → :39 w/ 200m breaks, 2k cool dn.	Off (sick)	Off (sick)	Off (sick)	10k @ 5:20/km	Easy 12k
3 (140km week)	10k @ 5:35/km	AM : 2k w/up, 12 x 200m @ :47 → :42 w/ 200m breaks, 2k cool dn.	Easy 25k @ ~5:35/km	20k @ 5:45/km	3k w/up, 5 x 3k w/ 5:00 breaks. 2k cool dn. @ 14:00 → 13:44	30k progression from 6:00 → 5:03/km	AM: 8k jog PM: Easy 16k
4 (51km week) ☹	Easy 9k @ 6:00/km	AM: 4k + 40 mins. pool. PM: 14k @ 5:40/km, finish at the track for 3 x 200m @ :47, :47, :45; 2 x 500m @ 1:55, 1:54.	Scheduled for an easy 30k. Did 0. I don't know why.	AM: 12k @ 5:55 → 4:52. PM: Pouring rain . Supposed to do 6 x 500m. Did 2 x 200m @ :47, 1 x 400m @ 1:44. Track too slippery. Quit.	1k warm-up, then some strides.	**Commonwealth Invitational 3,000m @ Harvard 12:12.** 5k warm-up. Out HARD (3:46, then 4:05, 4:20.) Ugh. Sick.	Clinic. About 2k of RW while demonstrating. Otherwise nada. (Sick)
5 (120km week)	Off (Sick)	4k w/up, 12 x 200m @ :46 → :41 w/200m breaks	20k progression from 5:25 → 4:59	15k @ 5:15/km	AM: 2k warm-up, then 8 x 1k @ 4:39 → 4:14, 2k cool dn. PM: Easy 12k.	AM: 2k w/up, 3k @ 15:00, 2k cool dn. PM: Easy 11k progression 6:00 → 5:30.	30k progression from 6:00 → 5:15
6 (125km week)	Very easy 5k	AM: 2k warm-up, then 2 x 200m; 4 x 400m; 2 x 200m @ :45 → :40 and 1:30 → 1:27 2k cool dn. PM: Easy 8k	30k @ 5:34/km	AM: Easy 5k PM: 4k w/up, then 8 x 200m @ :46 → :43 w/ 100m breaks.	**Millrose Games 1-Mile.** 2k warm-up, then **6:00.72 mile** (2:54 at the half.) Misjudged finish line. ☹	AM: 10k @ 5:00/km PM: Easy 15k	Easy 32k with Marc Varsano & Lucash Szela
7 (150km week)	Flew back from New York. PM: Gym	20k as 3k easy (5:40/km) then 14k @ 5:01/km, then 3k @ 6:15/km	AM: 25K @ 5:21/km PM: Easy 8k + gym	AM: 5k w/up, 4 x {100, 200, 300m} w/ 100m moving breaks PM: Easy 10k	Easy 25km	AM: Easy 12k @ 5:39/km PM: 2k w/up, then 8 x 2k @ 4:35/km w/ 2:00 min. breaks.	20k @ 5:30/km
8 (143km week)	Walking Magazine deadline. No time to train. `	AM: Easy 5k PM: 1k warm-up, then slam 15k @ 4:46/km	Easy 20k @ 5:35/km, then flew to Honolulu	AM: 2k warm-up, 5 x {30, 60, 90 secs.} PM: 10k @ 5:45/km uphill	7k hike	40k in 3:49:35 (5:44/km) with Gene Kitts	31k @ 6:00 → 5:30/km with Gene Kitts
9 (189km week)	2k warm-up, **8.25 mi. Aloha Run RW 56:48 = 6:53/mile! (~41:58 @ 10k)** PM: EZ 5k	AM: 23km in Kauai @ 5:35/km PM: "Strenuous" 21km Alakai Swamp Trail hike	AM: 3k hike, then 16km @ 5:20/km PM: 3k w/ up, 8 x 2:00 min. hill reps., 3k cool dn.	6-hour 17k Napali hike	AM: 25k @ 5:30/km PM: 10k @ 5:20/km	AM: Snorkle in Kona PM: Easy 8k with a couple of 1:38 400m reps. within.	32k @ 5:30/km up Kiluaea in Volcanoes Nat'l Park.

10 (111km week)	Easy 9k	AM:19-hour flight from Hawaii PM: 2k w/up, 2 x 200m @ :44, :43; 3 x 500m @ 1:56, 2:00, 1:58; 1k @ 4:04; 2k cool dn.	Easy 25k @ 5:30/km	AM: 2k w/up, then 5 x {100, 200, 300m} w/ 100m breaks PM: Easy 7km	AM: 12k @ 5:30/km PM: 3k + gym	**USATF Indoor 5,000m Championship 20:47.** Meh. PM: Easy 8k	Easy 20k (Feeling cruddy)
11 (156km week)	5k "just" walking.	AM: 5k w/up, then 8k tempo @ 4:29/km PM: 12k progression @ 5:33 → 4:59/km	30k progression, 5:36 → 4:49/km	AM: Sluggish 10km	AM: 8k jog in LaGrange PM: Easy 20k in Albuquerque, NM	AM: Easy 16k @ 6:00 → 5:45/k PM: 10 x 1 k @ 4:15 w/ 2:00 breaks	AM: Easy 21km PM: Easy 10km
12 (196km week)	Easy 35k hike	AM: 2k w/up, 8k @ 4:28/km, 2k cool dn. On the Bosque Trail. PM: Easy 10km	27k on the Tramway Trail @ < 5:30/km	15k @ 4:45/km on the Bosque Trail	AM: 15k @ 5:40/km PM: Very rugged 28km hike up and down Sandia Peak.	AM: 10k prog. @ 6:00 → 5:00/km. PM: 3 x {1k, 2k, 1k} @ 4:15/k for 1ks, 8:45 for 2ks.	AM: 1k w/up, **5k race in 22:41** , 1.5k cool dn., then 21 more kms @ ~5:50/km,
13 (115km week)	5k hike @ Petroglyphs Park	AM: 10k @ 5:30/km on Tramway Trail. PM: 8k tempo @ 4:24/km on the Bosque Trail	25k @ 5:30/k on the Bosque Trail	AM: 10k @ 6:00/km PM: 6 x 1k @ 4:23 → 4:09 at U. New Mexico track	10k @ 5:37/km Then flew to DC.	PM: Mostly easy 8k, but hit 4:22 for the last one, then some 30 sec. strides.	**20k race.** On 1:25:00 pace until 17k, then the wheels came off. **PR: 1:26:28**
14 (124km week)	AM: Easy 6k with Ian Whatley	AM: 2k jog, 40 minutes pool, 8k jog on grass. PM: 25k @ 4:54/km w/ Chinese walkers	20k @ 5:45/km	AM: Mod.18k w/ Zhao & Li in the mall. PM: 12 x 200 w/ 1:00 breaks :51 → :46.	AM: Easy 20k, then drove to Miami w/ the Chinese walkers & coaches.	AM: Easy 12k PM: 4k prog. W./-up, then 10 x 400m w/ Li @ 1:40 → 1:25 w/ 2:00 breaks	2k warm-up, then hot 5k race in 21:40.
15 (161k week)	16k @ 6:00/km, w/ Li, Zhao & Gao, then Gatorland & Disney	Easy 20k on the ATL Olympic course with Mr. Li.	AM: 5k PM: 20k @ 5:30/km	AM: 2k w/up, 2 x 8k @ 39:00, 37:30 w/ 5:00 break between. PM: 5k + pool	AM: 25k progression, 5:30 → 4:45/km PM: Gym	20k @ 5:30/km	AM: 40 x 400m @ 1:45 → 1:35 w/ 1:00 breaks. PM: Very easy 12km
16 (103km week)	30 minutes in the pool	AM: 5k + pool PM: 12k @ 5:30/km	2.5k w/up, 8 x 2k first 5 at 9:30; 6 & 7 at 9:00, 8th @ 8:15 w/ 2:00 breaks.	1.5k jog, 10k Easy with 5 x 200m @ :52 → :48, 1.5k jog.	AM: Very easy 6k 6:40 → 5:40. PM: Easy 6k progression 6:00 → 4:48/km.	AM: Easy 5k PM: 2k warm-up, 2 x 1k @ 4:35, 4:20.	**20k RACE!!! 1:24:29**

I started out writing what I was supposed to do, but then I figured let's be real! This is my build-up to my best 20k, in April of 1996—at the time it made me the 3rd fastest American ever at 20k, and only two seconds behind #2. This is the "all the warts" version. Sick days, bad workouts, etc. Your training doesn't have to be perfect for you to have good races, but it's important to be as consistent as possible. Mileage is king! Easy 6- to 8k walks or jogs can (should!) be added several days per week whenever possible. When doing doubles, the extra workouts should be separated from the main workout of the day by as long as possible. If the main workout is in the morning, the additional mileage should be done in the late afternoon, or vice versa. For the Monday cross-training days, I like long (2- to 6-hour) hikes whenever possible.

Intermediate 25k Training Schedule

Week	Mon.	Tues.	Wed.	Thurs.	Fri.	Sat.	Sun.
1	Off or easy cross-train	45-minute fartlek	Moderate 30 mins.	45-minute fartlek	Off or easy cross-train	Moderate 45 mins.	Easy 13 miles (or 21k)
2	Off or easy cross-train	50-minute fartlek	Easy 4-5 miles/5-8k	50-minute	Off or easy cross-train	Mod. 50 min.	"Not so easy" 9 miles/15k
3	Off or easy cross-train	60-minute fartlek	Easy 4-5 miles/6-8k	50 minute tempo	Off or easy cross-train	Mod. 60 min.	Easy 14 miles (or 22.5k)
4	Off or easy cross-train	60-minute fartlek	Easy 4-5 miles/6-8k	60-minute	Off or easy cross-train	Easy 60 min.	Easy 15 miles (or 24k)
5	Off or easy cross-train	60-minute	Easy 4-5 miles/6-8k	60 minute tempo	Off or easy cross-train	Mod. 60 min.	Easy 16 miles (or 26k)
6	Off or easy cross-train	60 minute tempo	Easy 5 miles/8k	60-minute	Off or easy cross-train	Mod. 60 min.	"Not so easy" 10 miles/16k
7	Off or easy cross-train	5-mile/8k tempo	Easy 5 miles/8k	60 minute tempo	Off or easy cross-train	Mod. 60 min.	Easy 17 miles (or 27.5k)
8	Off or easy cross-train	5-mile/8k	Easy 5 miles/8k	60-minute	Off or easy cross-train	Easy 60 min.	Easy 18 miles (or 29k)
9	Off or easy cross-train	Warm-up, then 8 x 400m @ 5k pace w/ 2:00 rests	Easy 5 miles/8k	5-mile/8k tempo	Off or easy cross-train	Mod. 60 min.	Easy 30k (or 18.6 miles)
10	Off or easy cross-train	5-mile/8k tempo	Easy 5 miles/8k	Wm.-up, drills, then 5 x 1 mi. @ 10k pace w/ 3:00 rests.	Off or easy cross-train	Mod. 60 min.	"Not so easy" 11 miles/18k
11	Off or easy cross-train	Warm-up, then 8 x 400m @ 5k pace w/ 2:00 rests	Easy 5 miles/8k	5-mile/8k tempo	Off or easy cross-train	Easy 60 min.	Easy 30k (or 18.6 miles)
12	Off or easy cross-train	5-mile/8k tempo	Easy 5 miles/8k	"" 3 x 1k @ 25k pace w/ 1:00 rests.	Off or easy cross-train	Easy 30 mins.	**20k time-trial!**
13	Off or easy cross-train	Warm-up, then 8 x 400m @ 5k pace w/ 2:00 rests	Easy 5 miles/8k	5-mile/8k tempo	Off or easy cross-train	Easy 60 min.	Easy 30k (or 18.6 miles)
14	Off or easy cross-train	5-mile/8k tempo	Easy 5 miles/8k	5 x 1 mile @ 10k pace w/ 3:00 rests.	Off or easy cross-train	Easy 60 min.	25k/15.5 miles progression
15	Off or easy cross-train	Warm-up, then 8 x 400m @ 5k pace w/ 2:00 rests	Easy 5 miles/8k	5-mile/8k tempo	Off or easy cross-train	Easy 30 mins.	10 miles with 6 easy, 4 at 30k pace
16	Off or easy cross-train	Warm-up, then 3 x 1 mile @ 25k pace w/ 1:00 rests.	Easy 3 miles/5k	Off!	Wm. up then 4 x 30 sec. sprints, cool dn., stretch.	**RACE!!!**	Off or easy 30 mins.

Since 25k races are such a rarity, and beginners are not likely to start their racing careers with such an odd distance, I've only included an intermediate 25k schedule. Race day is on Saturday to reflect the traditional race day for the Larry Fuselier 25k in New Orleans. The long tempo day has been moved from Thursday to every alternate Sunday because few people have the time or energy to do a "not so easy" 20k on a weekday.

CHAPTER 20: "THE WALL": 30K – 35K

The Wall is that mythical physical and mental collapse point that hits many poorly trained, poorly paced, and/or poorly fueled marathoners somewhere between 18 and 22 miles. But, as I wrote in *The Complete Guide to Marathon Walking,* "the wall appears wherever you decide to put it." When your pacing doesn't match up with your training and nutrition, it's possible to run out of energy in a long race well before the finish line. Of course properly trained, properly paced, and properly fueled walkers never hit the wall, but races of this duration can still be quite intimidating to some walkers. Even so, 30k, 20 miles, 21 miles and 35k are standard race distances: 30k is a national championship and national record-eligible racewalking distance in many countries, including the US, and north of the border, the Around the Bay 30k, first held in Hamilton, Ontario Canada in 1894, is the oldest road race in North America—yes, even older than the venerable Boston Marathon! The race is popular with faster walkers able to come in under the 4½-hour time limit (9:00 per kilometer, or about 14:30 per mile). 20 miles is a standard Nordic walking distance, and a classic racewalking distance, especially in the UK and Australia; 21 miles is a bit of an odd-ball distance, but it's the length of the Big Sur Power Walk held alongside the marathon of the same name in Big Sur, California; while 35 kilometers is widely regarded as the distance that levels the playing field between 20k and 50k racewalkers. 35 kilometers is also a world record-eligible racewalking distance, and either 30k or 35k will likely be the new Olympic long-distance event for racewalkers beginning in 2024. Finally, in the Land Down Under, "The Bloody Long Walk" is a 35k charity walk supporting The Mito Foundation,[57] which helps raise funds to "support people affected by mitochondrial disease (Mito), funds essential research into the prevention, diagnosis, treatment and cures of mitochondrial disorders, and increase awareness and education about this devastating disease."

Participants in Sydney, Australia's "Bloody Long Walk" to cure mitochondrial disease. Photo credit: Bloody Long Walk

[57] For information or to sign up for the Bloody Long Walk, head to www.bloodylongwalk.com.au/. My first-born son is affected by mitochondrial disease, so I support their mission 100%!

In terms of training for races in "The Wall" range, the idea is to push the wall beyond the race distance. What I mean by that is, if you're racing a 30k, ideally you want the wall to be safely located at 30.1k where it doesn't affect you. You obviously don't want to "crash and burn" before the finish line, but you also don't want to put the wall too far beyond the finish line, either, which would indicate that you didn't push hard enough in the race and got to the finish line with lots of fuel left in the tank.

When I graph out my best race paces over the course of my career, I get a very gradual, linear pace curve from one mile up to 20 kilometers. I call that the lactate part of the curve, where lactate buildup in the muscles dictates the decline in pace. My best one-mile race time was 6:00; my best 3k was 11:37, or 6:12 per mile; my 20:06 5k was 6:25 per mile; my best 10k was 6:36 per mile; and my 1:24:29 20k was 6:48 per mile. I only ever raced 25k once, so that pace (~7:30 per mile) probably isn't truly reflective, but I did race a number of 30k races. My best was only about 7:50 per mile, so my pace really fell off a cliff after 20k. (There seems to be another cliff after 35k, with my best marathon, or 42.195k, only coming in at about 8:19 per mile, but we'll get to that in the next chapter!) This sudden drop-off in pace after 20 kilometers isn't the lactate part of the graph anymore; I call it the "fuel mix" part of the pace curve. Basically carbohydrate depletion, rather than lactate buildup, becomes the issue after 20 kilometers about 90 minutes of hard walking, or 20 kilometers in my case. And the wall can come even earlier for undertrained or less experienced walkers. Your training before the race, and your pacing and fueling during the race, are the keys to "flattening the curve" so that your long-distance race paces aren't several minutes per mile slower than your 5 kilometer and 10 kilometer race paces. Your training for this range of race distances will teach your body to burn fat as a fuel preferentially over carbohydrates, which are in limited supply in your body, and the source of that nasty lactate stuff you've been reading about.

I've always been amazed that the top walkers in the world, who race 5,000m at under 6:00 per mile and 20k under 6:15 per mile, are able to race 30 to 35 kilometers at about 6:30 per mile, and 50k at 6:50 per mile—now that's a flat curve! With proper training (and pacing and fueling...) you'll be able to flatten your own curve, and push the wall to where it needs to be: somewhere beyond the finish line of your next race! The following schedules will show you exactly how to do that!

Beginners 30K/20-Mile/21-Mile/35k Training Schedule

Week	Mon.	Tues.	Wed.	Thurs.	Fri.	Sat.	Sun.
1	Off	45-minute fartlek	Moderate 30 mins.	45-minute fartlek	Off or easy cross-train	Moderate 45 mins.	Easy 6 miles (or 10k)
2	Off	45-minute fartlek	Easy 3-5 miles/5-8k	Easy 50 minutes	Off or easy cross-train	Mod. 50 mins.	Easy 9 miles (or 15k)
3	Off	10-min. warm-up, drills, then 8 x 30 sec. hill reps.	Easy 4-5 miles/6-8k	50-minute tempo	Off or easy cross-train	Mod. 60 mins.	Easy 10 miles (or16k)
4	Off	10-min. warm-up, drills, then 8 x 1:00 min. hill reps.	Easy 4-5 miles/6-8k	60-minute tempo	Off or easy cross-train	Mod. 60 mins.	Easy 11 miles (or 17.5k)
5	Off	10-min. warm-up, drills, then 8 x 1:30 hill reps.	Easy 4-5 miles/6-8k	60 minute tempo	Off or easy cross-train	Easy 60 mins.	"Not so easy" 8 miles/13k
6	Off	"" 8 x 2:00 min. hill reps.	Easy 5 miles/8k	Easy 60 minutes	Off or easy cross-train	Mod. 60 mins.	Easy 12 miles (or 19k)
7	Off	Track. 10 min. w/up then 8 laps of Turns & Straights	Easy 5 miles/8k	10k progression	Off or easy cross-train	Mod. 60 mins.	Easy 13 miles (or 21k)
8	Off	Track. 10 min. w/up then 10 laps of T&S	Easy 5 miles/8k	10-min. warm-up, drills, then 5-mile/8k tempo	Off or easy cross-train	Easy 60 mins.	"Not so easy" 10 miles/16k
9	Off	Track. 10 min. w/up then 12 laps of T&S	Easy 5 miles/8k	10-min. warm-up, drills, then 5 x 1 mile @ 10k pace w/ 3:00 rests	Off or easy cross-train	Mod. 60 mins.	Easy 14 miles (or 22.5k)
10	Off	"" 8 x 200m fast w/200m breaks	Easy 5 miles/8k	10k progression	Off or easy cross-train	Mod. 60 mins.	Easy 15 miles (or 25k)
11	Off	"" 6 x 400m @ goal race pace, w/ 200m breaks	Easy 5 miles/8k	"" 5-mile/8k tempo	Off or easy cross-train	Easy 60 mins.	"Not so easy" 10 miles/16k
12	Off	"" 10 x 200m fast w/200m breaks	Easy 5 miles/8k	"" 5 x 1 mile @ 10k pace w/ 3:00 rests	Off or easy cross-train	Mod. 60 mins.	Easy 25k (15.5 miles)
13	Off	"" 8 x 400m w/ 200m breaks	Easy 5 miles/8k	"" 3 x 1k @ 30k pace w/ 3:00 rests	Off or easy cross-train	Easy 30 mins.	**20k time-trial!**
14	Off	"" 12 x 200m fast w/200m breaks	Easy 5 miles/8k	"" 5 x 1 mile @ 10k pace w/ 3:00 rests	Off or easy cross-train	Easy 60 mins.	25k/15.5 miles progression
15	Off	"" 6 x 400m w/ 200m breaks	Easy 8k	8k tempo @ 30-35k race pace	Off or easy cross-train	Easy 30 mins.	15k with 10k easy, 5k at 30k-35k race pace
16	Off	"" 5k @ 30-35k pace	Easy 3 miles/5k	"" 3 x 1k @ 30-35k race pace w/ 1:00 rests	Off!	Wm. up then 4 x 30 sec. sprints, cool dn., stretch.	**RACE!!!**

The US 30k Racewalk Championship, the Around the Bay 30k, and the Big Sur 21-mile Power Walk, are held on Sundays, so this, and the schedules to follow, point toward a Sunday race day. The weekend long day, whether "easy" or "not so easy," needs to be easy enough for you to actually get through it! Keep track of your paces in your training log. Start very easy but progress faster as you near the end. Once you've rested up and put some carbs back into your brain, calculate your average pace for the entire workout, then start your next long day at that pace.

Intermediate 30K/20-Mile/21-Mile/35k Training Schedule

Week	Mon.	Tues.	Wed.	Thurs.	Fri.	Sat.	Sun.
1	Off or easy cross-train	45-minute fartlek	Moderate 30 mins.	45-minute fartlek	Easy 8k or cross-train	Moderate 45 mins.	Easy 13 miles (or 21k)
2	Off or easy cross-train	50-minute fartlek	Easy 3-5 miles/5-8k	Easy 50 minutes	Easy 8k or cross-train	Easy 50 mins.	"Not so easy" 9 miles/15k
3	Off or easy cross-train	60-minute fartlek	Easy 4-5 miles/6-8k	50-minute tempo	Easy 8k or cross-train	Mod. 60 mins.	Easy 14 miles (or 22.5k)
4	Off or easy cross-train	60-minute fartlek	Easy 4-5 miles/6-8k	60-minute tempo	Easy 8k or cross-train	Mod. 60 mins.	Easy 15 miles (or 24k)
5	Off or easy cross-train	60-minute progression	Easy 4-5 miles/6-8k	60 minute tempo	Easy 8k or cross-train	Mod. 60 mins.	Easy 16 miles (or 26k)
6	Off or easy cross-train	60-minute tempo	Easy 5 miles/8k	Easy 60 minutes	Easy 8k or cross-train	Easy 60 mins.	"Not so easy" 10 miles/16k
7	Off or easy cross-train	Warm-up, then 8 x 400m @ 5k pace w/ 2:00 rests	Easy 5 miles/8k	10k progression	Easy 8k or cross-train	Mod. 60 mins.	Easy 17 miles (or 27.5k)
8	Off or easy cross-train	"" 5-mile/8k tempo	Easy 5 miles/8k	"" 5-mile/8k tempo	Easy 8k or cross-train	Mod. 60 mins.	Easy 18 miles (or 29k)
9	Off or easy cross-train	"" 5-mile/8k tempo	Easy 5 miles/8k	"" 5-mile/8k tempo	Easy 8k or cross-train	Mod. 60 mins.	Easy 30k (or 18.6 miles)
10	Off or easy cross-train	"" 5-mile/8k tempo	Easy 5 miles/8k	"" 5 x 1 mile @ 10k pace w/ 3:00 rests.	Easy 8k or cross-train	Easy 60 mins.	"Not so easy" 11 miles/18k
11	Off or easy cross-train	Warm-up, then 8 x 400m @ 5k pace w/ 2:00 rests	Easy 5 miles/8k	"" 5-mile/8k tempo	Easy 8k or cross-train	Mod. 60 mins.	Easy 32k (or 20 miles)
12	Off or easy cross-train	"" 5-mile/8k tempo	Easy 5 miles/8k	"" 3 x 1 mile @ 30k pace w/ 1:00 rests.	Easy 8k or cross-train	Easy 30 mins.	**20k time trial**
13	Off or easy cross-train	Warm-up, then 8 x 400m @ 5k pace w/ 2:00 rests	Easy 5 miles/8k	"" 5-mile/8k tempo	Easy 8k or cross-train	Mod. 60 mins.	Easy 35k (or 21.7 miles)
14	Off or easy cross-train	""5-mile/8k tempo	Easy 5 miles/8k	"" 5 x 1 mile @ 10k pace w/ 3:00 rests.	Easy 8k or cross-train	Easy 60 mins.	25k/15.5 miles progression
15	Off or easy cross-train	"" 12 x 200m w/ 200m breaks	Easy 8k	8k tempo @ 30-35k race pace	Easy 8k or cross-train	Easy 30 mins.	15k with 10k easy, 5k at 30k-35k race pace
16	Off or easy cross-train	"" 5k @ 30-35k pace	Easy 3 miles/5k	"" 3 x 1k @ 30-35k race pace w/ 1:00 rests.	Off!	Wm. up then 4 x 30 sec. sprints, cool dn., stretch.	**RACE!!!**

Advanced 30K/20-Mile/21-Mile/35k Training Schedule

Week	Mon.	Tues.	Wed.	Thurs.	Fri.	Sat.	Sun.
1	Off or easy cross-train	45-minute fartlek	Moderate 30 mins.	45-minute fartlek	Easy 10k	Moderate 10k	Easy 13 miles (or 21k)
2	Off or easy cross-train	50-minute fartlek	Easy 3-5 miles/5-8k	50-minute progression	Easy 10k	Easy 10k	"Not so easy" 9 miles/15k
3	Off or easy cross-train	60-minute fartlek	Easy 4-5 miles/6-8k	45-minute tempo	Easy 12k	Moderate 10k	Easy 14 miles (or 22.5k)
4	Off or easy cross-train	60-minute fartlek	Easy 4-5 miles/6-8k	60-minute progression	Easy 12k	Moderate 10k	Easy 15 miles (or 24k)
5	Off or easy cross-train	60-minute progression	Easy 4-5 miles/6-8k	60-minute tempo	Easy 12-15k	Moderate 10k	Easy 16 miles (or 26k)
6	Off or easy cross-train	60-minute tempo	Easy 5 miles/8k	12k progression	Easy 12-15k	Easy 10k	"Not so easy" 10 miles/16k
7	Off or easy cross-train	Warm-up, then 8 x 400m @ 5k pace w/ 2:00 rests	Easy 5 miles/8k	10k tempo	Easy 12-15k	Moderate 10k	Easy 17 miles (or 27.5k)
8	Off or easy cross-train	"" 5-mile/8k tempo	Easy 5 miles/8k	12k progression	Easy 12-15k	Moderate 10k	Easy 18 miles (or 29k)
9	Off or easy cross-train	"" 5-mile/8k tempo	Easy 5 miles/8k	10k tempo	Easy 12-15k	Moderate 10k	Easy 30k (or 18.6 miles)
10	Off or easy cross-train	"" 5-mile/8k tempo	Easy 5 miles/8k	"" 5 x 2k @ 20k pace w/ mod. 500m breaks	Easy 12-15k	Easy10k	"Not so easy" 11 miles/18k
11	Off or easy cross-train	Warm-up, then 8 x 400m @ 5k pace w/ 2:00 rests	Easy 5 miles/8k	10k tempo	Easy 12-15k	Moderate 10k	Easy 32k (or 20 miles)
12	Off or easy cross-train	"" 5-mile/8k tempo	Easy 5 miles/8k	"" 4 x 1k @ 20k pace w/ mod. 500m breaks	Easy 10k	Easy 30 mins.	**20k time-trial!**
13	Off or easy cross-train	Warm-up, then 8 x 400m @ 5k pace w/ 2:00 rests	Easy 5 miles/8k	10k tempo	Easy 12-15k	Moderate 10k	Easy 35k (or 21.7 miles)
14	Off or easy cross-train	""5-mile/8k tempo	Easy 5 miles/8k	"" 6 x 2k @ 20k pace w/ mod. 500m breaks	Easy 12-15k	Moderate 10k	25k/15.5 miles progression
15	Off or easy cross-train	"" 12 x 200m w/ 200m breaks	Easy 8k	10k tempo @ 30-35k race pace	Easy 10k	Easy 30 minute	15k with 10k easy, 5k at 30–35k race pace
16	Off or easy cross-train	"" 5k @ 30-35k pace	Easy 3 miles/5k	"" 3 x 1k @ 30-35k race pace w/ 1:00 rests.	Off!	Wm. up then 4 x 30 sec. sprints, cool dn., stretch.	**RACE!!!**

As with the advanced and elite 20k schedules, I really like the Monday cross-training day for long races to be a long or very long hike. It helps build endurance, but it also helps your recovery from the long walk the day before. This should not be a racewalk or fast power walk, but a true hike. Get away from your usual training courses and just go! When in hard training I'll go at least two hours, and sometimes as long as five or six hours.

CHAPTER 21: 40K, MARATHON & 50K

The 40K has been a national championship racewalk distance in the United States since the 1930s, but it is otherwise rarely contested. Marathons, however, at 42.195 kilometers (26 miles 385 yards), a bit less than 1½ miles longer than 40k, appear on literally every continent on earth, and somewhere within each inhabited continent every weekend of the year. Many have competitive walk divisions, or are at least walker-friendly. The marathon, the classic Olympic long distance (running) race, and the 50k, the longer of the two standard Olympic and World Athletics Championships events for racewalkers, are seen by many as the pinnacles of endurance foot racing. Although the heyday of marathon walking was peaking around the time that I wrote *The Complete Guide to Marathon Walking* in the year 2000, it is still a popular pursuit among

1986 New York City Marathon elite racewalk division—one of my favorite race photos. US 50k record-holder and three-time Olympian **Curt Clausen** is 4th from the left; 1980 Olympic 50k silver medalist **Jordi Llopart** is partly obscured in front of Clausen; 3-time Olympian **Jim Heiring** towers over Llopart; 3-time Olympian (7th place in Los Angeles) **Marco Evoniuk** is to the right of Heiring in the photo; 1984 Olympic 50k silver medalist **Bo Gustafsson**, head turned and wearing a visor is at the rear of the pack; **Ann Jansson**, 1981 and 1986 World Championships silver medalist, and **Ann Peel**, 1987 Pan Am Games silver medalist and 1988 Pan Am Cup Champion, lead the pack; **the author** is to the far right in Team USA kit. Photo credit: Howard Jacobson many walkers, especially those who are fundraising for charities. *Competitive* marathon walking has lost a lot of great events over the past two decades, however. The New York City Marathon featured an elite racewalk division throughout the 1980s and 1990s. Olympic and world champion walkers were flown in from around the world, put up at the swanky meet hotel with the invited elite runners, transported to the start line on the same VIP buses and corralled in the same separate VIP staging area as the elite runners. We usually started just behind the elite female runners, or some years, we had a separate start ten minutes before the regular start. Somehow I managed to win the 1993 edition, and the giant engraved Tiffany crystal bowl that went with it, in a comparatively pedestrian time of 3:44:05. (The winning times most years were usually under 3:30.) I also have two fabulous ceramic Mickey Mouse statues for winning the racewalk divisions of the 2001 and 2002 Walt Disney World Marathons. There were also racewalk awards at the Portland, Los Angeles, Honolulu, Mardi Gras (New Orleans), Jersey Shore, and First Light (Mobile, AL) marathons, among others. Even though many of these events no longer present racewalk awards, you can walk in just about any marathon, as long as you're fast enough to come in under the time limit, which will earn you the same finisher's medal that is bestowed upon the runners. A few marathons have time limits as stringent as five hours, but the majority of the most popular marathon courses stay open for six, eight, or ten hours, or longer. For a list of walker-friendly marathons, head to: www.marathonguide.com/news/exclusives/WalkerFriendlyMarathons.cfm

Much more common in Europe, and really anywhere else in the world, opportunities to race 50 kilometers have really dropped off in recent years in the United States. Long gone are the US Olympic Festival 50k, and the John Evans 50k in Houston, TX. Even so, there are still plenty of running "ultra" races on the roads and trails that permit walkers. Some even give walk awards, judged by power walking, rather than racewalking, standards. For legitimate racewalkers there is still the US 50k Championship held every January or February, or the Olympic Trials held in Olympic years, also in January of February. In most years there will also be an open/international 50k held in conjunction with the USATF 30k and 40k Racewalk Championships, both usually held in September or October, and of course there is the We Walk! 50k (and marathon) held every September in Minnesota. For information on any of these races head to the USATF website at usatf.org/.

I think in large part due to my long-standing issues with dehydration—I sweat about 12x more than a normal person in races—I was never able to keep enough fluids down to put together a really good 50k. I made a number of international teams, but that says more about the lack of domestic depth in the event than it does about my skill at the distance. I've forever had coaches tell me I could be a great 50k walker, but … the puking. It's really, really tough to start hurling 25k into a 50k and keep going. I always had to pace my races sub-maximally. Racing a minute per mile slower than the pace charts said I was capable of was enough for me to make three World Cup teams, a couple of Pan Am Cups, and five Olympic Trials at 50k, but it's no way to make an

Olympic team. Anyway, enough about me… You're far better off taking 50k advice from someone who really *did* master the event than from me. Philip Dunn was just such a guy. He was a solid 1:26 to 1:27 20k walker, but man was he able to keep cranking out the miles in a 50k! (It's no wonder he named his son "Miles.") ☺ A three-time Olympian and Pan Am Games medalist with a personal best of 3:56:13, Philip was Mr. Consistency at the 50k during the 2000s, making every Olympic, World Championships, and World Cup team during the decade. Philip says:

> *"The 50 kilometer walk is unlike any other event in track and field. It's a constant mental battle and brutally long at 31 miles, though the best in the world are routinely able to walk the distance in under four hours. The key to walking a good 50k is superior mental and physical preparation; the two have to go hand-in-hand. When training for a 50k I would regularly walk 80-100 miles a week, training seven days a week, often doing "daily doubles" (two workouts per day). Twice a week, on Tuesdays and Thursday, I would do speed work with my coach and teammates. One of our more punishing workouts was 4 x 5 kilometers on the track at 15 to 20 seconds per km faster than race pace. 50 laps of fun! My long walk for the week usually fell on a Saturday and would range from 30 to 42 kilometers at goal race pace for 50k. One of my training secrets was a mental trick I used at the end of all my long walks. Normal people finish a long workout and think, "Oh, I'm so glad that's over; I can go drink a beer and lie down now. I don't think I could have gone another step." Well, my secret was to lie to myself. When I finished a grueling 35km workout, I would tell myself, "15km to go! I feel awesome! I can start to pick it up and finish strong!" And wouldn't you know it, on race day when I got to 35km I would hear that same voice in my head telling my how awesome I felt and how strong I would finish."*

With that terrific advice to pack away in your toolkit, a bit about the training schedules… My working title for *The Complete Guide to Marathon Walking* was *Walking a Marathon in 42,195 Easy Steps.* Okay, it was a bit tongue-in-cheek, but in reality, training to *finish* a marathon or 50k is not as difficult as some people make it out to be. In over twenty-five years of coaching thousands of walkers to complete marathons, I've never had anyone NOT finish! (50ks are another story, but we'll get to that…) When the mind is ready, the body will follow.

Obviously a big part of 40k, marathon or 50k training is the progressive build-up of a mileage base to prepare the body to race 24.8 to 31.1 miles. Certainly that would include the sixteen-week base training schedule, which should be completed before moving on to the race-specific 40k/marathon or 50k schedules. The mileage build-up is about all there is to the beginner's "Just Finish" marathon and 50k schedules. The intermediate schedules, however, introduce long sub-threshold ("long not-so-easy") days and speed work, as do the advanced schedules, albeit at a higher mileage volume. Rest is really critical for these long races, so days off, or easy recovery and/or easy cross-training days are baked into the mix. Finally, before beginning training for a marathon or 50-kilometer race, please consult with a doctor—preferably a psychiatrist. ☺

First-timers "Just Finish" Marathon Schedule							
Week	**Mon.**	**Tues.**	**Wed.**	**Thurs.**	**Fri.**	**Sat.**	**Sun.**
1	Off or easy cross-train	45-minute fartlek	Easy 3 miles	45 minutes "not so easy"	Off	Moderate 30 mins.	Easy 9 miles
2	Off or easy cross-train	45-minute fartlek	Easy 3 miles	4 miles "not so easy"	Off	Moderate 3 miles	Easy 10 miles
3	Off or easy cross-train	45-minute fartlek	Easy 3-4 miles	4 miles "not so easy"	Off	Moderate 3 miles	Easy 11 miles
4	Off or easy cross-train	45-minute fartlek	Easy 3-4 miles	5 miles "not so easy"	Off	Moderate 4 miles	Easy 10 miles
5	Off or easy cross-train	45-minute fartlek	Easy 4 miles	5 miles "not so easy"	Off	Moderate 4 miles	Easy 12 miles
6	Off or easy cross-train	45-minute fartlek	Easy 4 miles	5 miles "not so easy"	Off	Moderate 5 miles	Easy 13 miles
7	Off or easy cross-train	45-minute fartlek	Easy 4-5 miles	5 miles "not so easy"	Off	Moderate 5 miles	Easy 14 miles
8	Off or easy cross-train	45-minute fartlek	Easy 4-5 miles	5 miles "not so easy"	Off	Moderate 5 miles	Easy 12 miles
9	Off or easy cross-train	45-minute fartlek	Easy 5 miles	5 miles "not so easy"	Off	Moderate 5 miles	Easy 15 miles
10	Off or easy cross-train	45-minute fartlek	Easy 5 miles	5 miles "not so easy"	Off	Moderate 5 miles	Easy 16 miles
11	Off or easy cross-train	45-minute fartlek	Easy 5 miles	3 miles "not so easy"	Off	20-min. warm-up, then 4 x 30 seconds fast, then stretch!	**8k-10k "test race"**
12	Off or easy cross-train	45-minute fartlek	Easy 5 miles	5 miles "not so easy"	Off	Moderate 5 miles	Easy 18 miles
13	Off or easy cross-train	45-minute fartlek	Easy 5 miles	5 miles "not so easy"	Off	Moderate 5 miles	Easy 20 miles
14	Off or easy cross-train	45-minute fartlek	Easy 5 miles	5 miles "not so easy"	Off	Easy 5 miles	12 miles at goal pace
15	Off or easy cross-train	45-minute fartlek	Easy 5 miles	5 miles "not so easy"	Off	Moderate 5 miles	Easy 20 miles
16	Off or easy cross-train	45-minute fartlek	Easy 5 miles	5 miles "not so easy"	Off	Easy 5 miles	Easy 15 miles, but push last 5
17	Off or easy cross-train	45-minute fartlek	Easy 5 miles	5 miles "not so easy"	Off	Easy 5 miles	8 miles at goal pace.
18	Off	20-minute fartlek	Easy 4 miles	3-mile tempo @ marathon pace	Off	10 min. warm-up, 4 x 30 seconds fast, then stretch.	**RACE!!!**

The goal here is to build up gradually to 20 miles in training. If you can do that, you can finish a marathon! The "test race" in week 11 is a chance to test out your pre-race routine: foods, drinks, clothing, etc. Distances are in miles instead of kilometers for the marathon schedules because the vast majority of marathon courses in the US are laid out as English (26.2 miles) rather than metric (42.195 kilometers) events with mile markers, rather than kilometer markers.

Intermediate Marathon Schedule—Goal: Better Previous Best							
Week	**Mon.**	**Tues.**	**Wed.**	**Thurs.**	**Fri.**	**Sat.**	**Sun.**
1	Off or easy cross-train	45-minute fartlek	Easy 3-4 miles	4 miles at goal pace	Off or easy cross-train	Moderate 30-min.	Easy 12 miles
2	Off or easy cross-train	50-minute fartlek	Easy 3-4 miles	4 miles at goal pace	Off or easy cross-train	Easy 3 miles	10 miles at goal pace
3	Off or easy cross-train	60-minute fartlek	Easy 4-5 miles	4 miles at goal pace	Off or easy cross-train	Moderate 3 miles	Easy 13 miles
4	Off or easy cross-train	60-minute fartlek	Easy 5 miles	5 miles at goal pace	Off or easy cross-train	Easy 4 miles	10 miles at goal pace
5	Off or easy cross-train	60-minute fartlek	Easy 5 miles	5 miles at goal pace	Off or easy cross-train	Moderate 4 miles	Easy 14 miles
6	Off or easy cross-train	60-minute fartlek	Easy 5 miles	5 miles at goal pace	Off or easy cross-train	Easy 4 miles	10 miles at goal pace
7	Off or easy cross-train	60-minute fartlek	Easy 5 miles	5 miles at goal pace	Off or easy cross-train	Moderate 4 miles	Easy 15 miles
8	Off or easy cross-train	60-minute fartlek	Easy 5 miles	5 miles at goal pace	Off or easy cross-train	Easy 5 miles	12 miles at goal pace
9	Off or easy cross-train	10-min. warm-up, drills, then 8 x 30 sec. hill repeats	Easy 5 miles	5 miles at goal pace	Off or easy cross-train	Moderate 5 miles	Easy 16 miles
10	Off or easy cross-train	10-min. warm-up, drills, then 8 x 1 min. hill repeats	Easy 5 miles	5 miles at goal pace	Off or easy cross-train	Easy 5 miles	12 miles at goal pace
11	Off or easy cross-train	10-min. warm-up, drills, then 8 x 90 sec. hill repeats	Easy 5 miles	5 miles at goal pace	Off or easy cross-train	Moderate 5 miles	18 miles
12	Off or easy cross-train	Wm. up, drills, then 12 x 200m fast w/ 200m breaks	Easy 5 miles	5 miles at goal pace	Off or easy cross-train	Easy 5 miles	12 miles at goal pace
13	Off or easy cross-train	60-minute fartlek	Easy 5 miles	5 miles at goal pace	Off or easy cross-train	Moderate 5 miles	Easy 20 miles
14	Off or easy cross-train	"" 12 x 200m fast w/ 200m breaks	Easy 5 miles	5 miles at goal pace	Off or easy cross-train	Easy 5 miles	12 miles at goal pace
15	Off or easy cross-train	60-minute fartlek	Easy 5 miles	5 miles at goal pace	Off or easy cross-train	Moderate 5 miles	Easy 20 miles
16	Off or easy cross-train	"" 8 x 400m @ 5k pace w/ 200m breaks	Easy 5 miles	5 miles at goal pace	Off or easy cross-train	Easy 5 miles	Easy 10 miles, then 5 at goal
17	Off or easy cross-train	45-minute fartlek	Easy 5 miles	5 miles at goal pace	Off or easy cross-train	Easy 5 miles	8 miles at goal pace
18	Off	20-minute fartlek	Easy 4 miles	3 miles at goal pace	Off	10 min. warm-up, 4 x 30 seconds fast, then stretch.	**RACE!!!**

The Intermediate Marathon Schedule is for any walker hoping to better a previous best marathon time. With that in mind, there is more speed and tempo training than in the beginner schedule, but of course the main focus is still on building endurance to get through the distance.

Advanced Marathon Schedule

Week	Mon.	Tues.	Wed.	Thurs.	Fri.	Sat.	Sun.
1	Off or easy cross-train	45-minute fartlek	Easy 6 miles	Moderate 5 miles	Easy 6 miles	Moderate 5 miles	Easy 16 miles
2	Off or easy cross-train	50-minute fartlek	Easy 6 miles	Moderate 5 miles	Easy 6 miles	Easy 5 miles	12 miles "not-so-easy"
3	Off or easy cross-train	60-minute fartlek	Easy 6 miles	Moderate 5 miles	Easy 6 miles	Moderate 5 miles	Easy 17 miles
4	Off or easy cross-train	60-minute fartlek	Easy 6 miles	5 miles at goal pace	Easy 6 miles	Easy 5 miles	12 miles "not-so-easy"
5	Off or easy cross-train	60-minute fartlek	Easy 6 miles	Warm-up, drills, then 8 x 1k @ 20k pace w/ mod. 200m breaks	Easy 6 miles	Moderate 6 miles	Easy 18 miles
6	Off or easy cross-train	60-minute fartlek	Easy 6 miles	6-mile progression	Easy 6 miles	Easy 6 miles	12 miles "not-so-easy"
7	Off or easy cross-train	60-minute fartlek	Easy 6 miles	"" 5 x 1 mile @ 20k pace w/ mod. 400m breaks	Easy 6 miles	Moderate 6 miles	Easy 19 miles
8	Off or easy cross-train	60-minute fartlek	Easy 6 miles	6-miles tempo	Easy 6 miles	Easy 6 miles	15 miles "not-so-easy"
9	Off or easy cross-train	10-min. warm-up, drills, then 8 x 30 sec. hill repeats	Easy 6 miles	""4 x 2k @ 20k pace w/ 500m mod. breaks	Easy 6 miles	Moderate 6 miles	Easy 20 miles
10	Off or easy cross-train	10-min. warm-up, drills, then 8 x 1 min. hill repeats	Easy 6 miles	6 miles at goal pace	Easy 6 miles	Easy 6 miles	15 miles at goal pace
11	Off or easy cross-train	10-min. warm-up, drills, then 8 x 90 sec. hill repeats	Easy 6 miles	""3 x 3k @ 20k pace w/ 500m mod. breaks	Easy 6 miles	Easy 5 miles	20 miles—push last 5
12	Off or easy cross-train	Wm. up, drills, then 12 x 200m fast w/ 200m breaks	Easy 6 miles	6 miles at goal pace	Easy 6 miles	Easy 5 miles	15 miles at goal pace
13	Off or easy cross-train	60-minute fartlek	Easy 6 miles	""6 x 1 mile @ 20k pace w/ 400m mod. breaks	Easy 6 miles	Moderate 5 miles	Easy 22 miles
14	Off or easy cross-train	Wm. up, drills, then 12 x 200m fast w/ 200m breaks	Easy 6 miles	6 miles at goal pace	Easy 6 miles	Easy 5 miles	15 miles at goal pace
15	Off or easy cross-train	60-minute fartlek	Easy 6 miles	""5 x 2k @ 20k pace w/ 500m mod. breaks	Easy 6 miles	Moderate 5 miles	22 miles—push last 5
16	Off or easy cross-train	Wm. up, drills, then 8 x 400m @ 5k pace w/ 200m breaks	Easy 6 miles	6 miles at goal pace	Easy 6 miles	Easy 5 miles	Easy 10 miles, then 5 at goal
17	Off or easy cross-train	45-minute fartlek	Easy 6 miles	5 miles at goal pace	Off or easy cross-train	Easy 5 miles	8 miles at goal pace
18	Off	4 miles at goal pace	Easy 4 miles	""2 x 1 mile @ goal pace w/ 400m mod. break	Off	10 min. warm-up, 4 x 30 seconds fast, then stretch.	**RACE!!!**

Although most advanced long-distance racewalkers will only do marathons as training opportunities for 50k races, there are plenty of advanced power walkers who do marathons, and of course the marathon is a championship and record-eligible distance for Nordic walkers. There is more total volume, and more, and longer, long days than in the intermediate schedule, but otherwise it follows the same basic pattern.

Beginners 50k Training Schedule

Week	Mon.	Tues.	Wed.	Thurs.	Fri.	Sat.	Sun.
1	Off, hike or easy cross-train	45-minute fartlek	Easy 6-8 km	45 minutes "not so easy"	Off	Moderate 30 mins.	Easy 15k
2	Off, hike or easy cross-train	45-minute fartlek	Easy 6-8 km	6k "not so easy"	Off	Moderate 3 miles	Easy 16k
3	Off, hike or easy cross-train	45-minute fartlek	Easy 6-8 km	6k "not so easy"	Off	Moderate 3 miles	Easy 17k
4	Off, hike or easy cross-train	45-minute fartlek	Easy 8k	8k "not so easy"	Off	Moderate 4 miles	Easy 16k
5	Off, hike or easy cross-train	45-minute fartlek	Easy 8k	8k "not so easy"	Off	Moderate 4 miles	Easy 20k
6	Off, hike or easy cross-train	45-minute fartlek	Easy 8k	8k "not so easy"	Off	Moderate 5 miles	Easy 21k
7	Off, hike or easy cross-train	45-minute fartlek	Easy 8k	8k "not so easy"	Off	Moderate 5 miles	Easy 23k
8	Off, hike or easy cross-train	45-minute fartlek	Easy 8k	8k "not so easy"	Off	Moderate 5 miles	Easy 20k
9	Off, hike or easy cross-train	45-minute fartlek	Easy 8k	8k "not so easy"	Off	Moderate 5 miles	Easy 25k
10	Off, hike or easy cross-train	45-minute fartlek	Easy 8k	8k "not so easy"	Off	Moderate 5 miles	Easy 28k
11	Off, hike or easy cross-train	45-minute fartlek	Easy 8k	5k "not so easy"	Off	20-min. w/up, 4 x 30 secs. fast, then stretch!	**8k-10k "test race"**
12	Off, hike or easy cross-train	45-minute fartlek	Easy 8k	8k "not so easy"	Off	Moderate 5 miles	Easy 30k
13	Off, hike or easy cross-train	45-minute fartlek	Easy 8k	8k "not so easy"	Off	Moderate 5 miles	Easy 32k
14	Off, hike or easy cross-train	45-minute fartlek	Easy 8k	8k "not so easy"	Off	Easy 5 miles	Easy 25k, push last 8k
15	Off, hike or easy cross-train	45-minute fartlek	Easy 8k	8k "not so easy"	Off	Easy 5 miles	Easy 35k
16	Off, hike or easy cross-train	45-minute fartlek	Easy 8k	8k "not so easy"	Off	Easy 5 miles	Easy 25k, push last 8k
17	Off, hike or easy cross-train	45-minute fartlek	Easy 8k	8k "not so easy"	Off	Moderate 5 miles	Easy 35k
18	Off, hike or easy cross-train	45-minute fartlek	Easy 8k	8k "not so easy"	Off	Easy 5 miles	Easy 25k, push last 8k
19	Off, hike or easy cross-train	45-minute fartlek	Easy 8k	8k "not so easy"	Off	Easy 5 miles	15k at goal pace
20	Off	20-minute fartlek	Easy 6k	6k tempo @ 50k race pace	Off	10 min. w/up, 4 x 30 secs. fast, then stretch!	**RACE!!!**

Beginners should not do 50k races! I recommend training for and racing many shorter distance races for at least two years before jumping up to a 50k. But if you're a beginner and want to walk a 50, this schedule will ensure you're well prepared. You'll notice a return to kilometer distances since most 50k walking races, other than some ultra-running races with walk divisions, are measured in kilometers. Most 50k race walks are held on short loop courses, between 1 kilometer and 2 kilometers in length. Otherwise the pattern is similar to the marathon schedules, albeit with somewhat longer long days.

Intermediate 50k Training Schedule

Week	Mon.	Tues.	Wed.	Thurs.	Fri.	Sat.	Sun.
1	Long hike or easy cross-train	45-minute fartlek	Easy 5-6k	6k at goal pace	Off or easy cross-train	Moderate 30-min.	Easy 20k
2	Long hike or easy cross-train	50-minute fartlek	Easy 5-6k	6k at goal pace	Off or easy cross-train	Easy 5k	Easy 22k
3	Long hike or easy cross-train	60-minute fartlek	Easy 6-8k	6k at goal pace	Off or easy cross-train	Moderate 5k	Easy 24k
4	Long hike or easy cross-train	60-minute fartlek	Easy 8k	8k at goal pace	Off or easy cross-train	Easy 6k	16k at goal pace
5	Long hike or easy cross-train	60-minute fartlek	Easy 8k	8k at goal pace	Off or easy cross-train	Moderate 6k	Easy 26k
6	Long hike or easy cross-train	60-minute fartlek	Easy 8k	8k at goal pace	Off or easy cross-train	Easy 6k	18k at goal pace
7	Long hike or easy cross-train	60-minute fartlek	Easy 8k	8k at goal pace	Off or easy cross-train	Moderate 6k	Easy 28k
8	Long hike or easy cross-train	60-minute fartlek	Easy 8k	8k at goal pace	Off or easy cross-train	Easy 8k	20k at goal pace
9	Long hike or easy cross-train	60-minute fartlek	Easy 8k	8k at goal pace	Off or easy cross-train	Moderate 8k	Easy 30k
10	Long hike or easy cross-train	60-minute fartlek	Easy 8k	8k at goal pace	Off or easy cross-train	Easy 8k	20k at goal pace
11	Long hike or easy cross-train	60-minute fartlek	Easy 8k	8k at goal pace	Off or easy cross-train	Moderate 8k	Easy 32k
12	Long hike or easy cross-train	Wm. Up, drills, 12 x 200m fast w/ 200m breaks	Easy 8k	8k at goal pace	Off or easy cross-train	Easy 8k	25k at goal pace
13	Long hike or easy cross-train	60-minute fartlek	Easy 8k	8k at goal pace	Off or easy cross-train	Moderate 8k	Easy 35k
14	Long hike or easy cross-train	"" 12 x 200m fast w/ 200m breaks	Easy 8k	8k at goal pace	Off or easy cross-train	Easy 8k	20k at goal pace
15	Long hike or easy cross-train	60-minute fartlek	Easy 8k	8k at goal pace	Off or easy cross-train	Moderate 8k	**EASY 40k or marathon**
16	Long hike or easy cross-train	"" 8 x 400m @ 5k pace w/ 200m breaks	Easy 8k	8k at goal pace	Off or easy cross-train	Easy 8k	Easy 16k, then 8k at goal
17	Long hike or easy cross-train	45-minute fartlek	Easy 8k	8k at goal pace	Off or easy cross-train	Easy 8k	15k at goal pace
18	Off	20-minute fartlek	Easy 6k	6k at goal pace	Off	10 min. warm-up, 4 x 30 seconds fast, then stretch	**RACE!!!**

I've put in an easy 40k (24.8 miles) workout or marathon race three weeks before race day. If you have a local marathon within 3-6 weeks of your 50k, it's a great training opportunity—just don't push too hard! Backing off as little as 30 seconds to one minute per mile from 50k race pace will make recovery much, much easier than pushing all-out in the marathon. That will be enough if the race is four to six weeks before, but if you put the 40k three weeks before your goal 50k race, be sure to take it very easy—1:30 to 2:00 minutes per mile slower than your 50k race pace.

Advanced 50K Training Schedule

Week	Mon.	Tues.	Wed.	Thurs.	Fri.	Sat.	Sun.
1	Long hike or easy cross-train	45-minute fartlek	Easy 10k	Moderate 8k	Easy 10k	Moderate 5 miles	Easy 25k
2	Long hike or easy cross-train	50-minute fartlek	Easy 10k	Moderate 8k	Easy 10k	Easy 5 miles	20k "not-so-easy"
3	Long hike or easy cross-train	60-minute fartlek	Easy 10k	Moderate 8k	Easy 10k	Moderate 8k	Easy 27k
4	Long hike or easy cross-train	60-minute fartlek	Easy 10k-15k	8k at goal pace	Easy 10k-15k	Easy 8k	20k "not-so-easy"
5	Long hike or easy cross-train	60-minute fartlek	Easy 10k-15k	Warm-up, drills, then 8 x 1k @ 20k pace w/ mod. 200m breaks	Easy 10k-15k	Moderate 10k	Easy 30k
6	Long hike or easy cross-train	60-minute fartlek	Easy 10k-15k	10k progression	Easy 10k-15k	Easy 10k	20k "not-so-easy"
7	Long hike or easy cross-train	60-minute fartlek	Easy 10k-15k	"" 5 x 1 mile @ 20k pace w/ mod. 400m breaks	Easy 10k-15k	Moderate 10k	Easy 32k
8	Long hike or easy cross-train	60-minute fartlek	Easy 10k-15k	10k tempo	Easy 10k-15k	Easy 10k	25k "not-so-easy"
9	Long hike or easy cross-train	60-minute fartlek	Easy 10k-15k	""4 x 2k @ 20k pace w/ 500m mod. breaks	Easy 10k-15k	Moderate 10k	Easy 35k
10	Long hike or easy cross-train	60-minute fartlek	Easy 10k-15k	10k at goal pace	Easy 10k-15k	Easy 10k	25k at goal pace
11	Long hike or easy cross-train	60-minute fartlek	Easy 10k-15k	""3 x 3k @ 20k pace w/ 500m mod. breaks	Easy 10k-15k	Easy 8k	35k—push last 8k
12	Long hike or easy cross-train	Wm. Up, drills, 12 x 200m fast w/ 200m breaks	Easy 10k-15k	10k at goal pace	Easy 10k-15k	Easy 8k	25k at goal pace
13	Long hike or easy cross-train	60-minute fartlek	Easy 10k-15k	""6 x 1 mile @ 20k pace w/ 400m mod. breaks	Easy 10k-15k	Easy 6k	**"Easyish" 40k (or marathon)**
14	Long hike or easy cross-train	"" 12 x 200m fast w/ 200m breaks	Easy 10k-15k	10k at goal pace	Easy 10k-15k	Easy 8k	25k at goal pace
15	Long hike or easy cross-train	60-minute fartlek	Easy 10k-15k	""5 x 2k @ 20k pace w/ 500m mod. breaks	Easy 10k-15k	Easy 8k	35k—push last 8k
16	Long hike or easy cross-train	"" 8 x 400m @ 5k pace w/ 200m breaks	Easy 10k-15k	10k at goal pace	Easy 10k-15k	Easy 8k	Easy 17k, then 8k at goal
17	Long hike or easy cross-train	45-minute fartlek	Easy 10k	8k at goal pace	Off	Easy 8k	15k at goal pace
18	Off	20-minute fartlek	Easy 6k	6k at goal pace	Off	10 min. warm-up, 4 x 30 seconds fast, then stretch.	**RACE!!!**

As in the advanced 30 to 35k schedule, I really like the Monday cross-training day to be a long hike. It helps build endurance, but also helps your recovery from the long walk the day before. This should not be a racewalk or fast power walk, but a true hike. Get away from your usual training courses and just go! When in hard training I'll go at least two hours, and sometimes as long as five or six.

Elite 50K Training Schedule							
Week	**Mon.**	**Tues.**	**Wed.**	**Thurs.**	**Fri.**	**Sat.**	**Sun.**
1	Long hike or easy cross-train	45-minute fartlek	Easy 15k	Warm-up, drills, then 4 x 3k @ 20k pace w/ mod. 200m breaks	Easy 15k	Moderate 5 miles	Easy 25k
2	Long hike or easy cross-train	50-minute fartlek	Easy 15k	10k at goal pace	Easy 15k	Easy 5 miles	20k "not-so-easy"
3	Long hike or easy cross-train	60-minute fartlek	Easy 15-20k	"" 8 x 1 mile @ 20k pace w/ mod. 400m breaks	Easy 15-20k	Moderate 8k	Easy 27k
4	Long hike or easy cross-train	5k wm, up, drills, 12 x 200m fast w/ 200m breaks	Easy 15-20k	10k at goal pace	Easy 15-20k	Easy 8k	20k "not-so-easy"
5	Long hike or easy cross-train	60-minute fartlek	Easy 15-20k	""7 x 2k @ 20k pace w/ 500m mod. breaks	Easy 15-20k	Moderate 10k	Easy 30k
6	Long hike or easy cross-train	"" 4 x {100m, 200m, 300m} w/ 100m breaks	Easy 15-20k	10k at goal pace	Easy 15-20k	Easy 10k	20k "not-so-easy"
7	Long hike or easy cross-train	60-minute fartlek	Easy 15-20k	""5 x 3k @ 20k pace w/ 500m mod. breaks	Easy 15-20k	Moderate 10k	Easy 30k
8	Long hike or easy cross-train	"" 8 x 400m @ 5k pace w/ 200m breaks	Easy 15-20k	10k at goal pace	Easy 15-20k	Easy 10k	25k "not-so-easy"
9	Long hike or easy cross-train	60-minute fartlek	Easy 15-20k	""3 x 5k @ 20k pace w/ 1k mod. Breaks	Easy 15-20k	Moderate 10k	Easy 32k
10	Long hike or easy cross-train	"" 12 x 200m fast w/ 200m breaks	Easy 15-20k	10k at goal pace	Easy 15-20k	Easy 10k	25k at goal pace
11	Long hike or easy cross-train	60-minute fartlek	Easy 15-20k	""8 x 2k @ 20k pace w/ 500m mod. breaks	Easy 15-20k	Easy 8k	35k—push last 8k
12	Long hike or easy cross-train	"" 5 x {100m, 200m, 300m} w/ 100m breaks	Easy 15-20k	10k at goal pace	Easy 15-20k	Easy 8k	30k at goal pace
13	Long hike or easy cross-train	60-minute fartlek	Easy 15-20k	""6 x 3k @ 20k pace w/ 500m mod. breaks	Easy 15-20k	Easy 6k	**Easy 40k (or marathon)**
14	Long hike or easy cross-train	"" 8 x 400m @ 5k pace w/ 200m breaks	Easy 15-20k	10k at goal pace	Easy 15-20k	Easy 8k	30k at goal pace
15	Long hike or easy cross-train	60-minute fartlek	Easy 15-20k	""4 x 5k @ 20k pace w/ 500m mod. breaks	Easy 15-20k	Easy 8k	35k—push last 8k
16	Long hike or easy cross-train	"" 12 x 200m fast w/ 200m breaks	Easy 15-20k	10k at goal pace	Easy 15-20k	Easy 8k	Easy 17k, then 8k at goal
17	Long hike or easy cross-train	45-minute fartlek	Easy 15k	""4 x 2k @ 20k pace w/ 500m mod. breaks	Off	Easy 8k	15k at goal pace
18	Off	20-minute fartlek	Easy 6k	6k at goal pace	Off	10 min. warm-up, 4 x 30 seconds fast, then stretch.	**RACE!!!**

The above schedule averages about 65 to 70 miles per week. I'm a bit limited by the teeny, tiny boxes so it's not written in, but most days can/should be double workout days. Adding an additional 8k/5-mile workout five days per week can bump that closer to 100mpw. These should always be very easy miles.

CHAPTER 22: ULTRA RACES: 50 MILES – 100 MILES/24 HOURS

For some walkers, a 26.2-mile marathon is just a warm-up, and a 50k is a sprint. To ultra-walkers, "real" racing starts at 50 miles, and the classic race distance is 100 miles. In Nordic walking, world records are kept at 50 miles, 100 kilometers, 100 miles, 12 hours and 24 hours. There are also multi-day Nordic walking races at 500 kilometers, 500 miles, 1,000 kilometers, 1,000 miles, 48 hours, and six-days.

Although not technically racing, on February 9th, 1963, Attorney General of the United States, Robert Kennedy, accepted a challenge from his brother, President Kennedy, to walk 50 miles in one day. At 5:00am he set out on his march along the C&O Canal towpath from Great Falls, VA to Harper's Ferry, WV, with four of his aides and his 100+ lb. Newfoundland, Brumus. Two of his colleagues called it a day at 25 miles, and by 35 miles all but Kennedy had packed it in. To the last of his aides to drop off, Kennedy said: "You're lucky your brother isn't president of the United States!" (Presumably meaning that he, himself, didn't have the luxury of quitting…)

Bobby Kennedy and Brumus taking a break from their 50-mile walk.

Kennedy's march started a fad resulting in thousands of people completing 50-mile walks in the US and abroad during the early 1960s. Many "Kennedy Marches" became annual events. The JFK 50 Mile in Washington County, MD, has been held every year since the spring of 1963, as has the Kennedy-Mars (March) Sittard in Sittard, Netherlands, which attracts several thousand walkers every year. Most Kennedy Marches are Saturday events—some starting as early as 3:00am on Saturday, but still, Saturday—so the training schedule will reflect that. Moving up in distance, the IAAF (now WA) has recognized 100 kilometers as a record-eligible racewalking distance since 1991. Dan Pierce, an old training partner of mine, and a solid but not stellar 50k walker, knocked his only attempt at 100k out of the park, walking 9:36:33—the equivalent of two consecutive 4:48:16 50ks! Even more astounding, another old friend, Viktor Ginko from Belarus, walked 8:38:07 for 100km in 2002—that's two 4:19 50ks! 100k is also a Nordic walking record-eligible event, as is the 12-hour event, which is at the highest level, close to the same thing. (The 100k Nordic walking world record is 12:50:38.) Having said all that... 100k and 12-hour walking races are almost non-existent, and when they are held they are very small events specifically set up to break the world or American record. Training for such an event would have to be tailored specifically to that athlete for that event,[58] so I have not included specific 100k or 12-hour schedules here, but have combined them with the 50-mile schedule.

As mentioned in Chapter 15, "Centurion" is the moniker applied to the rare endurance walker who has completed 100 miles in less than 24 hours. As of this writing, there are only 94 US Centurions—athletes from any country who have walked 100 miles under 24 hours on US soil. (And only 61 of the "US Centurions" are US citizens.) It's a short list considering that the US Centurion rolls date all the way back to 1878. There are a whopping 1,211 British Centurions, but it's not a fair comparison since they had a head start on us, as J. E. Fowler-Dixon received Centurion Badge "C1" a year earlier, in 1877. ☺ The "Continental" Centurion Club, based in the Netherlands, has 486 members; there are 80 Australian Centurions; 39 African Centurions; 27 New Zealand Centurions; and 40 Malaysian Centurions, although they haven't held an event since 2007. So there you have it. In 143 years fewer than 2,000 walkers worldwide have achieved Centurion status. Want to join this illustrious group? Read on to find out how to train for a 24-hour or 100-mile race! Not quite ready? The 24-Hour schedule is also appropriate for races as "short" as the 85-mile "Parish Walk" on the UK's Isle of Man, and if you're feeling a bit more ambitious, as long as 28-hour races like "Les 28 Heures de Roubaix" held every September in Roubaix, France. Roubaix has been held every year since 1954—even in 2020 when most other races worldwide were cancelled due to Covid-19. Roubaix is a qualifier for Paris-to-Alsace (Chapter 23), so I imagine there was some added pressure to keep the streak going. The race starts with an 18.5-kilometer tour of Roubaix, ending at Barbiex Park where competitors walk repeated 1.982-kilometer loops in the park. The loop encompasses a 400-meter track where lap-counters, aid tables, and tents are set up. It's an excellent venue for a (very!) long walk in le parc! Unlike the multi-loop Roubaix race, the Parish Walk is a single 85-mile loop, which traverses each of the Isle's 17 parishes. The storied race traces its roots back to 1853, and in its current form, to 1913. For many years participants were required to touch the front door of each of the seventeen parish churches to be recorded, but in the modern age the race is chip timed. Ok, enough yammering... On to the schedules!

[58] I know a guy who does that sort of thing... https://racewalking.org/coaching.html

First-Timers 50-Mile/12-Hour/100k Training Schedule

Week	Mon.	Tues.	Wed.	Thurs.	Fri.	Sat.	Sun.
1	Off or very easy cross-train	Moderate 5 miles	Easy 6 miles	Moderate 5 miles	Off	Mod. 3-6 miles	3 hours. Don't worry about the pace!!!
2	Off or very easy cross-train	Moderate 5 miles	Easy 6 miles	Moderate 5 miles	Off	Mod. 3-6 miles	3.5 hours. Don't worry about the pace!!!
3	Off or very easy cross-train	Moderate 5 miles	Easy 6 miles	Moderate 5 miles	Off	Mod. 3-6 miles	4 hours. Don't worry about the pace!!!
4	Off or very easy cross-train	5 miles	Easy 6-10 miles	5-mile progression	Off	Mod. 3-6 miles	3 hours. Don't worry about the pace!!!
5	Off or very easy cross-train	5 miles	Easy 6-10 miles	5-mile progression	Off	Mod. 3-6 miles	4.5 hours. Don't worry about the pace!!!
6	Off or very easy cross-train	5 miles	Easy 6-10 miles	5-mile progression	Off	Mod. 3-6 miles	5 hours. Don't worry about the pace!!!
7	Off or very easy cross-train	5 miles	Easy 6-10 miles	5-mile progression	Off	Mod. 3-6 miles	5.5 hours. Don't worry about the pace!!!
8	Off or very easy cross-train	5 miles	Easy 6-10 miles	5-mile progression	Off	Mod. 3-6 miles	20 miles at goal pace
9	Off or very easy cross-train	5 miles	Easy 6-10 miles	5-mile progression	Off	Mod. 3-6 miles	6 hours. Don't worry about the pace!!!
10	Off or very easy cross-train	5 miles	Easy 6-10 miles	5-mile progression	Off	Mod. 3-6 miles	22 miles at goal pace
11	Off or very easy cross-train	5 miles	Easy 6-10 miles	5-mile progression	Off	Mod. 3-6 miles	6.5 hours. Don't worry about the pace!!!
12	Off or very easy cross-train	Easy 5 miles	Easy 6-10 miles	5-mile progression	Off	Mod. 3-6 miles	24 miles at goal pace
13	Off or very easy cross-train	Easy 5 miles	Easy 6-10 miles	5-mile progression	Off	Mod. 3-6 miles	7 hours. Don't worry about the pace!!!
14	Off or very easy cross-train	Easy 5 miles	Easy 6-10 miles	5-mile progression	Off	Mod. 3-6 miles	"Fun" marathon or 25 miles at goal pace.
15	Off or very easy cross-train	Easy 5 miles	Easy 6-10 miles	5-mile progression	Off	Mod. 3-6 miles	7.5 hours. Don't worry about the pace!!!
16	Off or very easy cross-train	Easy 5 miles	Easy 8 miles	5-mile progression	Off	Mod. 3-6 miles	25 miles. Any pace is fine. Goal would be nice, but do it to finish—at any pace.
17	Off or very easy cross-train	Easy 5 miles	Easy 10 miles	5-mile progression	Off	Mod. 3-6 miles	8 hours. Don't worry about the pace!!!
18	Off or very easy cross-train	Easy 5 miles	Easy 5-10 miles	5-mile progression	Off	Mod. 3-6 miles	Last-chance EASY 6 hours. Any pace is fine. Practice drinking/eating on the go.
19	Off or very easy cross-train	Easy 5 miles	Easy 5-10 miles	5-mile progression	Off	Mod. 3 miles	12.5 miles at goal 50-mile/100k race pace
20	Off or very easy cross-train	Easy 5 miles	Easy 3-mile progression	Easy 3 miles, then stretch	Off	**RACE!!!**	Sleep! ☺

50-milers are tricky. At half the distance of a hundred-miler you would be forgiven for thinking your pace will be considerably faster than it would be in a century race, but at more than 50% longer than a 50k, you'll be much slower than you would be in a race of "only" 31 miles. The pace will be very easy for you; it's a matter of sustaining it, and sustaining your energy, for the better part of a day. The same thing goes for 12-hour and 100k races. Pay close attention to your food and drink. Write everything down during training to confirm what works for you. You only have one shot to get it right on race day!

100 Miles in 24 Hours Centurion Qualifying Schedule							
Week	**Mon.**	**Tues.**	**Wed.**	**Thurs.**	**Fri.**	**Sat.**	**Sun.**
1	Off or very easy cross-train	Moderat e 5 miles	Easy 6 miles	Moderate 5 miles	Off	Easy 3 hours. Don't worry about the pace!!!	Easy 12 miles
2	Off or very easy cross-train	Moderat e 5 miles	Easy 6 miles	Moderate 5 miles	Off	Easy 3½ hours. Don't worry about the pace!!!	12 miles at goal pace.
3	Off or very easy cross-train	Moderat e 5 miles	Easy 6 miles	Moderate 5 miles	Off	Easy 4 hours. Don't worry about the pace!!!	15 miles at goal pace
4	Off or very easy cross-train	5 miles	Easy 6-10 miles	5-mile progression	Off	20 miles at goal pace	Very easy 3 miles
5	Off or very easy cross-train	5 miles	Easy 6-10 miles	5-mile progression	Off	Easy 4.5 hours. Don't worry about the pace!!!	15 miles at goal pace
6	Off or very easy cross-train	5 miles	Easy 6-10 miles	5-mile progression	Off	Easy 5 hours. Don't worry about the pace!!!	20 miles at goal pace.
7	Off or very easy cross-train	5 miles	Easy 6-10 miles	5-mile progression	Off	25 miles at goal pace	Very easy 3 miles
8	Off or very easy cross-train	5 miles	Easy 6-10 miles	5-mile progression	Off	Easy 5.5 hours. Don't worry about the pace!!!	20 miles at goal pace.
9	Off or very easy cross-train	5 miles	Easy 6-10 miles	5-mile progression	Off	25 miles at goal pace	Very easy 3 miles
10	Off or very easy cross-train	5 miles	Easy 6-10 miles	5-mile progression	Off	Easy 6 hours. Don't worry about the pace!!!	20 miles at goal pace.
11	OFF!!!	5 miles	Easy 6-10 miles	5-mile progression	Off	25 miles at goal pace	Very easy 5 miles
12	Off or very easy cross-train	Easy 5 miles	Easy 6-10 miles	5-mile progression	Off	Easy 6.5 hours. Don't worry about the pace!!!	20 miles at goal pace.
13	OFF!!!	Easy 5 miles	Easy 6-10 miles	5-mile progression	Off	25 miles at goal pace	Very easy 6 miles
14	Off or very easy cross-train	Easy 5 miles	Easy 6-10 miles	5-mile progression	Off	Easy 7 hours. Don't worry about the pace!!!	Easy 5 miles
15	Off or very easy cross-train	Easy 5 miles	Easy 6-10 miles	5-mile progression	Off	25 miles at goal pace.	Easy 5 miles
16	Off or very easy cross-train	Easy 5 miles	Easy 8 miles	5-mile progression	Off	Easy 7.5 hours. Don't worry about the pace!!!	Easy 10 miles
17	Off or very easy cross-train	Easy 5 miles	Easy 10 miles	5-mile progression	Off	25 miles at goal pace	Easy 10 miles
18	Off or very easy cross-train	Easy 5 miles	Easy 5-10 miles	5-mile progression	Off	Last-chance EASY 8 hours. Any pace is fine. Practice drinking/eating on the go.	Easy 5 miles
19	Off or very easy cross-train	Easy 5 miles	Easy 5-10 miles	5-mile progression	Off	Easy 8 miles	Easy 5 miles
20	Off or very easy cross-train	Easy 3 miles	Off!	Easy 3 miles, then stretch	Sleep! ☺	**RACE!!!**	

I really believe that for races of 100 miles and longer, the specific details of the training schedule are less important than your mindset, and your fueling. That's certainly not to say that training plays no role. Of course it does! But there are diminishing returns after the first 20 to 25 miles or so of a training walk. Just as most marathoners don't do more than 20, or at most 22 miles in training, and most 50k walkers don't do more than 35k (21.7 miles), or at most, an occasional 40k (24.8 miles), prospective 100-mile (and longer!) walkers certainly don't do 100-mile workouts, or anything even close to it. In general, a solid 50k training schedule will get you more or less *physically* ready for a 100-miler. Ah, but the mental side… You will probably want to go somewhat longer than 35 or 40k for your long day, but walking 50- or 75-milers is neither practical nor necessary! 30 miles or 50k is sufficient to get yourself physically ready to race, but if it's your first 100-miler, I think a few 8-hour walks at your goal race pace or faster are necessary to mentally prepare yourself to walk a sub-24-hour 100, as well as to sort out your hydration and fueling. Having said that, I did a *50-mile* walk before my failed Centurion attempt. I'm convinced now that it probably did more harm than good to walk so far in training, especially given the pace. It wasn't that it wore me out for the race—I recovered very well and quickly from the workout. It's that it gave me the *over*-confidence to think I could walk a sub-19-hour 100-miler because I was able to do 50 miles in under 9½ hours in training. On race day I attacked the first eight hours despite very hot weather and paid the price in the second half.

Assuming your goal is 100 miles in 24 hours, goal pace is only 14:24 per mile/~8:56/km. You should do a lot of your training at, and faster than that pace. If at all possible, your training should take place at all hours, including at night. Long easy workouts will be an opportunity to test out different feeding/drinking strategies. Keeping fueled will be critical if you hope to walk for 24 hours straight. According to Rob Robertson, hands-down the most prolific Centurion in America in this era:

"My best Centurion walks were when I trained 56 miles per week. One 28-mile [45 kilometers] day on Sundays, a twelve-mile day on Wednesday, and four miles every other day of the week except Friday, which I took off. I made a point to always walk sub-twelve-minute miles. I did not need the speed for a Centurion. By making the training hard and fast (by my standard!) a Centurion pace of 13:50 felt easy. I wanted my Centurion race to feel easy for as long as possible. I never cut training and never cut mileage. The reward was to finish. The same with a Centurion race. The mindset was never stop,

Rob Robertson's British, US, Continental, Australian, African and New Zealand Centurion badges.

always finish. As to diet, I ate a whole food diet. Absolutely no sugar. I trained my body to burn fat. Then during a race I ate sweets. They were like high-octane fuel. In several Centurion races, Coke got me to the finish line!"

Adding to Rob's tips, here is some additional advice from the Australian Centurion Club:

> *"...it is really a question of consistent daily training, previous experience, common sense and guts. From a time and distance standpoint, training is similar to that of a 50k walker..., which includes a weekly long walk (in the region of 3-4 hours). With such a preparation behind you, you are well on the way to completing a 100 miler. All you have to do is add a couple of very long walks (nice slow pace and make a day of it...) of at least 8 hours to really prepare the body for the event."*

I've included just such a plan in the Centurion Qualifying training schedule, so we're good there, but at least as important as the actual training for the event are the logistical preparations. It is absolutely imperative in a long race to have someone competent and clear-headed manning your aid table through the day and night. It's simply not possible to think clearly when carb-depleted. (Yes, I'm speaking from experience!) It's critical to have someone in your corner who will be able to do the thinking for you, making sure you stick to your pacing and drinking/fueling plan, or advise you on how to sensibly deviate from it if conditions warrant. Your plan should include carb-loading before, and carb ingestion during the race, which are absolutely necessary. The "recommended dose" of carbs is 1gm/kg of body mass/hour (ideally consisting of glucose and fructose in a 2:1 ratio). I'm tipping the scales at right around 80 kilograms these days, so that means 80gm/hour of carbohydrate. At four calories per gram (kilocalories per gram, actually...) that means taking in 320 calories of carbs per hour. There are two problems here:

1. I love to eat, but taking in that many calories during a race is not easy! Gatorade, for example, has "only" 50 calories per 8 oz. serving. To onboard 320 calories I would need to drink 51.2 ounces of Gatorade per hour. For 24 hours. Barf! ☺ Coke has 103 calories per 8 ounces, so that's a bit easier. I would "only" need to drink 25 ounces of Coke, but Coke is really tough on the stomach. Again, Barf! Gels are a much better solution. At about 110 calories each, I would only need to eat three per hour. For 24 hours...
2. As bad as all that is, the bigger problem is that the human body—and that's the kind I have—can only absorb about 240 to 280 calories per hour, so no matter what you do you're always going to run a deficit.

The solution to both problems is to eat, not just drink. Gels are ok for the first four hours or so, but after that you'll want to take on real food. Figuring out what your stomach can tolerate is the key. Many energy bars offer a 4:1 carb to protein mix, which is exactly what you're looking for. Other quick hits are pretzels, and bananas or other fruit, but you'll probably need "real" food during the second half of the race. Boiled, baked or mashed potatoes, soup, and turkey or peanut butter and jelly sandwiches are some old and reliable favorites. Your race pace will necessarily be much slower than it is in a shorter race, so it is somewhat easier to hold down food and drink, but it will still take some practice. Even if you don't need it to get through that particular workout, you should experiment and practice eating and drinking some of the aforementioned foods and drinks during your longest training walks. It takes some trial-and-error—and tracking everything in your training log—to get it right, but it will be well worth the effort if it helps you to get things right on race day. If you *don't* get it right it's not the end of the world. You'll just have put up with some nausea, dizziness, stomach or intestinal cramps, vomiting, and diarrhea, that's all. ☺

CHAPTER 23: PARIS-TO-ALSACE AND OTHER MULTI-DAY RACES

The storied Paris-to-Alsace walk began in 1926 as a 504 kilometer (313 miles) race from Paris to Strasbourg, France. Over the years, distances and even directions have changed, but it has always been a grueling multi-stage, ultra-long-distance challenge. In 1981 the endpoint moved 75 kilometers south to Colmar, and from 2015 through 2019, the competitors made their way from Paris to Ribaeauvillé, a town 16km north of Colmar. The 2020 edition, rebranded as Paris-to-Alsace, was slated to finish in Kaysersberg Vignoble,[59] but was not held—yet another victim of the Covid-19 pandemic.

Strasbourg is the capital and largest city of the Grand Est region of France, located at the border with Germany in the historic region of Alsace, as are Colmar, Ribaeauville, and Kaysersberg

The start of the 1957 "Paris-to-Colmar" race, departing from Strasbourg.

[59] If Kaysersberg Vignoble sounds vaguely familiar, it is best known as the site of Anthony Bourdain's suicide in his room at Relais et Châteaux Le Chambard.

Vignoble. A shorter women's race was added in 1988, following the last two days of the veteran men's race. Current races in the event are the 426-kilometer (264 miles) "*La Mythique*" for veteran men; the 303km (188 miles) *"La Vosgéene"* for women and first-time men; and the 227km (141 miles) *"La Nocéene"* for both men and women who did not qualify for the longer races by posting superior 24- or 28-hour race performances.

Training for such a grueling event is at least as much about the mental as the physical, but there is still the need for a lot of walk training. According to Erin Taylor-Talcott—a Paris-to-Colmar veteran from Owego, New York, who placed 4th in *La Vosgéene* in 2018—preparing for the event was a matter of already being in excellent 50k racing shape, and then adding some longer training walks—up to 60 kilometers sometimes. Another key to her success was improving the efficiency of her "pedestrian" walking, since it can be very difficult to use straight-legged racewalking technique for more than 50k at a time. Finally, working on her feeding plan, and gathering a top-notch support crew—including her husband, Dave Talcott, America's 3rd fastest Centurion ever, and Paris-to-Alsace veterans including John Constandinou, Emmanual Tardi, and Karen Davies—were the final critical elements. Erin's support crew followed her in a well-stocked camper van the entire time, and Dave walked a lot of miles with her during the race to keep her motivated and give her advice through the bad patches that inevitably come in such a long race. The van came in handy for bathroom stops, which were frequent, as Erin had a lot of GI issues during the race. Erin claims Dave can eat a double cheeseburger during a 20k—a talent I share with Mr. Talcott ☺—but that her stomach is a lot more sensitive. Yogurt was her go-to food during the race because it provided both carbs and protein and was one of the few things she could keep down.

I'm a big believer in specificity of training. Paris-to-Alsace requires several days of walking, and lots of it, with little sleep, so your training, to some extent, should reflect that. I recommend "cluster training"—consecutive long days to mimic the experience of multi-day racing. And when I do have consecutive long days scheduled, I like my athletes to put them as close together as possible, so if you're scheduled for an eight-hour walk on Saturday and 20 miles on Sunday, I prefer the eight-hour to be as late as possible on Saturday—noon to 8:00pm, for example—and then the 20-miler to be as early as possible on Sunday morning. That doesn't leave a whole lot of time for recovery, rehydration and carb repletion, but that's kind of the point, isn't it?

Of similar scale to Paris-to-Alsace are 48-hour races. They are a rarity, and most are running races, but since they are fixed-time, not distance, races, walkers are generally welcome. One of the more popular "running" events among walkers is the "Across the Years" festival of races in Phoenix, AZ, so named because the 10-day event begins on December 28th and ends on January 7th. In addition to the 48-hour race, the festival features 24-, and 72-hour, as well as 6- and 10-day races. Anyone wishing to train for the 48-hour race should follow the women's Paris-to-Alsace schedule, since finish times for that race generally range from 40 to 50 hours; anyone training for the 72-hour race should follow the Paris-to-Alsace men's schedule, since those finish times are generally around 60 hours—a bit shorter than 72, but in the ballpark.

If three days of walking is not enough for you, there are ultra-ultra races from six to ten days, and even the ultra-race of ultra-ultra races, the Sri Chinmoy 5,000 kilometer (3,100 mile) race in Queens, NY where athletes navigate a single square city block for 52 days straight, from 6:00am to midnight. Since this is, as the title suggests, a book about *competitive* walking, I will not specifically cover training for a number of grueling events which, although impressive in their own right, are non-competitive hikes, rather than races. Such adventures include the Appalachian Trail (2,190 miles), Pacific Crest Trail (2,650 miles) and Continental Divide Trail (3,100 miles) in the US; traversing the entire US from coast to coast (2,500 to 3,100 miles); northern Spain's Camino de Santiago de Compostela (~500 miles) and of course the Great Wall of China (3,728 miles). Maybe some day I'll write *The Complete Guide to Long-Distance Hiking*, but until then we'll get some advice on training for and racing six-day races and even the Sri Chinmoy 3,100 from the Walking Diva herself, Yolanda Holder—"holder" of world records for 6 days, 10 days, and 3,100 miles. But first, let's start small with training schedules for events lasting "just" 141, 188, and 264 miles:

La Nocéene and *La Vosgéne* Paris-to-Alsace Training Schedule

Week	Mon.	Tues.	Wed.	Thurs.	Fri.	Sat.	Sun.
1	Off or very easy cross-train	Moderate 5 miles	Easy 6 miles	Moderate 5 miles	Off	Easy 3 hours. Don't worry about the pace!!!	Easy 12 miles
2	Off or very easy cross-train	Moderate 5 miles	Easy 6 miles	Moderate 5 miles	Off	Easy 3½ hours. Don't worry about the pace!!!	12 miles at goal pace.
3	Off or very easy cross-train	Moderate 5 miles	Easy 6 miles	Moderate 5 miles	Off	Easy 4 hours. Don't worry about the pace!!!	15 miles at goal pace
4	Off or very easy cross-train	5 miles	Easy 6-10 miles	5-mile progression	Off	20 miles at goal pace	Very easy 5 miles
5	Off or very easy cross-train	5 mile	Easy 6-10 miles	5-mile progression	Off	Easy 5 hours. Don't worry about the pace!!!	15 miles at goal pace
6	Off or very easy cross-train	5 miles	Easy 6-10 miles	5-mile progression	Off	Easy 6 hours. Don't worry about the pace!!!	20 miles at goal pace.
7	Off or very easy cross-train	5 miles	Easy 6-10 miles	5-mile progression	Off	25 miles at goal pace	Very easy 5 miles
8	Off or very easy cross-train	5 miles	Easy 6-10 miles	5-mile progression	Off	Easy 7 hours. Don't worry about the pace!!!	15 miles at goal pace.
9	Off or very easy cross-train	5 miles	Easy 6-10 miles	5-mile progression	Off	25 miles at goal pace	Very easy 6 miles
10	Off or very easy cross-train	5 miles	Easy 6-10 miles	5-mile progression	Off	Easy 8 hours. Don't worry about the pace!!!	15 miles at goal pace.
11	OFF!!!	5 miles	Easy 6-10 miles	5-mile progression	Off	25 miles at goal pace	Very easy 8 miles
12	Off or very easy cross-train	Easy 5 miles	Easy 6-10 miles	5-mile progression	Off	Easy 8 hours. Don't worry about the pace!!!	15 miles at goal pace.
13	Off or very easy cross-train	Easy 5 miles	Easy 6-10 miles	5-mile progression	Off	25 miles at goal pace	Very easy 10 miles
14	OFF!!!	Easy 5 miles	Easy 6-10 miles	5-mile progression	Off	Easy 8 hours. Don't worry about the pace!!!	20 miles at goal pace.
15	Off or very easy cross-train	Easy 5 miles	Easy 6-10 miles	5-mile progression	Off	25 miles at goal pace.	Easy 20 miles
16	Off or very easy cross-train	Easy 5 miles	Easy 8 miles	5-mile progression	Off	Easy 8 hours. Don't worry about the pace!!!	Easy 25 miles
17	Off or very easy cross-train	Easy 5 miles	Easy 10 miles	5-mile progression	Off	Easy 25 miles	25 miles at goal pace
18	Off or very easy cross-train	Easy 5 miles	Easy 5-10 miles	5-mile progression	Off	Last-chance long day. EASY 20 miles. Practice drinking/eating on the go.	Easy 15 miles
19	Off or very easy cross-train	Easy 5 miles	Easy 5-10 miles	5-mile progression	Off	Easy 8 miles	Easy 5 miles
20	Off or very easy cross-train	Easy 3 miles	Off!	Easy 3 miles, then stretch	Sleep! ☺	**RACE!!!**	

Women and first-time men qualifiers "only" walk about 303 kilometers (188 miles) compared to the veteran men's 426km (264 miles) race. Non-qualifiers may participate in the 227km (141 miles) race. The training for the three is more or less identical other than the timing of the races. The short races take ~2 to 2½ days while veteran men take ~3 days to finish.

La Mythique Veteran Men's Paris-to-Alsace Training Schedule							
Week	**Mon.**	**Tues.**	**Wed.**	**Thurs.**	**Fri.**	**Sat.**	**Sun.**
1	Off or very easy cross-train	Easy 5 miles	Moderate 5 miles	Off or very easy cross-train	Easy 5 miles	Easy 3 hours. Don't worry about the pace!!!	Easy 12 miles
2	Off or very easy cross-train	Easy 5 miles	Moderate 5 miles	Off or very easy cross-train	Easy 5 miles	Easy 3½ hours. Don't worry about the pace!!!	12 miles at goal pace.
3	Off or very easy cross-train	Easy 5 miles	Moderate 5 miles	Off or very easy cross-train	Easy 5 miles	Easy 4 hours. Don't worry about the pace!!!	15 miles at goal pace
4	Off or very easy cross-train	Easy 5 miles	5-mile progression	Off or very easy cross-train	Easy 5 miles	20 miles at goal pace	Very easy 5 miles
5	Off or very easy cross-train	Easy 5 miles	5-mile progression	Off or very easy cross-train	Easy 5 miles	Easy 5 hours. Don't worry about the pace!!!	15 miles at goal pace
6	Off or very easy cross-train	Easy 5 miles	5-mile progression	Off or very easy cross-train	Easy 5 miles	Easy 6 hours. Don't worry about the pace!!!	20 miles at goal pace.
7	Off or very easy cross-train	Easy 5 miles	5-mile progression	Off or very easy cross-train	Easy 5 miles	25 miles at goal pace	Very easy 5 miles
8	Off or very easy cross-train	Easy 5 miles	5-mile progression	Off or very easy cross-train	Easy 5 miles	Easy 7 hours. Don't worry about the pace!!!	15 miles at goal pace.
9	Off or very easy cross-train	Easy 5 miles	5-mile progression	Off or very easy cross-train	Easy 5 miles	25 miles at goal pace	Very easy 6 miles
10	Off or very easy cross-train	Easy 5 miles	5-mile progression	Off or very easy cross-train	Easy 5 miles	Easy 8 hours. Don't worry about the pace!!!	15 miles at goal pace.
11	OFF!!!	Easy 5 miles	5-mile progression	Off or very easy cross-train	Easy 10 miles	25 miles at goal pace	Very easy 8 miles
12	Off or very easy cross-train	Easy 5 miles	5-mile progression	Off or very easy cross-train	Easy 10 miles	Easy 8 hours. Don't worry about the pace!!!	15 miles at goal pace.
13	Off or very easy cross-train	Easy 5 miles	5-mile progression	Off or very easy cross-train	Easy 10 miles	25 miles at goal pace	Very easy 10 miles
14	OFF!!!	Easy 5 miles	5-mile progression	Off or very easy cross-train	Easy 10 miles	Easy 8 hours. Don't worry about the pace!!!	20 miles at goal pace.
15	Off or very easy cross-train	Easy 5 miles	5-mile progression	Off or very easy cross-train	Easy 10 miles	25 miles at goal pace.	Easy 20 miles
16	Off or very easy cross-train	Easy 5 miles	5-mile progression	Off or very easy cross-train	Easy 5 miles	Easy 8 hours. Don't worry about the pace!!!	Easy 25 miles
17	Off or very easy cross-train	Easy 5 miles	5-mile progression	Off or very easy cross-train	Easy 10 miles	Easy 25 miles	25 miles at goal pace
18	Off or very easy cross-train	Easy 5 miles	5-mile progression	Off or very easy cross-train	Easy 10 miles	Last-chance long day. EASY 20 miles. Practice drinking/eating on the go.	Easy 15 miles
19	Off or very easy cross-train	Easy 5 miles	5-mile progression	Off or very easy cross-train	Easy 10 miles	Easy 8 miles	Easy 5 miles
20	Off or very easy cross-train	Easy 3 miles	Easy 3 miles, then stretch	Sleep! ☺		**RACE!!!**	

Six-day races and beyond

Six-day pedestrian races hit their peak in the late 1870s. By the early 1890s, eclipsed by bicycle racing, they were no longer drawing the enormous crowds they attracted just a few years earlier. Prize money dried up and the races simply disappeared—even in cities that hadn't outlawed them for their brutality. There was a brief resurgence of multi-day pedestrian races in the 1920s as trans-continental stage races became a "thing," but that fad, too, petered out. In 1980 ultra-runner Don Choi decided to resuscitate ultra-long-distance pedestrian racing, hosting on a track in Woodside, California, the first six-day race in over half a century. Choi won the race with a total of 401 miles. Running. Not bad, but keep in mind that Daniel O'Leary regularly walked over 500 miles in six days the 1880s, and the go-as-you-please record from 1888 was 623 miles 1,320 yards. The success of the Woodside race led to the hosting of the first "Edward Payson Six-Day Track Race" a few weeks later in Philadelphia, and six-day racing was once again "off to the races" in the US, as well as the UK, France, and Australia.

Today, the Sri Chinmoy Self-Transcendence Six-Day (as well as ten-day and 52-day/3,100 miles) in Queens, NY, and the Across the Years festival of races in Phoenix are long-standing annual events in the US. Newer additions to the calendar are the "Six Days in the Dome" races held indoors, first in 2014 at the Alaska Dome in Anchorage, and in 2019 at the Pettit Ice Center in Milwaukee, WI. (The 2020 race in Milwaukee was cancelled due to Covid-19.)

Training for a six-day race is a mixed bag. As I mentioned previously, there are diminishing returns after a certain point. A physiology professor once told me that that body learns everything it needs to learn (about burning fat vs. carbs as a fuel, building capillary density, elevating hemoglobin levels, etc.) after the first three hours. Presumably he was talking about running, and of course he was neither a competitive walker nor a runner, but still. The point is that a lot of the changes you need to occur in your body do happen before twenty miles. There's no need to walk 60, 70, 80 miles per day in training to be able to walk four or five hundred miles in six days (or 3,100 miles in 52 days…) I believe in relatively high weekly mileage, and consecutive long days, to prepare the body and mind for multi-day races. Yolanda Holder, the undisputed Queen of multi-day walk races simply walks 30 miles every day. Most people don't have that luxury, so "cluster training"—back-to-back or occasionally back-to-back-to-back long workouts on the weekends every few weeks—are the best way to get ready for the rigors of a multi-day race. I've already laid out such a plan for Paris-to-Alsace, and the Six-Day schedule is very similar because again, once the body is ready to race 50k, there's not much more you need other than somewhat longer long days to prepare it to walk 100k, 100 miles, or six days. Get through that training and the difference between finishing or not finishing is your fueling, and your mental game. According to Yolanda Holder herself: "Race walking a six-day race takes determination and a strong belief in yourself, even when everything is going wrong, to keep moving forward. Find a way to enjoy parts of the race and SMILE."

Six-Day Race Training Schedule							
Week	**Mon.**	**Tues.**	**Wed.**	**Thurs.**	**Fri.**	**Sat.**	**Sun.**
1	Off or very easy cross-train	Easy 5 miles	Moderate 5 miles	Off or very easy cross-train	Easy 5 miles	Easy 3 hours. Don't worry about the pace!!!	Easy 12 miles
2	Off or very easy cross-train	Easy 5 miles	Moderate 5 miles	Off or very easy cross-train	Easy 5 miles	Easy 3½ hours. Don't worry about the pace!!!	12 miles at goal pace.
3	Off or very easy cross-train	Easy 5 miles	Moderate 5 miles	Off or very easy cross-train	Easy 5 miles	Easy 4 hours. Don't worry about the pace!!!	15 miles at goal pace
4	Off or very easy cross-train	Easy 5 miles	5-mile progression	Off or very easy cross-train	Easy 5 miles	20 miles at goal pace	Very easy 5 miles
5	Off or very easy cross-train	Easy 5 miles	5-mile progression	Off or very easy cross-train	Easy 5 miles	Easy 5 hours. Don't worry about the pace!!!	15 miles at goal pace
6	Off or very easy cross-train	Easy 5 miles	5-mile progression	Off or very easy cross-train	Easy 5 miles	Easy 6 hours. Don't worry about the pace!!!	20 miles at goal pace.
7	Off or very easy cross-train	Easy 5 miles	5-mile progression	Off or very easy cross-train	Easy 5 miles	25 miles at goal pace	Very easy 5 miles
8	Off or very easy cross-train	Easy 5 miles	5-mile progression	Off or very easy cross-train	Easy 5 miles	Easy 7 hours. Don't worry about the pace!!!	15 miles at goal pace.
9	Off or very easy cross-train	Easy 5 miles	5-mile progression	Off or very easy cross-train	Easy 5 miles	25 miles at goal pace	Very easy 6 miles
10	Off or very easy cross-train	Easy 5 miles	5-mile progression	Off or very easy cross-train	Easy 5 miles	Easy 8 hours. Don't worry about the pace!!!	15 miles at goal pace.
11	Off or very easy cross-train	Easy 5 miles	5-mile progression	Off or very easy cross-train	Easy 10 miles	25 miles at goal pace	Very easy 8 miles
12	Off or very easy cross-train	Easy 5 miles	5-mile progression	Off or very easy cross-train	Easy 10 miles	Easy 8 hours. Don't worry about the pace!!!	15 miles at goal pace.
13	Off or very easy cross-train	Easy 5 miles	5-mile progression	Off or very easy cross-train	Easy 10 miles	25 miles at goal pace	Very easy 10 miles
14	Off or very easy cross-train	Easy 5 miles	5-mile progression	Off or very easy cross-train	Easy 10 miles	Easy 8 hours. Don't worry about the pace!!!	15 miles at goal pace.
15	Off or very easy cross-train	Easy 5 miles	5-mile progression	Off or very easy cross-train	Easy 10 miles	25 miles at goal pace.	Easy 20 miles
16	Off or very easy cross-train	Easy 5 miles	5-mile progression	Off or very easy cross-train	Easy 5 miles	Easy 8 hours. Don't worry about the pace!!!	Easy 5 miles
17	Off or very easy cross-train	Easy 5 miles	5-mile progression	Off or very easy cross-train	Easy 10 miles	Easy 25 miles	15 miles at goal pace
18	Off or very easy cross-train	Easy 5 miles	5-mile progression	Off or very easy cross-train	Easy 10 miles	Last-chance long day. EASY 20 miles. Practice drinking/eating on the go.	Easy 5 miles
19	Off or very easy cross-train	Easy 5 miles	Easy 3	Off	Easy 3 miles	3 miles at goal pace, then stretch	Sleep! ☺
20	**RACE!!!**						

CHAPTER 24: NATIONAL SENIOR GAMES DOUBLE: 1,500M FOLLOWED BY 5K

The National Senior Games is the largest multi-sport event in the world for seniors (adults over age 50). The National Senior Games Association is a non-profit member of the United States Olympic Committee dedicated to motivating senior men and women to lead healthy lifestyles through the senior games movement. Annual Senior Games competitions are offered in many sports through all of NSGA's individual state member organizations. Due to a lawsuit over the "Olympics" name, most states use the "Senior Games" name ("Texas Senior Games") but states that were using the term "Senior Olympics" before the lawsuit were "grandfathered" (pun definitely intended…) and allowed to continue using the name ("Arizona Senior Olympics").

Competitors at the 2019 National Senior Games 1,500m power walk.

Photo credit: National Senior Games

The NSG offer both racewalking and power walking, featuring 1,500m and 5k races, both nationally and at most state Senior Games/Senior Olympics track and field meets. Athletes qualify for the National Senior Games through their home state, or in any state that allows out-of-state competitors. State Games held in even-numbered years are qualifying competitions for the Nationals, which are held in odd-numbered years (2019, 2021). Awards are presented to men and women in five-year age groups starting at 50-54 and going up to 100+. For information on the National Senior Games or your individual state Senior Games, visit http://www.nsga.com.

The NSG meet schedule is not out for the 2021 Games as of this writing. The Senior Games double has in the past been, I believe, backwards. The track meet, which includes the 1,500m walks, is held on the final weekend of the Games; The 5k road event usually took place on Thursday, two days before the Saturday 1,500m races. I understand the reasoning behind this scheduling of the events, but athletes recover faster from a 1,500m than a 5k, so it's less than ideal for the 1,500m race to come after the 5k. In 2019 NSG switched to a Saturday 1,500m and a Monday 5k. Much better! Hopefully this will be the schedule for 2021, and the training schedule here reflects that hope/assumption. Whichever way the races are scheduled, your competitors will be facing the same schedule, and like any other challenge, the body can be trained for either scenario.

In my mind a good walker is a good walker is a good walker. If you're in shape for a 5k you'll be able to race a competent 1,500m, and vice versa. To be at your best for both events, however, your mileage has to be at a reasonable level, you need to sharpen your speed, and to be able to race both distances 48 hours apart, you'll need to practice recovering form a hard speed effort and then go right into a hard tempo workout two days later. Your training schedule for the 1,500m/5k double will reflect this reality. Your diet, stretching routine, and any bodywork (massage, etc.), will also play a part.

My racewalking "twin," David Swarts of Norvell, Michigan, who shares my birthday and year, understandably has similar ideas about training for track meets with two or more races in a row. At the 2017 World Masters Games in Aukland, New Zealand, David walked 1,500m/3,000m/5,000m in four days, setting M50 Games records of 6:30.62, 13:36.33 and 23:20.40. I asked David how he trains for sprint doubles and triples like the World Masters, Huntsman, and this chapter's featured event, the National Senior Games double:

"With multiple races, I take each one individually. When training for an upcoming double or triple event, I train for the longest distance I'll be racing. Strength carries me from race to race. I want to do well in all of them. The road miles and longer track workouts build strength and the shorter ones polish off the process. Do the strength work first, stay consistent, and build a good base. I typically do my longer training efforts (10k to 20k) at a faster pace than my short (5k to 8k) efforts. The short days are my recovery days. I also take one day completely off every week. I work full-time, so I'm only a 55-70k (34-43 miles) a week athlete. With six weeks to go, I add long fartlek workouts to my schedule. A typical workout might be 2k

easy with 13k of 1-minute hard/1-minute easy. With four weeks to go, I'll add quicker track workouts to get leg turnover up, and work on pace. I'll do 10k of 400m fast/200m easy for a couple of weeks, then drop it down to something really fast the week of competition, like 12 x 200m as fast and relaxed as possible. Also during the last week, I do not drop my mileage down. I do slow the pace a little, working on recovery and rest. Between race days, I'll rest but I also have the need to keep moving. I'll get out for a few easy kilometers to loosen up sore muscles and get some stretching in, but I'll also get out and pedestrian walk (sight-see) for a while, making sure I stay hydrated."

The NSG, Huntsman, US Masters, and World Masters schedules incorporate a lot of David's suggestions, although I diverge a bit in terms of tapering for race day—I'm a firm believer in rest! They also assume you've completed one of the base-training schedules in Chapter 16. Otherwise it will be difficult to jump right into hill training. The hill intervals (walked on a gentle 3-5% grade) are designed to build strength and serve as a transition into the faster track intervals to follow, but also to improve your walking technique, be it racewalking or power walking. Many state-level Senior Games meets are somewhat more open to non-racewalkers in the racewalk events than USA Track and Field events. At the National Senior Games level, the racewalk judging is generally on par with USA Track & Field judging, but at state qualifying events it can be a mixed bag, with many states qualifying walkers with questionable technique on to the national level. Nothing can be more frustrating than spending a ton of money on travel and hotels to get to a track meet and then be disqualified, so you have a choice: Make sure you have passable racewalking technique, or enter the power walk which has much less stringent judging. In either case, racewalking or power walking, training with the following schedule will ensure that you're well prepared for the rigors of the NSG double!

National Senior Games 5k/1,500m Double Training Schedule

Week	Mon.	Tues.	Wed.	Thurs.	Fri.	Sat.	Sun.
1	Off or easy cross-train	45-minute fartlek	Easy 30 minutes	45-minute fartlek	Off or easy cross-train	Moderate 30-min.	Easy 5 miles/8k
2	Off or easy cross-train	20 min. w/up, drills, then 10 x 30 sec. hill reps. "Hike" down after each	Easy 3 miles/5k	45-minute fartlek	Off or easy cross-train	Easy 3 miles/5k	Easy 6 miles/10k
3	Off or easy cross-train	"" then 10 x 30 sec. hills	Easy 3 miles/5k	45-minute fartlek	Off or easy cross-train	Easy 3 miles/5k	Easy 6 miles/10k
4	Off or easy cross-train	"" 10 x 30 sec. hill repeats	Easy 3 miles/5k	10-min. w/-up, drills, then 30-min. progression	Off or easy cross-train	Easy 3 miles/5k	Easy 6 miles/10k
5	Off or easy cross-train	"" then 5 x 300m @ race pace, w/ 200m breaks	Easy 3 miles/5k	"" 30-minute tempo—steady, hard effort	Off or easy cross-train	Easy 3 miles/5k	Easy 6 miles/10k
6	Off or easy cross-train	"" 6 x 300m @ race pace w/ 400m breaks	Easy 3 miles/5k	"" 30-min. progression	Off or easy cross-train	Easy 3 miles/5k	Easy 6 miles/10k
7	Off or easy cross-train	"" 5 x 400m w/ 400m easy breaks	Easy 3 miles/5k	"" 4 x 800m @ current → goal 5k pace w/ easy 400m breaks	Off or easy cross-train	Easy 3 miles/5k	Easy 6 miles/10k
8	Off or easy cross-train	""4 x 500m w/ 400m easy breaks	Easy 3 miles/5k	"" 30-minute tempo—steady, hard effort	Off or easy cross-train	Easy 3 miles/5k	Easy 6 miles/10k
9	Off or easy cross-train	""6 x 400m w/ 400m easy breaks	Easy 3 miles/5k	"" 4 x 1,000m @ current → goal 5k pace w/ 400m breaks	Off or easy cross-train	Easy 3 miles/5k	Easy 6 miles/10k
10	Off or easy cross-train	""5 x 500m w/ 400m easy breaks	Easy 3 miles/5k	"" 6k progression	Off or easy cross-train	Easy 3 miles/5k	Easy 6 miles/10k
11	Off or easy cross-train	""6 x 400m w/ 400m easy breaks	Easy 3 miles/5k	"" 3 x 1,600m @ current → goal 5k pace w/ 400m breaks	Off or easy cross-train	Easy 3 miles/5k	Easy 5 miles/8k
12	Off or easy cross-train	""1,500m time-trial!	Easy 3 miles/5k	"" 5k time-trial!!	Off or easy cross-train	Easy 3 miles/5k	Easy 6 miles/10k
13	Off or easy cross-train	"" 1 x 800m; 2 x 400m @ 1,600m pace; 1 x 200m fast! All w/ 200m breaks	Easy 3 miles/5k	"" 3 x 2,000m @ current → goal 5k pace w/ 400m breaks	Off or easy cross-train	Easy 3 miles/5k	Easy 6 miles/10k
14	Off or easy cross-train	6 x 400m w/ 400m easy breaks	Easy 3 miles/5k	"" 30-min. progression	Off or easy cross-train	Easy 3 miles/5k	Easy 6 miles/10k
15	Off or easy cross-train	"" 1 x 800m; 2 x 400m @ 1,600m pace; 1 x 200m fast! All w/ 200m breaks	Easy 3 miles/5k	"" 3k tempo; 2k @ current 5k pace; 1k @ goal 5k pace w/ 400m breaks	Off or easy cross-train	Easy 3 miles/5k	Easy 5 miles/8k
16	OFF	"" 3 x 300m @ 1,500m race pace w/ 100m breaks	Off!	Easy 10-15 min.	"" 4 x 30 sec. sprints, cool dn., stretch	**NSG 1,500m!**	"" 4 x 30 sec. fast, cool dn., stretch
17	**NSG 5k!**	Easy 20 to 30-minute stroll	Off	Easy 30-minute stroll	Off	Easy 30 mins.	Easy 4 miles

We're back to sprint racing here, so complete warm-ups, including flexibility drills (Chapter 34), are critical! If you're entered in the NSG, you're, by definition, no spring chicken. ☺ If you feel overly tired, or you're not progressing, take it very easy on the Monday and Friday cross training days, and even consider taking Wednesday off instead of doing the easy 3 miles/5k.

CHAPTER 25: THE HUNTSMAN WORLD SENIOR GAMES 1,500; 3,000; 5,000M TRIPLE

The Huntsman World Senior Games take place in St. George, UT every October. Like the National Senior Games, Huntsman is an all sports, Olympic-style sports festival open to athletes age 50 and up. Unlike the National Senior Games, Huntsman is an international event, welcoming athletes from all nations to take part. The track and field competition features 1,500m, 3,000m and 5,000m racewalks and power walks held on consecutive days.

In addition to the various athletic events, the Huntsman Games promote health by providing screenings for serious health threats such as breast cancer, colon cancer, prostate cancer, glaucoma, diabetes, high blood pressure, elevated cholesterol, and decreased bone density. Concerts, dances, and awards socials for each sport are also part of the package, bringing athletes and guests together in a social atmosphere where they share in, and congratulate each other for, their achievements, whether or not they win a medal. Women's health & fitness advocate, and Huntsman World Senior Games ambassador, Bonnie Parrish-Kell[60] embodies the values of the Huntsman Games, which in turn abide by the Olympic ideal spelled out by Pierre de Coubertain, founder of the modern Olympic Games: "*The important thing… is not to win, but to take part; the important thing in Life is not triumph, but the struggle; the essential thing is not to have conquered but to have fought well.*" Bonnie says:

> *"Sometimes, I'm the last woman to finish a power walk or racewalk competition. But I'm okay with that because my success in walking races isn't about winning medals or having fast times. If it were, I'd have quit after my 5k power walk race at the 2013 Huntsman World Senior Games. I was the last woman to cross the finish line, and more than fifteen minutes behind the overall winner. Instead, I was inspired by all the women who passed me, many of whom were at least ten years, if not twenty years, older than me. If they can do it, then I can do it! This motivates me to get up in the morning for my walk and strength training sessions, to eat more healthfully, and get more hours of sleep each night. I want to be like them at their age—walking, staying active, and enjoying their friendship at senior games competitions. Today, so many years after that first race, I'm physically stronger and healthier, have more stamina and endurance, have gotten a bit faster despite getting older, and still striving to better my times. Success doesn't get any better than that!"*

---

[60] Bonnie is the publisher and "Chief Diva" of the SlowpokeDivas.com & GoSpeedyDivas.com websites and Facebook pages/groups.

Training for the Huntsman Games triple is similar to what is required for the National Senior Games double, only with minor differences in the scheduling of interval and tempo sessions. There will be some weeks where an economy (short intervals) day will be followed by a longer interval day, which will be followed by a tempo day. Not every week, but enough to get the body and mind accustomed to walking fast on three consecutive days. The key to both training for and racing at Huntsman is recovery between workouts and events. Cooling down properly, replenishing fluids and carbs, stretching, and maybe getting a massage are great ways to speed recovery between each hard effort.

Huntsman World Senior Games Training Schedule

Week	Mon.	Tues.	Wed.	Thurs.	Fri.	Sat.	Sun.
1	Off or easy cross-train	45-minute fartlek	Moderate 30 minutes	45-minute fartlek	Off or easy cross-train	Moderate 30 minutes	Easy 6 miles (or 10k)
2	Off or easy cross-train	10-min. warm-up, drills, then 8 x 1:00 min. hill reps.	Mod. 30 mins.	45-minute fartlek	Off or easy cross-train	Mod. 30 mins.	Easy 6 miles (or 10k)
3	Off or easy cross-train	"" then 8 x 1:30 min. hill reps.	Mod. 30 mins.	45-minute fartlek	Off or easy cross-train	Mod. 30 mins.	Easy 6 miles (or 10k)
4	Off or easy cross-train	"" 8 x 200m fast w/200m breaks	Mod. 30 mins.	45-minute fartlek	Off or easy cross-train	Mod. 30 mins.	Easy 6 miles (or 10k)
5	Off or easy cross-train	"" 4 x {100m/200m/300m} w/ 100m breaks	Mod. 30 mins.	Warm-up, drills, then 6 x 400m @ 3,000m race pace, w/ 200m easy walk breaks	Off or easy cross-train	Mod. 30 mins.	Easy 6 miles (or 10k)
6	Off or easy cross-train	"" 8 x 300m @ 1,500m pace w/200m breaks	Mod. 30 mins.	""6 x 500m @ race pace, w/ 300m easy walk breaks	Off or easy cross-train	Mod. 30 mins.	Easy 6 miles (or 10k)
7	Off or easy cross-train	"" 10 x 200m fast w/200m breaks	Mod. 30 mins.	"" then 20-minute tempo—steady, hard effort	Off or easy cross-train	Mod. 30 mins.	Easy 6 miles (or 10k)
8	Off or easy cross-train	"" 4 x {100m/200m/300m} w/ 100m breaks	Mod. 30 mins.	""6 x 500m @ current race pace, w/ 300m easy walk breaks	Off or easy cross-train	Mod. 30 mins.	Easy 6 miles (or 10k)
9	Off or easy cross-train	"" 6 x 300m @ 1,500m pace w/200m breaks	""6 x 500m @ 3,000m pace, w/ 300m breaks.	"" then 25-minute hard progression	Off or easy cross-train	Mod. 30 mins.	Easy 6 miles (or 10k)
10	Off or easy cross-train	"" 12 x 200m fast w/200m breaks	Mod. 30 mins.	""6 x 500m @ current race pace, w/ 300m easy walk breaks.	Off or easy cross-train	Mod. 30 mins.	Easy 6 miles (or 10k)
11	Off or easy cross-train	"" 4 x {100m/200m/300m} w/ 100m breaks	Mod. 30 mins.	""4k/2.5-mile progression.	Off or easy cross-train	Mod. 30 mins.	Easy 6 miles (or 10k)
12	Off or easy cross-train	"" 6 x 300m @ 1,500m pace w/200m breaks	""6 x 500m @ 3,000m pace, w/ 300m breaks	"" then 25-minute hard progression	Off or easy cross-train	Mod. 30 mins.	Easy 6 miles (or 10k)
13	Off or easy cross-train	"" 6 x 200m fast w/200m breaks	Mod. 30 mins.	"" 1,600m; 800; 400m @ 3,000m pace, then 200m fast! w/ 200m breaks.	Off	10-min. w/up, 4 x 30 sec. sprints, cool dn., stretch.	**5k time-trial/ "test race"**
14	Off or easy cross-train	"" 4 x {100m/200m/300m} w/ 100m breaks	Mod. 30 mins.	""6 x 500m @ current race pace, w/ 300m easy walk breaks	Off or easy cross-train	Mod. 30 mins.	Easy 6 miles (or 10k)
15	Off or easy cross-train	"" 6 x 300m @ 1,500m pace w/200m breaks	""6 x 500m @ 3,000m pace, w/ 300m easy walk breaks.	10-min. warm-up, drills, then 25-minute hard progression	Off or easy cross-train	Mod. 30 mins.	Easy 5 miles (or 8k)
16	Off or easy cross-train	"" 10 x 200m fast w/200m breaks	Easy 30 mins.	Off or easy cross-train	"" 3 x 300m @ 1,500m pace w/ 200m breaks	Off	10-min. w/up, 4 x 30 sec. sprints, cool dn., stretch.
17	**Huntsman 1,500m!**	**Huntsman 3,000m!**	**Huntsman 5000m!**	Easy 30-minute stroll	Off	Easy 30 mins.	Easy 5 miles

CHAPTER 26: US MASTERS CHAMPIONSHIPS DOUBLE: 5,000M FOLLOWED BY 10K

The USA Track & Field Masters National Championships take place every July. The meet includes a 5,000m track walk on Friday followed by a 10k road walk on Sunday. The World Masters Athletics (WMA) World Outdoor Championship, held in alternate years, features a 5,000m track race followed by a 10k road walk, followed by a 20k road walk. In both meets, many walkers choose to do the 5,000m/10k double.

Although in Chapters 17 and 18 I labeled the 5,000m race a sprint and the 10k a middle distance event, both require a mix of speed and endurance, so the training for each of the two races is similar. The combination of the two simply requires a bit more speed work than is required for 10k training alone, or a bit more distance work than what is required for 5k training alone, plus the ability to recover between quality training sessions and races.

As a US and world masters championship-level double, it can be assumed that all walkers attempting the double are "advanced" level athletes, so as with many of these doubles, I've only included one training schedule here. It will prepare you well for the event, but by all means feel free to modify to your own particular situation with respect to age, sex and ability level. As always, the schedule assumes you have completed a solid base-training phase as laid out in Chapter 16. As with all of the doubles, extra attention needs to be paid to diet, flexibility training, and rest, to allow sufficient recovery between high-quality training session and of course between the races themselves.

Champion masters racewalkers, David Swarts and Matt DeWitt, battling it out at the 2019 US Masters 10,000m.
Photo credit: Rob D'Avellar

Masters Championships 5,000m/10k Double Training Schedule

Week	Monday	Tuesday	Wednesday	Thursday	Friday	Saturday	Sunday
1	Off or easy cross-train	45-minute fartlek	Moderate 30-mins.	45-minute fartlek	Off or easy cross-train	Moderate 30-mins.	Easy 7 miles (or 11k)
2	Off or easy cross-train	10-min. warm-up, drills, then 8 x 1:00 min. hill reps.	Mod. 35 mins.	45-minute fartlek	Off or easy cross-train	Mod. 35 mins.	Easy 7.5 miles (or 12k)
3	Off or easy cross-train	"" then 8 x 1:30 min. hill reps.	Mod. 40 mins.	45-minute fartlek	Off or easy cross-train	Mod. 40-mins.	Easy 8 miles (or 13k)
4	Off or easy cross-train	"" 8 x 2:00 min. hill reps.	Mod. 45 mins.	10-min. warm-up, drills, then 40-min. progression	Off or easy cross-train	Mod. 45 mins.	Easy 6 miles (or 10k)
5	Off or easy cross-train	"" 10 x 200m fast w/200m breaks	Mod. 45 mins.	"" 45-minute tempo—steady, hard effort.	Off or easy cross-train	Mod. 45 mins.	Easy 9 miles (or 14k)
6	Off or easy cross-train	"" 8 x 400m @ 5,000m race pace, w/ 200m breaks.	Mod. 45 mins.	"" 50-min. progression.	Off or easy cross-train	Mod. 45 mins.	Easy 9.5 miles (or 15k)
7	Off or easy cross-train	"" 4 x {100m/200m/300m} w/ 100m breaks	Mod. 45 mins.	"" 4 x 1,600m @ current → goal 10k pace w/ easy 400m breaks.	Off or easy cross-train	Mod. 45 mins.	Easy 10 miles (or 16k)
8	Off or easy cross-train	"" 12 x 200m fast w/200m breaks	Mod. 45 mins.	"" 10k tempo	Off or easy cross-train	Mod. 45 mins.	Easy 8 miles (or 13k)
9	Off or easy cross-train	"" 10 x 400m w/ 200m breaks	Mod. 45 mins.	"" 5 x 1,600m @ current → goal 10k pace w/ easy 400m breaks.	Off or easy cross-train	Mod. 45 mins.	Easy 10 miles (or 16k)
10	Off or easy cross-train	"" 4 x {100m/200m/300m} w/ 100m breaks	Mod. 45 mins.	10k progression	Off or easy cross-train	Mod. 45 mins.	Easy 10 miles (or 16k)
11	Off or easy cross-train	"" 12 x 200m fast w/200m breaks	Mod. 45 mins.	"" 6 x 1,600m @ current → goal 10k pace w/ easy 400m breaks.	Off or easy cross-train	Mod. 45 mins.	Easy 10 miles (or 16k)
12	Off	"" 6 x 400m w/ 200m breaks.	Mod. 30 mins.	**"" 10k time-trial!!**	Off or easy cross-train	Mod. 45 mins.	Easy 8 miles (or 13k)
13	Off or easy cross-train	"" 4 x {100m/200m/300m} w/ 100m breaks	Mod. 45 mins.	"" 5 x 2K @ current → goal 10k pace w/ easy 400m breaks.	Off or easy cross-train	Mod. 45 mins.	Easy 10 miles (or 16k)
14	Off or easy cross-train	"" 12 x 200m fast w/200m breaks	Mod. 45 mins.	10k progression	Off or easy cross-train	Mod. 45 mins.	Easy 10 miles (or 16k)
15	Off or easy cross-train	"" 10 x 400m w/ 200m breaks.	Mod. 45 mins.	"" 3k @ 10k pace; 1k @ 5k pace w/ easy 2:00 min. break	Off or easy cross-train	Mod. 30 mins.	Easy 5 miles
16	Off	10 min. warm-up, then 1 x 2k @ 10k pace, 1 x 1k @ 5k pace w/ 1:00 break	Off	10 min. w/ up, 4 x 30 sec. sprints, cool dn., then stretch	**5,000m RACE!!!**	w/ up, 4 x 30 sec. sprints, cool dn., then stretch	**10k RACE!!!**

CHAPTER 27: WMA CHAMPIONSHIPS TRIPLE: 5,000M TRACK, 10K ROAD, 20K ROAD WALKS

The World Masters Athletics (WMA) World Championship features a 5,000m track walk, followed by a road 10k, followed by a road 20k. It's a tough triple that requires both speed and endurance, and the ability to recover quickly between races. The timing is such that the 5,000m is on Monday, Tuesday, Wednesday or Thursday, depending on your age group,[61] with the 10k on Saturday and the 20k the following Thursday.

Start of the 2019 World Masters Championships 10k. #872 is, incidentally, Canadian two-time Olympian Marcel Jobin. Photo credit: Emmanuel Tardi

[61] Women age 35-49 and 70+ are on Monday, women age 50-69 and men age 75+ are on Tuesday, men age 35-59 are on Wednesday, and men age 60-74 are on Thursday.

WMA Championships Triple Training Schedule-M60-M70							
Week	**Mon.**	**Tues.**	**Wed.**	**Thurs.**	**Fri.**	**Sat.**	**Sun.**
1	Off or easy cross-train	45-minute fartlek	Moderate 30-mins.	45-minute fartlek	Off or easy cross-train	Moderate 30-mins.	Easy 8 miles (or 13k)
2	Off or easy cross-train	10-min. warm-up, drills, then 8 x 1:00 min. hill reps.	Mod. 35 mins.	45-minute fartlek	Off or easy cross-train	Mod. 35 mins.	Easy 8 miles (or 13k)
3	Off or easy cross-train	"" then 8 x 1:30 min. hill reps.	Mod. 40 mins.	45-minute fartlek	Off or easy cross-train	Mod. 40-mins.	"Not so easy" 5 miles/8k
4	Off or easy cross-train	"" 8 x 2:00 min. hill reps.	Mod. 45 mins.	Warm-up, drills, then 40-min. progression	Off or easy cross-train	Mod. 45 mins.	Easy 9 miles (or 15k)
5	Off or easy cross-train	"" 10 x 200m fast w/200m breaks	Mod. 45 mins.	"" 45-minute tempo (steady, hard effort)	Off or easy cross-train	Mod. 45 mins.	"Not so easy"' 6 miles/10k
6	Off or easy cross-train	"" 8 x 400m @ 5k pace, w/ 200m breaks	Mod. 45 mins.	"" 50-min. progression	Off or easy cross-train	Mod. 45 mins.	Easy 9 miles (or 15k)
7	Off or easy cross-train	"" 4 x {100/200/300m} w/ 100m breaks	Mod. 45 mins.	"" 4 x 1,600m @ current → goal 10k pace w/ 400m breaks	Off or easy cross-train	Mod. 45 mins.	Easy 10 miles (or 16k)
8	Off or easy cross-train	"" 12 x 200m fast w/200m breaks	Mod. 45 mins.	"" 10k tempo	Off or easy cross-train	Mod. 45 mins.	"Not so easy" 8 miles/13k
9	Off or easy cross-train	"" 10 x 400m w/ 200m breaks	Mod. 45 mins.	"" 5 x 1,600m @ current → goal 10k pace w/ 400m breaks	Off or easy cross-train	Mod. 45 mins.	Easy 11 miles (or 17k)
10	Off or easy cross-train	"" 4 x {100/200/300m} w/ 100m breaks	Mod. 45 mins.	10k progression	Off or easy cross-train	Mod. 45 mins.	Easy 12 miles (or 19k)
11	Off or easy cross-train	"" 12 x 200m fast w/200m breaks	Mod. 45 mins.	"" 6 x 1,600m @ current → goal 10k pace w/ 400m breaks	Off or easy cross-train	Mod. 45 mins.	"Not so easy" 9 miles/15k
12	Off	"" 6 x 400m w/ 200m breaks.	Easy 30 mins.	**"" 10k time-trial!!**	Off or easy cross-train	Mod. 45 mins.	Easy 12 miles (or 19k)
13	Off or easy cross-train	"" 4 x {100/200/300m} w/ 100m breaks	Mod. 45 mins.	"" 5 x 2K @ current → goal 10k pace w/ 400m breaks	Off or easy cross-train	Mod. 45 mins.	Easy 13 miles (or 21k)
14	Off or easy cross-train	"" 12 x 200m fast w/200m breaks	Mod. 45 mins.	10k progression	Off or easy cross-train	Mod. 45 mins.	"Not so easy" 10 miles/16k
15	Off or easy cross-train	"" 10 x 400m w/ 200m breaks.	Mod. 45 mins.	"" 3k @ 10k pace; 1k @ 5k pace w/ 2:00 min. break	Off or easy cross-train	Mod. 30 mins.	6 mi. w/ 3 EZ, 3 at 20k pace
16	W/up, 1 x 2k @ 10k pace, 1 x 1k @ 5k pace w/ 1:00 break	Off	W/up, 4 x 30 sec. sprints, cool dn., stretch	**5,000m RACE!!!**	W/up, 4 x 30 sec. cool dn., stretch	**10k RACE!!**	Easy 30 min. walk/hike
17	Off	"" 6 x 400m @ 20k race pace, w/ 1:00 min. breaks.	W/up, 4 x 30 secs., cool dn., stretch	**20k RACE!!!**	Easy 30-min. stroll.	Off!	Easy 5 miles

WMA has made this chapter unnecessarily complicated… ☺ The above schedule is only for men in the 60-64, 65-69 and 70-74 age groups—M60, M65 and M70, in WMA parlance. These age groups compete in the 5,000m on the Thursday preceding the road 10k. The next schedule is for M35 through M55 who race the 5,000m on Wednesday; the 3rd schedule is for M75+ and women W50-W65 who race the 5,000m on Tuesday; and the final schedule is for W30-45 and W70+ who race the 5,000m on the Monday preceding the road 10k.

WMA Championships Triple Training Schedule-M35-M55							
Week	**Mon.**	**Tues.**	**Wed.**	**Thurs.**	**Fri.**	**Sat.**	**Sun.**
1	Off or easy cross-train	45-minute fartlek	Moderate 30-mins.	45-minute fartlek	Off or easy cross-train	Moderate 30-mins.	Easy 8 miles (or 13k)
2	Off or easy cross-train	10-min. warm-up, drills, then 8 x 1:00 min. hill reps.	Mod. 35 mins.	45-minute fartlek	Off or easy cross-train	Mod. 35 mins.	Easy 8 miles (or 13k)
3	Off or easy cross-train	10-min. warm-up, drills, then 8 x 1:30 min. hill reps.	Mod. 40 mins.	45-minute fartlek	Off or easy cross-train	Mod. 40-mins.	"Not so easy" 5 miles/8k
4	Off or easy cross-train	"" 8 x 2:00 min. hill reps.	Mod. 45 mins.	10-min. warm-up, drills, then 40-min. progression	Off or easy cross-train	Mod. 45 mins.	Easy 9 miles (or 15k)
5	Off or easy cross-train	"" 10 x 200m fast w/200m breaks	Mod. 45 mins.	"" 45-minute tempo (steady, hard effort)	Off or easy cross-train	Mod. 45 mins.	"Not so easy"' 6 miles/10k
6	Off or easy cross-train	"" 8 x 400m @ 5,000m race pace, w/ 200m breaks	Mod. 45 mins.	"" 50-min. progression	Off or easy cross-train	Mod. 45 mins.	Easy 9 miles (or 15k)
7	Off or easy cross-train	"" 4 x {100m/200m/300m} w/ 100m breaks	Mod. 45 mins.	"" 4 x 1,600m @ current → goal 10k pace w/ easy 400m breaks.	Off or easy cross-train	Mod. 45 mins.	Easy 10 miles (or 16k)
8	Off or easy cross-train	"" 12 x 200m fast w/200m breaks	Mod. 45 mins.	"" 10k tempo	Off or easy cross-train	Mod. 45 mins.	"Not so easy" 8 miles/13k
9	Off or easy cross-train	"" 10 x 400m w/ 200m breaks	Mod. 45 mins.	"" 5 x 1,600m @ current → goal 10k pace w/ easy 400m breaks.	Off or easy cross-train	Mod. 45 mins.	Easy 11 miles (or 17k)
10	Off or easy cross-train	"" 4 x {100m/200m/300m} w/ 100m breaks	Mod. 45 mins.	10k progression	Off or easy cross-train	Mod. 45 mins.	Easy 12 miles (or 19k)
11	Off or easy cross-train	"" 12 x 200m fast w/200m breaks	Mod. 45 mins.	"" 6 x 1,600m @ current → goal 10k pace w/ easy 400m breaks	Off or easy cross-train	Mod. 45 mins.	"Not so easy" 9 miles/15k
12	Off	"" 6 x 400m w/ 200m breaks	Easy 30 mins.	**"" 10k time-trial!!**	Off or easy cross-train	Mod. 45 mins.	Easy 12 miles (or 19k)
13	Off or easy cross-train	"" 4 x {100m/200m/300m} w/ 100m breaks	Mod. 45 mins.	"" 5 x 2K @ current → goal 10k pace w/ easy 400m breaks	Off or easy cross-train	Mod. 45 mins.	Easy 13 miles (or 21k)
14	Off or easy cross-train	"" 12 x 200m fast w/200m breaks	Mod. 45 mins.	10k progression	Off or easy cross-train	Mod. 45 mins.	"Not so easy" 10 miles/16k
15	Off or easy cross-train	"" 10 x 400m w/ 200m breaks	Mod. 45 mins.	"" 3k @ 10k pace; 1k @ 5k pace w/ easy 2:00 min. break	Off or easy cross-train	Easy 30 mins.	W/up, 1 x 2k @ 10k pace, 1 x 1k @ 5k pace w/ 1:00 break
16	Off	W/up, 4 x 30 sec. sprints, cool dn., stretch	**5,000m RACE!!!**	Easy 30 minutes	W/up, 4 x 30 sec. sprints, cool dn., then stretch	**10k RACE!!!**	Easy 30 min. walk (not racewalk, just walk)
17	Off	"" 6 x 400m @ 20k race pace, w/ 1:00 min. breaks	W/up, 4 x 30 sec. sprints, cool dn., stretch	**20k RACE!!!**	Easy 30-min. stroll.	Off!	Easy 5 miles

WMA Championships Triple Training Schedule-M75+, W50-W65

Week	Mon.	Tues.	Wed.	Thurs.	Fri.	Sat.	Sun.
1	Off or easy cross-train	45-minute fartlek	Moderate 30-mins.	45-minute fartlek	Off or easy cross-train	Moderate 30-mins.	Easy 8 miles (or 13k)
2	Off or easy cross-train	10-min. warm-up, drills, then 8 x 1:00 min. hill reps.	Mod. 35 mins.	45-minute fartlek	Off or easy cross-train	Mod. 35 mins.	Easy 8 miles (or 13k)
3	Off or easy cross-train	"" then 8 x 1:30 min. hill reps.	Mod. 40 mins.	45-minute fartlek	Off or easy cross-train	Mod. 40-mins.	"Not so easy" 5 miles/8k
4	Off or easy cross-train	"" 8 x 2:00 min. hill reps.	Mod. 45 mins.	10-min. warm-up, drills, then 40-min. progression	Off or easy cross-train	Mod. 45 mins.	Easy 9 miles (or 15k)
5	Off or easy cross-train	"" 10 x 200m fast w/200m breaks	Mod. 45 mins.	"" 45-minute tempo—steady, hard effort.	Off or easy cross-train	Mod. 45 mins.	"Not so easy"` 6 miles/10k
6	Off or easy cross-train	"" 8 x 400m @ 5,000m race pace, w/ 200m breaks.	Mod. 45 mins.	"" 50-min. progression.	Off or easy cross-train	Mod. 45 mins.	Easy 9 miles (or 15k)
7	Off or easy cross-train	"" 4 x {100m/200m/300m} w/ 100m breaks	Mod. 45 mins.	"" 4 x 1,600m @ current → goal 10k pace w/ easy 400m breaks.	Off or easy cross-train	Mod. 45 mins.	Easy 10 miles (or 16k)
8	Off or easy cross-train	"" 12 x 200m fast w/200m breaks	Mod. 45 mins.	"" 10k tempo	Off or easy cross-train	Mod. 45 mins.	"Not so easy" 8 miles/13k
9	Off or easy cross-train	"" 10 x 400m w/ 200m breaks.	Mod. 45 mins.	"" 5 x 1,600m @ current → goal 10k pace w/ easy 400m breaks.	Off or easy cross-train	Mod. 45 mins.	Easy 11 miles (or 17k)
10	Off or easy cross-train	"" 4 x {100m/200m/300m} w/ 100m breaks	Mod. 45 mins.	10k progression	Off or easy cross-train	Mod. 45 mins.	Easy 12 miles (or 19k)
11	Off or easy cross-train	"" 12 x 200m fast w/200m breaks	Mod. 45 mins.	"" 6 x 1,600m @ current → goal 10k pace w/ easy 400m breaks.	Off or easy cross-train	Mod. 45 mins.	"Not so easy" 9 miles/15k
12	Off	"" 6 x 400m w/ 200m breaks.	Easy 30 mins.	**"" 10k time-trial!!**	Off or easy cross-train	Mod. 45 mins.	Easy 12 miles (or 19k)
13	Off or easy cross-train	"" 4 x {100m/200m/300m} w/ 100m breaks	Mod. 45 mins.	"" 5 x 2K @ current → goal 10k pace w/ easy 400m breaks.	Off or easy cross-train	Mod. 45 mins.	Easy 13 miles (or 21k)
14	Off or easy cross-train	"" 12 x 200m fast w/200m breaks	Mod. 45 mins.	10k progression	Off or easy cross-train	Mod. 45 mins.	"Not so easy" 10 miles/16k
15	Off or easy cross-train	"" 10 x 400m w/ 200m breaks.	Mod. 45 mins.	"" 3k @ 10k pace; 1k @ 5k pace w/ easy 2:00 min. break	Easy 30 mins.	W/up, 1 x 2k @ 10k pace, 1 x 1k @ 5k pace w/ 1:00 break	Off
16	W/up, 4 x 30 sec. sprints, cool dn., stretch	**5,000m RACE!!!**	Easy 30 minutes	"" 4 x 400m @ 10k race pace, w/ 1:00 min. breaks.	W/up, 4 x 30 secs. cool dn., then stretch	**10k RACE!!!**	Easy 30 min. walk (not racewalk, just walk)
17	Off	"" 6 x 400m @ 20k race pace, w/ 1:00 min. breaks.	W/up, 4 x 30 sec. sprints, cool dn., stretch	**20k RACE!!!**	Easy 30-min. stroll.	Off!	Easy 5 miles

WMA Championships Triple Training Schedule-W30-W45, W70+

Week	Mon.	Tues.	Wed.	Thurs.	Fri.	Sat.	Sun.
1	Off or easy cross-train	45-minute fartlek	Moderate 30-mins.	45-minute fartlek	Off or easy cross-train	Moderate 30-mins.	Easy 8 miles (or 13k)
2	Off or easy cross-train	10-min. warm-up, drills, then 8 x 1:00 min. hill reps.	Mod. 35 mins.	45-minute fartlek	Off or easy cross-train	Mod. 35 mins.	Easy 8 miles (or 13k)
3	Off or easy cross-train	10-min. warm-up, drills, then 8 x 1:30 min. hill reps.	Mod. 40 mins.	45-minute fartlek	Off or easy cross-train	Mod. 40-mins.	"Not so easy" 5 miles/8k
4	Off or easy cross-train	"" 8 x 2:00 min. hill reps.	Mod. 45 mins.	10-min. warm-up, drills, then 40-min. progression	Off or easy cross-train	Mod. 45 mins.	Easy 9 miles (or 15k)
5	Off or easy cross-train	"" 10 x 200m fast w/200m breaks	Mod. 45 mins.	"" 45-minute tempo—steady, hard effort.	Off or easy cross-train	Mod. 45 mins.	"Not so easy"' 6 miles/10k
6	Off or easy cross-train	"" 8 x 400m @ 5,000m race pace, w/ 200m breaks	Mod. 45 mins.	"" 50-min. progression	Off or easy cross-train	Mod. 45 mins.	Easy 9 miles (or 15k)
7	Off or easy cross-train	"" 4 x {100m/200m/300m} w/ 100m breaks	Mod. 45 mins.	"" 4 x 1,600m @ current → goal 10k pace w/ easy 400m breaks.	Off or easy cross-train	Mod. 45 mins.	Easy 10 miles (or 16k)
8	Off or easy cross-train	"" 12 x 200m fast w/200m breaks	Mod. 45 mins.	"" 10k tempo	Off or easy cross-train	Mod. 45 mins.	"Not so easy" 8 miles/13k
9	Off or easy cross-train	"" 10 x 400m w/ 200m breaks	Mod. 45 mins.	"" 5 x 1,600m @ current → goal 10k pace w/ easy 400m breaks	Off or easy cross-train	Mod. 45 mins.	Easy 11 miles (or 17k)
10	Off or easy cross-train	"" 4 x {100m/200m/300m} w/ 100m breaks	Mod. 45 mins.	10k progression	Off or easy cross-train	Mod. 45 mins.	Easy 12 miles (or 19k)
11	Off or easy cross-train	"" 12 x 200m fast w/200m breaks	Mod. 45 mins.	"" 6 x 1,600m @ current → goal 10k pace w/ easy 400m breaks	Off or easy cross-train	Mod. 45 mins.	"Not so easy" 9 miles/15k
12	Off	"" 6 x 400m w/ 200m breaks	Easy 30 mins.	**"" 10k time-trial!!**	Off or easy cross-train	Mod. 45 mins.	Easy 12 miles (or 19k)
13	Off or easy cross-train	"" 4 x {100m/200m/300m} w/ 100m breaks	Mod. 45 mins.	"" 5 x 2K @ current → goal 10k pace w/ easy 400m breaks	Off or easy cross-train	Mod. 45 mins.	Easy 13 miles (or 21k)
14	Off or easy cross-train	"" 12 x 200m fast w/200m breaks	Mod. 45 mins.	10k progression	Off or easy cross-train	Mod. 45 mins.	"Not so easy" 10 miles/16k
15	Off or easy cross-train	"" 10 x 400m w/ 200m breaks.	Mod. 45 mins.	"" 3k @ 10k pace; 1k @ 5k pace w/ easy 2:00 min. break	Easy 30 mins.	Off	W/up, 4 x 30 sec. sprints, cool dn., stretch
16	**5,000m RACE!!!**	Easy 30 minutes	Off	"" 4 x 400m @ 10k race pace, w/ 1:00 min. breaks.	W/up, 4 x 30 sec. sprints, cool dn., then stretch	**10k RACE!!!**	Easy 30 min. walk (not racewalk, just walk)
17	Off	"" 6 x 400m @ 20k race pace, w/ 1:00 min. breaks	W/up, 4 x 30 sec. sprints, cool dn., stretch	**20k RACE!!!**	Easy 30-min. stroll	Off!	Easy 5 miles

CHAPTER 28: WMA CHAMPIONSHIPS DOUBLE: 10K ROAD WALK FOLLOWED BY 20K ROAD WALK

Some walkers either can't stick around for 10 days to do the WMA triple, or simply prefer the longer races, choosing to "only" do the 10k/20k double. The two races are usually separated by about five days. Masters athletes do take a bit longer to recover than open athletes, so recovery will be a key element of training between hard efforts, often separated by the same four-day gap as the WMA events. Although speed is always important, the strength to handle such a double is also critical.

Male and female competitors from around the globe mixing it up during the 2018 World Masters Athletics 20k road walk in Malaga, Spain. Photo credit: Emmanual Tardi

I have only one schedule in this section because I'm presupposing that by competing at the World Masters Championship you are not likely to be a beginning walker! Mileage will be an important element, but high-end speed work (economy training) is important for technique development, and tempo training is important for the challenge of walking a sustained, fast pace as is required for successful 10k and 20k racing.

WMA Championships 10k/20k Double Training Schedule							
Week	**Mon.**	**Tues.**	**Wed.**	**Thurs.**	**Fri.**	**Sat.**	**Sun.**
1	Off or easy cross-train	45-minute fartlek	Moderate 30-mins.	45-minute fartlek	Off or easy cross-train	Moderate 30-mins.	Easy 8 miles (or 13k)
2	Off or easy cross-train	10-min. warm-up, drills, then 8 x 1:00 min. hill reps.	Mod. 35 mins.	45-minute fartlek	Off or easy cross-train	Mod. 35 mins.	Easy 9 miles (or 15k)
3	Off or easy cross-train	10-min. warm-up, drills, then 8 x 1:30 min. hill reps.	Mod. 40 mins.	45-minute fartlek	Off or easy cross-train	Mod. 40-mins.	"Not so easy" 6 miles/10k
4	Off or easy cross-train	"" 8 x 2:00 min. hill reps.	Mod. 45 mins.	10-min. warm-up, drills, then 40-min. progression	Off or easy cross-train	Mod. 45 mins.	Easy 10 miles (or 16k)
5	Off or easy cross-train	"" 10 x 200m fast w/200m breaks	Mod. 45 mins.	"" 45-minute tempo—steady, hard effort	Off or easy cross-train	Mod. 45 mins.	"Not so easy"' 6 miles/10k
6	Off or easy cross-train	"" 8 x 400m @ 5,000m race pace, w/ 200m breaks	Mod. 45 mins.	"" 50-min. progression.	Off or easy cross-train	Mod. 45 mins.	Easy 11 miles (or 17.5k)
7	Off or easy cross-train	"" 4 x {100m/200m/300m} w/ 100m breaks	Mod. 45 mins.	"" 4 x 1,600m @ current → goal 10k pace w/ easy 400m breaks	Off or easy cross-train	Mod. 45 mins.	Easy 12 miles (or 19k)
8	Off or easy cross-train	"" 12 x 200m fast w/200m breaks	Mod. 45 mins.	"" 10k tempo	Off or easy cross-train	Mod. 45 mins.	"Not so easy" 8 miles/13k
9	Off or easy cross-train	"" 10 x 400m w/ 200m breaks	Mod. 45 mins.	"" 5 x 1,600m @ current → goal 10k pace w/ easy 400m breaks	Off or easy cross-train	Mod. 45 mins.	Easy 13 miles (or 21k)
10	Off or easy cross-train	"" 4 x {100m/200m/300m} w/ 100m breaks	Mod. 45 mins.	10k progression	Off or easy cross-train	Mod. 45 mins.	Easy 14 miles (or 22.5k)
11	Off or easy cross-train	"" 6 x 1,600m @ current → goal 10k pace w/ 400m breaks	Mod. 45 mins.	"" 8 x 200m fast w/200m breaks	Off	Easy 20 mins., 4 x 30 sec. sprints	**15k time-trial. Solid effort!**
12	Off	"" 6 x 400m w/ 200m breaks.	Mod. 30 mins.	10k progression	Off or easy cross-train	Mod. 45 mins.	Easy 15 miles (or 24k)
13	Off or easy cross-train	"" 4 x {100m/200m/300m} w/ 100m breaks	Mod. 45 mins.	"" 6 x 2K @ 20k → goal 10k pace w/ easy 400m breaks.	Off or easy cross-train	Mod. 45 mins.	Easy 15.5 miles (or 25k)
14	Off or easy cross-train	10k progression	Mod. 45 mins.	"" 12 x 200m fast w/200m breaks	Off or easy cross-train	Mod. 45 mins.	"Not so easy" 11 miles/18k
15	Off or easy cross-train	"" 10 x 400m w/ 200m breaks	Mod. 45 mins.	"" 5k @ 20k pace; 3k @ 10k pace; 2k @ 5k pace w/ 2:00 min. breaks	Off or easy cross-train	Mod. 30 mins.	10k. w/ 6k EZ, 4k progress down to 20k pace
16	Off or easy cross-train	Easy 30 minutes	"" 2 x 1k @ 10k pace w/ 1:00 breaks	Off	W/up, 4 x 30 sec. sprints, cool dn., then stretch	**10k RACE!!!**	Easy 30 min. walk (not racewalk, just walk)
17	Off	"" 6 x 400m @ 20k race pace, w/ 1:00 min. breaks	W/up, 4 x 30 secs. cool dn., stretch	**20k RACE!!!**	Easy 30-min. stroll	Off!	Easy 5 miles

CHAPTER 29: PORTLAND-TO-COAST RELAY RACE

The Portland-to-Coast Walk Relay, an offshoot of the Hood-to-Coast Running Relay, is the largest walk-only relay in the world. Known as "The Mother of All Relays," the race from downtown Portland to the Oregon Coast at Seaside, pits 400 men's, women's, and mixed-sex eight- to twelve-member teams against one another along the last 24 legs and 130 miles of the Hood-to-Coast Running Relay. The race involves 18½ to 36+ hours of walking—and riding along in a van packed to the gills with your tired, sweaty, slaphappy teammates. Each participant in the relay walks two or three legs in rotation, averaging between 10 and 16 total miles per team member. Portland-to-Coast attracts teams of walkers from all over the US and beyond, including a number

2000's winning Portland-to-Coast masters team and, to this day, overall record-setting walk team (18:31:06) featuring some of the all-time greats of US masters racewalking.

Photo credit: Ian Whatley

of elite racewalkers. Nick Christie, Katie Burnett, Ian Whatley, Erin and Dave Talcott, Pablo Gomez, and Lydia McGranahan are notable alumni.

Training for the Portland-to-Coast Walk Relay is a bit of a crapshoot, since it depends a lot on which of the 3.4- to 7.8-mile legs you'll be racing. In many ways training will be like training for the US Masters or WMA Championships in that you'll be racing two or three races in succession, but in the case of Portland-to-Coast, the gap between races is much shorter. The most important components of PTC training may well be the mental and logistical elements. Some of your workouts should be done in the dark of night, preferably after not sleeping for many hours, or sleeping in a lumpy, malodorous, claustrophobia-inducing environment. If I were a member of a twelve-person team training for Portland-to-Coast, for example, I would walk a hard 8k in the late evening, sleep for a few hours in a closet on my mangy Labra-mongrel's bed, with loud music blaring on the radio while the TV is concurrently playing a series of bad soap operas, and then get up four hours later and walk a hard 10k. If I were a member of an eight-member team I would go back to the closet, sleep another couple of hours, then do another hard 8k. But that's just me… Ian Whatley, co-captain of the record-setting "Racewalkers Northwest-USA Masters" team, has some other, perhaps better, suggestions:

> *"Logistics will defeat your team three times more often than other teams will defeat you. Mini-van exchanges with your vans at opposite ends of the leg where you agreed to meet will cost you an hour, while getting your van stuck in a ditch or hung up on a pile of asphalt in a parking area will cost you a lot more. Enjoy your first PTC, and try to join an experienced team. Watch and learn from the old hands. Be ready for the shock of your night leg(s). Getting out of a van at 3:00 in the morning on a pitch dark country road surrounded by trees full of strange noises from the fauna, with legs still feeling sore from your first leg, and a few hours crammed in a slow moving vehicle, make for a very tough physical and mental challenge. Train with all your night gear (headlamp, flashers, reflective vest, etc.), at your expected leg time. Gauge your food intake carefully. Don't eat anything in the hour before your leg, and make sure to refuel and rehydrate immediately after your leg."*

Ian tells a great story about the superiority of experience and deviousness vs. youthful vigor in a long stage race like Portland-to-Coast:

> *"We started two hours after 398 other walking teams. We were up against a team of Canadians with several junior international team members who should have kicked our butts on paper, but we were racing on roads, not paper. Never bet against a group of racewalkers with that much experience! The Canadians put a very fast 18-year-old girl on leg one. We got our driver, Jerry, a shot-putter who racewalked in masters meets for fun at average speeds but with decent form, to warm up, wearing a bib number. With five seconds to go before the start, Jerry gave me the wristband and I gave the young lady a polite smile. She was done for*

before the gun went off. She clearly had in mind to go off fast and bury the chunky old guy. I was in about 1:32 20k shape, having just raced at the Olympic Trials, and she foolishly went with me for the first mile. I handed off about four minutes up on her and their next walker panicked. She went off like a bat out of Hell—there were still 125+ miles to go—chasing a very fit and sensible Dave Lawrence. She blew up a couple of miles in, the gap grew and the game was over. They finished an hour back with the second fastest time ever, and utterly dejected to have been beaten by a group of old men."

Results may vary, but it's always a good idea to race smart, no matter what condition you're in. Of course the best way to go into any race is in great shape, and specifically prepared for the conditions under which you'll be racing. The following schedules are perfect preparation for, on average, three five-mile legs, each separated by about eight hours for an eight-member team, or two five-mile legs separated by about 12 hours for a 12-member team. If you're looking for a good time with a bunch of your best walking friends, and are crazy enough to do this, good luck to you!

Portland-to-Coast Twelve-Team-Member Training Schedule							
Week	**Mon.**	**Tues.**	**Wed.**	**Thurs.**	**Fri.**	**Sat.**	**Sun.**
1	Off or easy cross-train	45-minute fartlek	Moderate 30 mins.	45-minute fartlek	Off or easy cross-train	Moderate 30 mins.	Easy 7 miles (or 11k)
2	Off or easy cross-train	10-min. warm-up, drills, then 8 x 1:00 min. hill reps.	Moderate 35 mins.	45-minute fartlek	Off or easy cross-train	Moderate 35 mins.	Easy 7.5 miles (or 12k)
3	Off or easy cross-train	"" 8 x 1:30 min. hill reps.	Moderate 40 mins.	45-minute fartlek	Off or easy cross-train	Mod. 40-min.	Easy 8 miles (or 13k)
4	Off or easy cross-train	"" 8 x 2:00 min. hill reps.	Moderate 45 mins.	10-min. warm-up, drills, then 40-min. progression	Off or easy cross-train	Mod. 45 mins.	Easy 6 miles (or 10k)
5	Off or easy cross-train	"" 10 x 200m fast w/200m breaks	Moderate 45 mins.	"" 45-minute tempo—steady, hard effort	Off or easy cross-train	Mod. 45 mins.	Easy 9 miles (or 14k)
6	Off or easy cross-train	"" 8 x 400m @ 5,000m race pace, w/ 200m breaks	Moderate 45 mins.	10-min. warm-up, drills, then 45-min. progression	Off or easy cross-train	Mod. 45 mins.	Easy 9.5 miles (or 15k)
7	Off or easy cross-train	"" 4 x {100m/200m/ 300m} w/ 100m breaks	Moderate 45 mins.	"" 4 x 1,600m @ current → goal 8k pace w/ easy 400m breaks	Off or easy cross-train	Mod. 45 mins.	Easy 10 miles (or 16k)
8	Off or easy cross-train	"" 12 x 200m fast w/200m breaks	Moderate 45 mins.	"" 45-minute tempo—steady, hard effort	Off or easy cross-train	Mod. 45 mins.	Easy 8 miles (or 13k)
9	Off or easy cross-train	"" 10 x 400m w/ 200m breaks	Moderate 45 mins.	"" 4 x 1,600m @ current → goal 8k pace w/ easy 400m breaks	Off or easy cross-train	Mod. 45 mins.	Easy 10 miles (or 16k)
10	Off or easy cross-train	Easy 45 minutes	Late afternoon / evening 8k tempo	Late night or early morning hilly 8k progression	Off or easy cross-train	Mod. 45 mins.	Easy 10 miles (or 16k)
11	Off or easy cross-train	"" 12 x 200m fast w/200m breaks	Moderate 45 mins.	"" 5 x 1,600m @ current → goal 8k pace w/ easy 400m breaks	Off or easy cross-train	Mod. 45 mins.	Easy 10 miles (or 16k)
12	Off	"" 6 x 400m w/ 200m breaks	Easy 30 mins.	**10-min. warm-up, drills, then 8k time-trial!!**	Off or easy cross-train	Mod. 45 mins.	Easy 8 miles (or 13k)
13	Off or easy cross-train	"" 4 x {100m/200m/ 300m} w/ 100m breaks	Moderate 45 mins.	"" 4 x 2K @ current → goal 8k pace w/ easy 400m breaks	Off or easy cross-train	Mod. 45 mins.	Easy 10 miles (or 16k)
14	Off or easy cross-train	Easy 45 minutes	Late afternoon / evening 8k tempo	Late night or early morning hilly 8k progression	Off or easy cross-train	Mod. 45 mins.	Easy 10 miles (or 16k)
15	Off or easy cross-train	"" 10 x 400m w/ 200m breaks	Easy 45 mins.	"" 4k tempo; 3k @ current 8k pace; 1k @ goal pace w/ easy 3:00 min. breaks	Off or easy cross-train	Easy 45 mins.	Easy 8 miles (or 13k)
16	Off	"" 3 x 1K @ 8k pace w/ 1:00 breaks	Off	"" 4 x 30 sec. sprints, cool dn., then stretch	**RACE!!!**		Sleep! ☺

Portland-to-Coast Eight-Team-Member Training Schedule

Week	Mon.	Tues.	Wed.	Thurs.	Fri.	Sat.	Sun.
1	Off or easy cross-train	45-minute fartlek	Moderate 30 mins.	45-minute fartlek	Off or easy cross-train	Moderate 30 mins.	Easy 7 miles (or 11k)
2	Off or easy cross-train	10-min. warm-up, drills, then 8 x 1:00 min. hill reps.	Moderate 35 mins.	45-minute fartlek	Off or easy cross-train	Moderate 35 mins.	Easy 7.5 miles (or 12k)
3	Off or easy cross-train	"" 8 x 1:30 min. hill reps.	Moderate 40 mins.	45-minute fartlek	Off or easy cross-train	Mod. 40-min.	Easy 8 miles (or 13k)
4	Off or easy cross-train	"" 8 x 2:00 min. hill reps.	Moderate 45 mins.	"" 40-min. progression	Off or easy cross-train	Mod. 45 mins.	Easy 6 miles (or 10k)
5	Off or easy cross-train	"" 10 x 200m fast w/200m breaks	Moderate 45 mins.	"" 45-minute tempo—steady, hard effort	Off or easy cross-train	Mod. 45 mins.	Easy 9 miles (or 14k)
6	Off or easy cross-train	"" 8 x 400m @ 5,000m race pace, w/ 200m breaks	Moderate 45 mins.	"" 45-min. progression	Off or easy cross-train	Mod. 45 mins.	Easy 9.5 miles (or 15k)
7	Off or easy cross-train	"" 4 x {100m/200m/300m} w/ 100m breaks	Moderate 45 mins.	"" 4 x 1,600m @ current → goal 8k pace w/ easy 400m breaks	Off or easy cross-train	Mod. 45 mins.	Easy 10 miles (or 16k)
8	Off or easy cross-train	"" 12 x 200m fast w/200m breaks	Moderate 45 mins.	"" 45-minute tempo—steady, hard effort.	Off or easy cross-train	Mod. 45 mins.	Easy 8 miles (or 13k)
9	Off or easy cross-train	"" 10 x 400m w/ 200m breaks	Moderate 45 mins.	"" 4 x 1,600m @ current → goal 8k pace w/ easy 400m breaks	Off or easy cross-train	Mod. 45 mins.	Easy 10 miles (or 16k)
10	Off or easy cross-train	Easy 45 minutes.	Moderate 45 mins.	Easy 45 minutes.	Off or easy cross-train	Morning 8k tempo, then afternoon/ evening 8k progression	Late night or early morning hilly 8k progression.
11	Off or easy cross-train	"" 12 x 200m fast w/200m breaks	Moderate 45 mins.	"" 5 x 1,600m @ current → goal 8k pace w/ easy 400m breaks.	Off or easy cross-train	Mod. 45 mins.	Easy 10 miles (or 16k)
12	Off	"" 6 x 400m w/ 200m breaks.	Easy 30 mins.	**10-min. warm-up, drills, then 8k time-trial!!**	Off or easy cross-train	Mod. 45 mins.	Easy 8 miles (or 13k)
13	Off or easy cross-train	"" 4 x {100m/200m/300m} w/ 100m breaks	Moderate 45 mins.	"" 4 x 2K @ current → goal 8k pace w/ easy 400m breaks	Off or easy cross-train	Mod. 45 mins.	Easy 10 miles (or 16k)
14	Off or easy cross-train	Easy 45 minutes	Moderate 45 mins.	Easy 45 minutes.	Off or easy cross-train	Morning 8k tempo, then afternoon/ evening 8k progression	Late night or early a.m. hilly 8k progression
15	Off or easy cross-train	""10 x 400m w/ 200m breaks	Easy 45 mins.	"" 4k tempo; 3k @ current 8k pace; 1k @ goal pace w/ easy 3:00 min. breaks	Off or easy cross-train	Easy 45 mins.	Easy 8 miles (or 13k)
16	Off	"" 3 x 1K @ 8k pace w/ 1:00 breaks	Off	10-min. w/ up, then 4 x 30 sec. sprints, cool dn., then stretch	**RACE!!!**		Sleep! ☺

CHAPTER 30: DISNEY'S "GOOFY" AND "DOPEY" CHALLENGES

In the Olden Days, Florida's Walt Disney World Marathon and Half-Marathon shared the same starting line and start time. It was really tough to race the full marathon because right around the 12-mile mark, everybody around you would start going faster and faster. Struggling to keep up, your confidence would begin to waver: "What's going on here?! Why the heck am I slowing down?" Then all of a sudden, after 12½ miles, 90% of the field would veer off to the half-marathon finish line, leaving you to suffer alone for the next 13½ miles after having just blown your gasket surging to keep up with the "quitters"—er, half-marathoners. ☺ In 2006 organizers solved the problem by moving the half-marathon to Saturday followed by the full marathon on Sunday to ease crowding on the course. What event organizers didn't realize was that many participants would decide to register for both events! Voilà! "Goofy's Race-and-a-Half Challenge" was born!

The challenge of racing a half-marathon followed by a full marathon the next day was an immediate success, aided in no small part by the extra medal bestowed upon completers of both events. Further changes allowed for the possibility of racing the 5k, 10k, half-marathon and full marathon on four consecutive days, for a total of 48.6 miles. Disney rolled with it, came up with yet another medal for those who complete all four races, and named their creation the "Dopey Challenge." What follows are training schedules for walking both the Goofy and Dopey Challenges. Much like training for the various other

The payoff for subjecting your body to the rigors of the Dopey Challenge: Hardware! Photo credit: rundisney.com

multi-event series in this section, a big part of your preparation for the Goofy or Dopey Challenges will be of the logistical and mental variety. Speeding your mental and physical recovery from each event will be paramount. With 5:30am start times for the half-marathon and marathon, it can be all too easy to say: "Screw it! I'm not doing this!" when the alarm clock rings at 3:00 or 3:30am each race morning. Caffeine, then, will be a critical component of your pre-race preparation; that, and maybe a little pixie dust. ☺ And now, bibbidi bobbidi boo, without further ado, on to the Most Magical Training Schedules on Earth!

Disney's Goofy Challenge Training Schedule

Week	Mon.	Tues.	Wed.	Thurs.	Fri.	Sat.	Sun.
1	Off or easy cross-train	45-minute fartlek	Easy 3-4 miles	4 miles at goal pace	Off or easy cross-train	Moderate 3 miles	Easy 12 miles
2	Off or easy cross-train	50-minute fartlek	Easy 3-4 miles	4 miles at goal pace	Off or easy cross-train	Easy 3 miles	10 miles at goal pace
3	Off or easy cross-train	60-minute fartlek	Easy 4-5 miles	4 miles at goal pace	Off or easy cross-train	Moderate 3 miles	Easy 13 miles
4	Off or easy cross-train	60-minute fartlek	Easy 5 miles	5 miles at goal pace	Off or easy cross-train	Easy 4 miles	10 miles at goal pace
5	Off or easy cross-train	60-minute fartlek	Easy 5 miles	5 miles at goal pace	Off or easy cross-train	Moderate 4 miles	Easy 14 miles
6	Off or easy cross-train	60-minute fartlek	Easy 5 miles	5 miles at goal pace	Off or easy cross-train	Easy 4 miles	10 miles at goal pace
7	Off or easy cross-train	60-minute fartlek	Easy 5 miles	5 miles at goal pace	Off or easy cross-train	Moderate 4 miles	Easy 15 miles
8	Off or easy cross-train	60-minute fartlek	Easy 5 miles	5 miles at goal pace	Off or easy cross-train	Easy 5 miles	12 miles at goal pace
9	Off or easy cross-train	10-min. warm-up, drills , then 8 x 30 sec. hill repeats.	Easy 5 miles	5 miles at goal pace	Off or easy cross-train	Moderate 5 miles	Easy 16 miles
10	Off or easy cross-train	"" 8 x 1 min. hill repeats.	Easy 5 miles	5 miles at goal pace	Off or easy cross-train	Easy 5 miles	12 miles at goal pace
11	Off or easy cross-train	"" then 8 x 90 sec. hill repeats.	Easy 5 miles	5 miles at goal pace	Off or easy cross-train	Moderate 5 miles	18 miles
12	Off or easy cross-train	"" 12 x 200m fast w/ 200m breaks	Easy 5 miles	5 miles at goal pace	Off or easy cross-train	8-mile prog. to goal pace	12 miles at goal pace
13	Off or easy cross-train	60-minute fartlek	Easy 5 miles	5 miles at goal pace	Off or easy cross-train	8-mile prog. to goal pace	Easy 20 miles
14	Off or easy cross-train	"" 12 x 200m fast w/ 200m breaks	Easy 5 miles	5 miles at goal pace	Off or easy cross-train	Easy 5 miles	12 miles at goal pace
15	Off or easy cross-train	60-minute fartlek	Easy 5 miles	5 miles at goal pace	Off or easy cross-train	8-mile prog. to goal pace	Easy 20 miles
16	Off or easy cross-train	""8 x 400m @ 5k pace w/ 200m breaks	Easy 5 miles	5 miles at goal pace	Off or easy cross-train	8-mile prog. to goal pace	Easy 10 miles, then 5 at goal
17	Off or easy cross-train	45-minute fartlek	Easy 5 miles	5 miles at goal pace	Off or easy cross-train	Easy 5 miles	8 miles at goal pace
18	Off or easy cross-train	Easy 45 mins.	3 miles at goal pace	Off	10 min. warm-up, 4 x 30 seconds fast, then stretch.	**Disney Half-Marathon**	**Disney Marathon!**

Disney's Dopey Challenge Training Schedule							
Week	**Monday**	**Tuesday**	**Wednesday**	**Thursday**	**Friday**	**Saturday**	**Sunday**
1	Off or easy cross-train	45-minute fartlek	Easy 3-4 miles	4 miles at goal pace	Off or easy cross-train	Moderate 3 miles	Easy 12 miles
2	Off or easy cross-train	50-minute fartlek	Easy 3-4 miles	4 miles at goal pace	Off or easy cross-train	Easy 3 miles	10 miles at goal pace
3	Off or easy cross-train	60-minute fartlek	Easy 4-5 miles	4 miles at goal pace	Off or easy cross-train	Mod. 3 miles	Easy 13 miles
4	Off or easy cross-train	60-minute fartlek	Easy 5 miles	5 miles at goal pace	Off or easy cross-train	Easy 4 miles	10 miles at goal pace
5	Off or easy cross-train	60-minute fartlek	Easy 5 miles	5 miles at goal pace	Off or easy cross-train	Mod. 4 miles	Easy 14 miles
6	Off or easy cross-train	60-minute fartlek	Easy 5 miles	5 miles at goal pace	Off or easy cross-train	Easy 4 miles	10 miles at goal pace
7	Off or easy cross-train	60-minute fartlek	Easy 5 miles	5 miles at goal pace	Off or easy cross-train	Mod. 4 miles	Easy 15 miles
8	Off or easy cross-train	60-minute fartlek	Easy 5 miles	5 miles at goal pace	Off or easy cross-train	Easy 5 miles	12 miles at goal pace
9	Off or easy cross-train	10-min. warm-up, drills, then 8 x 30 sec. hill repeats	Easy 5 miles	5 miles at goal pace	Off or easy cross-train	Mod. 5 miles	Easy 16 miles
10	Off or easy cross-train	"" 8 x 1 min. hill repeats	Easy 5 miles	5 miles at goal pace	Off or easy cross-train	Easy 5 miles	12 miles at goal pace
11	Off or easy cross-train	"" 8 x 90 sec. hill repeats	Easy 5 miles	5 miles at goal pace	Off or easy cross-train	Mod. 5 miles	18 miles
12	Off or easy cross-train	"" 8 x 200m fast w/ 200m breaks	Easy 5 miles	W./up, drills, then 5k tempo	10k progression	8-mile prog. To goal pace	12 miles at goal pace
13	Off or easy cross-train	60-minute fartlek	Easy 5 miles	W./up, drills, then 5k tempo	10k progression	8-mile prog. to goal pace	Easy 20 miles
14	Off or easy cross-train	"" 12 x 200m fast w/ 200m breaks	Easy 5 miles	5 miles at goal pace	Off or easy cross-train	Easy 5 miles	12 miles at goal pace
15	Off or easy cross-train	60-minute fartlek	Easy 5 miles	W./up, drills, then 5k tempo	10k progression	8-mile prog. to goal pace	Easy 20 miles
16	Off or easy cross-train	"" 8 x 400m @ 5k pace w/ 200m breaks	Easy 5 miles	W./up, drills, then 5k tempo	10k progression	8-mile prog. to goal pace	Easy 10 miles, then 5 at goal
17	Off or easy cross-train	45-minute fartlek	Easy 5 miles	5 miles at goal pace	Off or easy cross-train	Easy 5 miles	8 miles at goal pace
18	Off or easy cross-train	Off	10 min. warm-up, 4 x 30 seconds fast, then stretch	**Disney 5k!**	**Disney 10k!**	**Disney Half-Marathon!**	**Disney Marathon!**

Recovery after each race of the Dopey Challenge (and after the half-marathon of the Goofy Challenge) is critical. Taking in fluids, carbs., and a little protein, cooling your legs off in the pool, maybe getting a massage, and resting—not standing in line all day at the parks!—are important for race-to-race recovery. The WORST thing you can do is sit in the Jacuzzi with a beer. Or six. Alcohol is a diuretic, which hinders rehydration, and the warm water exacerbates inflammation and swelling. One of my former athletes (I was not coaching her at the time!) wound up in The Most Magical ER on Earth with dehydration and hyponatremia after nearly passing out in the Jacuzzi a few hours after her race. Don't let this happen to you!

CHAPTER 31: THE OLYMPIC-DOUBLE! 20K FOLLOWED BY 50K

Since 1956, when the 20-kilometer racewalk was added to the Olympic program, the Games have featured a men's 20k followed by the 50k, separated by about one week. (The men's 50k made its first Olympic appearance in 1932.) The scheduling of the most recent World Athletics Championships in Doha, Qatar, in late September/early October of 2019 saw the 50k first, followed by the 20k six days later. The women had it even tougher, with the 20k occurring just one day after the 50k![62] The World Athletics Team Championships and the Pan Am Race Walk Cup, with the 20k on Saturday and the 50k the very next morning, is marginally better, but still not at all an advisable double; I won't encourage such foolishness by creating training schedules for any of these scenarios. ☺ Recovery from a hard 50k takes weeks, or even months, not a day or days, so the focus of this chapter is the Olympic double. The *current* Olympic-double, that is... As of publication, there is a strong push by athletes to create parity between the sexes by adding a women's 50k event to the Olympics, but unfortunately an equally strong push-back from World Athletics, led by the IOC, to not only *not* add a women's 50k, but to shorten the championships distances for men and women to 10k and 30 or 35k! But for now, the 20/50 is the reality so let's talk about training for the current, traditional events!

Walking a hard 20k followed a week later by a 50k may seem like an impossible task, but not only is it possible, Poland's Robert Korzeniowski proved it's possible to *excel* in both races when he won gold in both the 20k and the 50k at the 2000 Sydney Olympics. Although many have tried, only a handful of other athletes have had the chops to succeed at the double at the Olympic-medal level. Mexican great Raúl González, silver medalist in the 20k and Olympic Champion in the 50k at Los Angeles in 1984, comes to mind. Aussie Jared Tallent's medal collection includes bronze and silver in the 2008 Olympic 20k and 50k, and a 7th in the 2012 Olympic 20k to go along with his gold medal in the 50k. Tallent has also used the 20k as a warm-up for the 50k in the World Championships, placing 6th in the 20k and 7th in the 50k in 2009, and placing 26th in the 20k and taking silver in the 50k in 2015. Another of the world's best doublers in recent years has been Ireland's Robert Heffernan, who was coached throughout much of his career by Korzeniowski, the undisputed greatest doubler of all-time. Robbie placed third in the 20k at the 2010 European Championships, then came back three days later to place fourth in the 50k; he placed ninth in the

[62] If I know World Athletics like I think I know World Athletics, this was to hurt participation in the women's 50k, figuring an underwhelming event would give them more leverage to kill the women's 50k. They failed miserably: The women's 50k was an incredible race!

50k at the 2012 London Olympics before taking the bronze medal in the 50k. The following year Rob beat the Russians on their home turf in Moscow, becoming World Champion in the 50k.

While researching for this chapter I asked Rob if he had any tips on training for the Olympic double. He told me to piss off, but that's just Robbie. ☺ With a little more cajoling, Rob gave me some insight into his training leading up to his London Olympics double. There's a lot more on the topic in Chapter 46, but Rob's Big Secret, not just in terms of the Olympic double, but woven throughout every aspect of his training, is rest. Rest after hard workouts and races, very easy tapers leading into races, and a complete break from training at the end of every season. Rob also emphasized the importance of periodizing his training throughout the year and always training at the right intensity, using both heart rate monitoring and lactate testing as guides. According to Rob, in a bit of a stream-of-consciousness phone message:

2013 World 50k Champion, Rob Heffernan.

> *"If you've trained and periodized your year right, when it comes to the time when you have to shine, you can really enjoy that part of the year. You're not mentally burnt out and you can enjoy having the whole winter behind you, enjoy—after doing all the right things—that you can really express yourself in the championships. Whereas a lot of people can get carried away with the intensity of the training, [some workouts are] meant to be a bit easier. It's not as quick, so more people are able to do them. But whereas the top fellas are doing it at 70%, 80% you've got the middle of the road athlete doing it at 90% to 100% thinking they're as good as the top athletes. Knowing what part of the year you're at, knowing when to be on, when to be off, when to relax; to realize how important recovery is, and mentally, when to attack the year and when to just get the work in and be able to just switch off, because if you don't recover right, you can't adapt from training. So that's where all your life choices come in. If you're going to be training really hard, and you're training to compete, you need know how to recover. You figure it out if you have a champion's mindset. There are athletes out there who just love training, they love the lifestyle, they just love getting out the*

door and they're happy about that, but guys who are training to win, you need to maximize everything... your diet, your sleep, everything. It's just so, so important."

2016 US Olympic Track & Field Team coach Troy Engle agrees. Troy is *so* old he remembers a time when the US Olympic Trials lined up with the Olympic schedule, with the 1984 20k trial held in Los Angeles on June 16th, and the 50k held one week later on the 23rd.[63] Troy not only *remembers* the '84 Trials, he competed in both the 20k and the 50k, finishing a solid 11th in the 20k and 6th in the 50k.[64] Several other walkers doubled as well, including the winner of *both* races, Marco Evoniuk, and eventual five-time Olympian Carl Schueler, 5th in the 20k and 3rd in the 50k. I wrote in the introduction to this section that a good walker is a good walker is a good walker, and the same holds true with regards to the double. If you're a solid 20k walker, with the right training you can become a pretty good 50k walker, and vice versa. It's no surprise then that Marco was able to win both races, or that so many other walkers—half the 50k field, and one-third of the 24 walkers in the 20k—were able to qualify for both races, and to at least attempt the double. In fact, every one of the top five finishers in the 20k came back to do the 50k a week later. Clearly they were all very fit individuals, but how did they come back so soon after a hard, hot-weather 20k and be ready to race another hard hot-weather race—a 50k, no less!—a week later? I have my own ideas, but considering his years of experience as a both a high-power coach, and as a 20k/50k athlete, I wanted to ask Troy for his thoughts on the Olympic double. (So I did.) ☺

"To try and double in both the 20k and 50k is without question one of the most challenging physical acts an athlete can attempt. Bear in mind that the total distance of these two races is greater than the cumulative distance of all other Olympic races (including the marathon) combined! From a physiological perspective, there is literally nothing you can do to enhance your conditioning [in the days between the two races]. *The name of the game is literally not screwing things up and doing everything you can to aid your system in the recovery process. That necessitates a concerted focus on muscular repair, energy system replenishment and psychological rejuvenation. It requires you to do just enough activity to stimulate blood flow to damaged muscles and to assist in the removal of metabolic waste. Nutrition should focus on replacement of glycogen stores and muscle repair. Most importantly perhaps is the need to focus on mentally "resetting" and relaxing*

---

[63] These days the 50k is held months before the track & field trials, to allow athletes plenty of time to recover from the 50k trial, have a spring 20k season, or race the 50k at the May World Cup/Team Championships, before racing the 20k Trials in June.

[64] Unlike Grandpa Troy, I was *so* young at the time that I competed in the Junior—under age 20—10,000m on the track in the Olympic Stadium the morning after watching the 50k trial. I placed 2nd, and the experience was so motivating that I immediately set my sights on qualifying for the '88 Olympic Trials—the 20k Trials, anyway!—and many more beyond!

to allow the body to sleep and repair. It's a bit of a tightrope that coach and athlete must walk to "wind down" and recover and then prepare the system for the intense, grueling effort of the 50k."

So a good walker is a good walker is a good walker, but that good walker needs to be very dedicated to his recovery between events. It's not as easy as it sounds, so it's the rare individual that can be among the best in the world at both distances, but certainly Rob Heffernan belongs in that rarefied group. In contrast to Perseus Karlström (Chapter 16), Rob really liked to periodize his years so that he was at his absolute peak just in time for the Olympics or World Championships. I can't possibly reproduce his entire two-year schedule leading up to these events, but here are some sample weeks to give an idea of how Rob trained for his London double in case you would like to do the same. ☺

Rob Heffernan's Olympic Double Schedule September/October						
Monday	**Tuesday**	**Wednesday**	**Thursday**	**Friday**	**Saturday**	**Sunday**
Active rest phase. No racewalking! Running about 40 miles per week, playing games, soccer, etc. Family time.						

November - February: Winter Base Training in Cork and Australia						
Mon.	**Tues.**	**Wed.**	**Thurs.**	**Fri.**	**Sat.**	**Sun.**
AM: Easy 12k PM: Easy 8k	AM: Easy 15k PM: Easy 8k	AM: Easy 25k PM: Easy 8k	AM: 10 x 2k/1k between 20k and 50k pace PM: Easy 8k	AM: Easy 12k PM: Easy 8k	"Easy" 40k	AM: Easy 10k PM: Easy 8k
Easy morning 12k, evening 8k	AM: Easy 15k PM: Easy 8k	AM: Easy 25k PM: 8k	AM: 8 x 3k/1k between 20k and 50k pace PM: Easy 8k	AM: Easy 15k PM: 8k	35k Tempo	AM: Easy 10k PM: Easy 8k

March – May: 20k Racing Season						
Mon.	**Tues.**	**Wed.**	**Thurs.**	**Fri.**	**Sat.**	**Sun.**
AM: Easy 12k PM: Easy 8k + Gym	AM: Easy 15k PM: 4k plus 2 x {100/200/300/200/100}	AM: 20k w/10k easy/10k hard PM: Easy 6k	AM: Easy 12k PM: Easy 6k + Gym	AM: 15k w/ last 5k as 100 fast/400 easy PM: 6-8km	AM: 8x2km/500m PM: Easy 6-8km	AM: Easy 12k
Easy morning 12k, evening 8k	AM: Hard 10 x 1k/400m PM: Easy 8k	AM: Easy 20k PM: 8k	AM: 8 x 3k/1k between 20k and 50k pace PM: Easy 8k	AM: Easy 8k	**World Cup, Saransk, Russia 20k 11th, 1:21:51**	AM: Easy 10k PM: Easy 8k

June-July: Altitude Camp in Spain						
Mon.	**Tues.**	**Wed.**	**Thurs.**	**Fri.**	**Sat.**	**Sun.**
AM: Easy 12k PM: Easy 8k	AM: Easy 15k PM: Easy 8k	AM: Easy 25k PM: Easy 8k	AM: 10 x 2k/1k between 20k and 50k pace PM: Easy 8k	AM: Easy 12k PM: Easy 8k	"Easy" 40k	AM: Easy 10k PM: Easy 8k
Easy morning 12k, evening 8k	AM: Easy 15k PM: Easy 8k	AM: Easy 25k PM: 8k	AM: 8 x 3k/1k between 20k and 50k pace PM: Easy 8k	Easy morning 15k Evening 8k	35k Tempo	AM: Easy 10k PM: Easy 8k

CHAPTER 32: THREE-DAY CHARITY WALKS AND FOUR-DAY "MARCHES"

This chapter is a bit of anomaly for this book since these are *non*-competitive walks—no times or place awards are given. But they are significant endurance challenges, they're very popular, and in the case of the Susan G. Komen Breast Cancer 3-Day walks, they're held for a very good cause that is worthy of all our support. The Komen walks take place in cities throughout the US, bringing thousands of women and men together to raise money for Susan G. Komen (formerly known as Susan G. Komen for the Cure, and prior to that, The Susan G. Komen Breast Cancer Foundation.) An offshoot of the now-defunct 39.3-mile Avon 2-Day Walks, the Komen 3-Days are 60-mile walks over three days that raise millions of dollars for breast cancer research, education, and community health programs. On the other side of the pond, the Nijmegen International Four-Day March, first held in 1909, is the largest multiple-day walking event in the world. Nearly 50,000 participants from over 70 nations walk 30, 40 or 50 kilometers per day for four consecutive days. On the final day,

Karen and Nick Bdera[65], looking great two days into New York City's 3-Day Walk. Karen is a veteran of three 3-Day and 16 2-day (39 miles) walks for breast cancer.

Photo courtesy of Karen Bdera

[65] Nick, by the way, was the oldest man to ever qualify for and compete in the US Track & Field Olympic Trials, when he walked 50 kilometers in 4:44:10 at the age of 55 in 2004. His longevity inspired me to go for my 9th Olympic Trials at age 55 in 2020. Now about that hat…☺

as participants near the finish, an enormous and enthusiastic crowd of spectators presents the walkers with gladiolus flowers, a symbol of victory since Roman times, when gladiators were similarly showered with the sword-shaped flowers. After crossing the finish line, finishers are presented with a military-style medal, the Cross of the Four Day Marches.

Training for these three- and four-day events will be more like training for a series of races than a true ultra-marathon since there are long breaks between the segments. There is really no need for speed here, but strings of consecutive long days will be crucial. As always, it's a good idea to start with several weeks of base training (Chapter 16) before moving on to the specific three-day or four-day schedules, but in the case of these non-competitive walks, it's not critical to do so.

For more information or to sign up for a Susan G. Komen 3-Day, head to www.the3day.org or call (800) 996-3DAY; to learn about or register for the Nijmegen Four-Day Marches, let your fingers do the walking to www.4daagse.nl/.

3-Day Walk for Breast Cancer 16-Week Training Schedule

Week	Monday	Tuesday	Wednesday	Thursday	Friday	Saturday	Sunday
1	Off	3 miles	Off	4 miles	30 minutes	5 miles	3 miles
2	Off	3 miles	15 minutes	5 miles	30 minutes	6 miles	5 miles
3	Off	3 miles	15 minutes	5 miles	30 minutes	7 miles	6 miles
4	Off	3 miles	15 minutes	5 miles	30 minutes	8 miles	6 miles
5	Off	3 miles	15 minutes	5 miles	30 minutes	10 miles	6 miles
6	Off	4 miles	30 minutes	5 miles	45 minutes	6 miles	5 miles
7	Off	4 miles	30 minutes	5 miles	45 minutes	12 miles	9 miles
8	Off	4 miles	30 minutes	5 miles	45 minutes	14 miles	10 miles
9	Off	4 miles	30 minutes	5 miles	45 minutes	15 miles	11 miles
10	Off	5 miles	45 minute	6 miles	45 minutes	17 miles	13 miles
11	Off	5 miles	45 minutes	6 miles	45 minutes	10 miles	6 miles
12	Off	5 miles	45 minutes	6 miles	45 minutes	18 miles	15 miles
13	Off	5 miles	45 minutes	6 miles	45 minutes	10 miles	8 miles
14	Off	6 miles	45 minutes	6 miles	45 minutes	18 miles	8 miles
15	Off	4 miles	45 minutes	5 miles	45 minutes	10 miles	8 miles
16	Off	5 miles	30 minutes	Off	**3-Day Walk! 20-20-20**		

As a non-competitive event, the only goal is to complete the 60 miles—and the training that will get you there! There is no need for speed work, but course-specific training is recommended. If your event is on a hilly course, you should do at least some of your training on hills.

3-Day Walk for Breast Cancer 24-Week Training Schedule							
Week	**Monday**	**Tuesday**	**Wednesday**	**Thursday**	**Friday**	**Saturday**	**Sunday**
1	Off	45 mins.	Off	45 mins.	Off	45 mins.	5 miles
2	Off	45 mins.	Off	45 mins.	Off	45 mins.	6 miles
3	Off	60 mins.	Off	60 mins.	Off	45 mins.	7 miles
4	Off	45 mins.	Off	45 mins.	Off	45 mins.	6 miles
5	Off	60 mins.	Off	60 mins.	Off	45 mins.	8 miles
6	Off	60 mins.	Off	60 mins.	Off	45 mins.	9 miles
7	Off	60 mins.	Off	60 mins.	Off	45 mins.	10 miles
8	Off	45 mins.	Off	45 mins.	Off	45 mins.	8 miles
9	Off	60 mins.	Off	60 mins.	Off	45 mins.	12 miles
10	Off	60 mins.	Off	60 mins.	Off	45 mins.	13 miles
11	Off	60 mins.	Off	60 mins.	Off	45 mins.	14 miles
12	Off	45 mins.	Off	45 mins.	Off	10 miles	10 miles
13	Off	60 mins.	Off	60 mins.	Off	45 mins.	15 miles
14	Off	60 mins.	Off	60 mins.	Off	45 mins.	16 miles
15	Off	60 mins.	Off	60 mins.	Off	45 mins.	17 miles
16	Off	45 mins.	45 mins.	Off	5 miles	12 miles	12 miles
17	Off	60 mins.	Off	60 mins.	Off	45 mins.	18 miles
18	Off	60 mins.	Off	60 mins.	Off	45 mins.	19 miles
19	Off	60 mins.	Off	60 mins.	Off	45 mins.	20 miles
20	Off	60 mins.	45 mins.	Off	5 miles	15 miles	15 miles
21	Off	60 mins.	Off	60 mins.	Off	15 miles.	20 miles
22	Off	60 mins.	Off	60 mins.	Off	15 miles	15 miles
23	Off	60 mins.	Off	60 mins.	Off	45 mins.	6 miles
24	Off	3 miles	Off	2 miles	**20-20-20-mile walk!!!**		

Although 16 weeks is enough time for most people to get ready to walk a Komen three-day, if you have enough lead-time, longer is better. This 24-week schedule will allow for a more gradual mileage build-up, as well as more three-day back-to-back-to-back long days to mimic the Komen schedule.

Nijmegen 4-Day 30k/Day 16-Week Training Schedule							
Week	**Monday**	**Tuesday**	**Wednesda**	**Thursday**	**Friday**	**Saturday**	**Sunday**
1	Off	60 mins.	Off	60 mins.	Off	14k	12k
2	Off	60 mins.	Off	60 mins.	Off	16k	12k
3	Off	60 mins.	Off	60 mins.	Off	18k	12k
4	Off	60 mins.	Off	60 mins.	Off	20k	15k
5	Off	60 mins.	Off	60 mins.	Off	22k	16k
6	Off	60 mins.	Off	60 mins.	Off	24k	15k
7	Off	60 mins.	Off	60 mins.	Off	26k	16k
8	Off	60 mins.	Off	60 mins.	Off	28k	16k
9	Off	60 mins.	Off	60 mins.	Off	30k	20k
10	Off	60 mins.	Off	60 mins.	Off	30k	25k
11	Off	60 mins.	60 mins.	Off	20k	20k	20k
12	Off	60 mins.	Off	60 mins.	Off	30k	30k
13	Off	45 mins.	Off	20k	20k	20k	20k
14	Off	45 mins.	Off	60 mins.	Off	20k	10k
15	Off	60 mins.	Off	60 mins.	Off	15k	10k
16	Off	30 mins.	Off	**30k-30k-30k-30k walk!!!**			

Nijmegen 4-Day 40k/Day 16-Week Training Schedule							
Week	**Monday**	**Tuesday**	**Wednesday**	**Thursday**	**Friday**	**Saturday**	**Sunday**
1	Off	60 mins.	Off	60 mins.	Off	14k	12k
2	Off	60 mins.	Off	60 mins.	Off	16k	12k
3	Off	60 mins.	Off	60 mins.	Off	18k	12k
4	Off	60 mins.	Off	60 mins.	Off	20k	15k
5	Off	60 mins.	Off	60 mins.	Off	22k	16k
6	Off	60 mins.	Off	60 mins.	Off	24k	15k
7	Off	60 mins.	Off	60 mins.	Off	26k	16k
8	Off	60 mins.	Off	60 mins.	Off	28k	16k
9	Off	60 mins.	Off	60 mins.	Off	32k	25k
10	Off	60 mins.	Off	60 mins.	Off	35k	25k
11	Off	60 mins.	60 mins.	Off	20k	30k	30k
12	Off	60 mins.	Off	60 mins.	Off	35k	35k
13	Off	45 mins.	Off	20k	20k	30k	20k
14	Off	45 mins.	Off	60 mins.	Off	25k	10k
15	Off	60 mins.	Off	60 mins.	Off	15k	10k
16	Off	30 mins.	Off	**40k-40k-40k-40k walk!!!**			

There's not much room for error, but it is possible to prepare for the Nijmegen 4 x 30k and 40k events in 16 weeks, especially if you come in having already completed the base-training schedule.

Nijmegen 4-Day 30k/Day 24-Week Training Schedule							
Week	**Monday**	**Tuesday**	**Wednesday**	**Thursday**	**Friday**	**Saturday**	**Sunday**
1	Off	45 mins.	Off	45 mins.	Off	6k	6k
2	Off	45 mins.	Off	45 mins.	Off	8k	8k
3	Off	60 mins.	Off	60 mins.	Off	10k	10k
4	Off	60 mins.	Off	60 mins.	Off	12k	10k
5	Off	60 mins.	Off	60 mins.	Off	14k	12k
6	Off	60 mins.	Off	60 mins.	Off	15k	12k
7	Off	60 mins.	Off	60 mins.	Off	16k	12k
8	Off	60 mins.	Off	60 mins.	Off	18k	12k
9	Off	60 mins.	Off	60 mins.	Off	20k	15k
10	Off	60 mins.	60 mins.	Off	10k	15k	10k
11	Off	60 mins.	Off	60 mins.	Off	22k	16k
12	Off	60 mins.	Off	60 mins.	Off	25k	15k
13	Off	60 mins.	60 mins.	Off	10k	20k	10k
14	Off	60 mins.	Off	60 mins.	Off	26k	16k
15	Off	60 mins.	Off	60 mins.	Off	28k	16k
16	Off	60 mins.	60 mins.	Off	10k	30k	10k
17	Off	60 mins.	Off	60 mins.	Off	30k	20k
18	Off	60 mins.	Off	60 mins.	Off	30k	25k
19	Off	60 mins.	60 mins.	Off	20k	20k	20k
20	Off	60 mins.	Off	60 mins.	Off	30k	30k
21	Off	45 mins.	Off	20k	20k	20k	20k
22	Off	45 mins.	Off	60 mins.	Off	20k	10k
23	Off	60 mins.	Off	60 mins.	Off	15k	10k
24	Off	30 mins.	Off	**30k-30k-30k-30k walk!!!**			

This is more like it! 24 weeks gives a lot more time to physically prepare for the rigors of Nijmegen, but also to take care of logistical planning. There's no point in me re-inventing the wheel here. William Hunter has an excellent website that lays out what to wear, what to eat, where to stay, etc. Do yourself a favor and head to: https://nijmegenmarchhowto.weebly.com/preparation.html/.

Nijmegen 4-Day 40k/Day Training Schedule

Week	Monday	Tuesday	Wednesday	Thursday	Friday	Saturday	Sunday
1	Off	45 mins.	Off	45 mins.	Off	6k	6k
2	Off	45 mins.	Off	45 mins.	Off	8k	8k
3	Off	60 mins.	Off	60 mins.	Off	10k	10k
4	Off	60 mins.	Off	60 mins.	Off	12k	10k
5	Off	60 mins.	Off	60 mins.	Off	14k	12k
6	Off	60 mins.	Off	60 mins.	Off	15k	12k
7	Off	60 mins.	Off	60 mins.	Off	16k	12k
8	Off	60 mins.	Off	60 mins.	Off	18k	12k
9	Off	60 mins.	Off	60 mins.	Off	20k	15k
10	Off	60 mins.	60 mins.	Off	10k	20k	10k
11	Off	60 mins.	Off	60 mins.	Off	22k	16k
12	Off	60 mins.	Off	60 mins.	Off	25k	18k
13	Off	60 mins.	60 mins.	Off	10k	22k	10k
14	Off	60 mins.	Off	60 mins.	Off	26k	20k
15	Off	60 mins.	Off	60 mins.	Off	28k	20k
16	Off	60 mins.	60 mins.	Off	10k	30k	25k
17	Off	60 mins.	Off	60 mins.	Off	32k	25k
18	Off	60 mins.	Off	60 mins.	Off	35k	25k
19	Off	60 mins.	60 mins.	Off	20k	30k	30k
20	Off	60 mins.	Off	60 mins.	Off	35k	35k
21	Off	45 mins.	Off	20k	20k	30k	20k
22	Off	45 mins.	Off	60 mins.	Off	25k	10k
23	Off	60 mins.	Off	60 mins.	Off	15k	10k
24	Off	30 mins.	Off	**40k-40k-40k-40k walk!!!**			

Nijmegen 4-Day 50k/Day Training Schedule							
Week	**Monday**	**Tuesday**	**Wednesday**	**Thursday**	**Friday**	**Saturday**	**Sunday**
1	Off	45 mins.	Off	45 mins.	Off	6k	6k
2	Off	45 mins.	Off	45 mins.	Off	8k	8k
3	Off	60 mins.	Off	60 mins.	Off	10k	10k
4	Off	60 mins.	Off	60 mins.	Off	12k	12k
5	Off	60 mins.	Off	60 mins.	Off	15k	12k
6	Off	60 mins.	Off	60 mins.	Off	18k	15k
7	Off	60 mins.	Off	60 mins.	Off	20k	15k
8	Off	60 mins.	Off	60 mins.	Off	22k	15k
9	Off	60 mins.	Off	60 mins.	Off	25k	15k
10	Off	60 mins.	60 mins.	Off	10k	26k	10k
11	Off	60 mins.	Off	60 mins.	Off	28k	16k
12	Off	60 mins.	Off	60 mins.	Off	30k	18k
13	Off	60 mins.	60 mins.	Off	10k	25k	15k
14	Off	60 mins.	Off	60 mins.	Off	32k	20k
15	Off	60 mins.	Off	60 mins.	Off	35k	20k
16	Off	60 mins.	60 mins.	Off	10k	35k	25k
17	Off	60 mins.	Off	60 mins.	Off	40k	25k
18	Off	60 mins.	Off	60 mins.	Off	45k	25k
19	Off	60 mins.	60 mins.	Off	20k	40k	30k
20	Off	60 mins.	Off	60 mins.	Off	45k	30k
21	Off	45 mins.	Off	20k	20k	35k	25k
22	Off	45 mins.	Off	60 mins.	Off	30k	10k
23	Off	60 mins.	Off	60 mins.	Off	15k	10k
24	Off	60 mins.	Off	**50k-50k-50k-50k walk!!!**			

CHAPTER 33: WALKING IN TRIATHLONS

As I pointed out just a couple hundred pages ago in Chapter 1, walking in triathlons is growing, and many of these tri-walkers discovered the sport in the same way: They start as die-hard runners who get themselves injured, which happens a lot to runners. ☺ The hobbled runners take up swimming, and then spin classes or cycling as cross training to recover from their injuries, or as a substitute when their orthopedists tell them: "If you keep running you'll be back for a knee replacement in a year!" The now *former* runners get hooked on swimming and cycling, a light bulb goes off, and... *Eureka!* "Hey! I'm doing all this swimming and biking, I'll sign up for a tri!" The budding triathletes begin training in earnest and soon realize why they started swimming and biking in the first place: They can't run anymore!

Ironman triathlete Mike Madigan has, in his words, "destroyed" his knees from years of running, yet he still competes by racewalking the "run" portion of his tris.

Photo courtesy of Mike Madigan

Although this is purely anecdotal, not statistical, evidence of triathlon-walking's growth, I've been watching the trend toward walking in triathlons develop over the years as more and more triathletes have been signing up for my racewalking/marathon walking clinics and camps. Twenty years ago I would get one or two triathletes per year; now I get walking triathletes at just about every one of my clinics. Their goal is usually not to have perfect racewalking form; it's to make their walking faster and more efficient so they can beat the strict race time limits—and some of their competitors!—at their triathlons. Mike Madigan is one such athlete. Mike is a former collegiate runner who had always wanted to complete an Ironman triathlon, but by the time he got around to it, he was no longer able to run. According to Mike, *"Doing an Ironman 140.6 was always on my bucket list, but by my late 40s, I couldn't run anymore—too many knee surgeries. Racewalking, and Dave's clinics, enabled me to complete one, which I did at age 58. I'm 66 now, and I'm still racing half-Ironman triathlons!"* (Mike attended several of my Mesa, AZ clinics, and eventually became my Tucson clinic host.)

Technique is certainly an important part of the equation when it comes to beating triathlon time limits by walking, but so is training. Um… And equipment. One of the great things about competitive walking is that it requires very little equipment. If that's a strong selling point for you, triathlon might not be your thing! Obviously you'll need a swimsuit (~$35 for men, $80 for women, and you'll probably need more than one); but also goggles ($20 - $25); swim cap ($5 - $10); various training aids like "pull buoys," fins and kick boards (figure $50 for the lot, but if you're lucky your gym will have these). Oh, right, gym membership ($50 - $100+ per month). That's just for the training. For your race you'll probably need a wetsuit (~$250). Ok, one event down, two to go! You'll need a bike. You can probably get a "crappy" one for $500, but real triathlon bikes run $3,000 and *way* up, and you'll want to get one of those because the thing about cyclists is they like to express their individuality by fitting in with everybody else. ☺ And that $3,000 bike won't work without special shoes ($75) and you'll *need* to know your power output because everyone on Strava and Slowtwitch.com will be asking (power meter $150, but why not go all-in? Get the power meter pedals for $2,150); and of course speed and cadence sensors ($75) which will display on your "bike computer" ($250). Of course you'll need sunglasses, but not just *any* sunglasses. No, you need to get *the right* glasses everyone else is wearing to, again, express your individuality. You already have your walking gear, so you're good for the third leg. Now let's talk entry fees… Want to do a full-Ironman? Set aside $750. For myself, coming from a walking background, it's all pretty daunting. I actually found an article on my bank's website—my *bank's* website—called "How to Manage the Costs of a Triathlon"—no joke![66] (Of course you could just take out a second mortgage. I hear rates are at historic lows, so it won't cost you much…) ☺ If you're still with me, what follows are training schedules for sprint, Olympic, half- and full-Ironman triathlons for walkers.

I hope you didn't get too excited when you read the word "sprint" there. If you're a terrible swimmer as I am, allow 12+ minutes for the swim; 45 minutes on the bike (unless you bought the crappy one, then figure a couple of minutes longer) ☺; 30 minutes for the walk if you're a pretty good racewalker, and closer to 45 if you're power walking, and let's say five minutes for each transition, and you're approaching two hours for your finish time. So even though a sprint is only about a quarter of the distance of a half-Ironman, and one-eighth of a full, it is absolutely an endurance event, which will require a bit of a time commitment. (And a big wallet.) ☺ According to Ken Lucchesi, National Triathlon Coach for the Crohn's & Colitis Foundation's Team Challenge:

---

[66] Seriously! It's here: https://www.chase.com/news/011817-cost-of-triathlon

> *"Walking is a great way to get the run portion of the triathlon done. I've had lots of my athletes do it. The most important thing to keep in mind is the race cutoff time. If you ace the swim and bike, you will be better off on the walk. It also depends on the length of your race—there is often a lot of walking going on during the run portion of a full Ironman."*

Ken suggests calculating your expected finish times for the swim, bike, and transitions, which are reasonably predictable once you have some training under your belt; then you can calculate the pace you will need to walk to finish under the cut-off time. You can then base your walk training on that pace. Good advice. Maybe it'll counter some of the not-so-good advice I gave in an article I wrote a while back based on my vast triathloning experience upon completing my second-ever triathlon:[67]

- Keep your head out of the water at all times. This will help you to see really well. As an added bonus, it keeps your feet low in the water, which will obviously help you swim faster.
- Don't wear a wetsuit in the swim. It will make your transition so much faster!
- Take your sweet time on the swim. It'll really speed up your transition to not have to figure out which bike is yours when it's the only one left on the rack.
- Bike shoes? Yeah, no. Those insane lock-on bike shoes are a friggin' menace! Whatever happened to regular ol' Schwinn bike pedals? Get yourself some normal pedals and you can just wear your walking shoes on the bike. Boom, boom, boom: Jump off the bike and start walking. Smooth transition! Why haven't any of these so-called pros and experts figured that one out?
- Don't even think about training for the bike portion. It's waaay too dangerous! Have you seen those cars out there? Those hills? Take it from me, save your cycling for the race.

Clearly I'm not a triathlon coach, but I have been around the sport for quite a while. I did my first tri in 1985—a year before my brother, the real triathlete in the family. He was a 9:41 Ironman competitor who has raced in the World Championships in Kona. He was Triathlon Magazine's 2004 and 2005 overall "Duathlete of the Year" (run-bike-run), and a triathlon coach. He's even owned a triathlon store. So I asked him for a little help with the following schedules. They are, for the most part, beginners' schedules. Obviously, beginners should not be attempting Ironman-distance tris, but even that schedule is written at a "just finish" level. If you're a more experienced triathlete, by all means, use whatever schedule from whichever source you're comfortable with. This is, after all, not a triathlon-training book, but hopefully it has opened your eyes to the possibility of walking your tri "runs"! With these schedules, and a bit of technique work, I'm confident you'll have what it takes to get to the finish line. Now on to the schedules!

---

[67] The complete article detailing the many lessons I learned from that debacle of a race is posted on my website here: www.racewalking.org/pdfs/Other%20Articles/Fun/triathlon.pdf/. Don't do any of this stuff!!

Sprint Distance Triathlon Walk Training Schedule							
Week	**Monday**	**Tuesday**	**Wednesday**	**Thursday**	**Friday**	**Saturday**	**Sunday**
1	Rest	Swim: 300yds.*	Bike: 20 mins.	Walk: 20 mins.	Swim: 300yds.	Bike: 25 mins.	Walk: 25 mins.
2	Rest	Swim: 400yds.	Bike: 25 mins.	Walk: 25 mins.	Swim: 400yds.	Bike: 30 mins.	Walk: 30 mins.
3	Rest	Swim: 500yds.	Bike: 30 mins.	Walk: 30 mins.	Swim: 500yds.	Bike: 35 mins.	Walk: 35 mins.
4	Rest	Swim: 600yds.	Bike: 35 mins.	Walk: 35 min	Swim: 600yds.	Bike: 30 mins./ walk 15 mins.	Walk: 40 mins.
5	Rest	Swim: 700yds.	Bike: 40 mins.	Walk: 40 mins.	Swim: 700yds.	Bike: 35 mins.	Walk: 45 mins.
6	Rest	Swim: 800yds.	Bike: 40 min with 5x1 min. intervals	Walk: 45 mins.	Swim: 800yds.	Bike: 45 mins.	Walk: 10 mins. easy, 10 fast, 10 easy
7	Rest	Swim: 600yds.	Bike: 45 mins. w/ 5 x 2:00 mins. hard	Walk: 30 mins.	Swim: 600yds.	Bike: 40 mins. W: 15 mins.	Walk: 45 mins.
8	Rest	Swim: 800yds.	Bike: 40 mins.	Walk: 50 mins.	Open-water swim 20 mins.	Bike: 50 mins.	Walk: 50 mins.
9	Rest	Swim: 200yds. easy, 600yds. alt. 25 easy/25yds. hard, 200 easy	Bike: 15 mins. easy, 20 mins. @ race pace,15 mins. easy	Walk: 55 mins.	Swim: 1,000yds.	Bike: 60 mins.	Walk: 10 mins. easy, 15 mins. fast, 10 mins. easy
10	Rest	Swim: 200yds. easy, 600yds. hard, 200yds. easy	Bike: 45 mins.	Walk: 60 mins.	Open-water swim 25 mins.	Bike: 45 mins. Walk 30 mins.	Walk: 60 mins.
11	Rest	Swim: 200yds. easy, 600yds. alt. 25 easy/25yds. hard, 200yds. easy	Bike: 50 min (15 easy, 20 race pace, 15 easy)	Walk: 45 min	Swim: 800yds.	Bike: 60 mins.	Walk: 35 min (10 easy, 15 fast, 10 easy)
12	Rest	Swim: 200yds. easy, 200yds. alt. 25 easy/25yds. hard, 200yds. easy	Bike: 30 mins.	Off	Walk 20 mins., then 4 x 30 secs. fast	**RACE!!!**	Off

There are variations, but a sprint triathlon typically consists of a 750-meter to half-mile swim, 20k to 20 miles on the bike, and a 3- to 4- mile "bipedal ambulatory activity." (I'll do anything to avoid calling it a "run"…) ☺ The standard is 750m/20k/5k, and that's what this schedule will be heading you toward. Like all of the schedules in this section, it's written at a beginner's "just finish" level. Having said that, you should NOT attempt a half-Ironman unless you have successfully completed several sprint and Olympic-distance tris, and you should not attempt a full Ironman unless you have successfully completed at least one half-Ironman.

---

*Apologies to my international readers. Most pools in the US are 25 yards, not meters, so I've written the swim workouts in yards. If your pool is 25m, do the same workout, but in meters instead of yards. (Do 800 meters instead of 800 yards.) Of course you'll be swimming about 8.3% longer than your US counterparts, but that's not such a bad thing, is it? ☺

Olympic Distance Triathlon Walk Training Schedule							
Week	**Mon.**	**Tues.**	**Wed.**	**Thurs.**	**Fri.**	**Sat.**	**Sun.**
1	Off	Swim: 800yds.	Bike: 30 minutes	Walk easy 4 miles	Swim: 800yds.	Bike: 30 minutes	Walk 4 miles
2	Off	Swim: 900yds.	Bike: 45 minutes	Walk easy 4 miles	Swim: 900yds.	Bike: 45 minutes	Walk 4.5 miles
3	Off	Swim: 1,000yds	Bike: 60 minutes	Walk easy 4.5 miles	Swim: 1,000yds	Bike: 60 minutes	Walk 5 miles
4	Off	Sw: 200yds. w/up, 600 yds., Alt. 25yds. hard/25 easy, 200 cool dn.	Bike: hilly 45 minutes	Walk easy 4 miles	Swim: 800yds.	Bike: 65 minutes	Walk 4 miles
5	Off	Sw: 200yds. w/up, 700 yds. alt. 25yds. hard/25 easy, 200yds. cool dn.	Bike: 65 minutes	Walk easy 5 miles	Swim: 1,100yds.	Bike: 70 minutes	Walk 5.5 miles
6	Off	Sw: 200yds. w/up, 800 yds., alt. 25yds. hard/25 easy, 200yds. cool dn.	Bike: hilly 60 minutes	Walk 15 min. w/up, 12 x 60 sec. fast/60 sec. mod., 15 min. cool dn.	Swim: 1,200yds.	B: 60 mins. W: 15 mins.	Walk 6 miles
7	Off	Sw: 200yds. w/up, 900 yds., alt. 50yds. hard/50 easy, 200yds. cool dn.	Bike: 70 minutes	Walk 5-mile progression	Swim: 1,200yds.	Bike: 75 minutes	Walk 6.5 miles
8	Off	Sw: 200yds. w/up, 800 yds., alt. 50yds. hard/50 easy, 200yds. cool dn.	Bike: hilly 60 minutes	Walk 15 min. w/up, 10 x 90 sec. fast/60 sec. mod., 15 min. cool dn.	Swim: 1,000yds.	Bike: 60 mins., walk 15 mins.	Walk 5 miles
9	Off	Sw: 200yds. w/up, 1,000 yds., alt. 75yds. hard/25 easy, 200yds. cool dn.	Bike: 75 minutes	Walk 5-mile tempo	Swim: 1,300yds.	Bike: 80 minutes	Walk 6 miles
10	Off	Sw: 200yds. w/up, 1,200 yds., alt. 75yds. hard/25 easy, 200yds. cool dn.	Bike: 10 mins. w/up, 2 x 10 mins. hard, w/ 10 min. easy break. 10 min. cool dn.	Walk 15 min. w/up, 8 x 2 mins. fast/60 sec. mod., 15 min. cool dn.	Swim: 1,400yds.	Bike: 90 mins., walk 15 mins.	Walk 7 miles
11	Off	Sw: 200yds. w/up, 1,200 yds., alt. 25yds. hard/25 easy, 200yds. cool dn.	Bike: hilly 75 minutes	Walk 5-mile progression	Swim: 1,500yds.	Bike: 1:45	Walk 8 miles
12	Off	Sw: 200yds. w/up, 800 yds., alt. 75yds. hard/ 25 easy, 200yds. cool dn.	Bike: 60 minutes	Walk 5 miles	Swim: 1,200yds.	Bike: 90 mins., walk 20 mins.	Walk 6 miles
13	Off	Sw: 200yds. w/up, 1,200 yds., alt. 25yds. hard/ 25 easy, 200yds. cool dn.	Bike: hilly 75 minutes	Walk 15 min. w/up, 8 x 2 mins. fast/60 sec. mod., 15 min. cool dn.	Swim: 1,600yds.	Bike: 90 mins., walk 40 mins.	Walk 9 miles
14	Off	Sw: 200yds. w/up, 1,200 yds., alt. 75yds. hard/ 25 easy, 200yds. cool dn.	B: 10 min. w/up, 2 x 10 min. hard, w/10 min. easy break. 10 min. cool dn.	Walk 5-mile progression	Swim: 1,600yds.	Bike: 90 mins., walk 45 mins.	Walk 9 miles
15	Off	Sw: 200yds. w/up, 1,000 yds., alt. 25yds. hard/ 25 easy, 200yds. cool dn.	Bike: 10 min. w/up, 10 min. hard, 10 min. cool dn.	Walk 15 min. w/up, 6 x 2 mins. fast/60 sec. mod., 15 min. cool dn.	Swim: 1,600yds.	Bike: 60 mins., walk 15 mins.	Walk 5 miles
16	Off	Sw: 200yds. w/up, 800 yds., alt. 25yds. hard/ 25 easy, 200yds. cool dn.	B:10 min. w/up, 10 min. @ race pace, 10 min. cool dn.	Walk 15 min. w/up, 4 x 400m @ race pace/w/ 60 sec. mod. breaks, 15 min. cool dn.	Sw: 200 yds. wm up, 400 alt. 25 easy/25 hard, 200 cool dn.	Bike: easy 20-mins.	**RACE!**

The Olympic triathlon distance is 1,500m (1,650yds.) swim, 40k bike, 10k "ambulation." Although this is a beginners' schedule, it assumes you're able to swim 800yds. continuously, cycle for 60 minutes, and walk for 45 minutes.

Half-Ironman Distance Triathlon Training Walk Schedule

Week	Mon.	Tues.	Wed.	Thur.	Fri.	Sat.	Sun.
1	Off	Bike: hilly 45 mins. Push hard on the hills.	Sw: 300yds. w/up, 800 alt. 25 hard/25 EZ, 300 cool dn., W: 45 min. FTLK	Bike: 60 mins.	Sw: 1,200yds.w/ 4 x 100 hard within W: 45 min.	B: 45 min. W: 15	Sw: 1,600yds. W: 60 min.
2	Off	Bike: hilly 60 mins. w/ 6 x 1-min. hard within.	300yds. w/up, 800 alt. 25 hard/25 easy, 300 cool dn. + walk 45 min. FTLK	Bike: 65 mins.	Swim: 1,400yds.w/ 5 x 100 hard within + 45 min. walk	Bike: 60 mins./ walk 15	Sw:1,600yds. B: 45 mins. W: 60 mins.
3	Off	Bike: hilly 50 mins. Push hard on the hills.	300yds. w/up, 850 alt. 75 hard/75 easy, 300 cool dn.+ walk 45 min. FTLK	Bike: 70 mins.	Swim: 1,600yds.w/ 4 x 150 hard within + 45 min. walk	Bike: 90 minutes	Sw: 1,800yds. W: 60 mins.
4	Off	Bike: hilly 60 mins. w/ 6 x 1-min. hard within.	300yds. w/up, 600 alt. 100 hard/100 easy, 300 cool dn.+ walk 50 min. FTLK	Bike: 1:15.	Swim: 1,700yds.w/ 4 x 150 hard within + 60 min. walk	B: 1:40 mins./ walk 15	Sw: 1,900yds. W: 45 mins.
5	Off	Bike: hilly 55 mins. Push hard on the hills.	300yds. w/up, 1,000 alt. 100 hard/100 easy, 300 cool dn., W: 60 min. FTLK	Bike: 1:20	Swim: 1,800ds.w/ 6 x 150 hard within + 60 min. walk	Bike: 1:45	Swim: 2,000yds.
6	Off	Bike: hilly 45 mins. w/ 6 x 1-min. hard within.	300yds. w/up, 800 alt. 100 hard/100 easy, 300 cool dn.+ walk 60 min. FTLK	Bike: 45 mins	Swim: 1,200yds.w/ 4 x 150 hard within + 60 min. walk	Bike: 60 minutes	Swim: 1,600yds.
7	Off	Bike: hilly 60 mins. Push hard on the hills.	300yds. w/up, 1,100 alt. 100 hard/100 easy, 300 cool dn., W: 60 min. FTLK	Bike: moderate 1:25	Swim: 1,800ds.w/ 6 x 150 hard within + 60 min. walk	Bike: 1:45/ walk 30	Sw:1,600yds. B: 45 mins. W: 60 mins.
8	Off	Bike: 60 mins. w/two very hard 3 min. pushes within the workout.	300yds. w/up, 1,200 alt. 100 hard/100 easy, 300 cool dn., W: 45 min. FTLK	Bike: moderate 1:30	Swim: 1,900ds.w/ 4 x 200 hard within + 60 min. walk	Bike: 60 mins./ walk 30	Sw: 250 EZ, 1,600 mod., 250 EZ W: mod. 1:40
9	Off	Bike: hilly 65 mins. Push hard on the hills.	300yds. w/up, 1,300 alt. 100 hard/100 easy, 300 cool dn., W: 60 min. FTLK	Bike: moderate 1:30	Swim: 300 easy, 1,400 w/ 3 x 300 tempo, 300 easy + mod. 1:00 walk	Bike: mod. 2:15	Sw: 250 EZ, 1,700 mod, 250 EZ, W: mod 1:45
10	Off	Bike: 60 mins. with two very hard 3 min. pushes within the workout.	300yds. w/up, 800 alt. 100 hard/100 easy, 300 cool dn.+ w. 45 min. FTLK	Bike: moderate 60 mins.	Swim: 300 easy, 1,000 w/ 2x400 tempo, 300 easy, W: mod. 60 min.	Bike: 30 mins.	Sw: 880yds B: 20k W: 5k OR sprint tri.
11	Off	Bike: hilly 70 mins. Push hard on the hills.	300yds. w/up, 1,300 alt. 100 hard/100 easy, 300 cool dn., W: 60 min. FTLK	Bike: moderate 1:30	Swim: 300 easy, 1,500 w/ 3 x 300 tempo, 300 easy + mod. 1:00 walk	Bike: mod. 2:30	Sw: 250 EZ, 1,800 mod., 250 EZ, W: mod 1:45
12	Off	Bike: 75 mins. with four very hard 3 min. pushes within.	300yds. w/up, 1,400 alt. 100 hard/100 easy, 300 cool dn., W: 60 min. FTLK	Bike: moderate 1:30	Swim: 300 easy, 1,500 w/ 2 x 400 tempo, 300 easy + mod. 1:00 walk	Bike: mod. 1:45	Sw: 2,400yds., B: 1:45 mins. W: 45 mins.
13	Off	Bike: 75 mins. with two hard 12 min. pushes within the workout.	300yds. w/up, 1,500 alt. 100 hard/100 easy, 300 cool dn., W: 60 min. w/ 16 hard	Bike: moderate 1:30	Swim: 300 easy, 1,500 w/ 2x400 tempo, 300 easy + mod. 1:45 walk	Bike: mod. 2:45	Sw: 250 EZ, 2,000 mod, 250 EZ, W: 1:45 mod
14	Off	Bike: mod. 45 mins. with 15 min. tempo within the workout.	Sw: 300yds. w/up, 1,200 alt. 100 hard/100 easy, 300 cool dn., W: 60 min. w/ 18 hard	Bike: moderate 60 mins.	Swim: 300 easy, 1,200 w/ 2 x 400 tempo, 300 EZ + W: mod. 60 min.	Bike: 30 mins.	Sw. 250 EZ, 1,600 mod., 250 EZ, W: mod 1:45
15	Off	Bike: mod. 70 mins. with 25 min. tempo within the workout.	Sw: 300yds. w/up, 1,500 alt. 100 hard/100 easy, 300 cool dn., W: 60 min. w/ 20 hard	Bike: moderate 1:40	Swim: 300 easy, 1,500 w/ 2x400 tempo, 300 easy + mod. 1:45 walk	Bike: mod. 3:00	Sw: 250 EZ, 2,000 mod., 250 EZ, W: 1:45 mod
16	Off	Bike: mod. 75 mins. with 15 min. tempo within the workout.	300yds. w/up, 1,500 alt. 100 hard/100 easy, 300 cool dn., W. 60 min. tempo	Bike: mod. 1:45	Swim: 300 easy, 1,500 w/ 2x400 tempo, 300 easy + mod. 1:15 walk	Bike: mod. 3:15	Sw: 200 EZ, 2,100 TT 200 EZ, W: 1:15 tempo
17	Off	Bike: 25 mins. with two hard 15 min. pushes within the workout.	300yds. w/up, 1,500 alt. 100 hard/100 easy, 300 cool dn., W: 60 min. tempo	Bike: moderate 1:45	Swim: 300 easy, 1,500 mod, 300 easy + mod. 1:15 walk	Bike: 2:15	Swim: 250 EZ, 1,500 mod, 250 EZ, W: 5-mi.
18	Off	Bike: 55 mins. with two hard 15 min. pushes within the workout.	300yds. w/up, 800 alt. 25 hard/25 EZ, 300 cool dn. W: 10EZ/10 tempo/10EZ	B: EZ 10 mins./ mod 25/ EZ 10	300yds. w/up, 500 alt. 25 easy /25 hard, 300 cool dn.	Bike: easy 20-mins.	**RACE!!!**

Although this is and the full-Ironman schedule are "beginner" schedules, no beginning triathlete should attempt either before first completing several Olympic-distance triathlons. Accordingly, both schedules start with fairly high swim, bike and run volumes. TT = Time-trial.

Ironman Distance Triathlon Walk Training Schedule							
Week	**Mon.**	**Tues.**	**Wed.**	**Thurs.**	**Fri.**	**Sat.**	**Sun.**
1	Off	B: 40 mins. w/ 6 x 20 sec. sprints, Sw: 1,000yds. w/ 8 x 25yds. hard	Walk: 5 miles	Sw: 1,000yds. w/ 4 x 100yds. hard B: Easy 40 mins.	Walk: 60 mins, with 6 x 30 sec. pick-ups within	Bike: 25 miles	Walk: 6 miles, Swim: 1,000yds.
2	Off	Bike: 40 mins. w/ 8 x 20 sec. sprints, swim 1,100yds. w/ 10 x 25yds. hard	Walk: 5 miles	Swim: 1,100yds. w/ 5 x 100yds. within Bike: Easy 45 mins.	Walk: 60 mins. with 8 x 30 sec. pick-ups within	Bike: 30 miles	Walk: 7 miles, Swim: 1,250yds.
3	Off	Bike: 40 mins. w/ 10 x 20 sec. sprints, Swim: 1,200yds. w/ 12 x 25yds. hard	Walk: 5 miles	Swim: 1,200yds. w/ 6 x 100yds. within, Bike: Easy 45 mins.	Walk: 60 mins. with 8 x 30 sec. pick-ups within	Bike: 35 miles	Walk: 8 miles, Swim: 1,500yds.
4	Off	. Bike: 40 mins. w/ 6 x 20 sec. sprints, Swim: 1,200yds. w/ 10 x 25yds. hard	Walk: 5 miles	Swim: 1,200yds. w/ 5 x 100yds. within, Bike: Easy 45 mins.	Walk: 60 mins. with 6 x 30 sec. pick-ups within	Bike: 30 miles	Walk: 6 miles, Swim: 1,200yd.
5	Off	Bike: 45 mins. w/ 15 mins. hard, Swim: 1,500m w/ 10 x 50m sprints	Walk: 6 miles	Swim: 1,500yds. w/ 4 x 150yds. within, Bike: Easy 45 mins.	Walk: 60 mins. with 6 x 1 min. pick-ups within	Bike: 40 miles	Walk: 9 miles, Swim: 1,700yds.
6	Off	B: 45 mins. w/ 8 x 1:00 min. hill sprints, Sw: 1,600 yds. w/ 8 x 50, 8 x 25 hard	Walk: 6 miles	Swim: 1,600yds. w/ 4 x 200yds. within, Bike: Easy 45 mins.	W: 60 mins. as 20 easy/20 tempo/20 easy	Bike: 45 miles	Walk: 10 miles, Swim: 1,800yds
7	Off	Bike: 50 mins. w/ 20 mins. @ tempo, Swim: 1,700yds. w/ 12 x 50yds. hard	Walk: 6 miles	Swim: 1,700yds. w/ 5 x 150yds. within, Bike: Easy 50 mins.	W: 60 mins. w/ 10 x 1 min. pick-ups within	B: 50 miles, W: 10 mins.	Walk: 11 miles, Swim: 2,100yds.
8	Off	Bike: 45 mins. w/ 6 x 90 sec. sprints, Swim: 1,500yds. w/ 16 x 50yds. hard	Walk: 6 miles	Swim: 1,500yds. w/ 8 x 100yds. within, Bike: Easy 50 mins.	W: 65 mins. w/ 20 easy/25 tempo/20 easy	Bike: 40 miles	Walk: 8 miles, Swim: 1,800yds.
9	Off	B: 55 mins. w/ 20 min. hard, W: 15 min. easy, Sw: 1,900yds. w/ 8 x 75 hard.	Walk: 6 miles	Swim: 1,900yds. w/ 4 x 250yds. within, Bike: Easy 50 mins.	Walk: 60 mins. with 8 x 2 min. pick-ups within	Bike: 55 mi., Walk: 10 mins.	Walk: 12 miles, Swim: 2,400yds.
10	Off	B: 55 min. w/ 20 mins. hard, W: 15 min. easy, Sw: 2,100 w/ 10 x 50, 10 x 25	Walk: 6 miles	Swim: 2,100yds. w/ 6 x 150yds. within, Bike: Easy 55 mins.	W: 70 min. w/ 20 easy/30 tempo/20 easy.	Bike: 60 mi., Walk: 15 mins.	Walk: 10 miles, Swim: 2,700yds.
11	Off	B: 60 min. w/ 20 min. hard, W: 15 min., Sw: 2,300 yds. w/ 10 x 75, 10 x 25 hard	Walk: 6 miles	Swim: 2,300yds. w/ 5 x 200yds. within, Bike: Easy 60 mins.	Walk: 60 mins. with 8 x 2 min. pick-ups within	Bike: 65 mi., Walk: 10 mins.	Walk: 13 miles, Swim: 3,000yds.
12	Off	B: 50 mins. w/ 8 x 1:00 min. sprints, W: 15 min. Sw: 1,800 w/ 15 x 50 hard	Walk: 6 miles	Swim: 1,800yds. w/ 12 x 100yds. Bike: Easy 50 mins.	W: 45 mins. w/ 15 easy, 15 tempo, 15 easy	Bike: 50 mi., Walk: 15 mins.	Walk: 10 miles, Swim: 2,400yds.
13	Off	B: 70 mins. w/ 20 min. hard W: 15 min. Sw: 1,500 w/ 18 x 50 hard	Walk: 7.5 miles	Swim: 2,500yds. w/ 4 x 300yds. within, Bike: Easy 50 mins.	W: 75 min. w/ 10 x 2 min. pick-ups within	Bike: 70 mi., Walk: 10 mins.	Walk: 14 miles, Swim: 3,000yds.
14	Off	B: 70 mins. w/ 10 x 2:00 min. sprints, W: 15 min., Sw: 2,600yds w/ 8 x 25 hard	Walk: 7.5 miles	Swim: 2,600yds. w/ 2 x 400, 4 x 100 hard, B: Easy 1:15	W: 80 mins. w/ 30 easy/30 tempo/20 easy	Bike: 55 mi., Walk: 20 mins.	Walk: 11 miles, Swim: 3,300yds.
15	Off	B: 75 min. w/ 25 min. hard, W: 15 min., Sw: 2,800yds. w/ 6 x 75, 6 x 50 hard.	Walk: 7.5 miles	Sw: 2,800yds. w/ 4 x 300, 4 x 100 hard, Bike: Easy 1:15	Walk: 85 mins. with 5 x 3 min. pick-ups within	Bike: 85 mi., Walk: 10 mins.	Walk: 16 miles, Swim: 3,800yds.
16	Off	B: 60 mins. w/ 10 x 2:00 min. sprints, W: 15 mins. Sw: 2,300 w/ 16 x 50 hard	Walk: 6 miles	Swim: 2,300 w/ 2 x 400/4 x 100 hard Bike: Easy 1:00	W: 60 mins. w/ 20 easy/20 tempo/20 easy	Bike: 50 mi., Walk: 15 mins.	W: 10 miles, Sw: 400 Easy/1,750 TT/400 easy
17	Off	B: 80 min. w/ 30 hard, W: 15 mins, Sw: 3,000yds. w/ 10 x 100, 10 x 50 hard	Walk: 7.5 miles	Swim: 3,000yds. w/ 4 x 400yds., Bike: Easy 1:20	Walk: 90 mins. with 3 x 5 min. pick-ups within	Bike: 100 mi., Walk: 10 mins.	Walk: 18 miles, Swim: 4,000yds.
18	Off	B: 80 min. w/ 3 x 5 min. hard, W: 15 min., Sw: 3,000 w/ 8 x 75/8 x 50/8 x 25 hard	Walk: 7.5 miles	Swim: 3,000yds. w/ 4 x 400yds., Bike: Easy 1:30	W: 90 mins. w/ 30 easy/30 tempo/30 easy	Bike: 70 mi., Walk: 60 mins.	Walk: 5 miles, Swim: 4,000yds.
19	Off	B: 60 min. w/ 20 min. hard, W: 15 min. Sw: 2,600 w/ 10 x 100/10 x 50 hard	Walk: 7.5 miles	Swim:: 2,600yds. w/ 4 x 400yds., Bike: Easy 1:00	Walk:: 60 mins. with 6 x 3 min. pick-ups within	Bike: 50 mi., Walk:: 10 mins.	Walk: 10 miles, Swim: 4,000yds.
20	Off	B: 45 mins. w/ 6 x 1 min. hard, Sw: 2,200yds. w/ 10 x 50yds. hard	Walk: 5 miles	Swim:: 1,600yds. w/ 4 x 300yds., Bike: Easy 30 mins.	Walk: easy 30 minutes	Bike: easy 20 mins.	**RACE!!!**

SECTION IV: SUPPLEMENTAL TRAINING

The thing that will help your walking the most is more walking. But to walk lots of miles, you need to be healthy, and that means taking care of your muscles and joints with flexibility training, strengthening and core work, and taking care of your head with mental training. When I "sort of" retired from high-level competition around 1998, I still loved to walk, but I stopped doing all the "other stuff" that I didn't like as much, but still needed to do—stretching, going to the weight room, cross-training like swimming, etc. Before long I lost flexibility and started accumulating injuries. (Getting into marathon and 50k walking sure didn't help matters, but that's a whole other story…) In addition to the aforementioned information on physical and mental training, there are also chapters on injury prevention, tools for training like heart monitors and GPS units, and even a chapter on fundraising for those who walk to raise money for causes near and dear to their hearts. Sure, it's "all about the walking," but it's also about all the other stuff, too! ☺

CHAPTER 34: FLEXIBILITY TRAINING

We propel ourselves forward when walking by *contracting* our muscles. After the contraction, the muscles relax, but over time, contraction after contraction after contraction, the muscles eventually get tighter, limiting your range of motion and making you more prone to developing injuries. Maintaining and improving flexibility, then, is a key supplemental component to your walk training.

This chapter is titled "Flexibility Training" instead of simply "Stretching" because flexibility training is more than just stretching! There are actually a number of ways to enhance flexibility beyond the static stretches that are all too familiar to most experienced walkers. No matter what type of competitive walking you practice you—and most other walkers—could benefit from some form of flexibility training. I say *most*, not *all*, because although some people are very tight, and some have moderate flexibility, a very lucky few are extremely flexible. Every sport has its own optimal range of motion. Walking, like any other physical activity, takes advantage of the natural elasticity of the muscles, the tendons that connect the muscles to bones, and the ligaments that connect the bones to each other. If you're the rare individual that's *too* flexible, or *hypermobile*, you're actually wasting energy every time you have to prematurely contract the muscles before the end of their natural range-of-motion, where the elastic rebound kicks in.[68] Even if you are relatively limber, that could change with many miles of walk training, so you should do some flexibility training to retain the range-of-motion of your muscles over time. On the other hand, if the muscles are too tight their range-of-motion will be limited. Your strides will likely be shorter than optimal, and you will probably end up injured before long.

To retain (or regain) flexibility, walkers should do *dynamic flexibility drills* before training, and stretch and/or use a foam roller after. Massage therapy, and even weight training, performed using lighter weights moved through a full range-of-motion, are additional ways to enhance flexibility.

Dynamic flexibility drills

Dynamic flexibility drills, which are usually performed before workouts or races, are active range-of-motion exercises used to get the body ready to move. They are best done after a gentle warm-up, such as ten minutes of easy walking. The limbs are then moved through a specific range-of-motion, gently at first, then progressively more vigorously—hence the name *dynamic* flexibility drills. After drills, I like to do a couple of quick, 30- to 40-meter bursts, to make sure everything is feeling good, then I'm ready to start my workout or race. Here are a few of my favorite dynamic flexibility drills:

[68] Picture how awkwardly many hyper-mobile gymnasts run when approaching the vault!

Leg Swings: Stand sideways next to a fence or other sturdy support, steadying yourself by holding on to it with one hand. Swing your outside leg front to back, bending the knee as it comes forward, straightening as it goes back, through a full range of motion. This is a great warm-up for the hamstrings, glutes and lower back. Do 15 to 20 swings, then turn around and repeat with the other leg. Swinging the free arm in the opposite direction of the leg will help develop bilateral coordination.

Side swings: Stand about two feet away from the fence with your feet about shoulder-width apart. Holding on to the fence with both hands, swing your right leg to the outside, then to the inside about 12 to 20 times to stretch the groin and outside of the hip. Repeat with the left leg about 12 to 20 times.

Swedish twists: Grab the fence again, standing about two feet away. The leg closest to the fence will be the support leg. Tuck the other foot behind the knee of the support leg, then rotate the knee toward the fence, then back, keeping the foot tucked behind the knee. Repeat 12 to 20 times, then repeat with the other leg. Great for the lower back and groin. Most drills are pretty universal, but I've only seen this one done in Sweden.

Hip Circles: Again, hold on to the fence with both hands, with your feet about shoulder-width apart. Keeping your arms outstretched, lean into the fence with your pelvis, then circumscribe a large circle with the hips to stretch the entire pelvic area. Do 10 to 12 circles clockwise, then 10 to 12 circles counter-clockwise.

Knee Pumps: Again, hold on to the fence, with feet together about four feet away from it. Stand on the balls of your feet without bending at the waist. Pump your knees forward and back quickly, rolling up onto the toes of the pumping foot, almost as if you were running in place. Pump each knee 12 to 20 times.

Hurdle Drill: Standing about three feet from the fence, lift one leg out to the side with the knee bent, as if lifting it over an imaginary hurdle. "Hurdle" five times with each leg. The hurdler drill is a great groin and lower-back flexibility exercise.

Knee circles: Stand flat on one foot with a straight leg, and on the ball of the other foot with the knee bent. Circumscribe a circle with a bent knee along the horizontal plane, just as you did when doing hip circles.

Toe Touches: Take a small step forward with your right foot. With the right leg straight, gently bend down and touch your toes, then stand up straight to stretch your lower back. Step forward with the left foot, then gently bend down and touch your toes again. Repeat at least five times on each leg.

Rock & Roll: Stand sideways to the fence. Balance on your heels with one foot about 18” in front of the other. Throw your pelvis forward, rolling up onto the toes of both feet. Rock back onto your heels, then repeat, rocking back and forth 12 to 15 times. Put your other foot forward, then rock and roll again about 12 to 15 more times.

Arm circles: With your palm facing outward and the elbow straight, "backstroke" with your arm, holding your shoulder close to your ear. Do 12 to 20 with each arm for upper body flexibility. Doing both arms at the same time, 180 degrees apart, is good for developing coordination.

Torso Twists: Stand with your feet shoulder-width apart, arms outstretched and parallel to the ground. Keeping the feet planted, twist the torso fully by swinging the arms to the left, then to the right. Repeat 12 to 20 times. Great for the lower back and shoulders.

Static stretches

Static stretches are the stretches familiar to most walkers, which are held for 20 to 30 seconds or more. They are best performed AFTER workouts when the muscles are very well warmed up. When performing static stretches, always follow these rules of the road:

- Never stretch a cold muscle. Muscles need adequate blood flow to relax, and only a relaxed muscle can be stretched safely and comfortably. Stretch immediately after working out, or walk very easily for five to ten minutes first, then stretch the muscles before moving on to more vigorous training.
- Stretch opposing muscle groups to maintain muscle balance. For instance, stretch the back and front of the lower legs with calf and shin stretches, and both sides of the upper legs with quadriceps and hamstring stretches.
- Keep your breathing even and slow, exhaling as you move into a stretch, and then breathing slowly in and out as you hold the stretch.

- Hold each stretch for at least 15 to 30 seconds. Consciously relax the muscle as you slowly breathe into the stretch. Stretches should be held longer for larger muscle groups.

Practice the following stretches, or if you prefer, take yoga or Pilates classes, or use yoga or stretching videos. Whatever it takes to get the job done!

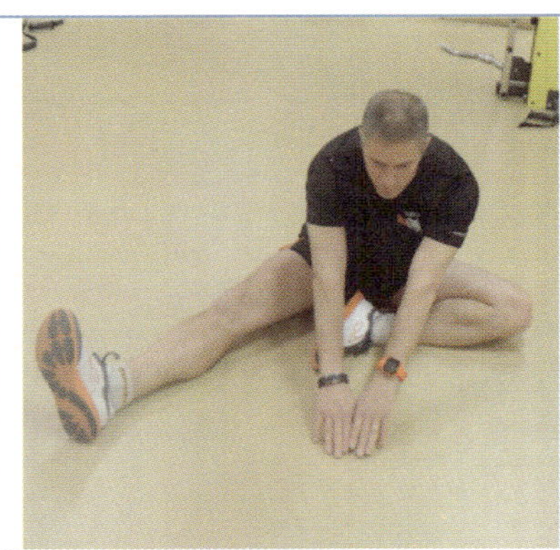
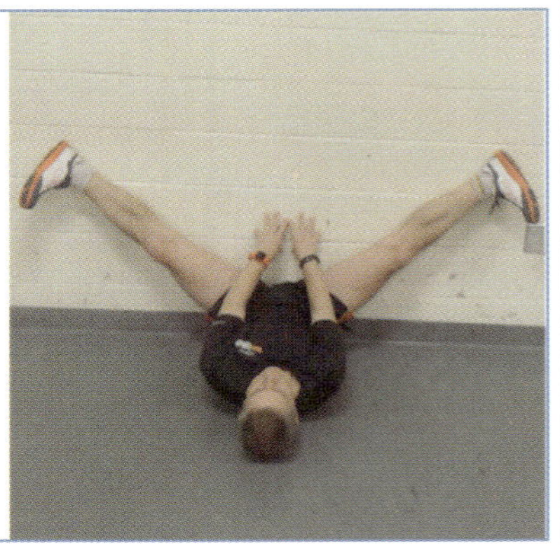

Three great groin/inner-thigh/adductor (gracilis) stretches

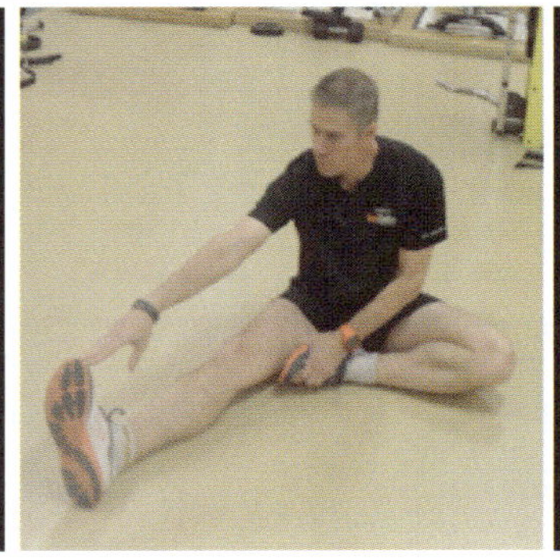
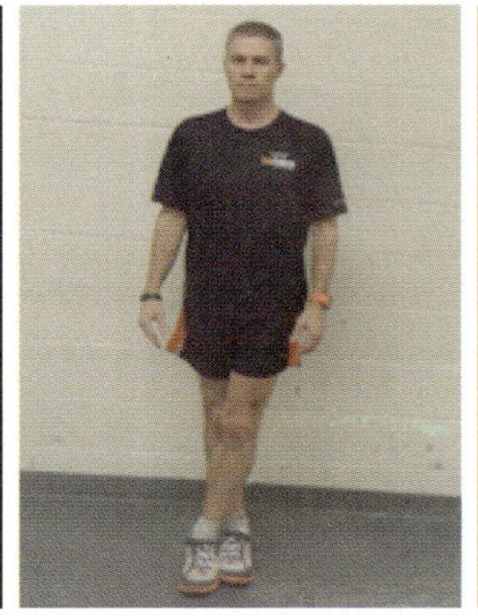
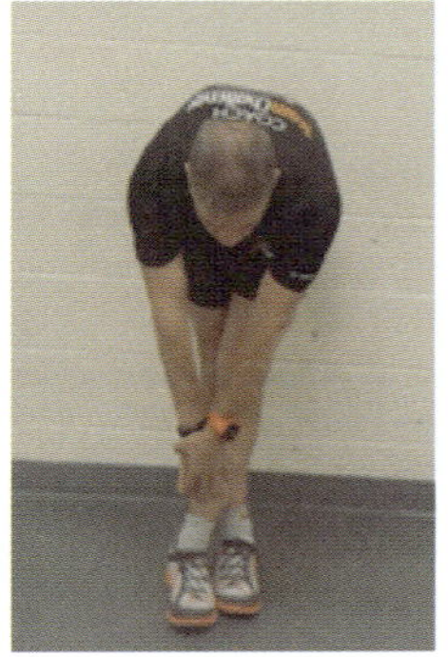

Seated two-leg and one-leg hamstring "toe-touches," and standing crossed-leg toe-touches. (For people who can touch their toes. In my case these are shin touches!)

Floor, and standing quad stretches

Hip-flexor, Iliopsoas and Iliotibial (IT) band stretches

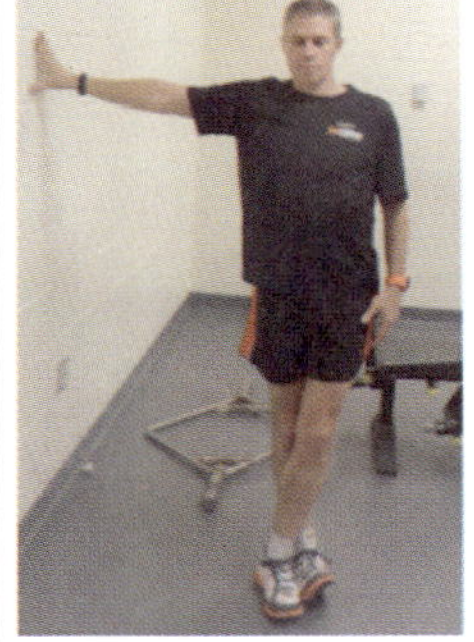
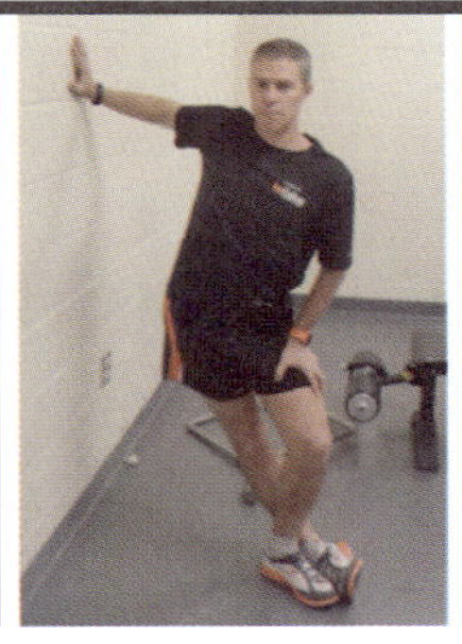

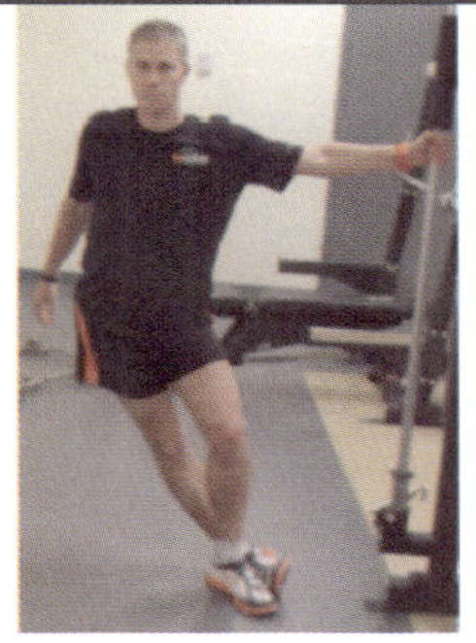
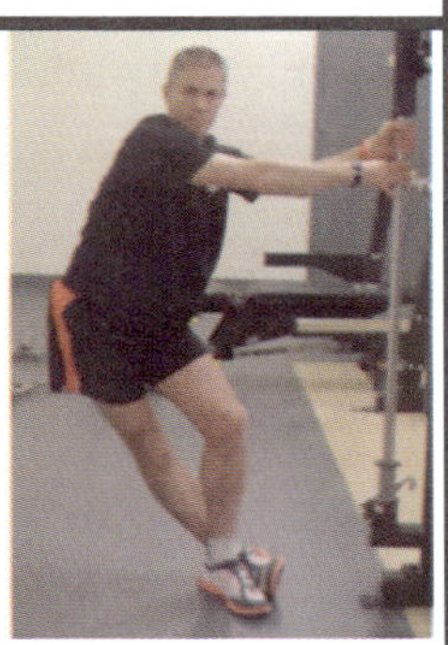

Iliotibial band stretches: Standing an arm's length away from a wall, cross the outside leg in front of the leg closest to the wall, then dip your hip into the wall. If you have something stable to hold onto, stand close to it, cross the leg nearest to the support in front, then allow your body to fall away from the support, putting your weight on the outside hip. To get an even better stretch, reach around with the free arm.

Side stretch sequence

Calf stretch

Lower calf/Achilles

Shin

Pectoralis/chest

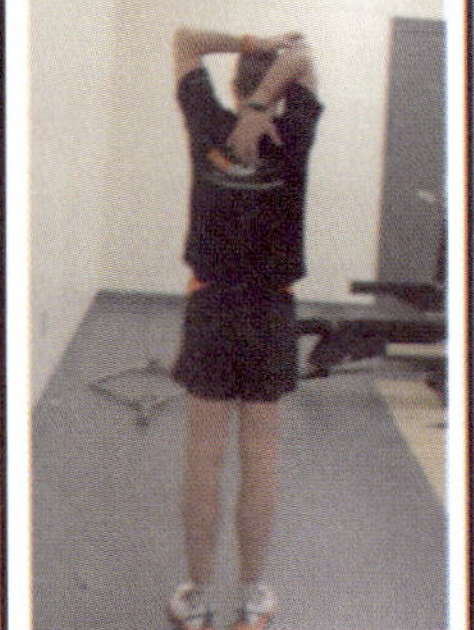

Shoulder

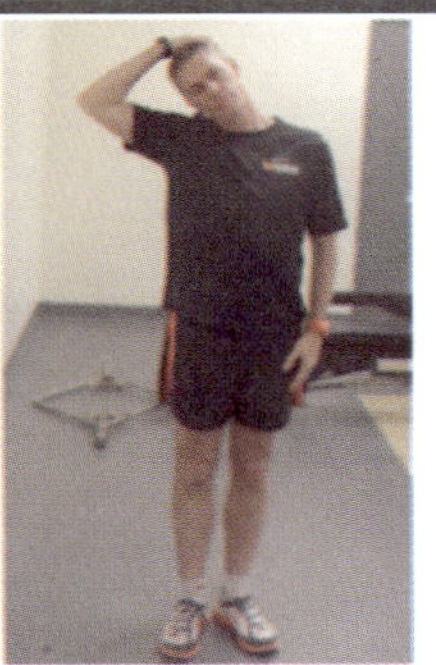

Neck

The preceding stretches are just a start. There are dozens of excellent books out there on stretching—Bob Anderson's *Stretching* is my go-to—and there are lots of web sites and YouTube videos as well. I even have my own YouTube video[69] showing both dynamic and static stretches. Whatever your source, you need to find the particular stretches that work for YOU. Experiment to see which positions get your own individual tight spots.

In addition to static and dynamic stretching, there are a number of other ways to work on flexibility. Competitive walkers can also work on flexibility in the weight room, for example. Instead of lifting very heavy weights through a limited range of motion, opt for lighter weights lifted through a full range of motion to enhance flexibility—see Chapter 35. Finally, you can enhance flexibility without "pulling" on the tendons (as stretching will do) by using a foam roller, getting a massage, or having a massage therapist or chiropractor perform ART (Active Release Therapy) on you. ART is a method of working out knots in the muscles while taking the limbs through a full range of motion.

As important as flexibility is as a component of overall fitness, it is no more important than muscular strength, a topic which we will delve into in the next chapter.

[69] The video is at this easy-to-remember link address: https://youtu.be/4xkeZhbxsiA

CHAPTER 35: STRENGTH TRAINING AND CORE WORK

Muscles propel your body forward. It stands to reason that strong muscles will propel it forward more easily than weak muscles. So developing overall muscular strength can directly help you to become a faster walker, but also indirectly, by helping to reduce the likelihood of injuries. Additionally, as was pointed out in Chapter 34, strength training is another way to enhance flexibility, which can not only help to prevent injuries, it can improve effective stride length. Beyond your walking, if you want to stay fit and healthy for a lifetime, strength training and core work should be a regular part of your training routine. It would be impossible to design a single, all-inclusive strength-training program for everybody since everyone has different strengths and weaknesses and access to different equipment; otherwise personal trainers would not exist! But the exercises that follow are easily performed in most reasonably well-equipped weight rooms, and many can be performed at home with limited equipment. The goal here is not to turn you into a professional body-builder or power-lifter; it's to help you to improve your walking. For most walkers, two or three sessions per week are sufficient to achieve that goal. If you're lifting more than that, then you probably have other motives. That's fine. Looking great at the beach is awesome, but if your primary goal is to improve your walking, two or three days per week is fine. If your schedule puts you in the gym on consecutive days (without a rest day in between), lift for the lower body/legs the first day and for the upper body on the next. On the other hand, if you can only get to the gym once per week, it's probably not worth going at all since any strength gains you make will be lost when gaps between sessions are so long that detraining occurs. I suggest working up to two or three sets with 10 to 15 reps of each exercise in a set. Don't overdo it! A strength-training program is about complementing your walking; it is not meant to detract from it by adding undue fatigue, or worse, injuries. The best way to determine the amount of weight to lift for a particular exercise is the RM method. An RM (Repetition Maximum) is the maximum number of times you can lift a weight before failure. Start light and find a weight that you are able to lift 10 to 15 times before you can't lift it any more. As training and fitness progress, weight can be added when doing 15 repetitions of a particular weight becomes easy.

Circuit training

Circuit training is weight training in which the rest intervals between different exercises are short. It's an attempt to combine weight training with some cardiovascular benefit, since heart rates can be pushed into the aerobic training range when rest breaks are very short. If you're performing daily aerobic training by walking there is probably no need to mix in a cardiovascular workout in the weight room, which will likely reduce the overall quality of the strength work. An exception would be when you are recovering from an illness or injury and have not been walking regularly.

Core work

The core refers to the muscles of the back, abs, hips and pelvic floor—basically everything other than your head, neck, and limbs. The core transfers force from the upper body to the lower body, and vice versa, and also supports the spine. If your core is weak and posture suffers, you'll begin using smaller muscles for propulsion. These smaller muscles are designed for "supporting roles" like rotating limbs internally or externally rather than driving the body forward. If the core is weak, smaller muscles can become overworked and eventually injured, so core work is critical for improving posture and preventing injuries. A focused core routine performed several times per week can really build strength with little or no special equipment. Some points to keep in mind when doing core and strength training exercises:

- Wear your walking training shoes—not racing flats—in the gym. Racing flats may not provide adequate support for weight training. On the other hand, don't wear anything with a very thick sole either, since these aren't good for your stability or alignment, and could lead to ankle sprains. Err on the side of less, rather than more cushioning.
- Warm up with some easy activity, such as walking on the treadmill, before lifting weights.
- Work to create symmetry between muscled groups; eliminate muscle imbalances, such as strong quadriceps straining weak hamstrings, which can lead to injuries.
- Work larger muscle groups before smaller ones.
- Breathe through a two- to three-second cycle; exhale on the exertion, inhale on the return.
- Use slow controlled motions and engage your core muscles to protect your back.
- Don't incur the wrath of gym attendants and personal trainers; never let weights stacks on machines bang together or drop heavy weights on the floor!

Strength Training Exercises

Leg (quadriceps) extensions

Seated hamstring curls

Seated leg press

Universal leg extensions

Universal hip flexion

Universal thigh adduction

Universal thigh abduction

Seated chest fly

Seated chest press

Bicep curls

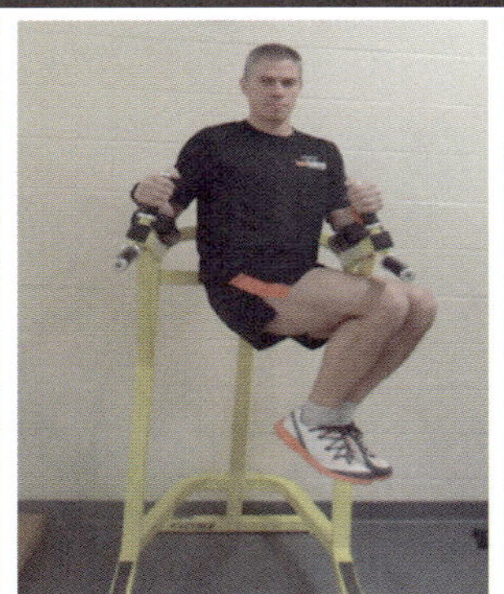
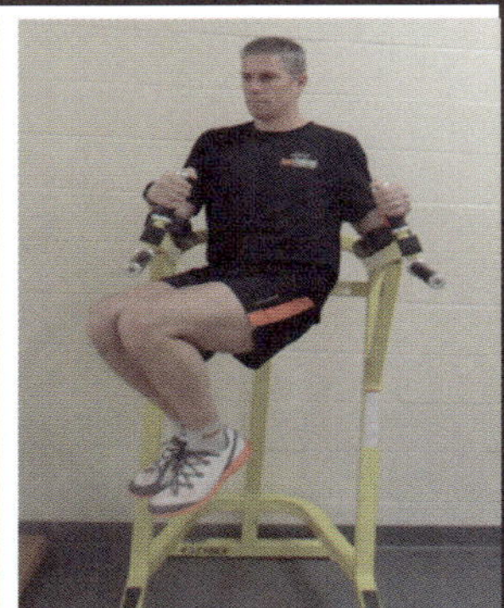

Roman chair crunches: Work through a rotation of straight, left and right curl-ups. Start with five of each, working up to 10 or more.

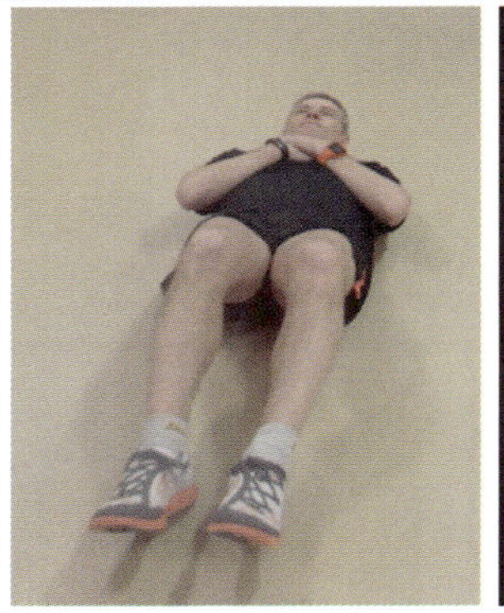

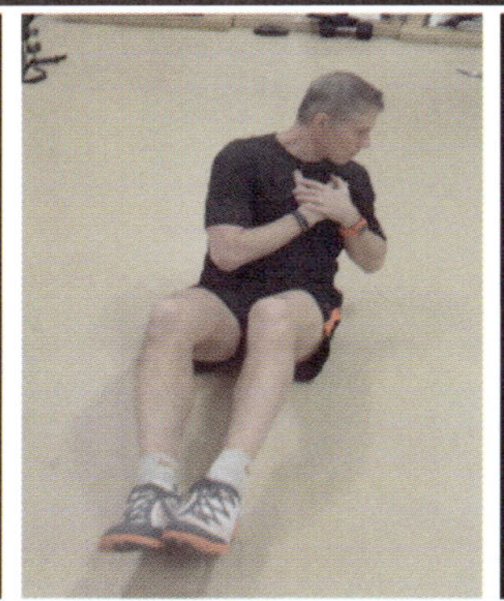
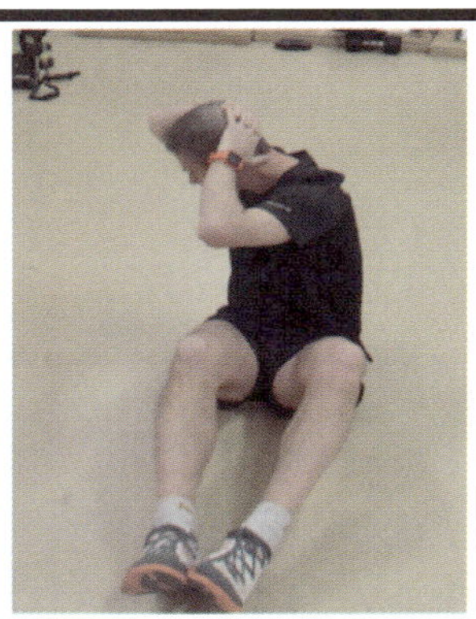

Crunches: Before curling up, be sure the lower back is flat on the floor to achieve a good pelvic tilt. Curl up slowly, hold at the top of the crunch for a count of three, then curl back down to the floor. To start, perform 10 straight crunches, then 10 oblique crunches on each side.

Variations include oblique crunches with bent knees, bicycles crunches…

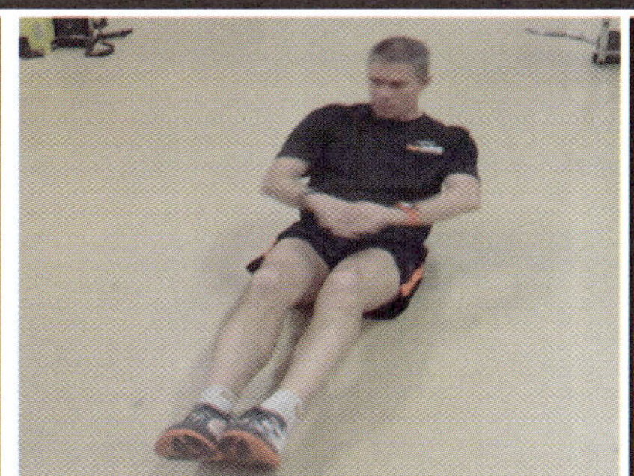

…and crunches with the legs raised or with the arms extended.

Reverse crunch: This is actually a bit of a variation on a reverse crunch. Start on your back with straight legs and both heels elevated six to eight inches off of the ground. Curl the knees up, pause, then shoot the legs upward. Pause, then come back to the curled-up position, then back to the start position. Repeat for 10 reps or more. Believe it or not, this one is not so easy! ☺

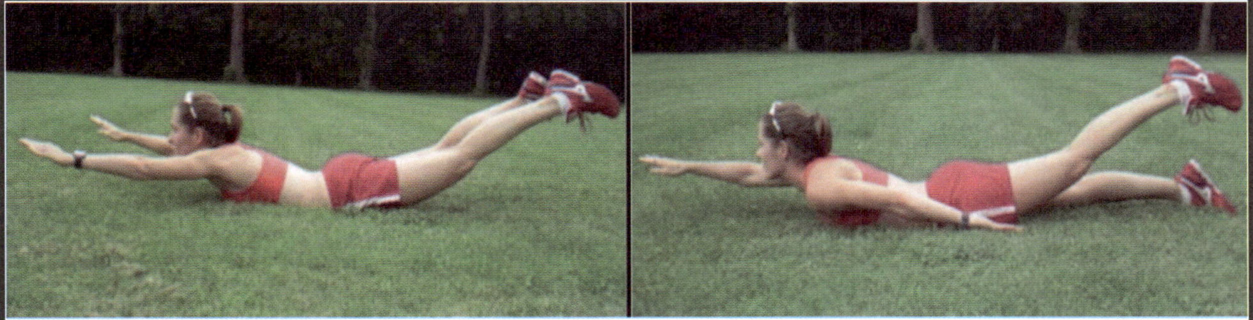

"Supermans": Lie flat on your belly with both feet and both arms raised. Hold for 20 seconds or more, rest, then repeat. A great variation is to do Supermans with alternating left leg/right arm and right leg/left arm lifted. (I would call these exercises "Supermen," but of course there is only ONE Superman!)

Planks: Start by resting on your forearms and toes with your back as straight as a plank of wood. The elbows should be bent at a 90-degree angle with the forearms held to the front, or crossed, as shown in the photo. Hold for 20 seconds, build to two minutes or more. Variations include side planks and straight-arm planks.

Heel dips, toe dips/raises: Standing on a step with your forefeet, let your heels dip below the plane of the step. Lift and raise your heels, alternating feet. For toe dips and raises stand with your heels on the step, then lift and lower the toes.

Elastic band exercises

The heel walking and toe walking exercises depicted in Chapter 12 are very good strengthening exercises for the shins and calves. I put them there because they are technique drills, but they are also very good lower leg strengtheners. The following are a number of other exercises to strengthen the legs, which can be performed with nothing more than a length of elastic band or tubing.

Glute/hamstring extension (L) and hip flexion (R) elastic band exercises: These are very similar to the dynamic flexibility exercises in Chapter 34 but with the added resistance provided by a thick elastic band. They are also similar to the Universal leg extension and Universal hip-flexion exercises performed on weight machines earlier in this chapter, but without the need for expensive machines. Several more elastic band exercises follow on the next page, but the number of exercises that can be performed with such a band is almost limitless.

Elastic band thigh abductor/adductor exercises: The adductors and abductors both play a role in driving the legs forward and pulling them back during the stride, but the abductors also limit excessive hip-drop, and can help prevent iliotibial (IT) band injuries.

Elastic band shin strengthener: The shins are incredibly important in competitive walking to keep the feet up and out of the way as the body is passing over them.

Elastic band calf (L) and peroneus (R) (outer lower leg) exercises: The calves are very important for propulsion at the end of the stride behind the body, and the peroneus muscles help to prevent the feet from pronating—flattening out—prematurely when walking. For the peroneus strengthener, loop the band around the feet, then separate the feet until there is tension in the band. "Princess wave" the feet, rotating around an imaginary vertical axis.

Plyometrics

Plyometric exercises are power exercises used to increase your speed, endurance, and strength. Also known as jump training, you may have seen plyometric exercises like high box jumps, which are better suited for explosive sport athletes—think football players, volleyball players or Olympic weight lifters. Plyos can, however, be used by competitive walkers wanting to develop a more explosive knee drive, better push-off from the back foot, and even a more powerful arm drive. Be very careful when introducing plyometric exercises to your training. As effective as they may be, plyometrics can be hard on the joints, especially the knees and ankles, so use with caution. If you feel you're up to the task, warm up well, start low and slow, and build gradually. Slowly increase the duration, difficulty, and intensity of any of the exercises. For example, backwards running can start as backwards walking with a short, low-to-the ground stride, then walking with a longer stride, then jogging with very short, low, shuffling steps, then finally, running with long strides reaching well behind the body. Start with just one session per week as part of your warm-up for intervals or other speed training. Although you can build to three sessions per week, two is probably sufficient for most walkers. Here are a few of my favorites:

Walking lunges: Keeping the rear foot far behind the body, extend the front foot so the front knee stays over the ankle. With your hands on your hips, squat straight down with the torso erect. "Walk" forward, then squat down on the "new" front foot. Repeat to lunge forward, walking down the track.

Step-ups: Starting at the bottom of a flight of steps, raise one foot one or two steps above the other foot. Quickly lift the rear foot one or two steps above the planted foot by driving the knee forward, then step back down with the same foot. Repeat several times before switching to the other leg. Whenever I walk up stairs I always take two at a time as an every-day strengthener.

Power skipping: Skip normally at first, then skip for height, pushing yourself up as high as possible, then skip for distance, being sure to slow your momentum after each powerful skip. Focus on a strong push through the toes of the back foot, keeping the back leg as straight as possible.

Butt-kicks: Run in place with a high back kick and a slight forward lean. Butt-kicks improve foot speed and help to strengthen the hamstrings.

Backward walking/backward running: Just as it sounds: Walk or run backwards. Start by walking backwards to establish coordination, then gradually transition to jogging with low, shuffling steps, building toward long strides and high knees.

Carioca or "grapevine" drill: Cross one foot over the other while twisting the torso in the opposite direction, again and again, moving sideways down the track. These are great for developing foot speed and strength, but also for strengthening many of the core support and propulsive muscles used in competitive walking.

Box Jumps: Just as it sounds. Jump from a standing position, with both feet together, up onto a box or other stable object. (No, a high-jump mat is not a stable object, but it's all I had at the time!) ☺

As critical as these supplemental physical exercises are for your competitive walking success, in many ways they pale in comparison to the mental side of training, especially for long distance races. So next up, let's take a look inside your head: mental training!

CHAPTER 36: MENTAL TRAINING

"If the mind is willing, the flesh could go on and on without many things." – **Sun Tzu**

It can be very difficult to separate the three elements of competitive walk preparation: technique, physical training, and psychology, because psychology weaves itself through all elements of training and competition. For example, you need to focus on technique while training, which requites concentration, a psychological tool. Although I'm hardly an expert in sport psychology, I have learned a few things over the years from some of the top experts in the field during our National Racewalk Team training camps at the U.S. Olympic Training Centers, and in classes I've taken with world-renowned sports psychologists at the University of Virginia. I've learned a lot about goal setting, relaxation, and visualization techniques, but to me the most important aspect of sport psychology is simple motivation. To excel you need to train. When it's hot or cold or raining or snowing you have to get out the door anyway. Sometimes you need to be a little creative, but you still need to get the mileage in. During summers when I was training in LaGrange, Georgia, or Mobile, Alabama, it was just too hot and humid to do good tempo workouts outdoors, so I often did them on a treadmill. If you think it's tough to hammer for two hours out on the roads, try it indoors on a treadmill—trust me on this one, it "builds character"! But more to the point, it requires a great deal of intrinsic motivation. This chapter will introduce the importance of goal setting, visualization, mental toughness, concentration, and relaxation in competitive walk training and competition.

Goal setting

The mind can be one of the most important weapons in a competitive walker's arsenal. It can also be his or her worst enemy. Monetary or other rewards are very sparse in the sport, so intrinsic motivation and non-tangible rewards are really all there is to keep you going. It is imperative to have concrete goals to keep yourself motivated. These goals should be ambitious enough to provide motivation, yet realistic enough to be attainable with proper, focused training. Sometimes, when the going gets tough, training well can become a game of mind over matter. Even with a great coach and supportive family and friends—if you're one of the lucky walkers who have those critical elements in place!—there's nobody forcing you out the door when you're tired, when the weather gets ugly, or you have to work late. You have to believe in your goals and your training plan and not let externalities like the weather, or distractions like television or social media, get in your way. Having a concrete goal in mind is often the only thing preventing you from hitting the snooze button, rolling over, and going back to bed, or spending the evening on the couch with Ben and Jerry instead of out training with Lefty and Righty, your walking shoes.

Commitment

Commitment to what you're doing is the key to achieving your goals. Sometimes it can be hard to train consistently when your target race is months away. You need to keep your eye on the ball, regardless. Long-term focus and faith in the program will get you through the hard training and to the starting line prepared to excel. That faith in the program is also what gives you the common sense and self-confidence to take a day off when needed, or the courage to get through tough workouts. Then, before an important race, you can look back on those months of training and have faith that you're ready.

The simple fact that you're reading this book shows a certain amount of commitment, but to achieve ambitious goals, you'll have to make walking an important part of your life. You'll need to make day-to-day decisions in your life based on how the outcome will affect your training and racing. Obviously you should choose the option that will help rather than hurt your walking. These are the "life choices" Rob Heffernan talked about in Chapter 31: Should you stay up to watch the "Dr. Pimple Popper Three-Hour Special" or go to bed so you can train in the morning? Do you keep a pair of training shoes in the car, or take them on business trips, or do you use not having them as an excuse to not train? Do you take the stairs instead of the elevator? Walk or bike, instead of driving the car? Should you eat that bacon double cheeseburger before or after your workout? (Or if you're me, *during* the workout.) ☺

You can't just be a walker or an athlete one or two hours a day while you're training. You have to have an athlete's mentality, an athlete's *commitment* 24 hours a day, every day, to be your best.

Individualize your goals

Commitment comes from believing that your goals are worthy, and believing that they are attainable. Television drills into our heads the idea that if you come in second you're a loser, that an Olympic silver medalist should somehow be apologetic. But it's not realistic for most people to set their goals at the Olympic medal level. Most elite walkers don't even have winning an Olympic gold medal as a goal—only three walkers on the planet can do so within any four-year period (two if Yusuke Suzuki decides to double!) So it's not realistic for everybody to have that goal. But whatever your goals may be, you need to believe that they are worthy, and that you have what it takes to achieve them.

Success doesn't always mean winning the race. It's a very individual thing, and it can mean anything from setting a personal record, to beating a rival, or just finishing a race feeling good and maintaining efficient technique. These are *your* goals; what's important is that they are important to *you*. It helps to be surrounded by supportive people who care about you and your goals, but often we have to train and race in anonymity. This is about *you*. If the local paper doesn't want to write about competitive walking or your co-workers don't understand what you're doing, screw 'em. What matters is that *you* believe what you're doing is important.

Evaluation

After every competition assess your situation. If you've achieved your objectives, decide where to go from there. If not, evaluate what went wrong. Look back in your training log. Were you undertrained? Overtrained? Was the initial goal overly ambitious, or was your "failure" simply caused by something beyond your control, such as bad weather, illness, or maybe just a competitor's superior performance?

If you didn't reach your goal, either train harder, or if you decide the original goal may have been overly ambitious, lower the bar a bit. Make sure the new goal is still challenging, but maybe a bit more realistic than your prior, unmet goal. If, however, you did achieve your goal, reward yourself with a favorite meal, drink, or maybe a small motivational purchase like a new pair of walking shoes. But don't rest on your laurels: Set your sights on new, loftier goals, then map out a course to achieve them.

Visualization

Visualization is one of the most important psychological tools at any athlete's disposal—especially for athletes involved in technique-intensive sports like racewalking or Nordic walking. Visualization is the act of programming your brain for the things you want to occur in the future by playing a positive virtual reality "movie" over and over again in your mind. The brain is where the neuromuscular signals that control your walking begin. It's also where pain messages are processed. Visualization works because you can trick your brain into believing something that isn't true—*yet!* If you constantly play the right messages over and over again in your head, you can help bring about that fast, efficient, walking future. Visualization can't replace hard physical training, but it can be very effective as a shortcut to learning efficient technique, as a confidence builder, and as a relaxation technique.

- **Skill learning**

  Technique improvements are most easily ingrained when you can first watch a good technique model, preferably in person. Watch, several times, noting what each body part is doing, and how they work together. Then replay the technique you've watched in your mind, and your body will learn to make the adjustments. If you don't have a good walking technique role model in your town, watch video of top walkers that you would like to emulate. Pick an athlete with a similar body type, and in your mind, play your own tape of you walking inside that person's body. Years ago, when trying to learn a more effective hip drive, I would often visualize my head on my good friend Olympic silver medalist Carlos Mercenario's body. I would see my own face, but the movements in my visualization were his. I would then imitate the actions while walking, still imagining Carlos's movements that I had seen in the video, and replayed in my head. After a while the actions felt comfortable and are now a part of my "natural" technique—I don't have to think about it any more while training or racing. Even today, when I want to work on a different element of my technique, I'll pick a good role model who exemplifies that particular technique component, and do the same thing. Try it; you'll be amazed at the results!

- **From dreams to reality**

Visualization can be a very important pre-competition confidence builder, Try to do your last workout before any important competition on the race course itself so you know the layout. By knowing the course you'll be able to create a mental image of yourself the night before the race—an image of yourself walking fast, efficiently and legally on the course during the next morning's race. Go over the tough parts of the course: the hills, the turns, etc., and focus on staying focused during those segments. Ask yourself what you want to occur during the race, then make it happen in your mind. You need to be able to see yourself winning or walking that big personal record first, or you'll never accomplish these goals in reality. The next morning, bring your "dreams" to life: Wake up and make your visualized scenario happen.

- **Relaxation**

Visualization can also be used as an excellent relaxation technique. If you feel yourself getting uptight before a race, tune out and take yourself away. Put yourself somewhere else, in a place where there are no worries. Perhaps you'd rather be at the beach or in a forest. Find a quiet spot away from your competitors and other distractions, making sure you have a friend or an alarm set to rouse you in case you drift off too deeply. Sit, or perhaps lie down under a tree, then think about that favorite beach or forest. Involve all your senses: See and hear the waves; feel the warm sand on your feet and the sun on your face, or listen to the birds and the cascading waterfall, and smell the trees in the forest. While you're taking yourself away, focus on your heart rate. Breathe deeply and slowly, attempting to bring your pulse rate down. You'll have plenty of time to get your heart rate back up during your warm-up, but use your pre-warm-up visualization session to calm and fully relax yourself.

Self-confidence

Self-confidence is the key to relaxation. You have to believe in yourself and constantly reinforce that belief to remain relaxed. If you still have worries before a race, write them down and look at your list rationally. What do you have control over? If you can't control it, don't bother thinking about it. If you do have some control over your problem, take steps to remedy the situation. If you're thinking, "Wow, I'm dehydrated," drink! If you're saying, "I feel really tight," stretch! When you can't control something, frame your thoughts about it in a positive way. Your competitors will be worried that the course has lots of hills, but you'll be thinking there are as many downhill sections as uphill sections. If your archrival shows up at a race unexpectedly you should be thinking, "Great! Now I have some good competition to pull me along." And as far as that archrival is concerned, it doesn't hurt to talk a little trash (to yourself) to get your confidence up. Be friendly, smile, shake hands with your competitor then, after he leaves, tell him how badly you'll kick his butt. Be as smug or "catty" as you need to be, as long as you're only talking to yourself: "Nice new shoes, Jack. Too bad they'll be finishing five minutes behind mine…"

Distraction control

You have enough psychological baggage to worry about when racing without getting hung up on *externalities*. Try to concern yourself only with the things you have some reasonable control over—your body and mind. Don't get flustered by anything that's beyond your control. If it's hot and humid, it's hot and humid for everybody. The person who will be affected the most is the person who is getting his blood pressure up worrying that it's hot and humid. If there's nothing you can do about it, don't waste your energy complaining. Whenever you feel these negative thoughts creeping in, talk them back to get yourself back on track. Learn to practice *distraction control.* It's okay to rationalize or lie to yourself if you have to. "It's not *that* hot out here. It'll get a lot better once the gun goes off." The only things worth thinking about are the things you can control. You can't control the weather or your competitors, but you can control how you react to them. Early in my career, there was one particular walker who would somehow always be around while I was warming up before races with some of the other athletes. Within 30 seconds of latching on to our group, he would start filing his excuses: "I can't believe I'm even here. I tore my hamstring during practice on Tuesday. Man, my back is killing me. I think I have a herniated disk... My glands sure are swollen. Are your glands swollen? I think I have a touch of that swine flu that's been going around…" Within five minutes of listening to this walking ball of negative energy we would all feel completely sapped, infected with his contagious hypochondria.[70] Before long we would be saying things like, "You know, my back kind of hurts too," or "I don't feel very good either. Maybe I'll just do this race as a workout—even if it *is* the national championship." If you run into one of these Negative Nellies—and you will—don't even bother with distraction control techniques. There's no way you'll be able to talk yourself down from a prolonged contact with such a black hole of negative energy. Don't allow yourself to get sucked into the void. Get away as quickly as possible. Duck into the nearest porta-potty if you have to, but get away. Negative

[70] Read all about "taperchondria" in Chapter 41.

energy is extremely contagious and it will affect your race if you allow it to. An iPhone with earbuds can be a very effective pre-race distraction-control device. If you need to tune out, *tune in* to your favorite playlist to block out negative influences, and to help you to focus on your own thoughts. Add a pair of dark sunglasses and you don't even need to have music playing for people to leave you alone when they see you getting your chill on.

Staying calm during judged races

About those judges—the people competitive walkers love to hate: They're your friends! Judges are out there on the course to help you by making sure *the other guy* isn't cheating! But just in case a judge decides to give you a "friendly advice" caution paddle or verbal warning, simply acknowledge it, then concentrate on your race. Trust your technique and relax! You've done your technique work, your drills, your economy intervals, so have confidence in your technique and keep moving. Don't let the judges or anyone else rattle you. Block them out of your mind and keep putting the pedal to the metal! If you think too much about the judges you'll wind up changing your technique when you go by them and risk doing something you haven't practiced in training; something that's potentially illegal. Although "common sense" may tell you otherwise, you shouldn't necessarily slow down if you get a caution. It can actually be counterproductive to do so: The slower your cadence, the easier it is for a judge to see what your feet or knees are doing. You may also wind up walking with a longer stride that can keep you off the ground even longer, and make it more difficult to straighten your knees if you're a racewalker. Maintaining that high cadence rate isn't just faster, it also looks better to most judges, so don't automatically assume that slowing down is the answer if you get a caution. If anything, spin your wheels even faster! ☺ And don't get into the mindset that a caution or red card necessarily means you've done something wrong. Have confidence in your technique, and remember to always frame things in the positive: One caution from one judge means you're doing great—you're at the very upper end of fast, legal technique. An actual "red card" isn't necessarily a good thing, but even collecting two red cards can be seen as a technically perfect race: borderline, but not out. You've pushed the limit of fast, legal technique without going overboard. Whatever happens, smile! What kind of cretin would disqualify a relaxed, smiling athlete?

Associative thinking

Successful athletes are *associative*—they are at all times aware of their bodies and their environment when competing. You should be alert, maintaining intense focus during your races. Don't race dissociatively, on "cruise control." It's easy to let the pace fall off or to let other athletes pull away from you when the going gets tough if you're not focused on your body and the race going on around you. I realize I've mentioned this before, but earbuds make it absolutely impossible to race associatively. 'Nuff said on that. (Until the next chapter. And the one after that…) ☺

A great sport psychologist once told me that you can only have one conscious thought going through your head at a time. The thought that needs to be going through your head during a race is "clop, clop, clop, clop, clop, clop, clop!" (Or whatever sound your feet make…) You need to remain focused to keep your cadence rate up despite fatigue or pain, and you can't do that if you're off in LaLa Land thinking about unicorns, hoping they'll magically make the pain go away. Racing is supposed to be difficult, but the pain is temporary. The gnawing afterthoughts of racing poorly in a big competition, however, can stay with you forever!

Body check

Challenge the negatives. If you're feeling pain, don't deny it, use it: "My legs are burning, but that means I'm working hard! I can handle more. Now I've got to maintain my cadence and keep hitting the splits." If you are pushing too hard, be aware of the situation. If you're laboring in the first few minutes of the race, don't keep hammering away only to blow up in the second half. Ease up a little. At regular intervals during the race, conduct a quick full-body technique assessment: "How are my shoulders?" "Good—nice and relaxed!" "How are the legs feeling?" "Just great, Dave! Really solid, and turning over quickly." "Lungs?" "No problem! Breathing's under control—I've got this thing sewn up!"

Watch your competitors

In addition to monitoring your own effort, it's also a good idea to try to gauge how your competitors are feeling. If someone you're racing looks like he's hurting, pick up the pace for a few minutes to break him or her. Try to make sure your own face is relaxed, though. It'll help keep you loose, and your competitor will think you're feeling much better than he or she is. You would be surprised how many walkers will settle for second place when you speed past them, if you do it looking strong and relaxed while they are hurting, or simply not focusing on staying competitive.

Keep your eye on to ball

Above all, use your mind to your advantage—don't let it use you. On a base level, there's no life-or-death reason to want to walk really fast. (Believe it or not, most people run away from danger, they don't walk.)[71] Since competitive walking isn't high on Abraham Maslow's hierarchy of human needs, you sometimes have to trick your mind into thinking that it really is a worthwhile pursuit—especially when it involves subjecting your body to the physical and psychological stresses of racing. To do so you must be able to focus on your body and how it's performing during the race.

---

[71] This point was scientifically proven by a Japanese variety show when they sent a small army of Samurai warriors to "attack" Olympic and world Champion Jefferson Perez while he was in the middle of an interval workout before the 2007 World Championships in Osaka, Japan. Although he probably could have walked faster, Jefferson ran for his life. ☺ The video is here: https://www.dailymotion.com/video/x4isx7

When the going gets tough, zero in on maintaining a high cadence rate and staying relaxed, and remind yourself why you're doing this: If your goal is to win the race, remind yourself of that goal if somebody tries to pass you in the final stages of the race. If you let him go because you're hurting, you're not going to win the race. If your goal is a time goal, on the other hand, watch the clock, not necessarily what the other guy is doing. Keep track of your splits, and force yourself to spin the wheels a little quicker if you find yourself falling off the pace.

Final thoughts

You're in control of your own destiny. Set ambitious but reasonable goals for yourself, make a plan to achieve them, visualize your goals becoming reality, then stick to your plan and make it so. Let each small victory motivate you to raise the bar a little higher, then visualize yourself achieving the next success. If you can't imagine walking fast and with perfect technique, and if you don't believe you can beat your rivals and your best times, you're probably right.

During competitions, stay alert and always in control of your mind. Challenge any negative thoughts with positives at all cost. Your brain will be trying to make you slow down when things start to hurt. Be ready for it, and don't let it happen. There are always two dueling influences in your head during competitions: the one that wants you to be a champion, and the one that wants you to go home and take a nap. It's up to you to decide which will come out on top. Billy Mills,[72] an unsung 10,000-meter runner, was given no chance of making the Olympic final in Tokyo in 1964, let alone winning. But he believed he could. Mills told himself every day that he could, and visualized every day that he would. Of course he did make the final, and going through the three mile mark of the 6.2-mile race only one second slower than his fastest three-mile ever, everyone assumed Mills would fall apart over the second half of the race. But Mills didn't. He believed. Going into the final lap in third place behind Mohamed Gammoudi of Tunisia, and Aussie Ron Clark, the World Record holder, Mills was falling behind. But he told himself again and again over that last lap, "One more try! One more try! Believe! Believe! Believe!" With one last push in the final thirty meters of the race, Mills blasted by Clarke and Gammoudi for the win, the first ever for an American at 10,000 meters. What the mind believes, the body achieves!

Whether you win or lose, self-evaluate after ever race. Write down in your training log what went right or wrong. Keep track of anything you did that seemed to help your race, as well as anything you may have done wrong that may have hurt it. If you don't know your own history, you're doomed to repeating your mistakes, and failing to replicate your successes.

Next up: What to do when you overdo it; a few words on walking-specific injuries.

---

[72] Incidentally, Billy's wife Pat attended my racewalking clinics in Sacramento during the early 2000s, so I've met Billy several times. What incredibly inspiring people they both are!

CHAPTER 37: WALKING: THE INJURY-FREE SPORT?

Competitive walking is often touted as an "injury-free" sport. And compared to what many runners go through, walkers do suffer from far fewer injuries. But anything done at a high level is liable to cause the occasional owie. When they do occur, walking injuries are nearly always of the overuse variety rather than traumatic ones (i.e., sprains and tears).[73] I've been lucky enough over the years to train through most of my injuries, but I have had my fair share of bad ones that have required medical attention. Most sports medicine specialists get fine educations in our medical schools, and receive lots of great on-the-job training treating a daily throng of synchronized swimmers, horseshoe pitchers, dog mushers and limbo dancers. The problem with many doctors, though, is that they work in generalities: If a doctor works with a lot of basketball players, a torn meniscus is probably a reasonable guess as the source of medial knee pain. Likewise, a sprain may be a likely diagnosis for a soccer player, and chondromalacia is fairly common among runners. Unfortunately most doctors don't see many racewalkers or Nordic walkers and aren't sure what kinds of assumptions they should make, so they'll often diagnose you with an injury they've seen a lot in their other patients.

Even with the best diagnostic imaging, things can go awry. For decades I've told people "don't get an MRI. You don't want to know what's going on in there!" In 1992 I was in heavy training for the Olympic Trials. I was noticing some pulling in my lower abdomen but tried my best to ignore it. I asked my GP what he thought. He said it *could be* an inguinal hernia but he wasn't sure. He sent me to a surgeon who diagnosed hernias on *both* sides. Since the Olympic Trials for the 20k were coming up we made a plan to repair one hernia, then come back to do the other one after the Trials. Well, it's been 28½ years and I still haven't felt the need to get the other side worked on. In hindsight I think the "hernias" were actually just tight iliopsoas muscles causing some pulling and pain "down there." I hope I really did need to have surgery, but seeing as I haven't felt the need to repair the other one almost 30 years after the fact, I'm thinking probably not. I suspect I could have actually trained all the way up to the Trials instead of having to take off for eight weeks after the surgery.[74]

[73] Although… The most commonly reported injuries among Nordic walkers are sprains of the ligament on the inside of the thumb, as well as shoulder dislocations, both related to accidental falls. www.mcmasteroptimalaging.org/blog/detail/blog/2014/09/21/lets-take-a-pole-who-wants-to-try-nordic-walking

[74] I came back pretty strong after the surgery, but I'm sure the layoff hurt me at the Trials. I was in third place with one kilometer to go but was passed by Jonathan Matthews and Ray Funkhouser heading into the stadium for

More recently, while training for the 2016 Olympic Trials, I dislocated my fibula (the smaller of the two lower leg bones) while running on grass, chasing after some helium balloons that had escaped my young son's grasp. Jumping for the balloons I heard a loud POP!—and it wasn't one of the balloons. After several days of pain I went to my chiropractor, who diagnosed the dislocation and popped it back into place. Instant relief! But in an overabundance of caution he convinced me to go in for my first-ever MRI. Long story short, it showed that in addition to the dislocated fibula, it seems I had been walking around (for months? Years?) with a 20% tear in my ACL, a torn and apparently completely detached (!) medial meniscus, a ruptured Baker's cyst, and a ganglion cyst growing through the ACL—none of which was causing any of the pain I had been feeling from the dislocation, and I haven't felt any pain ever since it was popped back into place. Fast-forward another four years to the time I tripped and slammed the same knee onto a concrete bike path while training for the most recent Olympic Trials. The knee wasn't too bad immediately after the fall, but for some reason it swelled up with fluid after a hard workout about 10 days after the initial injury, so I went to a doc who did a quick ultrasound then sent me for a CT scan. It revealed a bruised and bleeding patellar tendon, and a bunch of other stuff, but no mention of the meniscus, ACL or the cysts. I'm rambling here… The point is, walking is not necessarily an injury-free sport, but most of the injuries sustained by competitive walkers are overuse injuries that can be treated non-surgically with a little rest, ice, stretching, massage, etc. (And don't get an MRI on that wonky knee of yours. You don't want to know.) ☺

Origins and insertions

Competitive walking does a lot of great things for your body, but it does not enhance flexibility. Over time, muscles incrementally lose flexibility if they are not gently stretched following exercise. As a tight muscle shortens, it pulls at its origin and insertion points (at the tendons and fascial sheaths that connect the muscles to the bones). The only way to relieve the strain on the tendons is to stretch the muscles through massage, foam-roller work, dynamic flexibility exercises, and yes, stretching, all of which were outlined back in Chapter 34.

Having said all that, I've found that competitive walkers suffer relatively few serious injuries. Although torn meniscuses and the like do occur, tendinitis of the knee (iliotibial or sartorial), feet (plantar fasciitis or peroneal-cuboid syndrome), shins ("shin splints," anterior compartment syndrome, or posterior tibial myositis/tendinitis), or of the Achilles tendon are much more common overuse injuries in walkers. Bursitis of the hip or knee is also fairly common. The trick with tendinitis is to remember just what tendons are: They're tough fibrous sheaths that connect muscles to bones. Fortunately, 99% of the time there's nothing wrong with the tendon itself. It is

---

the finish. There's no telling how much higher I would have placed had I not lost that eight weeks of training after the surgery. ☹

simply being abused by a tight (and often, weak) muscle. As the muscle shortens, it pulls at its origin and insertion points (at the tendons, and fascial sheaths).

Tendinitis is a lot like someone is pulling your hair: Your hair doesn't hurt, it's the insertion point at your scalp.

Tendinitis is a lot like someone is pulling your hair. The hair itself doesn't hurt; it's the insertion point at the scalp that's making you scream. Anti-inflammatories, pain-killers, ice, and thinking happy thoughts may all help, but eliminating that "pulling" is ultimately the only way to make it stop hurting. Bursitis is the inflammation of a bursa (a fluid-filled sac that helps reduce friction in a joint). Like tendinitis, bursitis is caused by tight muscles, which cause friction and irritation of the bursae. Again, the only way to release the strain on the irritated tendon or bursa is to lengthen the muscle by stretching it, massaging it, foam-rolling it, etc.

The quick fix

Athletes are often seduced by the quick fix, Band-Aid approach to sports medicine: Rest, ice and anti-inflammatories will make the pain go away. All true to some extent, but these approaches attack the symptom and not the cause. The pain may be in the tendon or bursa, but the root cause is the tight, weak, neglected muscle. Treatment for these injuries needs to begin with identification of the muscle or muscles involved. Quite often you will notice discomfort and tightness in muscles that may lie far from the injured area. Don't ignore these sensations! They could be the source of the irritation. My first serious bout with tendinitis involved the insertion of my iliotibial band into the outside of my right knee. I felt a little tightness on the outside of my right hip as well, but thought nothing of it, since it was never very painful and was so far away from the hurting knee. The injury eventually forced me to take two months off and to pull out of the 1987 World Cup—my first international team as an open (over age 20) athlete. After a week or two off, the knee was fine for a couple of days, but when I tried to return to training, it would hurt just as much as the original injury after a few days on the road. Two months of on-and-off rest did nothing to cure the knee because I failed to attack the tight hip muscles and iliotibial band. The treatment that finally cured me involved having my physical therapist dig at the "necrotic" scar tissue in my hip and thigh with the back end of a screwdriver[75] to release the muscle and tendon, and then learning how to ward off further flare-ups with a sensible stretching routine.

An ounce of prevention is worth two in the bush (or something like that.) Do your flexibility drills before and stretch after every workout, especially anything long or fast. Take a yoga class. Get a massage. If the weather is too lousy to get out the door to train, stay inside and stretch! Attack those tight muscles before they turn into debilitating injuries.

Rehabilitation

Certainly stretching is an important first step in recovery, but gains in flexibility will be short-lived if the involved muscles are weak and atrophied. Strength training—Chapter 35—is equally critical in injury rehabilitation or preventative care. Whether using free weights, weight machines, elastic devices, or isometric exercises, the involved muscles should be worked through a range of motion that mimics the walking action as closely as possible. This may involve some improvisation with weight machines, or experimentation with postural changes until you find the perfect position. I like using a Universal weight machine to do a number of my flexibility drills with some added resistance. I'll put on a Velcro ankle cuff, hook it up to the cable and pulley attached to the stack of weights, and work each leg through a full range of motion. This improves strength and flexibility through the muscles' entire range of motion.

During rehabilitation, resistance should be just enough to cause minor fatigue without causing pain to the injured area. Work with very light weights initially, but as strength improves, work up to two to three sets of 10 to 12 RM, always allowing 48 hours for recovery between sessions on a particular muscle. Three days of light weight training per week is probably optimum, but if life gets in the way, two days per week is infinitely better than one day. I don't follow any particular rules about weight training on hard walking days vs. easy walking days: Some walkers like to do their weight training on their hard walking days to allow the body a full recovery on the easy days; others like to weight train on their easy walk days so they are not too tired from the weight-training to have a good walking workout that day, or vice versa.

RICE, MEAT, and a SCARIER method of injury treatment

Two acronyms familiar to many injured walkers are RICE and MEAT. RICE stands for Rest, Ice, Compression, Elevation, and MEAT means Movement, Exercise, Analgesics, and Treatment. Both are somewhat effective at treating walking injuries, but each on their own leaves out a few

[75] Could a more traditional massage tool have done the job? Probably. But my therapist (Marc Chasnov) apparently liked the shock value of attacking patients with construction tools. It worked, but what really kept me coming back was the chance to get treatments on the next table over from Irish World Champion and Olympic medalist, Eamonn Coghlan, a frequent patient.

important elements. I believe competitive walkers should try something SCARIER: Stretch, Compress, Anti-inflammatories, Rehydrate, Ice, Elevate, Rest.

Stretch the muscles. As mentioned above, most walking injuries are tendinitis or bursitis-type injuries. The root cause of these injuries is tight muscles that "pull" on tendon insertions. Stretching the tight muscles will relieve the strain on the tendon insertions.
Compress the sore spots with elastic bandages or compression socks or sleeves to push out excess fluids. Also "compress"—by massaging or using a foam roller—the tight muscles to work out any knots, and to break up scar tissue.
Anti-inflammatories like ibuprofen (Advil) or Aleve will further reduce swelling.
Rehydrate those dried out, beef-jerky muscles. Muscles are 90% water—a dry muscle is a tight muscle. DRINK!
Ice after training, 10 minutes on, 10 minutes off, for 30 minutes.
Elevate the feet whenever possible. Elevation will allow fluid to drain out of swollen areas.
Rest as a last resort. If at all possible, continue walking, but do take it easy. Warming up the muscles will allow you to get a better stretch, and will circulate lots of healing blood to the area. I don't think of it as training, but as "therapeutic walking."

While tendinitis-type injuries are the most serious injuries that a walker is likely to suffer, there are a number of other minor inconveniences that may befall you. You should be able to take care of these minor problems easily, without missing any training. Among these are:

- **Blisters-** Blisters form in places where the skin is rubbed repeatedly; usually by an ill-fitting shoe. Some walkers have success with double-layered socks. I've found that my feet slide around more with these socks, so they may actually cause more blisters than a single-thickness pair of socks would. Experiment with different sock thicknesses to see what works best for you, and never go out on a long workout in a pair of shoes or socks that you haven't first tested on several shorter workouts. If you already have a blister, I say pop it with a sterilized needle, then cover it with a Band-Aid or sterile gauze, although Ms. Kennedy, my old high school nurse, is apt to be very upset when she reads this.[76] I find that if I don't drain the fluid, the blister eventually tears open and then things get really ugly. Eventually, frequently blistered areas will thicken, forming a hard, scaly callus—so at least you have that to look forward to. As a last resort, some walkers have found that rubbing Vaseline on their feet before training will prevent blisters. This is definitely a case of the cure being worse than the ailment—see "chafing" for more on the subject. Others

[76] Come to think of it, by my calculation Ms. Kennedy would be about 113 years old now, so maybe she won't be reading this after all.

have used spray antiperspirant to reduce sweating, therefore preventing blisters. Never tried it, not going to start now. ☺

- **Black toenails-** Formed when blood collects in a blister under a traumatized toenail, these ugly buggers will really impress your friends. Although black toenails are most frequently caused by tight shoes, they can also form when your shoes are too big, so you're damned if you do, damned if you don't. The nail will eventually "die" and fall off, but if it really hurts you may want to see a podiatrist who will drill a hole in the nail to drain the blister. Me? I just pop a hole in the nail with a hot paper clip—a high-tech solution that costs about 300 bucks less than the D.P.M. version. Keeping your toenails clipped will help prevent black toenails from recurring.

- **Side stitches-** Not an injury, per se, but they can be pretty painful nonetheless. A side stitch is a temporary pain in the side, below or behind the rib cage, believed to be caused by an insufficient oxygen supply to the diaphragm—a muscle below the lungs that helps you breathe. If you get a stitch while training, bend sideways away from the side that hurts, while massaging the area. The theory behind the cure is that you're trying to get oxygen into the area—although simply stopping your walk to do the stretch will probably do as much good as the stretch itself. Eventually, as you get fitter, oxygen supply to the diaphragm increases and the stitches stop occurring.

- **Chafing-** Chafing is a nasty rash that occurs when you rub two pieces of skin together 140-210 times per minute. Chafing most commonly occurs when you're dehydrated—after you've stopped sweating and your skin is left covered with a film of sticky salt. Staying hydrated will help, as will wearing half-tights under your shorts—in the case of thigh chafing anyway. Losing weight may also help—enough said. As was the case with blisters, some walkers solve the problem by smearing the affected areas with Vaseline before training and racing, but I'm having a hard time imagining anything more awful than that fate. I'm not afraid of snakes, spiders, or rabid Rottweilers, but Vaseline on my thighs and armpits? Just no. That stuff gives me the willies! Body Glide (described in Chapter 3) is a more civilized alternative.

Coming back from an injury

Patience is the keyword when returning from an injury—don't rush things! Again, most walking injuries are overuse injuries. Your body is trying to tell you something: "Take it easy, dummy!" A certain amount of detraining will set in after any layoff. Speed is the first thing to go, but before long endurance is also degraded. The good news is that it takes a lot less time to return to top form than it took to get there in the first place, so relax! Don't rush your return to training.

I've often been told that it takes two weeks to come back from every week off, but I've found that it seems to take two weeks to return from any layoff of any duration. If I've been off for a month, the first two weeks back will feel like garbage, but then things will always "click" suddenly after about two weeks. One rule of thumb that I do believe, however, is that you shouldn't race after a layoff until you've gotten at least as much training in as you've lost. If you were off for two weeks, don't even think about racing unless you've gotten at least two good weeks under your belt after the break. If you were off for six weeks, get in six weeks of training before racing.

Injuries may be an inevitable part of competitive walk training, but if you know how to treat them, your down time will be measured in days rather than weeks or months. Now, speaking of time, let's talk about stopwatches and stuff!

CHAPTER 38: TRAINING TOOLS

Although there are certainly some walkers who like to keep things as simple as possible, walking by "feel" without the use of any modern technology to gauge their speed or level of exertion,[77] and others who are perfectly happy using nothing more than the timer on their smart phones, here in the 21st century where I live ☺ there are a wide variety of technological devices that can help motivate you and make your training more precise and effective. At the most rudimentary level, some form of stopwatch is a necessity for any walker even remotely serious about his or her training. If you have a goal to finish a 5k, half-marathon, or ultra in a particular time, it will be necessary to do at least some of your training at your goal pace. A stopwatch ensures that you are doing so. But for a simple stopwatch to be effective, you need to be training on some sort of measured course. As discussed in Chapter 6, tracks are one option. A standard outdoor high school or college track is 400 meters around, assuming you're walking close to the inner edge of lane one. That's just a hair less than a quarter mile, while 2.5 times around is exactly one kilometer (or 1,000 meters), and four times around is just a bit short of one mile. If you aren't diligent about walking near the rail on the inside of lane one and stay toward the outside of the lane instead, you will be walking very close to one mile every four laps. Tracks are great places to do the speed work laid out in Section III when you'll want to know the exact distance you're walking. They are also safe, controlled environments if you live in a busy area with lots of automobile traffic.

If you don't have access to a track it's still possible to walk on measured courses. Look to GPS mapping sites, like mapmywalk.com or the Charity Miles app on your smart phone, if you want to find or measure road courses. These sites and apps allow you to exactly measure distances on your computer or phone screen. You can then find landmarks out on the course to locate and mark mile or kilometer splits. Particular houses, trees, phone poles, manhole covers, road kill, mailboxes and the like are clearly visible from the air and are easily found out on the roads. (Okay, maybe the road kill won't still be there, but you get my point…) Alternately, there are a growing number of iPhone and Android applications that use your smartphone's GPS feature to measure speed and distance on the go. Many also allow you to be a part of a social community with other users with whom you can share your workouts if you choose. A few of the more popular are Polar Beat, Strava, MapMyWalk, RunKeeper, Dailymile, and Endomondo. I personally don't like the idea of people around the world knowing exactly what I'm doing (or more to the point, *not* doing!) every day, but to each his own. ☺

[77] These people are known as "Luddites." ☺

If you want to spend a couple of bucks (actually, more like 50 to 150 couples of bucks...), you can buy a GPS watch that will allow you to track your pace and distance without having to be on a previously measured course. A GPS (global position system) is a navigation system that uses satellite triangulation to precisely identify your location. Until the 1980s GPS systems were only available to the military. Now wrist-worn units, as well as phone-based GPS apps, have become widely available to the public, and many walkers use them to map out new routes on a smartphone or computer prior to training, or to determine their speed and distance on the fly while working out. In addition to using GPS technology, some watches link with "shoe pods" or use inertial sensors—accelerometers—to measure speed and distance and cadence. Much more than just a pedometer, the inertial sensor measures the acceleration of the monitor on your wrist or the foot pod worn on a shoe. Brands associated with these technologies include, but are not limited to: Polar, Garmin, Fitbit, Nike, Suunto, Apple, etc.

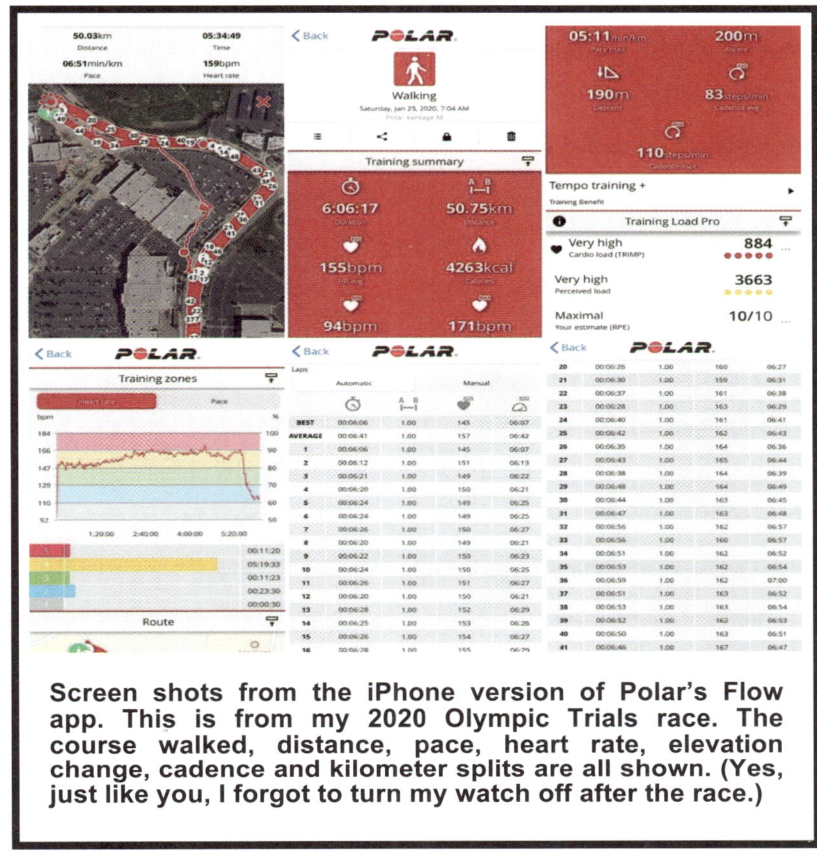

Screen shots from the iPhone version of Polar's Flow app. This is from my 2020 Olympic Trials race. The course walked, distance, pace, heart rate, elevation change, cadence and kilometer splits are all shown. (Yes, just like you, I forgot to turn my watch off after the race.)

Another rapidly evolving technology is optical wrist-based heart rate monitoring. Heart rate monitors allow you to train based on how your heart responds to training rather than just using how you feel—perceived exertion—which can be affected by many environmental and internal factors, or by using your walking pace, which can be affected by things like the weather or how well rested you happen to be. I've used a heart monitor with an electrode transmitter chest strap since the late 1980s, but never realized how much I hated the transmitter strap until reliable wrist-based monitors came out in 2018. These devices measure heart rate by shining light from a number of LEDs through the skin and measuring how it scatters off of your blood vessels. The vessels change color slightly as blood is pumped through them, and the optical sensors in the monitor are able to detect those color changes. Several companies sell heart rate monitors, most of which now include optical sensors. Among these are Polar, Timex, Garmin, Apple and Nike. Some of the low-end units simply give heart rate, but most are now combined units, known as "wearables," that have stopwatches, zone alarms, GPS or inertial speed and distance monitors, altimeters, thermometers, etc., etc., etc. The number of features will determine the cost of the wearable. Full disclosure: Polar is one of my long-time sponsors, and I wrote their user's manual for walkers, *Precision Walking,* back in 1995, so admittedly I'm biased. But Polar really is the best! ☺ Company founder Seppo Säynäjäkangas[78] invented heart rate telemetry devices for athletes in Finland way back in 1975, and Polar has always been among the most innovative companies in the field. If I ever have issues during the heart rate training tests at my walking clinics, it seems to almost always be with a participant's non-Polar device. (I won't mention any names, but monitors made by a company that rhymes with "nitwit" seem to be among the least reliable….) ☺ As far as GPS is concerned, Garmin is the best-known brand in the space, and was an early innovator, but all the major companies now use the same technology, satellites, and algorithms, resulting in comparable speed and distance results. But heart rate technology varies a great deal from company to company, as does the software used to display the heart rate, GPS, cadence, and other data.

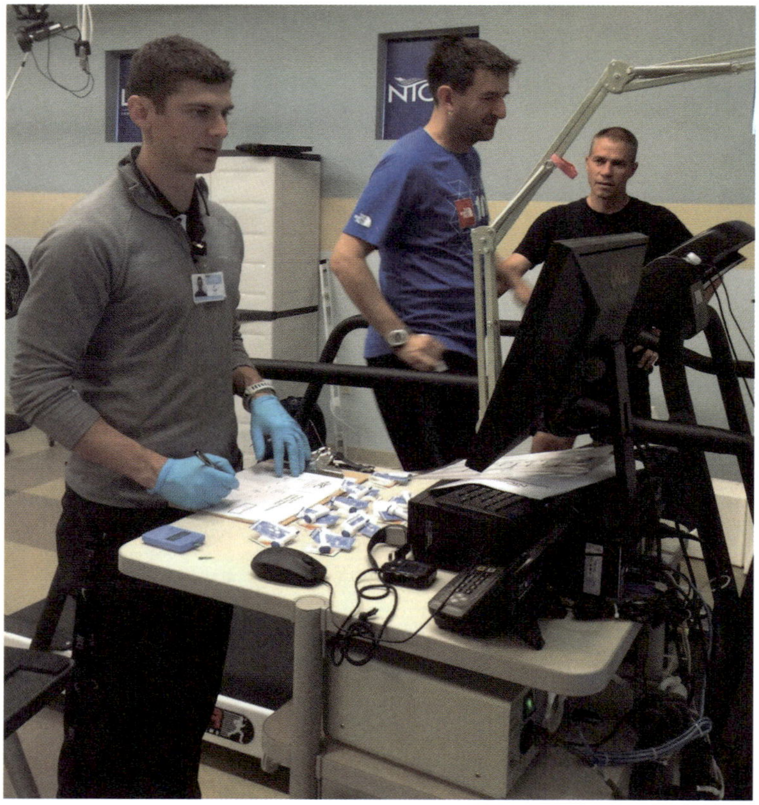

Coach Dave overseeing lactate threshold testing at a World Class Racewalking training camp.
Photo credit: Loretta McGovern

Most companies' monitors will link up to their own proprietary web- or app-based analysis software, such as Polar Flow or Garmin Connect,[79] which will allow you to track and analyze your training on your laptop or smartphone.

If you want to not just *track* your cadence, but set it to a particular beat, some athletes use a simple metronome, or music set to a precise number of beats-per-minute, to ensure they stay on pace. There are several smartphone apps that will allow you to set a particular cadence to walk to, including "Metronome Beats," and "Mobile Metronome." The downside is that if you pick a

[78] Say that three times fast!

[79] As I write this, Garmin is suffering a ransomware attack that has shut down the Connect interface.

beat that's too fast, you may end up artificially shortening your stride, and if it's too slow, you may end up either over-striding or training too slowly. With a little trial and error, however, metronome or music apps can be helpful training tools. While we're on the subject of music, I'll reiterate my advice from Chapter 7 to avoid wearing earbuds, or at least to not wear earbuds in both ears unless you're in a very safe, traffic-free location. I've never used music in training, so I know it's possible to walk many miles without it!

You may never get any more high-tech than a heart monitor/GPS wearable unit, but there are other training tools that high-level athletes use to improve the quality of their training. These include lactate threshold testing, $\dot{V}O_2$ max testing, and simulated-altitude training. Lactate and $\dot{V}O_2$ max testing generally occur in a physiology lab where athletes will walk a number of progressively faster intervals on a treadmill while technicians collect blood or exhaled gas samples. For lactate testing, a drop of blood is drawn after each interval to determine blood lactate levels, and for $\dot{V}O_2$ max testing a facemask is worn to collect exhaled carbon dioxide and oxygen levels. The mask is connected to a gas chromatograph, which tests the ratio of CO_2 to O_2, allowing the physiologist to determine the volume of oxygen inhaled and utilized by the athlete. The maximum level is the athlete's $\dot{V}O_2$ max. Measuring an athlete's percentage of $\dot{V}O_2$ max is a way of determining relative training intensity, much as percentage of maximum heart rate is used as a measure of training intensity. A university lab threshold test can be as cheap as \$50 for students to about \$100 to \$125 for the general public, while a commercial test will run \$175 to \$200. On the other hand, the price of a good portable lactate analyzer has come down in recent years, to the point where now they go for about \$400. I've used one in my own training for years. Lactate Pro, Lactate Scout, and Lactate Plus are the most popular brands. $\dot{V}O_2$ max testing can range from \$100 for a university test to up to \$250 for a commercial test. In my mind, knowing your $\dot{V}O_2$ max in milliliters of oxygen per kilogram of body mass per minute is nice for cocktail party conversation, but it's of limited use for prescribing training programs. Lactate threshold testing has a lot more real-world applicability.

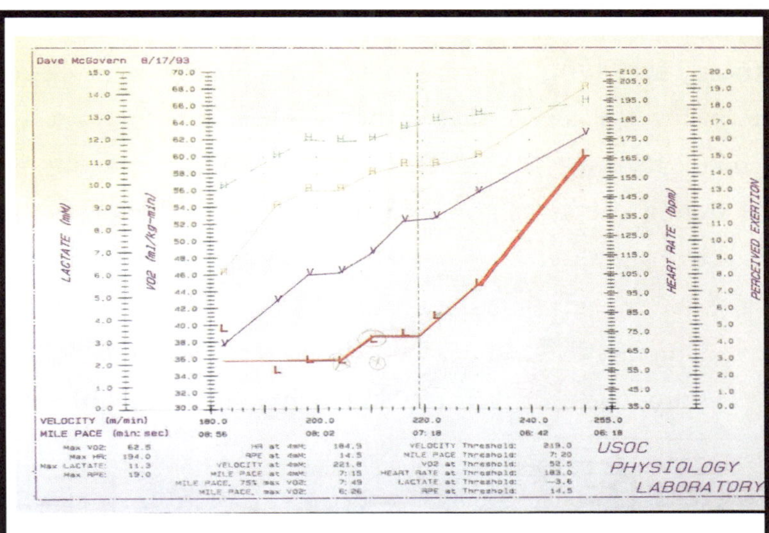

Results from one of the author's lactate/$\dot{V}O_2$ max tests from the US Olympic Training Center in Colorado Springs, Colorado.

Finally, simulated altitude hypoxic systems are used by elite athletes to "scrub" some of the oxygen out of the ambient air within a sealed tent, room, or an entire house. Normal air at any altitude contains 20.9% oxygen, but lower air pressure at higher elevations makes it "feel" like there is less oxygen in the air. By pumping nitrogen into the tent, an altitude system's generator can bring the oxygen level down to 16% to simulate the 7,000 ft. altitude of Flagstaff, AZ, 15% for Bogota, Colombia, or even 6.9% to simulate conditions at the top of Mt. Everest. Athletes sleep in the hypoxic tents, which can fit around a normal bed, over time causing the body to respond to the reduced oxygen level by boosting hemoglobin levels, and the number of red blood cells in the blood. At $3,000 to $6,000 for a tent system, this is probably a level of technology far beyond the reach of most non-elite athletes, but for those who have the funds but not the time to travel for extended periods, a hypoxic system can be more practical than travelling to a high-altitude location to train. For the more budget conscious, there are altitude-simulation masks, which allow athletes to train on a treadmill or exercise bicycle with reduced oxygen. That being said, I'm pretty sure you would be wasting the $50 to $100 you forked over to Amazon for one. There is approximately zero evidence that they work, other than possibly strengthening the diaphragm muscles as the mask restricts your breathing. Even so, the muscle-heads at my gym seem to have bought into the hype. Whenever I train on the treadmills, several of them will knuckle-walk their way out of the weight room, make a big show of putting on their masks, then hop onto the treadmills. After a few loud grunts to get everyone's attention, they'll sprint for about two minutes at 12mph, and just before getting shot off the back, they'll jump off the belt, grunt a few more times, then strut back to the weight room completely spent (while I reset my treadmill for another hour of "just" walking…) I have a general rule that seems to work pretty well for me: If the lunkheads in the gym are using it, don't. ☺

At the other extreme, in terms of both cost and effectiveness, are altitude houses like the five-bedroom model at the Australian Institute of Sport in the capital city of Canberra. The entire sealed house has nitrogen pumped in 24/7, simulating the hypoxic environment of 3,000 meters (nearly 10,000 ft.) of altitude. 2012 Olympic 50k racewalk gold medalist Jared Tallent is a frequent resident. Athletes will stay in the house for about three weeks at a time, spending most of the day and night living at simulated altitude, but then training in Canberra's 600-meter (< 2,000 ft.) elevation. The benefit of sleeping at simulated altitude, but training at or near sea level, is that you can train faster at the lower elevation while deriving the benefits of living at altitude during the 20+ non-training hours of the day.

Although I've had coaches who weren't fans of technological training tools,[80] I've always been a big proponent of their use. Looking around me, all of my competitors take advantage of every

[80] In 1994 I was invited to a training camp with Belorussian National Coach Boris Drazdov conducted at a very well equipped training facility in Northern Virginia. After we showed him around the gleaming weight room, the Olympic-size pool, and top-notch sports medicine lab, we asked Boris what he thought of the facilities. Without skipping a beat he said, "If we had all this stuff back in Belarus our guys would be walking 1:30, just like you." (The best Belorussians were at the time walking 1:19 for 20k…) Kind of a reverse Rocky IV, where Ivan Drago used all of the high tech tools and got his *zhopa* kicked by the chicken-chasing, wood-cutting, log-lifting, Sly Stallone. ☺

legal means available to help them to improve, so I think it would be foolish to not do so myself. You can expect to see improvement for the first year or two of your competitive walk training even with a somewhat scatter-shot approach, but the improvement curve does level off over time. More experienced walkers, and even beginners with ambitious goals, can benefit from a more precise approach to training using tools like stopwatches, GPS/speed-distance units and heart rate monitors. Your coach,[81] or the staff at your local running/walking specialty store, should be able to steer you toward the models that will best suit your needs.

[81] What? You don't have a coach?! I know a guy… https://www.racewalking.org/coaching.html

CHAPTER 39: FUNDRAISING

Lots of competitive walkers get their start in racing as a way to raise funds for a favorite charity. Over the years I've coached teams for the Leukemia and Lymphoma Society's "Team in Training," and was the National Coach for the Crohn's & Colitis Foundation's "Team Challenge" and the Paul Newman Foundation's "Team Serious Fun." In my experience, the two fears people have when signing up for such a program are that they won't be able to complete the half-marathon or marathon they've signed up for, and that they won't be able to meet their fundraising goal. The first is a snap. ☺ Over the years, the teams that I've coached have had a 99.7% completion rate. If a participant could make it to the starting line I could get them to the finish line. The problem for some people is *getting to* the starting line by successfully raising the $1,500 to $5,000 fundraising goal that many charities require for membership on the team.

The task of raising money, even for a great charity, can seem daunting at first. But with proper planning and a little bit of legwork, almost anybody can do it. I find that the first and most important step for most people is this: You need to change your attitude about asking people for money! When I was growing up, my father would take the family to my Irish immigrant grandparents' walk-up apartment in the Bronx for Sunday dinner. My grandfather ran a successful bar and grill, but he was by no means wealthy. As soon as my father left the room, "Pop" would pull out his wallet and hand each of the kids $5, telling us "go buy yourselves some ice cream." Whenever my father found out that we accepted money from Pop he would be furious! I've had a weird guilt about asking for or accepting money every since. Consequently, I always had a hard time with fundraising until someone explained it to me: You're not asking people for money. You're giving them the opportunity to support you and the charity you're helping. Mind-blowing, right?! If you have a personal connection to the charity—a spouse or child with a disease, for example—people feel terrible, but they also feel helpless. Your friends don't have any idea what they can do to help you. By allowing them to donate to your charity, you are helping *them* by easing that feeling of helplessness. So don't feel guilty about asking! People you ask are under no obligation to donate; they can always say no. You're just providing them with the opportunity to say YES!

The second thing you need to do when signing on to raise money for a non-profit, if you don't already have one, is to develop a personal connection to the charity. Most fundraising teams will pair you with an Honored Hero—someone who is affected by the disease for which you are raising money. The Honored Hero will often come to team functions and some group training sessions if you're part of a local team. If you're part of a group that meets via Zoom or some other remote video conferencing platform, you'll get to know your Honored Hero that way. By getting to know your Honored Hero, you'll develop a personal connection with both your hero, and to the charity itself. It puts a name, a face, and a story on the charity for you, making it that much easier for you to do what you'll need to do to seek out and collect those fundraising dollars.

Once you've accomplished those first two tasks, the rest is easy. There are literally thousands of ways to fundraise, but most professional fundraisers will tell you the most important thing is to put your personal stamp on whatever you do. Think about your hobbies: If you like going to bars, host a bar night; if you're a sports fan, sell Super Bowl boxes, or Final Four brackets before the NCAA tournament; if you like to bowl or play softball, host a charity bowling or softball tournament, etc., etc., etc. I'll get into all of that in a bit, but before heading down that road, the majority of most fundraisers' donations come from… Asking! So before deciding to plan an event, start your fundraising off by writing a great letter telling your friends and family about your charity and the race you'll be entering, and asking them for donations.

Letter writing

Most successful fundraising campaigns begin with a great fundraising letter. Your friends and family will be far more motivated to give when they see that you have a personal connection to the charity for which you are raising money. If you're fortunate enough to NOT be affected yourself, or to have a close relative or friend who is affected by a serious disease, your Honored Hero will be that personal connection. In your letter you'll talk about yourself, your loved one, or your Honored Hero and how the disease affects him or her. Once you've written your letter, send it out to at least 100 prospects. These can be your close friends and relatives, but don't be afraid to extend way beyond that inner circle. Many charity walkers have had success by sending letters out to anyone to whom they have given money in the past—their hairdresser, doctors, auto mechanic and landscaper, are all possibilities. Think about all the people for whom you have bought gifts over the years: friends' engagements, weddings, bridal showers, baby showers, graduations, etc. Don't feel uncomfortable asking these people to return the favor for a good cause—and a tax deduction! You probably don't know everything about your friends' personal lives. You may be surprised at all the people who have been touched by the charity for which you are raising funds, and the generosity they will bestow upon you for your efforts.

Beyond physical letters, send an email to everyone in your address book, even people you haven't spoken to in years. You'll be pleasantly surprised at how much many of them will donate! If 75 of the 100 people you send your letter to donate an average of $50 each then you will have raised $3,750! It really is that easy.

Including a self-addressed, stamped return envelope greatly increases the chance that your prospects will give. Pro Tip: keep a database of who you have sent letters to and who has donated. After about a month, send out a second letter or postcard with an update on your training to anyone you didn't hear from after sending out the first letter. A lot of times I'll receive a fundraising request in the mail, tell myself I need to write a check, then the letter winds up in The Pile. We all have one. It's the pile of mail we all know we need to get to eventually, but we never seem to get to it. That second letter though? When I get a second letter I IMMEDIATELY pull out the checkbook and send a check! I don't know what it is, but it gets me every time! Don't forget to send that second letter! Definitely send out those actual hard-copy letters, but also send a copy of your letter vie email to a wider group of friends, and update your email signature to include the link back to your fundraising page.

Social Media

Nowadays, getting your letter out to an even broader network is easy and free through the magic of social media. Sending your letter out on Facebook, Twitter, or via a link in your Instagram profile, and frequently updating with follow-up posts allows you to reach thousands, especially when you convince your friends to share your post to their social networks. When your friends do share, tactfully ask them to include a message indicating how they know you. That connection greatly increases the chance their friends will donate compared to your friends just sending the link with no message. Creating a Facebook event or group for your friends to follow your progress is another way to let your friends know you're serious about your training and fundraising. It creates a central location for all your fundraising updates and allows you to quickly and publicly thank donors, which can often prompt others to donate. Despite its flaws, Facebook has become a cornerstone of many charity fundraising campaigns. I've had a lot of success using Facebook "birthday" fundraisers to raise funds for a charity close to my own heart. It's another way to get the word out, and Facebook pays for all of your credit card transaction fees. And it's not just for birthdays! You can create a "birthday" fundraiser for any occasion. Finally, consider creating a video either for your initial ask, or for follow-up updates about your training and/or fundraising progress. Videos are shareable on most platforms (Facebook, Instagram, Twitter, Snapchat, TikTok, etc.) and they grab people's attention much more than text or photos can.

Matching gifts

Be sure to mention matching gifts in your fundraising letter and social media posts! Your donors can double, triple, or even quadruple their donation by asking their human resources departments at work about matching gifts. Many companies match employee donations to charities 1:1, but some larger companies match 2:1 or even 3:1. For example, ExxonMobil will triple-match employee donations up to $22,500, so a friend's $150 donation becomes a $600 donation! Lots of people don't even know about the programs their employers offer, so be sure to ask! If 25 of the above donors have companies that match gifts even at 1:1, then each of their $50 donations become $100 donations. That's another $1,250 simply by asking the question! Head to doublethedonation.com to find companies that match, and be sure to ask your friends about applying for the match if you know they work for a matching company.

Corporate Sponsorships

Corporate Sponsorships are another great source of funds. Once again, the most important thing is to ask! The worst thing that could happen is you'll be told no, but your company, or a friend or family's company, could very well say yes and write a check for $1,000, $5,000 or even $10,000! Many companies have sponsorship funds available to donate, and would love to receive the PR and tax benefits of sponsoring you. Maybe you won't get the $5,000 you ask for, but many companies will donate $1,000 without even batting an eye, and all it takes is a few minutes of your time to compose a sponsorship request letter—or less if you use the template in the Appendix section at the back of this book! ☺

Events

This is where you get to put the FUN in FUNdraising! There are countless ways to meet or at least put a big dent in your fundraising goal with events and mini-events that reflect your personality and interests. Here are just a few examples:

- **Bar night-** A "Take Over the Taps" event is not just fun, but it can also bring in a ton of money for your charity. The idea is to recruit local celebrities (the mayor, the school principal, the high school football coach, etc.) to act as guest bartenders to work for tips for your charity at a local pub. You and the bartenders invite all of your friends to the party, and advertise around town. In addition to your tips, bars will often make a donation to your cause since the events bring in lots of new customers. Bar nights can also be combined with other events like a silent auction or a 50/50. If you hold a silent auction, ask other local businesses to donate prizes that your guests will bid on. Depending on your prizes, you should expect anywhere from another $500 to several thousand dollars in auction bids! For a 50/50, all you need to do is buy a roll of raffle tickets from a party store. Have volunteers at the event or around town sell as many tickets as possible for $1-$5. As the name implies, the winning ticket drawn at the event wins half of the proceeds while you keep the rest as a donation for your charity!
- **Wine & cheese tasting party-** Ask local grocery stores and wine shops that you frequent to donate the wines and cheeses. Charge $20 admission and invite at least 50 people. If 35 show up, that's $700. This is another great venue for a silent auction and/or a 50/50.
- **Super Bowl squares or March Madness brackets-** With Super Bowl squares, you create a 10 by 10 grid of 100 individual boxes on poster board. Sell each box for $5 or $20 per square. Before the Super Bowl kicks off, participants purchase individual boxes until all

100 are sold. The numbers 0 through 9 are then assigned to the columns and rows (usually at random), giving two numbers to each individual cell. From here, the game can be played a few different ways. Typically, one axis represents the last digit of the NFC team's score and the other represents the last digit of the AFC team's score. Whoever has the correct digits of the final score wins the pot. If the final score is 28-21, for example, the winning square would be where the number eight on the NFC axis meets the number one on the AFC axis. With March Madness brackets you sell pre-printed bracket blanks for $5 to $20 for your friends and family to fill out. The bracket is the grid of all the teams in the tournament and the paths they have to follow to the Final Four and the championship game. Whoever comes closest to the correct path to the Final Four wins half the pot while you keep the other half for your charity.

- **Community yard sales-** Ask friends, family, and neighbors to donate items they would like you to take off their hands. For example, furniture, electronics, clothing, toys, etc. Then hold a yard sale, advertising in your community calendar that all proceeds will go to your charity. With a little work you can easily raise $1,000 with a home yard sale; with a lot of work, you can raise a LOT more! My wife and I, with the help of several volunteers, held a community yard sale at our local church and raised over $25,000 in one day! It took a lot of prep-work to round up donations, but it was obviously well worth the effort!
- **Dress-down-day at work-** All you have to do is get permission to hit up your co-workers to pay $5 to wear jeans to work on a random Friday. If 50 employees in your office take you up on it, boom! $250.

The fundraisers you could hold are only limited by your imagination. Some other ideas include:

- Art auction,
- Bachelor & bachelorette auction,
- Bake/book sales,
- Bingo night,
- Candy sale,
- Car wash,
- Coin canisters at local businesses,
- Craft sale/show or holiday bazaar,
- Dinner party,
- Lemonade stand,
- Pancake breakfast,
- Softball/bowling/golf tournament,

- Valentine carnation sale,
- Walk-a-thon.

Some key elements of hosting a successful fundraiser include:

- Start planning early! Planning is half the battle.
- Promote your event: Get the word out to everyone you know! You have to get people in the door to make your fundraiser a success. Use email and social media invites to spread the word quickly. Make posters for the venue and to post around town. Tell everyone to bring a friend or two.
- Do something you enjoy! Only host a dinner party if you enjoy cooking. Only organize a softball tournament if you love playing softball.
- For larger events, use bracelets or stamps at the door so you know who has paid. Ask the venue to provide discounted products to everyone with the bracelet/stamp.
- Thank your donors! Your charity will probably send official donation acknowledgements to donors. However, as your donations start coming in, it's important for you to thank your donors personally as well, by writing a note, sending an email, and/or thanking them in person.

To quote Forrest Gump, "That's all I have to say about that." Now let's move on to everything you need to know about racing!

SECTION IV: RACING!

Racing is the reward for all the hard work you do in training. The following chapters will delve into tips and tricks from the pros you can use in the weeks leading up to your competition, and during the race itself, to ensure that all your hard work in training is rewarded with a personal best on race day! So lace 'em up and let's go!

CHAPTER 40: RECONNAISSANCE AND ACCLIMATIZATION

One of the most important, yet widely overlooked and underutilized race-preparation tools available to competitive walkers is *acclimatization.* Acclimatizing means subjecting your body to conditions similar to what it will be subjected to during important races. This includes external factors like the weather and the topography of your race course, as well as internal ones like what you'll be drinking and eating during the race. Acclimatization tunes your body to these conditions so you'll be better prepared to compete at your absolute best, both physically and mentally.

The first step to effectively acclimating yourself leading up to a race is *reconnaissance.* Before any competition you need to find out as much as possible about the race, including the time of day, expected weather conditions, course layout, drink and gel sponsors, and if it's an out-of-town race the location of the start and finish lines in relation to your hotel, and any other factors that could affect your performance on race day. The process should start many months before the competition so you'll have plenty of time to expose yourself in training to the conditions you'll likely experience on race day.

2004 and 2012 Olympic walker—and now US Army First Lieutenant —John Nunn, on a reconnaissance mission.
Photo credit: Jonathan Weiser

Much of this information will be readily available on the race website. You'll be able to find links to many race websites, including sites for running races with power walk divisions, racewalking events, and many other walking races by searching USA Track & Field's calendar at usatf.org. Marathon and half-marathon sites can be located at marathonguide.com, while a specific list of walkable marathons and half-marathons is at: marathonwalking.com/marathons.html. Finally, for Nordic walking races, head to marathons.ahotu.com/calendar/nordic-walking/usa/. Of course you could also just Google the race by name if you already know which event you'll be entering. Most sites, even for relatively small races, will have links to the sports drink and gel sponsors' sites as well, enabling you to secure a supply of these products to test out during training. In addition to the race web site, and the sports drink and gel sponsor sites, it's also a good idea to head to weather.com to get a general idea of what weather you'll likely experience on race day to guide whether you'll need to be heat-acclimated or not.

Your reconnaissance will provide one of the most powerful tools in your training arsenal: Knowledge! Before each race, smart walkers will find out if the race will be indoors or out. If it's outdoors are the conditions likely to be hot and humid, or cool and dry? Will the competition be at sea level or altitude? Is the course hilly or flat? Track, trail, or road? If it's a road course, is the surface concrete or asphalt? Shaded or in full sun? Will the race begin at 6:00 a.m. or 5:00 p.m.? Athletes are sometimes told to ignore these factors because they affect everyone equally. Nonsense! Once the gun goes off, sure, you should do what you can to tune out these externalities. But the body and mind are adaptable to many deleterious environmental conditions, so the prepared, properly acclimated athlete will have a big advantage over his or her non-acclimated competitors. Planning ahead and adapting your body and mind to these conditions beforehand can give you the edge that may prove the difference between winning and losing. Here are just a few examples:

Weather- Extreme heat and humidity inhibit the body's ability to cool itself. But your body can quickly adapt to these conditions, with full adaptation occurring within 10 to 14 days. By training in hot and humid conditions, or by artificially creating these conditions by wearing an extra layer of clothing during workouts, an athlete can gain an advantage over competitors who do not specifically preparing for these weather extremes. 2008 Olympic racewalker Joanne Dow took her weather acclimation to the next level by dragging her NordicTrack onto the pool deck at the gym where she worked, and added three or four 45-minute sessions per week to her walk training schedule. The humidity in the pool area hovered around 80 percent. Joanne went on to win the Olympic Trials and placed a solid 31st in the 20-kilometer event in Beijing's stifling heat and humidity.

Altitude- Racing at altitudes over 5,000 feet poses unique challenges for endurance athletes who train at sea level. Until recently, the only practical way to prepare for a race at altitude was to train in these conditions for at least several weeks before the event. The good news is that most championship races are not held at altitude. But if you do want to or have to race at altitude, sea-level athletes have three choices:

- Get to the race site several weeks before your race to acclimate.
- Don't acclimate, but pace yourself appropriately. Plan to race at a pace 7-10% slower than you would be able to maintain at lower elevations.

- Buy or rent a hypoxic altitude-simulation tent system—see Chapter 38. Athletes sleep with their beds enclosed in hypoxic tents, which lower the oxygen concentration of the air within them by using generators that pump in nitrogen. Sleeping for eight hours per night in such an environment can boost your hemoglobin levels and induce other positive physiological changes similar to those that occur when living at altitude. They're expensive—at least $3,000 and up for the system—but something worth considering if you have the means. Be forewarned: it can get hot in the tent, so be prepared to blast the air conditioner!

Since altitude adaptation takes several weeks to occur, there is little point getting into town a week early to try to acclimate for a race at altitude. There is even some evidence that getting in as close to the race as possible—perhaps the night before—may be better than getting in a few days or a week before. Going the other way, athletes training full-time at altitude will have difficulty maintaining quick leg turnover during high-elevation workouts, so they may be unprepared for the faster pace of sea-level races. These athletes should incorporate sufficient short, fast economy work into their training to adapt to high-speed walking. Altitude-trained athletes also have thick, hemoglobin-rich blood, which is great for supplying the muscles with oxygen, but not very good at cooling the body. I probably blew my best chance of making an Olympic Team in 1996 by coming down from an altitude training camp in Mexico City too close to the hot, humid Olympic Trials in Atlanta. I was in the best shape of my life but raced horribly in the Trials because I was altitude-trained, but not acclimated to high heat and humidity. This after watching Tim Lewis, the best 20k walker in US history, do the same thing in 1992, coming down from Colorado Spring too close to the Olympic Trials in New Orleans and failing to make the team. Live and learn! Walkers living at altitude need to come down at least 10 to 14 days before racing in hot, humid conditions.

Circadian rhythms- Nothing can be more frustrating than going to bed a few hours early for a 6:00 a.m. race, only to lie awake all night tossing and turning with anticipation. Short of sleeping pills, the easiest solution is to go to bed earlier and earlier in the nights leading up to the race to synchronize the body's internal clock. Training rhythms should also be synchronized by doing workouts in the weeks before the race at or near the time of day that the race will be contested. Many athletes who normally train in the mornings find it difficult to get "energized" for an evening race; afternoon trainers are often tight and tired for morning races. Train at race time to get in synch. Meal times should be adjusted as well. Eat close to the same number of hours before and after sleeping, and training, as usual. If competing in a different time zone, be sure to calculate the time difference and take this into account when deciding when to sleep, eat, or train. It's also a good idea when flying to plan on getting to the race site one day early for every time zone you'll be crossing. If you live in New York and will be racing in California, plan on flying in three days before the race to account for the three time zones you'll be crossing. This will help you to adjust your body to California time.

While we're on the subject, if you're too excited to sleep the night before the race, don't stress out about it! I've walked some of my best times—including my fastest 20k ever—on no sleep. In fact I wasn't able to adjust to the time difference before competing in my personal record 20k in Békéscsaba, Hungary and lay awake all night for *two* consecutive nights before the race with no ill effects. As a last resort I've had some success using melatonin to regulate my sleep patterns when traveling. It sure didn't work on that trip, though!

Equipment- With the obvious exception of Nordic walkers, and ignoring the great technological tools discussed in Chapter 38, competitive walkers require very little equipment to compete. But every walker should be very comfortable with his shoes, shorts, singlet, sports bra, etc., before a race. (Did I just write *his* sports bra?) ☺ Always wear your racing shoes, socks and uniform/singlet/tech-shirt several times in pre-competition training sessions to make certain you'll be free of blisters or chafing during the race. Also, make sure you actually have that equipment with you at the starting line! If you tend to be nervous before traveling to a race you may become forgetful. Make a list: Shoes, uniform, sunglasses, water bottles, extra pins, toilet paper etc., should all be packed and ready to go the night before the race. Try everything on before packing it. Your intrepid author showed up at World Cup Trials one year, only to discover he had packed two left shoes! It was a stressful scramble to find an open running/walking store to find a new pair of shoes the night before the race! Do what I say, not what I do…[82]

Pin your numbers onto your uniform as soon as you get them, and walk around a bit while wearing them to make certain they are pinned on properly. This could save you from frantically re-pinning them at the starting line. You don't want to be the person standing at the starting line trying to figure out why you can't get into your racing top because you've accidentally pinned the front of your racing singlet to the back when you pinned on your race numbers! (Yes, this happens…)

Even if it's a cold day, it'll usually feel about 15 degrees warmer once the race starts: Don't overdress! Wear less than you think you'll need, not more. I always wear shorts and a racing top unless it's below 40 degrees. If it's very cold, I may go with a pair of light gloves, but a T-shirt or sweatshirt can become pretty uncomfortable once it's soaked in sweat.

Whatever the weather, don't wear sweat pants, dark-colored or patterned tights, or long shorts while racing, especially if you're a racewalker. The judges need to see your knees. If they can't, they may just turn in red cards on you without giving you the benefit of the doubt. Finally, it *is* a race, right? Be sure to wear your fastest, lightest, most flexible shoes when competing. And don't forget

[82] I did well enough to make the team, but I also had some pretty nasty blisters to show for it after having to race a 50k in brand-new shoes!

to double-tie the laces and tuck the ends in between the tongue and the laces. I've double-tied my shoes before some races but still had them come undone because I didn't tuck in the loose ends.

Training your gut- In warm races, especially those longer than 5k, you'll need to be able to drink on the go. I prefer to drink from bottles, but since most races hand out cups rather than bottles, you need to perfect the skill of drinking from a cup on the fly. Think it's hard to drink from a cup while power walking or racewalking? Now imagine doing it while holding walking poles! With or without poles, it's not easy, so practice drinking on the fly in training. Inhaling sports drink instead of drinking it isn't as much fun as it sounds. What I like to do after grabbing the cup is to pinch the top into a spout shape with my thumb and index finger. I then take a breath, and while holding my breath I pour the contents of the cup into my mouth. I hold the drink in my mouth until I get my breathing back under control and then, and only then, do I swallow.

In long races you'll need to take in a lot of fluids, possibly including carbohydrate-rich sports drinks, as well as energy gels, and/or other carbohydrate sources. You'll have to determine in training what works best for you, including what your gut will tolerate. Some athletes can't stomach a high volume of fluids, high-carb drinks, or other carbohydrate sources while walking. But this, like anything else, is trainable. Train using several different types of drinks on your longer workouts to see what works best for you, and over time, increase the volume. To determine how much you need to drink, do a sweat-rate test, as described in Chapter 5.

Consider a trial ~~run~~ walk- In addition to sharpening your training for a big competition, you should also be putting some thought into logistics. Decide what time you'll leave for the race course, who'll be driving, where you'll park, and so on. A trial run will help you to finalize your plans and reduce stress on race morning. If it's a local race, try completing one of your last workouts on the course to test out your race-day plan, and to learn what kind of terrain you'll encounter during the competition. Pack everything you'll take with you on race day, and head out early enough to get yourself to the course on time. Once there, warm up and stretch as usual, then walk the course noting any turns, hills, rough spots on the pavement and anything else that could affect your race. When timing your race-day departure time, keep in mind that there may be road closures and traffic diversions on race morning that you might not experience on your trial run and plan accordingly.

These are just a few of the things you should keep in mind. As a rule, don't experiment with *anything* just before or during a race. If someone gives you a magic pill the night before your race, don't take it! If it sounds like a good idea, try it in training one or two times first, then during an unimportant test race, before potentially using it during an important competition. What works for your training partner, or even the Olympic champion, might spell disaster for you—and you don't want to find that out in the middle of an important race.

CHAPTER 41: TAPERING

Most walkers, usually through trial and error, eventually settle on a training schedule that works best for them. Unfortunately, many of these same walkers become bewildered in the final weeks and days leading up to an important race, either training too much or too little. Some get worried that they haven't done enough training for their goal race so they try to "cram for the exam" by doing some last minute overly intense speed work, or a way-too-close-to-the-race long day to boost their confidence, but in doing so they severely undermine their ability to be at their best on race day. I've also coached far too many walkers—and runners!—who REALLY love to rest up for their races! After the last long day a few weeks before their goal race, they completely shut down, doing little or no training, leaving themselves a pound or five over their fighting weight, stale, and sluggish on race day. Like Goldilocks's search for the perfect porridge, the amount of work you do during the last week or two before your goal races needs to be juuust right!

Tapering is the process of getting your body and mind race-ready in the final weeks before an important competition. It's also part of the pay-off for all the hard work you've done all season in preparation for race day. It's a period of reduced mileage leading up to race day that allows your body to recover from, and adapt to, the months of hard training you've put in. Tapering often leads to improved conditioning, as your well-rested body is able to perform at its best on race day. For the nervous, late-training walker, any hoped-for fitness gained through additional hard training will be very limited in the last 10 to 14 days before the event, but improvements made due to the "rebound" effect brought on by *cutting back* on training can be considerable. Resting in the last few weeks, and "sharpening" with short, relatively intense efforts at, or slightly faster than race pace, can result in dramatic improvement in racing speed.

Trust your training

For better or worse, whatever training you've done in the months before a race will rise to the top on race day—if you allow it to. You need to have faith in your fitness going into a race—don't undermine your training by hammering yourself in the last week or two. Additional fitness gains will be minimal, and they will be overshadowed by the detriment of going into the race fatigued. It's okay to *not* taper—to "train through"—less-important races. Doing so will sacrifice your best possible performance in these minor races in exchange for higher-quality training for future, presumably more important competitions. It's a fair trade-off. If you want to perform at your absolute peak now, however, you must be rested. But what does "rested" mean?

Cutting back

Tapering has traditionally meant maintaining much the same schedule as usual in the final two weeks before a race, except with a ⅓ to ½ reduction in total weekly mileage, the number of intervals, etc. Less is definitely more at this point, but that doesn't mean completely putting an end to training either. Quite the contrary: An effective taper requires some high intensity training, albeit at a much lower volume than in the previous weeks and months. During the last few weeks of training you'll start cutting back on the distance of your long day and reducing your total weekly mileage. The duration of your taper will vary depending on the distance of the race you're training for. For races under 10k, a one-week taper is usually fine; for 10k to half-marathon, a one- to two-week taper is appropriate; for marathons and longer, plan on a three-week taper.

Assuming your last long workout is two weeks before your goal race, you'll cut back on your weekly mileage by about ⅓ the following week, and by ½ during the week leading into your competition. With fresher legs due to the reduced mileage, this is a good time for you to walk some race-pace efforts, but only for short bouts, with a total volume of no more than about 40% of your race distance. These short on-pace workouts will allow you to hone in on your race pace so you can learn the "feel" of that pace once the starter's gun fires on race day. Starting out too fast can kill your chance of a successful race, so these last few pace workouts can do a lot toward ingraining the correct race pace and preventing that bad outcome. Examples of mid-taper workouts are:

- Four or five x 400m within a week of a 5k race,
- Three x 1k about a week before a 10k,
- Or an 8k/5-mile tempo about ten days before a 20k or half-marathon.

Super taper?

Research during the 1980s with swimmers, and later with runners, found that an even greater reduction in mileage may be beneficial both in the short and the long term. Owen Anderson, writing in *Running Research News*,[83] discussed studies with runners who tapered by doing nothing, another group that cut their mileage back, but ran slowly every day, and a "super taper" group that tapered with a drastic reduction in total mileage, but with a limited number of short, high-intensity intervals every day in the week leading up to the race. These intervals—run at slightly faster than 5-kilometer race pace—amounted to just 12% of their usual weekly mileage in the final week, with just enough easy mileage added to ensure sufficient warm-ups and cool-downs. For walkers training 40 miles per week, this would amount to about five miles of intervals in the week before the race. The bulk of these intervals should be completed in the first few days of the taper, with

[83] Peakendurancesport.com has an update of the article here: www.peakendurancesport.com/endurance-training/training-structure-and-planning/tapering-training-improve-athletes-endurance/.

the number of intervals descending through the week. About 800 meters of warm-up and 800 meters of cool-down should be incorporated into each workout, increasing the total mileage for the week to 12. This may seem like a absurdly low mileage total for the week if you've been training for a half-marathon or marathon—or even a 5k, for that matter!—but remember the primary purpose of a taper: Rest! The group of runners using the very low-mileage, high-intensity taper improved their race times by a staggering 22% over the no-mileage runners, and 16% over the slow-mileage taperers! Much of the difference can probably be explained by the slow- and no-mileage control groups' loss of fitness during the taper, but in other studies with control groups using a traditional taper, the super-taperers still showed a 6% improvement over the control group. That would be the equivalent of a 30-minute 5k walker posting a 28:12 on race day! Anderson attributed the increase to both the additional rest as well as the neuromuscular benefits of the up-tempo running. What does this mean to a walker? Such a taper, coupled with copious stretching and rest, should mean enhanced flexibility, more economical technique, increased metabolic enzyme activity, and more glycogen storage in the leg muscles—and quite possibly, surprisingly fast race times while doing less work!

A typical "super-taper" for a 40-mile-per-week walker training for an important 5k race would be as follows:

Sunday- Easy 800m warm-up with flexibility drills, stretch, then 6 x 400 meters @ between 3k and 5k race pace. 800m easy cool-down, then stretch any tight spots.
Monday- Warm-up and cool-down as above. 5 x 400 meters—again at slightly faster than 5k pace.
Tuesday- "" 4 x 400 meters.
Wednesday- "" 3 x 400 meters.
Thursday- "" 2 x 400 meters, 1x 200 meters.
Friday- "" 2 x 400 meters.
Saturday- "" 1 x 400 meters.
Sunday- Personal Best Race!

I tried Anderson's "super taper" a few times during my peak years as an athlete with some success. After a disappointing sixth-place finish at the National 20k Championship, I decided to try the "new" taper before my next two races that summer. The results: a strong second place finish at the U.S. Olympic Festival 20k three weeks later, and a win at the National 10k Championship less than one week after that. In both races my legs felt fresher and faster than they had before the first race when I used a more traditional taper, with no apparent loss in fitness.

"Taper Madness" and "Taperchondria"

Whichever taper method you choose, the goal is to arrive at race day rested and well tuned for the race. More than any other time, it's critical that you stick to your training schedule as much as possible. With reduced time spent training, though, there's more time to do stupid stuff. It is so common for endurance athletes to do crazy things during their tapers that there's actually a name for it: "Taper Madness." Taper Madness is when the little gremlin on your shoulder tries to convince you that it's a great time to take up skydiving, or to clean the gutters on your roof, or to take part in a daredevil mountain biking race.[84] The loudest of the gremlins will also try to convince you to do one last long, hard workout, or to suddenly do an "easy" over-distance 15-mile day to make sure you can get through your half-marathon, or a hard tempo workout to test your pace for your 10k. Or maybe, says the Gremlin, it's a great time to add a crazy new stretching routine. DON'T! Another common phenomenon that befalls tapering endurance athletes is "Taperchondria." With a big race coming up, most walkers become hyper-aware of their bodies, blowing out of proportion every ache, pain, and sniffle. During any other time of the year you wouldn't even notice these very routine muscle and joint pains, or give another thought to a meaningless sneeze or sniffle, but with a full-blown case of pre-race taperchondria, inexperienced walkers elevate these feelings to the point where they become—in their minds—race-ending injuries or life-threatening illnesses.

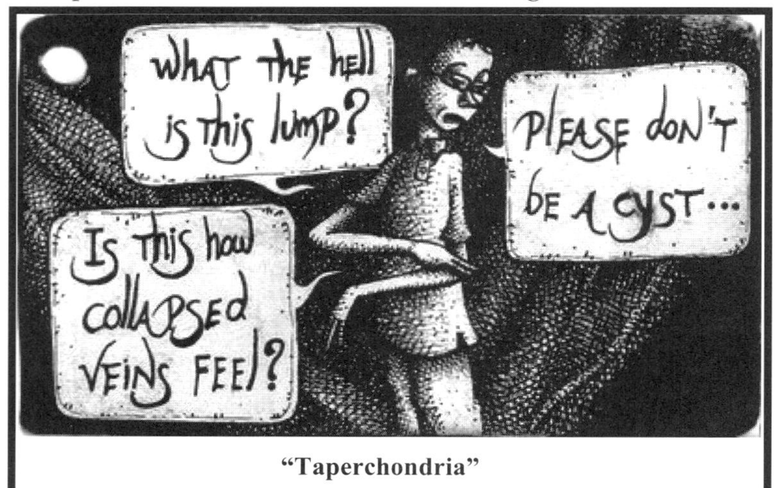

"Taperchondria"

Food and drink

"Carbo-loading" before important races lasting longer than 90 minutes is advisable. In the Olden Days (the 1970s) proponents suggested a "depletion" phase about a week before important races. After a hard glycogen-depleting workout like a hard 10-miler a week before the goal race, athletes would adopt a high-protein, low-carbohydrate diet for two or three days to make the muscles "hungry" for glycogen. They then switched over to a high-carbohydrate diet for the next four days to "load" the muscles with glycogen. More recent research has determined that the depletion phase is probably unnecessary. You simply need to maintain a high-carbohydrate diet in the three days before the competition without the depletion phase beforehand.

---

[84] These are all true stories involving athletes I've coached… The skydiving incident turned out just fine, but the gutter cleaner broke his ankle, and the mountain biker broke his collar bone a week before his race!

Carbo-loading does *not* mean carbo-bloating. The percentage of carbohydrate you eat should rise a bit beyond the day-to-day standard of 60% carbohydrates, 25% fat, and 15% protein but total caloric intake should not increase. In fact, since mileage will be tapering down during the final week or weeks, you might even cut back on total calories a bit during the taper. As always, make sure you have experimented with this type of diet several times in training before attempting to "load" before an important race. Drastic changes in your diet could lead to gastric or bowel distress during your race.

Conclusion

Consistently subjecting your body to race-like training conditions in the months before; undergoing environmental, dietary and circadian adaptation in the weeks before; and getting plenty of rest, while still doing some low-volume, high-intensity training in the days before competition are the keys to reaching your full potential. When tapering, remember that rest, glycogen storage, enzymatic adaptation, and high economy are the goals. In the final week, mileage should be reduced to the lowest level possible to ensure that your legs are rested and fully glycogen-loaded, while still doing a limited number of fast economy intervals to stoke enzymatic and neuromuscular activity. The time for hard mileage has passed—the final week should feel very easy, leaving you "champing at the bit" for a fast race. If in doubt, always do less! Building endurance and sharpening speed take many months of hard work. Last minute attempts to "catch up" on missed training will only make you tired for the big race. Once you've done your hard training, the "rest" is easy. ☺

CHAPTER 42: TRAVELLING TO YOUR EVENT

Let's face it, despite the persistent rumors of an impending "Walking Boom," there still aren't millions of us competitive walkers out there clogging the roads and bike paths of the world. Since we are still relatively few and far between, you may find it necessary to travel out of town to find good competitive opportunities. Racing in a national or regional championship or in a big city marathon, can be a great experience. Although you've probably heard from people who haven't "been there" that "getting there" is half the fun, traveling a considerable distance by car or plane to get to a race can take a heavy toll on your body and your mind. Knowing the ins and outs of travel could very well make or break your race. This chapter may help to ease some of the hardships of pre-race travel.

Driving

As a national park junkie, I have always loved heading out on the highway from time to time for long cross-country road trips. But sitting cramped in a car for an extended period of time can leave you feeling pretty beat up. Maybe I'm being paranoid, but have you noticed how many walkers and walking clubs there are in the Detroit area? I'm beginning to believe that large numbers of competitive walkers—our competitors—have infiltrated GM, Ford and Chrysler and have specifically designed automobile seats to cripple the rest of us as we drive to compete against them.

If you have to drive for more than an hour or so to get to your race, you can easily wind up trashing your hip-flexors, hamstrings, and lower back if you're not careful. If the race is more than an hour distant you should seriously consider driving in the day before and staying in a hotel. After checking in, walk for at least 20 minutes, do your drills, stretch, then finish off with a few quick sprints to make sure everything is loosened up. And no matter how long before the race you drive in to get to the race site, if you have to drive more than two hours, be sure to stop every hour or two to stretch and walk around a bit. If the race is more than an eight-hour drive, you should either break the trip up over two days, or seriously consider flying—there's no way you'll be able to race well if you've beaten yourself up with a marathon drive the day before.

Flying

Travelling to a distant race by air presents many of the same challenges as driving, as well as a number of other potential pitfalls that are unique to air travel. Among these are:

- **Dehydration-** Jet cabins are pressurized to the equivalent of about 8,000 feet of altitude, leading to an extremely dry environment. The pressure is not quite low enough to cause altitude sickness in most travellers, but the very dry air it causes can lead to rapid evaporation of body fluids, including sweat, but also saliva. As a result, your mouth may feel dry. Yes, do drink water, but don't drink gallons trying to counter dehydration. Aim for eight ounces of water per hour that you're in the air. There's no added benefit, and there are considerable dangers, in drinking too much water, so stick to eight ounces per hour. Carry your own water bottle with you—those little plastic cups of Coke or orange juice aren't going to cut it, and using your own bottle will allow you to keep better track of how much you're drinking. Getting up to refill your bottle or to use the lavatory will also give you a chance to stretch your legs from time to time, and selecting an aisle seat will give you the freedom to get up when you need to. Be sure to refill your bottle with bottled water from the drink cart, NOT from the spigots in the galley or lavatory! These "water" sources are only half a step above raw sewage. They are more often than not contaminated with high levels of E. coli and fecal coliform bacteria, among other biohazards. Consider drinking sports drinks, not just water, since sports drinks will not only provide you with carbohydrates, but also sodium, potassium and other electrolytes. You won't be able to pass through the TSA security checkpoint with a bottle of sports drink. My solution is to travel with a drink bottle containing nothing more than a pre-measured amount of sports drink powder that I reconstitute with water from a safe water source once I pass through security.

- **Carrying luggage-** Pay special attention to packing. Airlines are in business to mess with your head. When United winds up sending your luggage to Lhasa, Tibet (LXA) instead of Los Angeles (LAX), you'll want your shoes, socks, singlet, shorts, Body Glide, etc.—essentially anything irreplaceable that you want with you during the race—to be carried with you on the plane, not checked, where it could be misplaced or misdirected. Even so, that doesn't mean you should take *everything* with you onto the plane. If you have lots of luggage, check the larger bags so you don't fatigue your back, neck, and shoulders lugging your *impedimenta* through

Lhassa Gonggar International Airport, Lhasa, Tibet.

the airport when making connecting flights. Of course if you are flying with this much baggage, you might want to ask yourself why you need so much stuff for a quick weekend race trip!

- **Relax!** When the airline does send your luggage to Tibet, your flight is delayed or cancelled by the weather, or you get seated next to a screaming baby, hyper-ambitious multi-level marketer, or an overly talkative person of the opposing political party, try to stay calm. Remember Chapter 36: If you have no control over the situation, don't allow it rattle you; if you do have some control over the problem, stay calm, and take whatever steps you need to take to defuse or remedy the unpleasant situation. (Hint: Screaming at the flight attendant or punching the baby's parents are generally not the most effective solutions to these problems.)
- **Crossing time zones-** As mentioned in Chapter 40, jumping across time zones can be problematic if you allow it to be. Try to adjust for the time differences in the days before your trip by sleeping and training at appropriate times to synchronize yourself to the new zone. As mentioned in the last chapter, a good rule of thumb is to arrive at your race site one day ahead of time for every time zone you cross.

Whichever mode of transportation you choose to get yourself to your race, be sure to allow plenty of time for the inevitable delays that crop up on long trips, including, but not limited to bad weather, holiday or weekend traffic, TSA strikes, natural disasters, cattle or a jack-knifed watermelon trucks on the highway, yaks on the airport runway, or extra long lines at the rest stop TCBY counter. By allowing plenty of time for these delays, and getting in a nice long warm-up before the race, you'll be able to counter many of the ill effects that come with automobile or air travel.

Now it's almost race time… Next up: your pre-competition routine!

CHAPTER 43: THE PRE-COMPETITION ROUTINE

The first rule of pre-race preparation is to find a routine that works for you and stick with it. The goal is boring predictability. Think Bill Murray in *Groundhog's Day*. (Without the bad driving or the toaster in the bathtub.) Before any important competition you need to have your mind free to relax, and to concentrate on your race plan. You can't waste valuable mental energy trying to figure out what to do before the gun goes off. By race day, what to do in the hours leading up to the start should be rote. Settle on a routine that works for you, practice it many times in training, and then use the same routine before every race. If something isn't working, change it. Practice the new routine, then use it at your next race.

Your race-day preparation begins well before race morning. If at all possible pick up your "bib" number(s)—the large identifying number or numbers you'll wear on your racing top— and registration packet the day before the race. Pin your numbers to your racing shirt or singlet and make sure all the clothes you'll wear during the race fit properly, from your hat, if you'll be wearing one, all the way down to your shoes and socks. Once I try everything on I like to do a couple of sprints down the hotel hallway outside of my room, or in front of my house if I'm racing locally, as one last pick-me-up for my legs, and to make sure my racing gear feels just right. Then I'll stretch for a few minutes while going over any last-minute information contained in the packet put together by the race director, or on the race web site. Having done all that, set a couple of wake-up alarms—call me paranoid, but I set the bedside alarm clock, my smartphone, and my watch alarms, just to be sure! Then get to bed at a reasonable hour. Don't hit the hay too much earlier than usual, though, because pre-race jitters could prevent you from falling asleep right away and you'll end up staring at the ceiling until four in the morning. I find that reading a good book at bedtime—like this one, for example!— helps me to fall asleep. (Although a *bad* book might work even better if the goal is the conk out early in anticipation of an early wake-up alarm!)

Get up early enough on race morning so you're not rushing around while preparing to go to the course. I'll try to drink enough water the night before the race so I'll have to wake up and use the bathroom in the middle of the night. While I'm up I'll eat a banana or some other light breakfast, then go back to sleep. Once I wake up for good I like to take a shower to help me wake up, and to "condition" myself for the race—literally. I'll put some hair conditioner anywhere skin may rub together and cause chafing, and then rinse it off. It leaves my skin just a little bit "slippery" and almost always prevents chafing without me having to resort to Body Glide or Vaseline. Works for me! I'll usually have an energy bar or other light "meal" to get my GI system

"Official" porta-potties (top), and Coach Dave with the Mother Lode of secret porta-potties at the start of the Las Vegas Marathon. Photo credit: Jon Cheris

moving, and then hit the bathroom. I'll head out to the race course with the goal of arriving 60 minutes before the scheduled race start to allow myself plenty of time for check-in and for a complete mental and physical warm-up. I use the same warm-up routine that I use before any fast effort, including speed and tempo workouts, time trials, and of course, races. If you do the same warm-up before all of your hard workouts, it will be second nature come race day.

The following pre-competition routine has always worked well for me. The goal of such a routine is to get yourself to the starting line loose, warmed up, and ready to race. Try this routine as-is, or tweak it if you think you can come up with something that will work even better for you:

1. **Warm up-** An easy 10- to 20-minute walk, or a combination of jogging then walking helps to work out the kinks and pumps some blood into the muscles to facilitate drills and stretching.
2. **Potty break?** By now your GI system should be awake, so head to the porta-potty and see if you can "lighten the load." Most people wait until much too close to the race start and have to wait on long lines at the porta-johns, stressing out about whether the line will move fast enough for them to get their turn before the start of the race.[85]
3. **Dynamic flexibility drills-** Perform five or 10 minutes of drills from Chapter 34 to prepare your neuromuscular system and extend your walking muscles' range of motion.

[85] If you're at a big race and need a porta-john close to the start of the race but the lines are too long, there's *always* a magic hidden john somewhere near the starting line. One of my self-designated responsibilities as a coach is to find the hidden potty so my athletes won't have to wait in line. ☺

4. **Accelerations-** Three or four 30- to 40-meter accelerations will further enhance the range-of-motion of your walking-specific muscles. Be sure to get up to race speed to make sure your technique feels good at competition pace.
5. **Stretch any problem areas-** If anything still feels uncomfortable, spend a few minutes stretching the tight spots.
6. **Go!** But don't go nuts. You're warmed up, loose, and full of adrenaline—start the race at what feels like a very comfortable pace and you'll probably be right on. Go out too hard and you'll pay for it in the second half of the race.

When you find a pre-race routine that works for you, use it every time you race. You'll always be loose, relaxed and ready to go. The last thing you want to do is show up at the starting line stressed-out because you're still tying your shoes and pinning on your number when the gun goes off. Not that that's ever happened to me…

CHAPTER 44: PACING AND RACING STRATEGIES

If you've trained for, then tapered for a big race, you're ready and rested. You've done a number of short, fast intervals in the days before the race to keep your muscles metabolically "alive," and if the race means anything at all to you, you'll have lots of adrenaline coursing through your veins as the starter's gun goes off. The result: unless you really control yourself, you're liable to start out too fast. 90% of your competitors will also start off too fast which is additional motivation to push too hard. DON'T! The first two or three minutes of your race, whether it's 1,500 meters or a marathon, can decide whether you end up with a personal record or a personal disaster.

The way to get around this is to consciously start out about 10% slower than what you judge your race pace to be. Factoring in everything, you'll probably be right on pace anyway. But even if you've started a bit slower than your goal pace, and the first half of the race seems easy, it will gradually get more difficult as you progress through the race, and that increasing difficulty will be amplified if you start out too fast. Studies have found that most world records at distances from five to 50k were set by athletes whose second half of the race was faster than the first. It works! The physiological benefits are certainly part of the equation, but it can also be a huge psychological boost to spend the last few kilometers of the race flying by dozens of burned out stragglers who started out too fast.

Practice is the only way to ingrain a reliable sense of pace. By training on the track or on marked courses you eventually develop a sense of pace. Once it's locked in, you'll be able to get a general idea of how fast you're going based on your breathing and other physiological factors, and to "hear" how fast you're going by listening to your footfalls. After a while you develop a sort of metronome in your head where you know exactly what a certain pace sounds like. When I was training at a high level I could always feel and hear the difference between paces down to within a few seconds per kilometer within my normal training range of 4:00 to 6:00 minutes per kilometer. I wasn't as good at estimating paces much slower than that. Why? Because I didn't have much experience walking slower than about 5:45 per kilometer. In more recent years I've gotten much better at predicting paces between 6:00 and 7:00 minutes per kilometer because I've done a lot more training between those paces in the past decade as I've morphed into a fat old 50k walker. ☺ You learn to do by doing…

Since stride length remains fairly constant through a wide range of paces, cadence rate is the major factor affecting your walking speed. If you learn the "sounds" of your various paces by keeping track of your splits on marked courses, then listening for the right sound during races, you should always be able to zero in on the right pace.

Racing strategies

With your well-honed sense of pace dialed in, there are a number of different ways to pace your way through a race. The distance of the race, your experience level, your goals for the race, how stiff the competition is, and your degree of confidence in your own abilities and current conditioning will all influence which strategy you'll use to pace yourself during a race. In general terms, there are five different pacing strategies you can employ: You can go out hard and hang on as long as you can; you can try to maintain a steady pace; you can start out at a comfortable pace then ratchet up the pace throughout the race to "negative split" it; you can "stick and kick" by letting someone else set the pace, hoping to pass the leader at the very end; or you can shift gears throughout the race, covering the moves of your competitors or changing paces depending on how you're feeling.

- **Blast & burn out-** This is the strategy of choice for the rank beginner. In the running world, it's the guy wearing basketball shorts over his sweatpants who leads the New York Marathon for the first 400 meters to get himself on TV, then winds up flooded with lactate, curled up in the fetal position next to a fire hydrant somewhere in Queens. I won't name names, but there are certainly corollaries in the walking world. ☺ The idea is to go out hard to break your competitors, then to hang on as long as you can—hopefully to the finish line. This strategy only works if you're far superior to your competitors anyway, in which case you would have won no matter what strategy you used, so you might as well have used a smarter one. If you like lactic acid and rigor mortis, this is the strategy for you. if you like personal records and winning races, don't even think about it.
- **Steady pace-** Remember *The Tortoise and the Hare?* (Hint: The Turtle wins.) If you've been diligent about your interval training and tempo walks you should have a pretty good idea of the pace you'll be able to handle for whatever distance you're racing. The goal here is to start out at very close to that pace and carry it through to the finish line. By walking at a steady pace you should be reasonably comfortable through most of the race, only feeling physiological stress in the final stages—if you've judged your starting pace correctly.
- **Negative split-** You've probably already guessed, I'm partial to this strategy! Most championship races are won by a negative-splitting walker—one who takes the pace out relatively conservatively, then accelerates throughout the race. This strategy gives your body a good chance to warm up in the early going, and allows you to save the hardest walking for the end of the race. To negative split you should start out just a little bit conservatively, letting the other walkers fight for position in the first few laps or

kilometers, depending on the distance of the race. Then you consciously accelerate throughout the remainder of race by slightly increasing your cadence rate every lap, kilometer, or mile. Since things will be getting tougher and tougher over the last few laps or kilometers, and your stride rate may be decreasing from muscle tightness, you may not actually be picking up the pace very much, but the end of the race will still *feel* much faster. This strategy is very good psychologically since you'll be passing other walkers throughout the race. I like to break any race into thirds. In *The Complete Guide to Racewalking* I wrote about *control* in the first third of the race—not starting out too fast, and being patient for the first third of the race; *maintaining* your pace during the second third as you start feeling fatigue creep in; and *hammering* the final third as you feel the finish line getting closer.

- **Stick & kick-** Sticking and kicking—hanging on to another walker's pace throughout most of the race then blowing by him or her in the end—is a very "easy" pacing strategy since the other walker does all of the pacing work. It's a good way of taking some of the stress out of racing, but it does have its drawbacks. First, you're saving yourself for a blazing finishing kick, which could lead to disqualification in judged races. Also, because you've saved all your effort for that kick, your finish time may not be as fast as it would have been had you pushed the pace the whole way—and you can never be completely certain that you'll actually be able to out-kick your rival. Despite the drawbacks, if your goal is simply to beat a particular competitor, and you're confident that you have a fast, *legal* finishing kick, this strategy may be a viable option for you.

The author racing against kids half his age at the 2013 Millrose Games/US 1-Mile Championship.
Photo Credit: Jeff Salvage

- **Shifting gears-** One of my favorite memories from late in my career was the 2008 Millrose Games—my last walk at Madison Square Garden. I was pushing 43 years old, lining up against kids half my age in a one-mile race—a distance that favors younger legs. The old Garden track was eleven laps to the mile, with very tight, high banked turns. It was always difficult to pass anyone on the turns because to do so you had to climb uphill on the bank. I was in a mischievous mood that night, so battling the inexperienced kids, lap after lap, I would accelerate on the straightaways, then ease off heading into the turns. The kids figured the old man was running out of steam so they would try to pass me. When I felt them on my shoulder I would move out toward the outside of lane one, and sometimes even into lane two, to make them go high on the bank to try to pass me. As soon as they tried to make a move I would slowly accelerate just enough to hold them off, then put it into high gear again down the straightaway. Shifting gears is a great way to wear out your competitors, both physically and mentally. Just be careful that you don't wear yourself out in the process!

Age-grading

Whichever pacing strategy you choose, your finish time and place aren't always the end of the story. Many races now "handicap" the races and award prizes based on *age-grading*. Age-grading is a way to level the playing field by weighting every finisher's time based on the age and sex of the competitor. Essentially, your time is compared to the best times of the top walkers in the world in your age group. You are then assigned an age-grade percentage (basically your race pace as a percentage of the world record pace for your age). For example, if the 5k world-record for your age is 20:00 minutes and you walked 25:00, your pace was 80% of the world record pace, so your age-grade percentage is 80%. Alternately, or additionally, your time may be *age-adjusted*, so the 25:00 5k you walked would be worth 23:45 if you're a 40-year-old man, 21:54 for a 50-year-old man and 18:22 for a 70-year-old woman! Age-grade percentages are based on age-grade tables for every age from age eight to 100 and for just about every possible race distance. To find your own age-grade percentages and time conversions, the World Masters Athletics age-grade calculator can be found online at: www.howardgrubb.co.uk/athletics/wmawalk18.html/.

Hopefully you've paced yourself wisely through this book and have saved some energy for a very detailed chapter chock-full of great information on race course logistics!

CHAPTER 45: COURSE LOGISTICS

Chapter 39 covered the importance of researching the race web site to learn about, and acclimate to, the course and weather conditions you will likely experience on race day. Here we'll go over some details about what you were preparing yourself for, from start to finish, and beyond. We'll start with some information applicable to local 5k road races with a few hundred participants, or racewalks with 50 participants, then explore the organized chaos of very large races like big-city half-marathons and marathons.

Checking in

When arriving at a smaller event, like a local running race with a walk division, a Nordic walking event, or a track or road power walk or racewalk, there will usually be a check-in tent where you will pick up your "bib" number or numbers. Running races generally only provide one bib number, worn on the front of your shirt, while most walking races will give you a second number for your back to make it easier for walking judges to identify you. The check-in will normally open about an hour before the scheduled race time, and it's always a good idea to arrive early. Pins will usually be provided to pin your numbers on your front and back, but if you want to look like a pro, always bring your own. ☺ Most of the larger races these days use telemetric timing systems. You'll be provided with a timing tag which will be attached to the back of your front bib number, or if the race director is "old school," a timing "chip" which you will need to attach to your shoe. The tag or chip will record when you cross the electronic timing mat at the starting line and when you cross the mat at the finish line. "Chip timing" ensures a fair start for everyone no matter how far back in the pack they start, so there is no reason for slower walkers to nudge their way up closer to the starting line. Your chip time will be based on your actual start—when *you* cross the starting line, not when the starting gun is fired, which may have been several minutes earlier.

Incidentally, there will often be timing mats at other points on the course as well, to ensure that nobody cuts the course. Miss a mat and you could be disqualified. I recall a timing mat about five miles into the New Orleans Marathon along St. Charles Avenue, a wide boulevard bisected by the iconic St. Charles Streetcar's tracks. The dirt path on the median along the tracks was much less crowded than the road, and the dirt was much easier on the feet than the hot, pot-hole-riddled asphalt of the road, so a lot of runners and walkers chose to use the median instead of the road. That section of the course was a long dogleg where runners and walkers went out along one side of St. Charles, then took a turn at about the 5.5-mile mark and returned along the other side of the boulevard. At any point during that long section of the race someone could have easily cut across the street and blended in with the runners and walkers who had already made the turn, cutting off up to seven miles of the half-marathon or marathon! To prevent that sort of blatant cheating, there was a timing mat at about the five-mile mark. Anyone running or walking on the median at that point would have missed the mat, leading to their disqualification, and on that day several hundred did, and were. Always stay on the road!

Once your numbers and timing tag/chip are attached, it will be time to start your warm-up! Use the pre-competition routine you've practiced in training, as outlined in Chapter 43, to get yourself ready to race, then head to the starting line—after one last trip to the porta-johns, of course!

The starting line

Even in small races, but certainly in larger ones, there will be a wide range of walking and running abilities represented. Most races will attempt to "corral" athletes of similar ability together based on their predicted finish times. This allows the smoothest possible race, ensuring that the speed demons don't knock down slower runners and walkers as they bolt from the starting line, or that slower walkers and runners don't impede the speed demons, depending on your point of view. ☺ Lining up with the appropriate pace cohort works to your advantage, because it will help you stick to your race plan. Participants who line up too close to the front may find themselves getting caught up in a sprint at the start and going out too fast, while anyone lining up too far to the back of the pack in a large race will find that they have to weave unnecessarily around thousands of other runners and walkers to get up to the appropriate pace group. If the race doesn't have a corral system, there will probably be signs marking suggested pacing areas: 5:00 milers near the starting line, then 6:00 milers, then 7:00s, all the way through the teens. Smaller races will have no such corral system, relying instead on the honor system, with athletes lining up according to their own self-assessed ability level. Top runners will line up in

Outside the corrals at the Walt Disney World Marathon. I'm not bragging here, just indicating the location of Corrals A-H to the left, and after the sign changed, Corrals I-P straight ahead.

the front row, followed by progressively slower runners and walkers. In track races you will usually be lined up according to your "seed time" (your previous best, or recent best, time for the distance you'll be racing).

Each corral will hold between a few hundred to a few thousand walkers and runners, depending on the size of the race, and each is separated from the other corrals by snow fencing or a rope. When the starting gun fires, the race starts and the first corral takes off! And the rest of the corrals… wait. After Corral A is cleared, the rope or fencing behind it is dropped and the athletes in Corral B move ahead into Corral A to wait for their start, about 90 seconds later. Then the athletes from Corral C move ahead into Corral B, D moves ahead into C, E moves into D and so on. When timing your warm-up before the race, be sure to adjust for the amount of time it will take you to get from your corral to the starting line. If you're assigned Corral "J" for example, it will likely take you 15 to 20 minutes to get to the starting line. (J is the 10th letter of the alphabet x 90 seconds to two minutes per corral = 15 to 20 minutes.) This is assuming about 500 athletes per corral. It could take much longer if the corrals hold thousands, rather than hundreds of athletes, so be sure to check the race website for a time estimate, or make your own calculations depending on how many athletes are staged in each corral. (The website should list bib number ranges for each corral. (Bibs 1-25 for the Elite start, bibs 1000-1,500 for Corral A, 1,501-2,000 for Corral B, etc.)

Aid stations

Aid stations are the water, sports drink, and "personal aid" tables you will encounter out on the race course. The race web site will usually include a map laying out the locations of the aid tables and what will be served. A standard pattern is to place aid tables about every 1.5 miles or so, often alternating water-only stations with water and sport drink stations. Usually there will be several tables, with water at the first set of tables, then sports drink at the next set of tables, but sometimes that can be reversed. There will be lots of filled cups (or more likely half-filled cups!) laid out on the tables, as well as volunteers handing out cups. Grabbing a cup on the fly and learning how to drink without aspirating Gatorade is a learned skill, so make sure to practice in training!

At about 10 miles into a half-marathon, or 18 to 20 miles into a full marathon, there will often be an energy gel table at that aid station. For the love of all that's holy, do not confuse this aid station with the first-aid tents that you're also likely to see out on the course! PowerBar[86] was one

[86] After the 2016 Olympics, PowerBar took their entire "Team Elite" budget and used it to bestow redemption upon disgraced swimmer, Ryan Lochte, after his arrest for vandalizing a gas station bathroom and filing a false police report attempting to cover up the crime. It was one of a string of bad decisions the company made after Nestlé sold the brand to Post in 2014. They were a great sponsor under their original owner, founder Brian Maxwell, and under Nestlé as well. I'm grateful for their support throughout most of their career. Post, on the other hand… Not so much. I'd love to boycott Post, but their brands include Fruity Pebbles, Oreos, and Sour Patch Kids, so that would be damned near impossible. ☺

of my sponsors for over twenty years, so I was always able to pass out energy gel samples to my training groups leading up to their events. One season, after consulting with the course map, I told my group that there would be a gel table at the nineteen-mile mark of the San Diego Marathon, the race we were training for all season. One of my walkers loved gels and was *really* looking forward to the gel stop during the race. So much so that when he arrived at a first-aid station near the *eighteen*-mile mark and saw volunteers handing out tongue depressors slathered with goo, he eagerly grabbed one and popped it into his mouth. It took him several miles to get the taste of Vaseline out of his mouth... First-aid tents, clearly identified by their red and white color scheme and red-cross logos, are valuable on-course amenities, but please do not mistake them for nutritional aid stations!

Most road-course racewalking events are laid out on repeated 1km to 2km loops which will usually include a water table on one side of the course and a "personal aid" table on the other side, where each athlete may lay out sport drinks, gels, ice and any other legal refreshments. The walker can grab the aid off of the table by him/herself, or have the items handed off by a coach or other designated aid person. Easy access to your own personal choice of on-course refreshment is one of the great benefits of doing a racewalk-only event!

Thinking (and walking) tangentially

After almost every road race I hear or read accounts online where a walker complains that his or her time was "X" but it would have been "Y" had the course not been .57, or .84 or 1.12 miles "too long." Sometimes I will have walked in the same race, and although there may have been 40,000 participants in the race, I spent much of my time alone. Even when there were plenty of people walking or running at my pace, almost all of them spent much of the race waaaay over on the other side of the road. To me, walking the shortest distance in a race is second nature. I've done it for years in training so I see the straightest line from turn to turn without even thinking about it. Sometimes I even catch myself doing it when driving—not recommended! Most beginners however, and even some more experienced walkers, blindly follow the crowd or the curves of the road instead of walking the shortest distance from point to point on the course—incidentally, the way the courses are measured and certified.

Walking the shortest distance from point to point on the course is known as "cutting the tangents," and it derives from simple geometry: the shortest distance between two points is a straight line. Yet many walkers often walk many meters longer per turn because they always keep to the right-hand side of the road, or stay on the same side of the road as their last turn, regardless of where the next turn in the road may be. In long races with a lot of turns, not following the straightest line can add up to a mile or more of extra distance walked over the course of a marathon. So your GPS wasn't lying... You really did walk 27.3 miles in your last marathon, even though the course was an accurately measured 26 miles, 385 yards/42.195 kilometers. But that was your own fault, not the race director's!

A little junior high school geometry: The circumference of a circle = 2π x r. If a road is 10 meters wide and makes a 90-degree turn (¼ of a circle) and the radius of the circle from the origin (center point) to the outside edge of the road is 50 meters,[87] the difference in distance travelled is [2π x r]/4 of the outer edge of the road along the turn (which is ¼ of the radius of a full circle) – [2π x r]/4 of the inner edge of the road. So the distance saved by walking along the inner edge of the road rather than the outer edge of the road is [2π x 50 meters]/4 - [2π x 40 meters]/4 or 78.5m – 62.8m = 15.7 meters. At fifteen minutes per mile (1.8 meters per second) that's eight seconds. That's eight FREE seconds just by taking the shortest distance along that one turn! Now multiply that eight seconds by the dozens of similar turns you'll encounter throughout the race and you can see how consciously walking the shortest possible distance consistently during the race can really add up.

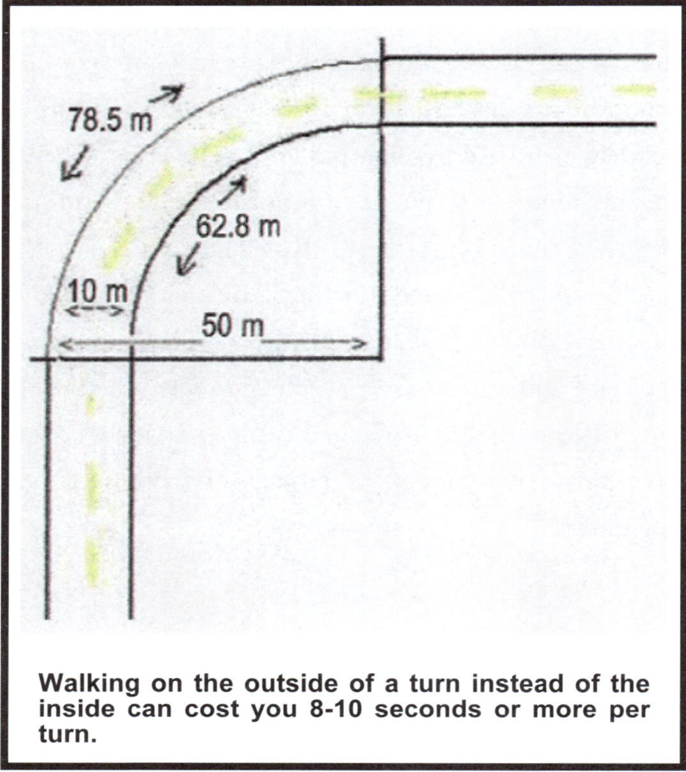

Walking on the outside of a turn instead of the inside can cost you 8-10 seconds or more per turn.

Walking the shortest distance is a pretty easy process, but it does take some practice before it becomes locked in so you do it automatically whenever you race. A few *how-tos:*

- Look far ahead down the road to where the walkers or runners ahead of you are disappearing around the next turn. Head in a straight-line for that point.
- Whenever possible hug the inside of turns.
- When coming out of a turn look ahead to the point where the next turn disappears and head in a straight line for that point.
- Try to anticipate what the people ahead of you are doing so you don't have to suddenly scramble the long way around packs of walkers.

---

87 The standard lane width in the US is 12ft. (3.7 meters), so a four-lane road would be ~15 meters wide, curb-to-curb.

Let's say you've just turned right, hugging the curb on a road course, and the next turn is a left-hand turn 400 meters ahead. Ideally you should walk in as straight a line as possible to the curb of the upcoming turn, gradually crossing the road diagonally to reach that point. Most of the people around you will immediately cross the street, like lemmings, and then walk along the curb on the far side of the road. You may not be able to walk in the middle of the road at home during training, but in a race, with the road closed to traffic this is unnecessary and doing so will add 20 to 30 meters to the distance walked. Again, multiply that 10 to 20 meters by 20 turns and you've saved 200 to 400 meters (1:30 to 3:00 minutes at 12:00 pace) over the course of the race.

One final note: Cutting the tangents is not cheating, but not doing so is cheating yourself! Races are measured on the tangents, so if the course is advertised as a 10k, it is a 6.2-mile race, measured along the shortest possible distance. The elite runners and faster walkers will be walking a 10k, but somewhere in the middle of the pack things break down and a lot of the slower walkers and runners start wandering the course along the curves which results in the slower athletes actually walking a much longer distance than the faster athletes. Racing is hard! A marathon—or a 10k or 5k—is a long way to go. Why walk 27.3 miles or 6.48 or 3.24 when you can walk 26.2 or 6.2 or 3.1? Even if you can't be fast, at least you can be smart! Cut the tangents!

On-course etiquette

My boys, at the ripe old ages of 11, 9 and 6, are fiercely "anti-noob." Newbs, or newbies, are beginners at Roblox, or whatever video game they happen to be playing this week. Newbs are fine. But *noobs*—and yes, there is a distinction!—noobs are mocked and shunned. They are beginners who think they're awesome, but don't know what they're doing, and don't care to learn the subtle etiquette conventions of the game. Don't be a noob! Learning a few "rules of the road" will go a long way toward keeping other competitors from rolling their eyes like my kids when they see you coming. ☺

I went over a bit of track etiquette in Chapter 6. Road racing etiquette follows many of the same conventions. Walkers have all of the same rights that runners do, but in mixed races, walkers will follow most of the same rules as slower runners, simply because even the fastest walkers are slower than the fastest runners. Some of these include:

1. When the race does not have assigned corrals, walkers should not line up in the front few rows at the start line. Obey pace markers and line up accordingly, or at least line up behind the faster runners to avoid impeding anyone's progress. This makes for a smoother, faster start for everyone and is safer for all.
2. Don't walk more than two people abreast. This leaves room for other participants to pass you.

3. If you are stopping at water stations, stay as far to the side (left or right) of the road as you can. This way runners and walkers who are not stopping have a safe and clear space to pass.
4. When drinking at an aid station, look before you throw your cup away to make sure you're not throwing it in the path of another participant.
5. On loop courses, be predictable! Cut the tangents, but if you feel the need to "be courteous" and move out of the way of an athlete who is lapping you, don't do it suddenly like a squirrel in traffic. Move out well before the athlete is about to pass you because he or she has already made his or her own calculations concerning your speed and distance and has already plotted out the best path to get around you that results in the least amount of deviation from a straight line for him- or herself. If you move suddenly you're just making that athlete suddenly change course and walk farther than he or she had to. The best course, really, is just to race your own race and athletes will be perfectly happy to just pass you without incident.
6. In judged events, don't piss off the judges! View yellow paddles as free technique advice! And even if you happen to get disqualified, don't yell at the judges, kick course-marking cones, or overturn water tables or police barricades. (Yes, I've seen all of the above…) None of this will get you reinstated and will certainly not have that/those judges on your side in the next race.
7. Be sure to thank the volunteers before, during, and after the event—especially the judges! ☺

Now hear this!

As you probably gathered from Chapter 7 (and 36, and 37, and 38…) I'm not a fan of headphones or earbuds—or whatever the heck the kids are calling them these days—when training, and definitely not when racing. Safety is always a concern, but races are supposed to be fun, right? Ignoring track races for a moment, there are things to see, and in longer races at somewhat slower paces, interesting people you may want to get to know through the long lost art of verbal communication—talking! If you're wearing earbuds you're not going to be aware of what's going on around you when it comes to both scenery and people.

There's also the matter of *performance.* As mentioned in Chapter 36, the best athletes are *associative,* meaning they are in-tune with their own bodies while racing. Top athletes control their pace by being intimately aware of their breathing, the sound of their own footfalls, their technique, as well as being aware of what their competitors are doing. Playing music while racing can keep you from pushing as hard as you could have, or motivate you to walk *too* fast early in the race, leading to ugly drop-offs in pace in the second half.

Finally, racing with earbuds *may* be illegal. Although RRCA permits—but strongly discourages—earbud use, and USA Track & Field modified its long-standing blanket ban of headphones/earbuds in 2008 to leave it up to individual race directors whether to ban them or not, USATF Rule 144.3 (b) *does* ban "portable listening devices" for those competing in championships for awards, medals, or prize money, so if you think you're in the "running" for such, leave the buds at home, Bud. ☺

The finish line

As you approach the finish, you may find that you have some energy left for a blazing finishing "kick." This is <u>not</u> a good idea in a judged race! Start a controlled, progressive acceleration well before the finish to avoid drawing unwanted attention from judges. There may be a finish line photographer, especially in bigger races. Smile! Pump your fist in the air! Strike your best Usain Bolt "Lightning Bolt" pose! But whatever you do, don't look down at your watch, unless you want a fabulous keepsake photo of the top of your head.

After crossing the finish line, sure, stop your watch. After that, volunteers will generally be there to steer you to what's next. In actual chip-timed races, a volunteer will help you to remove the chip from your shoe; in telemetry-timed races with a tag on the back of your number instead of an actual chip, you will not need to turn over the tag. It's yours to keep or toss it in the trash. In hand-timed races, there may be a pull-tab on the bottom of your bib that's used to record your finish place, which a volunteer will pull off. In all cases you will then be directed to any post-race amenities. Most longer races (half-marathons and marathons) will award you with a finisher's medal. After having the medal hung around your neck, there will often be another post-race photographer to take your photo, usually in front of the event's "step and repeat" backdrop. Smaller races will generally not have such amenities, but most races of any size will help you on your way to recovery with post-race food and beverages like bananas, bagels, sport drinks, or sometimes a post-race party with more substantial fare. Smaller races will generally have an award ceremony as soon as the results are sorted out. It's always polite to stick around for the awards even if you're not expecting to win anything. (In which case random door prizes are often awarded as well as a way to keep you around...) If nothing else, the award ceremony will give you a little time to get rehydrated and get some food into yourself to start you on your way to post-race recovery. But more on that in the next chapter…

CHAPTER 46: POST-RACE RECOVERY

Competitive walking is difficult. That's why we do it. After completing a race of any distance, your body may be a little beat up and you'll need to let it recover. For shorter races, recovery might mean doing a nice cool-down, eating some carbs and a little protein, drinking some water or sports drink, and getting some sleep. For longer races, full recovery may take days or weeks. A general rule of thumb is that you should allow one day of recovery for every mile raced, so after a 5k you should avoid any speed work or hard mileage for at least three days; allow two weeks after a half-marathon, and 3-4 weeks for a full marathon.

Just because a race isn't a "walk in the park," that doesn't necessarily mean you'll be sore and wrecked for weeks afterwards. In fact, walking a 5k, 10k, or even a marathon shouldn't leave you much more beat up or depleted than you were after some of your longest hard training walks, and it didn't take you a month to recover from those, did it? If it did, how would you, or anyone, ever be able to walk a 5k/10k double at the National Masters Championship, or a "Goofy" or "Dopey" Challenge at the Disney Marathon? Your body knows how to repair the damage you inflict upon it when training and racing. Your job is to facilitate that repair process by doing all of the right things before, during, and after your event. But what are these elusive "right things" that will speed your recovery?

Before the race

The surest way to speed your recovery from a race is to train adequately for the distance you'll be covering in the first place. Competitive walking is an endurance activity. That means you need to maintain a reasonably high weekly mileage level, and do a long day (yes, long is relative…) every week. I've seen double-your-race-distance-type rules for calculating the distance of your long day, but they break down for anything longer than a 10k. I don't believe there is an "if this, then that" rule for how long you should go, but I think something on the order of six to eight miles for a 5k, eight to ten miles for a 10k, 15 to 18 miles for a 20k/half-marathon, and 20 to 22 miles for a marathon or 50k are reasonable numbers to land on. Most coaches agree that something in the ballpark of 20 miles is the required distance for your long day for a marathon, but what if you only get up to 15 miles? If you're walking (rather than running or even racewalking) chances are you'll probably finish the race, but you can probably expect to be sore or even injured afterward. You really do need to get those long walks in to strengthen your muscles and connective tissues, and to teach your body to burn fat instead of carbohydrates during the marathon. The physiology is a little different for shorter races, but the general idea is the same: Mileage protects your body from damage during the race, and allows for a speedier recovery afterward.

During the race

Of equal importance to what you do before the race, what you do *during* the race has a lot to do with how you'll feel afterward. Smart pacing is not just a way to ensure a fast finish time, it's also one of the keys to quick post-race recovery. Starting out too fast in longer races prompts your body to burn a higher percentage of carbohydrates during the race. If that happens you'll likely become carbohydrate-depleted toward the end of the race—or sooner—and you'll "hit the wall." At that point your muscles will become very inefficient at burning fat as a fuel so you'll end up catabolizing muscle protein. Ouch! If you hit the wall and keep walking you'll actually start breaking down muscle tissue to use as a fuel source. It's certainly not fatal, and you'll eventually recover, but you'll feel beat up for weeks after the race rather than days.

Luckily, the wall is easily avoidable for long-distance walkers. All you need to do is train properly, then start the race at a reasonable pace and you'll set your muscles up to burn fat rather than carbs. In a marathon or 50k, for example, if you're feeling really good after 10 or 12 miles, you can start picking up the pace. If you've started at the right pace you should be able to pick it up even more over the final five or 10k. Your overall time will be much faster than it would have been had you started out too fast and crashed, and your recovery after the race will be much faster. Taking in roughly eight ounces of fluid every 15 minutes—or whatever amount your sweat-rate test indicated—and drinking or eating carbohydrates during the race, are other good ways to ensure a fast post-race recovery. Staving off dehydration, and supplementing your carbohydrate stores will keep your muscles working efficiently, ensuring that you'll be burning fats and carbohydrates instead of muscle protein in the later stages of the race.

Similarly, post-race recovery after shorter races can be facilitated by proper pacing and hydration. Starting out too fast in a 5k or 10k can lead to a crash just as it can in a marathon—albeit for different reasons. Spiking lactate levels are usually the cause for tanking in a 5k or 10k. Sustained high lactate levels before the crash can cause damage to the muscles, so again, pacing properly, even in shorter races, can help speed post-race recovery. Dehydration, too, is hard on the body. Although it's more of an issue in longer races, dehydration, and the muscle damage that comes with it, can occur in races as short as 10 kilometers in hot, humid conditions. Fluid stations are there for a reason. It doesn't take long to grab a cup of water or sports drink during your race. Staying hydrated will help you to race faster, but will also help to speed your post-race recovery. Drink!

After the race

What you do in the first few minutes after the race can really help to reduce your post-race recovery time. After you cross the finish line, walk around slowly to gradually bring your heart rate down. Whatever you do, don't sit down! If you don't keep moving, your muscles may stiffen up and you'll feel much worse once you try to get up again. Try to start drinking immediately, preferably a sports drink to replenish carbohydrates, but water is also fine if it's all you can find. If your stomach can handle it, it's also a good idea to try to eat some fruit or an energy bar as soon as you can. Your muscles are most receptive to carbohydrates within the first 15 minutes to two hours of finishing your race. A little protein will help your muscles to store even more carbs and will help to repair damaged muscles.

You may be tempted to soak in a hot tub after the race, but please avoid doing so! You don't necessarily need to subject yourself to a cold shower, but try to avoid very hot water. Heat will dilate your blood vessels, causing swelling in your sore muscles. If your GI system tolerates it well, an anti-inflammatory like Advil or Aleve will help to keep some of the swelling down. After the shower, take a short—or not so short—nap. Then get up and take an easy walk, and keep drinking water and/or sports drink to keep from tightening up too much—you'll need to get those legs working again if you want to dance at the post-race party! Keep a bottle of water with you and continue hydrating the rest of the day and night. If you do attend a party, it's okay to have a few "adult beverages." But continue drinking water—at least one glass of water or sports drink for every "other" beverage you consume.

When the evening winds down, unplug the alarm clock, turn the ringer on your phone off, draw the shades tight, and tuck yourself in for a nice long rest. Try to sleep in as late as possible. If you do get up to use the bathroom, drink another glass of water before going back to bed. You've had a long day, so you'll need a long night of sleep (or two or three) to begin the process of healing your tired muscles.

Getting back to normal

You'll probably be a little stiff and sore the day after a hard race, but most of the aches and pains will go away after a few days of rest. That can be a double-edged sword. You may feel so good after the race that you'll want to jump right back into training. That's probably ok after a short race, but after a half-marathon, marathon or longer you'll want to take some time off. You may be tempted to get right back out there and start walking long distances again, or even get back into racing shorter races—why let all that hard training go to waste, right? Wrong! A good rule of thumb is to take it easy—nothing too long or too fast—one day for every mile you raced.[88] That would be about six days for a 10k, almost two weeks after a 20k or half-marathon, and three to four weeks after a marathon. I've never sustained an injury in a marathon, but I have wound up with more than a few in the first week or two after the race because I didn't respect the distance. I felt good after the race so I jumped right back into training. You may feel great, but your muscles and joints will be weakened from the hard effort.

---

[88] I've also seen this rule as one day off for every *two* miles you raced, but that would mean you're ready to start banging out hard workouts a day and a half after a 5k, three days after a 10k, six days after a 20k or half-marathon and less than two weeks after a marathon. Um, no. At least not for inexperienced walkers.

For the first few weeks after a hard race, especially after a 20k or longer, continue doing the same good things that helped you to get through your training:

- Continue drinking water,
- Maintain a high-carbohydrate diet for at least three to five days after the race to fully reload your muscles with glycogen,
- Gently stretch to regain your range of motion,
- Spring for a massage to speed healing of overused muscles,
- Consider taking supplements like Vitamin C and echinacea to help boost your immune system.

After the first two weeks you'll probably start to miss training. You'll miss the camaraderie of walking with your training buddies, or the tranquility of your long walks alone. At this point it's probably safe to get back into training. If you do decide that you're up for another long-distance challenge, get out a calendar to start plotting your next race. Then follow the same rules that got you to the finish line of your last race. You won't have to start from scratch—your last long day, after all, was 13.1 or 26.2 or 31 miles, depending on what distance you just raced! With all the valuable experience you've gained—and all those miles under your belt—your next race is sure to be a personal record! Just make sure you don't overdo it. If the race you just completed was your first marathon or 50k, give yourself a full six months before doing another. With more experience you can safely walk a marathon or longer once every two to three months or so, but doing more than three or four per year can cause "burnout" or injury. Unless… You're a maniac! The Marathon Maniacs is a group of walkers (and runners) who enjoy doing several marathons per month, even on consecutive days. There is also a 50 States + DC club that endeavors to race a marathon in every state in the US + Washington, DC, and even a subset of the group that attempts to do at least one marathon on every continent on the globe. The key for most of them is to go slow—a finish is a win! So I don't want to get too much detail because this is a book about *competitive* walking and most Marathon Maniacs (and their half-marathon loving group, the "Half Fanatics") are only competing against the logistical goal of racking up lots of races in as short a time as possible, not against the clock during the races themselves. The point is, your body *can* recover very quickly from a race, even from a marathon, if you go at a reasonable pace. That's not an option if your goal is to race all-out, but if you have the goal of racing on consecutive days or doing two or more races within a few days of each other, you can recover very quickly and do very well in the subsequent race or races. All you have to do is back off just a little bit in the first race, then do everything mentioned above to speed your recovery, to be ready to go again on subsequent days.

Reverse taper

The reverse taper is a specific way of ramping your training back up again after your race. It means gradually increasing your mileage, following the kind of taper you used to reduce your volume leading up to the race, only in reverse. For a half-marathon, for example, you probably did your last long day about two weeks before the race, before gradually decreasing your mileage until the last three to five days when you probably only walked about ⅓ of your usual mileage. Your reverse taper should begin with probably just an easy 15-minute warm-up then some gentle stretching a day or two after the race, then maybe 30 minutes three or four days after. You first "long" day will probably be about half of what you would normally do, a week after the race. By two weeks after a half-marathon your long day will probably be back up to your normal level; three weeks after for a marathon and four for a 50k. You'll gradually reintroduce speed and tempo work as well, after two or three weeks.

With the proper training for your race, pacing and nutrition during the race, and a sensible recovery plan post-race, you'll be able to ramp your training back up again, and be ready to race again in no time. Which is great, because this racing stuff is addicting, isn't it?! ☺

CHAPTER 47: FINISH LINE THOUGHTS

Writing this book has been a prolonged labor of love. My first two full-length books, *The Complete Guide to Racewalking,* and *The Complete Guide to Marathon Walking* each took me about six to eight *weeks* to write. I started writing this bad boy in 2009… I let the racewalking book go out of print about 10 years ago, thinking I could knock this one off in a couple of months to replace it. Well, the first saved file in my computer for this book, containing a roughed out table of contents and few rudimentary chapters fleshed out, is dated June 7th, 2009. Not coincidentally, my first son was born two weeks earlier, on May 22nd, 2009… And so goes writing with a family.

I write best when I sit down to write and get up fourteen hours later when I'm hungry, have to pee, or can't keep my eyes open any longer. If I have an hour to write, I need to go back to see where I left off, and in doing so notice I don't like a font size, or that my word processor has eaten a photo, so I spend most of the hour changing the fonts or tracking down the lost photo instead of actually *writing.* With a new baby in the house, finding even an uninterrupted hour to write is a rarity, let alone four or fourteen. By 2012 I had made some progress, but then another baby came along, then another in 2014, and another in 2018. In 2020 came… Covid-19. It's been horrific, taking beloved family members, and making it impossible for me to travel to do clinics, but the small silver lining is that the pandemic has finally given me the chance to sit down and write again. The ensuing eleven years since starting this tome have given me a great deal of perspective. I made my last international team in 2010 and have allowed myself to become more of a coach and part-time recreational athlete than a full-time elite athlete—my participation in the 2012, 2016 and 2020 Olympic Trials notwithstanding. ☺

My goal in writing this book—like that of my other books—was to take the information gleaned over the ups and downs of a 40-year career as a reasonably competitive athlete, and to pass it on to others. As I've been saying at my "World Class Racewalking" clinics for many years, it's a whole heck of a lot easier to help you guys get faster than it is to try get this beat up, broken down old body to go faster than it did at its peak. I'm an eternal optimist, but also a realist. I'm pretty sure I'll never break 6:00 for a mile or 20:00 for 5k at this point,[89] but if your goal is to racewalk a 5k under 30:00, make the podium in your next 10k Nordic walk, medal in the powerwalk at the Huntsman Games or National Senior Games, or finish under the time limit in an Ironman or half-Ironman triathlon without running a single step, yeah, I think I can get you there.

[89] I do still think I can break 20 *hours* for 100 miles though, and probably make another Olympic Trials, too! There's always another mountain to climb. ☺

As with any lofty goal, it'll take some work on your part, but with the information and training schedules spelled out in the preceding chapters, I'm sure I can help you to achieve your competitive walking goals, whatever they may be.

Now put this book down and get out and walk! With writing finally out of the way, I'll be doing the same. Even after four decades of training and racing, there's always room for improvement! With any luck, maybe I'll see you at a race somewhere down the road.

Happy walking!

SECTION V: APPENDICES

APPENDIX I: TRAINING SCHEDULE DEFINITIONS & ABBREVIATIONS

100m: 100 meters = One straightaway, or one turn on a standard outdoor high school or college track.

200m: 200 meters = halfway around a standard high school/college track in lane one. 12 x 200m @ 5k pace w/ 200m recoveries means walk fast halfway around the track, then walk slowly the other half. Repeat 12 times. 5k pace is your fastest pace in a 5k (3.1-mile) race. If you've never raced, these 200m intervals should be fast, steady efforts, but not all-out sprints.

400m: 400 meters = one lap around a high school/college track in lane one.

4 x {100m, 200m, 300m}: An example of a rhythm or economy workout. On a track, walk 100m fast, then 100m easy; then 200m fast/100m easy; then 300m fast/100m easy. Repeat the set four times.

Acceleration: A workout that starts at an easy to moderate pace then gradually builds to a very fast finish. These could be very short accelerations (10 to 30 seconds) or longer progression workouts. Usually when I write "acceleration" on the schedule I'm referring to very short, fast accelerations.

Cross-train or XT: Aerobic workouts other than walking or running workouts using any enjoyable activity like swimming, cycling, elliptical trainer, group classes, etc. These days are intended to give your walking/running muscles a break, so don't push! Non-aerobic workouts like yoga or Pilates classes can also be substituted on these days.

Easy or **EZ:** Comfortable, "conversational" pace. Train, don't strain! Most of your workouts should be done at this easy pace.

Fartlek or FTLK: A varied pace workout. Start moderate for a few minutes, accelerate to race pace for a few minutes, slow back down, etc. Some days they can be "easy" fartleks, but usually these are fairly hard workouts, just without the stress of doing timed intervals.

Hill reps: Walk fast up a hill (with perfect technique!), slowly walk back down, repeat.

Moderate or Mod.: A not-so-easy, but not killer workout. Approaching, but not quite at, tempo pace.

Not-so-easy: Basically a long tempo workout; a sustained hard effort. These workouts start coming into play for half-marathon training and beyond after a solid foundation of long easy days has been laid down.

Progression or Prog.: A long "tempo acceleration" such as a five-miler starting at comfortable distance workout pace and building to half-marathon pace or faster.

Sw/B/W: Swim, bike, walk.

Tempo: A fast paced workout. For half-marathons these are workouts like 8k to 10k (five to six miles) workouts at a steady, fast pace approaching goal half-marathon pace, or longer workouts at a pace about 30 seconds per mile slower than goal race pace. I tend to call longer tempo workouts "not-so-easy" distance days.

Time Trial or TT: A time trial is a fast effort, treated like a race, but without other competitors. Take a couple of days easy before, warm-up fully, and try for your best effort.

Turns & Straights or T&S: On a track, walk easy on the turns, very fast down the straightaways. This is a great introduction to economy training for beginners.

W/up: Warm-up. The duration of your warm-up depends on the duration or speed of the workout or race. As a general rule, the faster the effort, the longer the warm-up. I would often warm up for five kilometers before a 1-mile race, but only a few minutes before a 50k.

"": Ditto. When I don't have room to write the same thing over and over again! For example, after the first few weeks on the training schedules writing "10 minute warm-up, then drills, then…" I'll start writing "10 min. w/up, then drills…" and eventually, just "".

→: From this to that. For example, I like my athletes to start their longer interval workouts at current race pace and then work down to goal pace, so I'll often write "… @ current → goal pace."

APPENDIX II: PACE CHART

	1500 meters	3,000 meters	5,000 meters	8k	5 miles	10k	15k	10 miles	20k	half-marathon	25k	30k	marathon	50k	50 miles	100 miles
6:00	5:35	11:11	18:38	29:49	30:00	37:17	55:56	1:00:00	1:14:34	1:18:39	1:33:12	1:51:51	2:37:19	3:06:25	5:00:00	10:00:00
6:10	5:44	11:29	19:09	30:39	30:50	38:19	57:29	1:01:40	1:16:38	1:20:50	1:35:48	1:54:57	2:41:41	3:11:35	5:08:20	10:16:40
6:20	5:54	11:48	19:40	29:20	31:40	39:21	59:01	1:03:20	1:18:42	1:23:01	1:38:23	1:58:04	2:46:03	3:16:46	5:16:40	10:33:20
6:30	6:03	12:07	20:11	30:07	32:30	40:23	1:00:35	1:05:00	1:20:47	1:25:13	1:40:58	2:01:10	2:50:25	3:21:57	5:25:00	10:50:00
6:40	6:12	12:25	20:42	30:53	33:20	41:25	1:02:08	1:06:40	1:22:51	1:27:24	1:43:34	2:04:16	2:54:48	3:27:07	5:33:20	11:06:40
6:50	6:22	12:44	21:13	31:39	34:10	42:28	1:03:41	1:08:20	1:24:55	1:29:35	1:46:09	2:07:23	2:59:10	3:32:18	5:41:40	11:23:20
7:00	6:31	13:02	21:44	32:26	35:00	43:30	1:05:15	1:10:00	1:27:00	1:31:46	1:48:44	2:10:29	3:03:32	3:37:29	5:50:00	11:40:00
7:10	6:40	13:21	22:15	33:12	35:50	44:32	1:06:48	1:11:40	1:29:04	1:33:57	1:51:20	2:13:36	3:07:54	3:42:39	5:58:20	11:56:40
7:20	6:50	13:40	22:47	33:58	36:40	45:34	1:08:21	1:13:20	1:31:08	1:36:08	1:53:55	2:16:42	3:12:16	3:47:50	6:06:40	12:13:20
7:30	6:59	13:58	23:18	34:45	37:30	46:36	1:09:54	1:15:00	1:33:12	1:38:19	1:56:30	2:19:48	3:16:38	3:53:01	6:15:00	12:30:00
7:40	7:08	14:17	23:49	35:31	38:20	47:38	1:11:27	1:16:40	1:35:17	1:40:30	1:59:06	2:22:55	3:21:01	3:58:12	6:23:20	12:46:40
7:50	7:18	14:36	24:20	36:17	39:10	48:40	1:13:01	1:18:20	1:37:21	1:42:41	2:01:41	2:26:01	3:25:23	4:03:22	6:31:40	13:03:20
8:00	7:27	14:54	24:51	37:04	40:00	49:43	1:14:34	1:20:00	1:39:25	1:44:53	2:04:16	2:29:08	3:29:45	4:08:33	6:40:00	13:20:00
8:10	7:36	15:13	25:22	37:50	40:50	50:45	1:16:07	1:21:40	1:41:29	1:47:04	2:06:52	2:32:14	3:34:07	4:13:44	6:48:20	13:36:40
8:20	7:46	15:32	25:53	38:36	41:40	51:47	1:17:40	1:23:20	1:43:34	1:49:15	2:09:27	2:35:21	3:38:29	4:18:54	6:56:40	13:53:20
8:30	7:55	15:50	26:24	39:23	42:30	52:49	1:19:13	1:25:00	1:45:38	1:51:26	2:12:02	2:38:27	3:42:52	4:24:05	7:05:00	14:10:00
8:40	8:04	16:09	26:55	40:09	43:20	53:51	1:20:47	1:26:40	1:47:42	1:53:37	2:14:38	2:41:33	3:47:14	4:29:16	7:13:20	14:26:40
8:50	8:14	16:28	27:26	40:55	44:10	54:53	1:22:20	1:28:20	1:49:47	1:55:48	2:17:13	2:44:40	3:51:36	4:34:26	7:21:40	14:43:20
9:00	8:23	16:46	27:57	41:17	45:00	55:55	1:23:53	1:30:00	1:51:51	1:57:59	2:19:49	2:47:46	3:55:58	4:39:37	7:30:00	15:00:00
9:10	8:32	17:05	28:28	42:28	45:50	56:58	1:25:26	1:31:40	1:53:55	2:00:10	2:22:24	2:50:53	4:00:20	4:44:48	7:38:20	15:16:40
9:20	8:41	17:23	28:59	43:14	46:40	58:00	1:27:00	1:33:20	1:55:59	2:02:21	2:24:59	2:53:59	4:04:43	4:49:58	7:46:40	15:33:20
9:30	8:51	17:42	29:30	44:01	47:30	59:02	1:28:33	1:35:00	1:58:04	2:04:32	2:27:35	2:57:05	4:09:05	4:55:09	7:55:00	15:50:00
9:40	9:00	18:01	30:01	44:47	48:20	1:00:04	1:30:06	1:36:40	2:00:08	2:06:43	2:30:10	3:00:12	4:13:27	5:00:20	8:03:20	16:06:40
9:50	9:09	18:19	30:33	45:33	49:10	1:01:06	1:31:39	1:38:20	2:02:12	2:08:55	2:32:45	3:03:18	4:17:49	5:05:30	8:11:40	16:23:20
10:00	9:19	18:38	31:04	46:20	50:00	1:02:08	1:33:12	1:40:00	2:04:16	2:11:06	2:35:21	3:06:25	4:22:11	5:10:41	8:20:00	16:40:00
10:10	9:28	18:57	31:35	47:06	50:50	1:03:10	1:34:46	1:41:40	2:06:21	2:13:17	2:37:56	3:09:31	4:26:33	5:15:52	8:28:20	16:56:40
10:20	9:37	19:15	32:06	47:52	51:40	1:04:13	1:36:19	1:43:20	2:08:25	2:15:28	2:40:31	3:12:37	4:30:56	5:21:03	8:36:40	17:13:20
10:30	9:47	19:34	32:37	48:39	52:30	1:05:15	1:37:52	1:45:00	2:10:29	2:17:39	2:43:07	3:15:44	4:35:18	5:26:13	8:45:00	17:30:00
10:40	9:56	19:53	33:08	49:25	53:20	1:06:17	1:39:25	1:46:40	2:12:34	2:19:50	2:45:42	3:18:50	4:39:40	5:31:24	8:53:20	17:46:40
	1500 meters	**3,000 meters**	**5,000 meters**	**8k**	**5 miles**	**10k**	**15k**	**10 miles**	**20k**	**half-marathon**	**25k**	**30k**	**marathon**	**50k**	**50 miles**	**100 miles**

	1500 meters	3,000 meters	5,000 meters	8k	5 miles	10k	15k	10 miles	20k	half-marathon	25k	30k	marathon	50k	50 miles	100 miles
10:50	10:05	20:11	33:39	50:11	54:10	1:07:19	1:40:58	1:48:20	2:14:38	2:22:01	2:48:17	3:21:57	4:44:02	5:36:35	9:01:40	18:03:20
11:00	10:15	20:30	34:10	54:40	55:00	1:08:21	1:42:32	1:50:00	2:16:42	2:24:12	2:50:53	3:25:03	4:48:24	5:41:45	9:10:00	18:20:00
11:10	10:24	20:48	34:41	55:30	55:50	1:09:23	1:44:05	1:51:40	2:18:46	2:26:23	2:53:28	3:28:10	4:52:47	5:46:56	9:18:20	18:36:40
11:20	10:33	21:07	35:12	56:20	56:40	1:10:25	1:45:38	1:53:20	2:20:51	2:28:34	2:56:03	3:31:16	4:57:09	5:52:07	9:26:40	18:53:20
11:30	10:43	21:26	35:43	57:09	57:30	1:11:27	1:47:11	1:55:00	2:22:55	2:30:45	2:58:39	3:34:22	5:01:31	5:57:17	9:35:00	19:10:00
11:40	10:52	21:44	36:14	57:59	58:20	1:12:30	1:48:44	1:56:40	2:24:59	2:32:57	3:01:14	3:37:29	5:05:53	6:02:28	9:43:20	19:26:40
11:50	11:01	22:03	36:45	58:49	59:10	1:13:32	1:50:18	1:58:20	2:27:03	2:35:08	3:03:49	3:40:35	5:10:15	6:07:39	9:51:40	19:43:20
12:00	11:11	22:22	37:16	59:39	1:00:00	1:14:34	1:51:51	2:00:00	2:29:08	2:37:19	3:06:25	3:43:42	5:14:38	6:12:49	10:00:00	20:00:00
12:10	11:20	22:40	37:48	1:00:29	1:00:50	1:15:36	1:53:24	2:01:40	2:31:12	2:39:30	3:09:00	3:46:48	5:19:00	6:18:00	10:08:20	20:16:40
12:20	11:29	22:59	38:19	1:01:19	1:01:40	1:16:38	1:54:57	2:03:20	2:33:16	2:41:41	3:11:35	3:49:54	5:23:22	6:23:11	10:16:40	20:33:20
12:30	11:39	23:18	38:50	1:02:08	1:02:30	1:17:40	1:56:30	2:05:00	2:35:21	2:43:52	3:14:11	3:53:01	5:27:44	6:28:21	10:25:00	20:50:00
12:40	11:48	23:36	39:21	1:02:58	1:03:20	1:18:42	1:58:04	2:06:40	2:37:25	2:46:03	3:16:46	3:56:07	5:32:06	6:33:32	10:33:20	21:06:40
12:50	11:57	23:55	39:52	1:03:48	1:04:10	1:19:45	1:59:37	2:08:20	2:39:29	2:48:14	3:19:21	3:59:14	5:36:28	6:38:43	10:41:40	21:23:20
13:00	12:07	24:14	40:23	1:04:37	1:05:00	1:20:47	2:01:10	2:10:00	2:41:33	2:50:25	3:21:57	4:02:20	5:40:51	6:43:53	10:50:00	21:40:00
13:10	12:16	24:32	40:54	1:05:27	1:05:50	1:21:49	2:02:43	2:11:40	2:43:38	2:52:36	3:24:32	4:05:26	5:45:13	6:49:04	10:58:20	21:56:40
13:20	12:25	24:51	41:25	1:06:17	1:06:40	1:22:51	2:04:16	2:13:20	2:45:42	2:54:48	3:27:07	4:08:33	5:49:35	6:54:15	11:06:40	22:13:20
13:30	12:34	25:09	41:56	1:07:06	1:07:30	1:23:53	2:05:50	2:15:00	2:47:46	2:56:59	3:29:43	4:11:39	5:53:57	6:59:26	11:15:00	22:30:00
13:40	12:44	25:28	42:27	1:07:56	1:08:20	1:24:55	2:07:23	2:16:40	2:49:50	2:59:10	3:32:18	4:14:46	5:58:19	7:04:36	11:23:20	22:46:40
13:50	12:53	25:47	42:58	1:08:46	1:09:10	1:25:57	2:08:56	2:18:20	2:51:55	3:01:21	3:34:53	4:17:52	6:02:42	7:09:47	11:31:40	23:03:20
14:00	13:02	26:05	43:29	1:09:36	1:10:00	1:27:00	2:10:29	2:20:00	2:53:59	3:03:32	3:37:29	4:20:59	6:07:04	7:14:58	11:40:00	23:20:00
14:10	13:12	26:24	44:00	1:10:25	1:10:50	1:28:02	2:12:02	2:21:40	2:56:03	3:05:43	3:40:04	4:24:05	6:11:26	7:20:08	11:48:20	23:36:40
14:20	13:21	26:43	44:31	1:11:15	1:11:40	1:29:04	2:13:36	2:23:20	2:58:08	3:07:54	3:42:39	4:27:11	6:15:48	7:25:19	11:56:40	23:53:20
14:30	13:30	27:01	45:02	1:12:05	1:12:30	1:30:06	2:15:09	2:25:00	3:00:12	3:10:05	3:45:15	4:30:18	6:20:10	7:30:30	12:05:00	24:10:00
14:40	13:40	27:20	45:34	1:12:54	1:13:20	1:31:08	2:16:42	2:26:40	3:02:16	3:12:16	3:47:50	4:33:24	6:24:33	7:35:40	12:13:20	24:26:40
14:50	13:49	27:39	46:05	1:13:44	1:14:10	1:32:10	2:18:15	2:28:20	3:04:20	3:14:27	3:50:26	4:36:31	6:28:55	7:40:51	12:21:40	24:43:20
15:00	13:58	27:57	46:36	1:14:34	1:15:00	1:33:12	2:19:48	2:30:00	3:06:25	3:16:38	3:53:01	4:39:37	6:33:17	7:46:02	12:30:00	25:00:00
15:10	14:08	28:16	47:07	1:15:24	1:15:50	1:34:14	2:21:22	2:31:40	3:08:29	3:18:50	3:55:36	4:42:43	6:37:39	7:51:12	12:38:20	25:16:40
15:20	14:17	28:34	47:38	1:16:13	1:16:40	1:35:17	2:22:55	2:33:20	3:10:33	3:21:01	3:58:12	4:45:50	6:42:01	7:56:23	12:46:40	25:33:20
15:30	14:26	28:53	48:09	1:17:03	1:17:30	1:36:19	2:24:28	2:35:00	3:12:38	3:23:12	4:00:47	4:48:56	6:46:23	8:01:34	12:55:00	25:50:00
15:40	14:36	29:12	48:40	1:17:53	1:18:20	1:37:21	2:26:01	2:36:40	3:14:42	3:25:23	4:03:22	4:52:03	6:50:46	8:06:44	13:03:20	26:06:40
15:50	14:45	29:30	49:11	1:18:42	1:19:10	1:38:23	2:27:35	2:38:20	3:16:46	3:27:34	4:05:58	4:55:09	6:55:08	8:11:55	13:11:40	26:23:20
16:00	14:54	29:49	49:42	1:19:32	1:20:00	1:39:25	2:29:08	2:40:00	3:18:50	3:29:45	4:08:33	4:58:15	6:59:30	8:17:06	13:20:00	26:40:00
16:10	15:04	30:08	50:13	1:20:22	1:20:50	1:40:27	2:30:41	2:41:40	3:20:55	3:31:56	4:11:08	5:01:22	7:03:52	8:22:17	13:28:20	26:56:40
	1,500m	**3,000m**	**5,000m**	**8k**	**5 miles**	**10k**	**15k**	**10 miles**	**20k**	**Half-marathon**	**25k**	**30k**	**marathon**	**50k**	**50 miles**	**100 miles**

	1,500m	3,000m	5,000m	8k	5 miles	10k	15k	10 miles	20k	Half-marathon	25k	30k	marathon	50k	50 miles	100 miles
16:20	15:13	30:26	50:44	1:21:12	1:21:40	1:41:29	2:32:14	2:43:20	3:22:59	3:34:07	4:13:44	5:04:28	7:08:14	8:27:27	13:36:40	27:13:20
16:30	15:22	30:45	51:15	1:22:01	1:22:30	1:42:32	2:33:47	2:45:00	3:25:03	3:36:18	4:16:19	5:07:34	7:12:37	8:32:38	13:45:00	27:30:00
16:40	15:32	31:04	51:46	1:22:51	1:23:20	1:43:34	2:35:21	2:46:40	3:27:07	3:38:29	4:18:54	5:10:41	7:16:59	8:37:49	13:53:20	27:46:40
16:50	15:41	31:22	52:17	1:23:41	1:24:10	1:44:36	2:36:54	2:48:20	3:29:12	3:40:40	4:21:30	5:13:47	7:21:21	8:42:59	14:01:40	28:03:20
17:00	15:50	31:41	52:49	1:24:30	1:25:00	1:45:38	2:38:27	2:50:00	3:31:16	3:42:52	4:24:05	5:16:54	7:25:43	8:48:10	14:10:00	28:20:00
17:10	16:00	32:00	53:20	1:25:20	1:25:50	1:46:40	2:40:00	2:51:40	3:33:20	3:45:03	4:26:40	5:20:00	7:30:05	8:53:21	14:18:20	28:36:40
17:20	16:09	32:18	53:51	1:26:10	1:26:40	1:47:42	2:41:33	2:53:20	3:35:25	3:47:14	4:29:16	5:23:07	7:34:28	8:58:31	14:26:40	28:53:20
17:30	16:18	32:37	54:22	1:27:00	1:27:30	1:48:44	2:43:06	2:55:00	3:37:29	3:49:25	4:31:51	5:26:13	7:38:50	9:03:42	14:35:00	29:10:00
17:40	16:28	32:56	54:53	1:27:49	1:28:20	1:49:47	2:44:40	2:56:40	3:39:33	3:51:36	4:34:26	5:29:19	7:43:12	9:08:53	14:43:20	29:26:40
17:50	16:37	33:14	55:24	1:28:39	1:29:10	1:50:49	2:46:13	2:58:20	3:41:37	3:53:47	4:37:02	5:32:26	7:47:34	9:14:03	14:51:40	29:43:20
18:00	16:46	33:33	55:55	1:29:29	1:30:00	1:51:51	2:47:46	3:00:00	3:43:42	3:55:58	4:39:37	5:35:32	7:51:56	9:19:14	15:00:00	30:00:00
18:10	16:55	33:51	56:26	1:30:18	1:30:50	1:52:53	2:49:20	3:01:40	3:45:46	3:58:09	4:42:12	5:38:39	7:56:18	9:24:25	15:08:20	30:16:40
18:20	17:05	34:10	56:57	1:31:08	1:31:40	1:53:55	2:50:52	3:03:20	3:47:50	4:00:20	4:44:48	5:41:45	8:00:41	9:29:35	15:16:40	30:33:20
18:30	17:14	34:29	57:28	1:31:58	1:32:30	1:54:57	2:52:26	3:05:00	3:49:54	4:02:31	4:47:23	5:44:51	8:05:03	9:34:46	15:25:00	30:50:00
18:40	17:23	34:47	57:59	1:32:47	1:33:20	1:55:59	2:53:59	3:06:40	3:51:59	4:04:43	4:49:58	5:47:58	8:09:25	9:39:57	15:33:20	31:06:40
18:50	17:33	35:06	58:30	1:33:37	1:34:10	1:57:01	2:55:32	3:08:20	3:54:03	4:06:54	4:52:34	5:51:04	8:13:47	9:45:07	15:41:40	31:23:20
19:00	17:42	35:25	59:01	1:34:27	1:35:00	1:58:04	2:57:05	3:10:00	3:56:07	4:09:05	4:55:09	5:54:11	8:18:09	9:50:18	15:50:00	31:40:00
19:10	17:51	35:43	59:32	1:35:17	1:35:50	1:59:06	2:58:39	3:11:40	3:58:12	4:11:16	4:57:44	5:57:17	8:22:32	9:55:29	15:58:20	31:56:40
19:20	18:01	36:02	1:00:04	1:36:06	1:36:40	2:00:08	3:00:12	3:13:20	4:00:16	4:13:27	5:00:20	6:00:24	8:26:54	10:00:40	16:06:40	32:13:20
19:30	18:10	36:21	1:00:35	1:36:56	1:37:30	2:01:10	3:01:45	3:15:00	4:02:20	4:15:38	5:02:55	6:03:30	8:31:16	10:05:50	16:15:00	32:30:00
19:40	18:19	36:39	1:01:06	1:37:46	1:38:20	2:02:12	3:03:18	3:16:40	4:04:24	4:17:49	5:05:30	6:06:36	8:35:38	10:11:01	16:23:20	32:46:40
19:50	18:29	36:58	1:01:37	1:38:35	1:39:10	2:03:14	3:04:51	3:18:20	4:06:29	4:20:00	5:08:06	6:09:43	8:40:00	10:16:12	16:31:40	33:03:20
20:00	18:38	37:17	1:02:08	1:39:25	1:40:00	2:04:16	3:06:25	3:20:00	4:08:33	4:22:11	5:10:41	6:12:49	8:44:23	10:21:22	16:40:00	33:20:00
	1,500m	**3,000m**	**5,000m**	**8k**	**5 miles**	**10k**	**15k**	**10 miles**	**20k**	**Half-marathon**	**25k**	**30k**	**marathon**	**50k**	**50 miles**	**100 miles**

APPENDIX III: SAMPLE FUNDRAISING LETTER

[Charity logo]

Dear Family and Friends,

I have decided to take on a new challenge that will require a great deal of dedication, determination and perseverance. I can hardly believe it myself, but I've decided to walk my first marathon (26.2 miles!) and raise **[insert fundraising goal]** to find a cure for **[name of charity or disease].** I will attempt to complete the **[insert name of race]** on **[insert race date]** with **[insert name of fundraising team],** a fundraising program for the **[insert name of charity].**

PHOTO HERE
You training
and/or honoree

[insert a paragraph or two about what your charity does for its patients].

I hope my effort makes a difference in fighting a disease that affects so many people. This is where I need your help; I can't do this alone. Please consider supporting me in this effort by making a tax-deductible donation to the **[insert name of charity].** Would you consider donating $5 for every mile I walk? How about $1?

Every dollar counts and I will also accept ice packs, Advil and prayers! Enclosed is a donation form and return envelope. Please make checks out to **[insert name of charity].** You can also donate online to my fundraising website at: **[fundraising page url].**

My personal fundraising deadline is **[insert fundraising deadline date].** Please help me reach my goal by then!

With gratitude and appreciation,

[insert your name]

APPENDIX IV: SAMPLE CORPORATE SPONSORSHIP LETTER

[Charity logo]

[Recipient's address]
[Your address and contact details]

[Date]

[Objective of letter – Charity sponsorship]

[Dear Mr./Mrs./Ms./Miss insert full name],

My name is **[insert full name]** and I will be taking part in **[activity and date]**. I am completing this event to raise money for **[insert name of charity and brief description]** and the event involves **[Brief description of event].** I feel passionate about this charity because **[state your motives for doing this event].**

I am looking for sponsorship to help this charity and to support me through the event itself. I believe that together, **[company name]** and I can change lives by raising as much money as possible for this great charity. In return I will wear your company's logo with pride on my racing jersey to show everyone what a great supporter the company is and there will be a banner with the company's logo and slogan shown throughout the event increasing awareness of, and creating more interest for you company.

I appreciate your taking the time to consider sponsoring me and I hope to hear from you in the near future by using the contact details above.

Yours sincerely,

[insert your name]

RESOURCES

Affleck, John. "Don't Run (And Don't Laugh): The Little-known History Of Racewalking." HuffingtonPost.com, August 17, 2016, huffpost.com/entry/dont-run-and-dont-laugh-t_b_11570334/. Accessed April 19, 2020.

Algeo, *Matthew. Pedestrianism: When Watching People Walk was America's Favorite Spectator Sport.* Chicago Review Press, 2014.

American Nordic Walking Association. "The History of Nordic Walking." www.americannordicwalking.com/nordic-walking-today. Accessed October 17, 2018.

Asp, Karen. "Nordic Walking Is My Favorite Form of Cardio—Here's Why You Should Try It." Self.com, February 19, 2019. self.com/story/nordic-walking-favorite-cardio-heres-why Accessed April 29, 2019.

Bohlen, Brent. *Boomerwalk: Why Baby Boomers Should Replace Running and Jogging with Racewalking*, Walking Promotions, Medford, NJ, 2009.

Bompa Tudor O., *Periodization Training for Sports*, Human Kinetics, 1999.

Burke LM, Sharma AP, Heikura IA, Forbes SF, Holloway M, et al. "Crisis of confidence averted: Impairment of exercise economy and performance in elite race walkers by ketogenic low carbohydrate, high fat (LCHF) diet is reproducible." PLOS ONE 15(6): e0234027. doi.org/10.1371/journal.pone.0234027 2020.

Burroughs, Roger and John Fitzgerald. "The Women's 10 Kilometres Race Walk Event," New Studies in Athletics, Vol. 5:3, September 1990, pp. 39-44.

Cairns, M. et al. "A biòmechanical analysis of racewalking gait." *Medicine and science in sports and exercise* 18 4 446-53 1986.

Cavagna, Giovanni A., and P. Franzetti. "Mechanics of Competition Walking," *Journal of Applied Physiology*, Vol. 81, 1981, pp. 243-251.

Chen, Y. et al. "OR-030 Influences of Four Weeks Intermittent Hypoxic Training on Aerobic Ability of High-Level Race Walking Athletes." www.semanticscholar.org/paper/OR-030-Influences-of-Four-Weeks-Intermittent-on-of-Chen-Qiu/7083177e09222a6017743aa13d06893f6a76e77c 2018. Accessed 8 October, 2020.

Colbert, LH, Hootman, JH, and Carol A. Macera. "Physical Activity-Related Injuries in Walkers and Runners in the Aerobics Center Longitudinal Study." *Clinical Journal of Sport Medicine* 10:4, 2000, pp. 259-263.

Damilano, Sandro. *100 Years of Racewalking,* Graph Art, Manta-Cuneo, Italy, 2002.

De Angelis, M. and Menchinelli, C. "Times of Flight, Frequency and Length of Stride in Race Walking," in Rodano, R. ed. *Proceedings of the X International Symposium of Biomechanics in Sports.* Milan: Edi-Ermes, January, 1992.

Erickson, Tim. "A Potted History of the Rules of Racewalking." www.vrwc.org.au/vrwchistrules.shtml/.

Fenker, Richard M. "Imagery Training for Olympic Athletes," unpublished.

Fenton, Mark, and Dave McGovern. *Precision Walking*, Polar Electro, Port Washington, NY, 1995.

Gosztyla, Metk. "One step at a time: Former UNH athlete Joanne Dow takes one last shot at Olympics," 6 July, 2008, fosters.com/article/20080706/GJSPORTS_01/90830587/. Accessed 14 July 2020.

Hagburg, James M., and Edward F. Coyle. "Physiological Comparison of Competitive Racewalking and Running," *International Journal of Sports Medicine*, Vol. 5, No. 2, pp. 74-77, 1984.

Hagburg, James M., and Edward F. Coyle. "Physiological Determinants of Endurance Performance as Studied in Competitive Racewalkers," *Medicine and Science in Sports and Exercise*, Vol. 15, No. 4, pp. 287-289, 1983.

Hagner-Derengowska M, Kałużny K, Hagner W, Plaskiewicz A, Bronisz A, Borkowska A, Budzyński J. "The Effect of a 10-Week Nordic Walking Training Program on the Level of GH and LH in elderly women." *Climacteric,* 18(6):835–840, 2015.

Hall, Harry. *The Pedestriennes: America's Forgotten Superstars*, Dog Ear Publishing, Indianapolis, IN, 2014.

Hamilton, Andrew. "Tapering Training to Improve Athlete's Endurance." peakendurancesport.com/endurance-training/training-structure-and-planning/tapering-training-improve-athletes-endurance/ Accessed 14 July, 2020.

Hanley, Brian. *Biomechanical Analysis of Elite Race Walking* - A thesis submitted in partial fulfillment of the requirements of Leeds Metropolitan University for the degree of Doctor of Philosophy. 2014.

Hanley, Brian. "Using Biomechanics to Improve Race Walking Performances, Coaching and Judging." University of Huddersfield Sport, Exercise and Nutrition Seminar Series, DOI:10.13140/RG.2.2.13622.24646 2019.

Hanley, B., Tucker, C. B., and Bissas, A. "Assessment of IAAF Racewalk Judges' Ability to Detect Legal and Non-legal Technique." *Front. Sports Act. Living*, at https://doi.org/10.3389/fspor.2019.00009 2019.

Hausleber, J. "Race Walking Technique," *Track and Field Journal*, Vol. 33, Spring 1987, pp. 5-8.

Heffernan, Rob. *Walking Tall: The Autobiography of a World Champion and Olympic Medalist*, Collins Press, Cork, Ireland, 2016.

Hilliard, Craig. "Weight Training and Conditioning for Walkers," *Modern Athlete and Coach*, Vol. 29:2, April 1991, pp. 36-38.

Hoga-Miura K, Ae M, Fujii N, Yokozowa T. "A Three-Dimensional Kinematic Analysis of Men's 20-km Walking Races Using an Inverted Pendulum Model." *Gazzetta Medica Italiana Archivo per le Scienze Mediche,*175(7-8), 2016, pp. 297-307.

Hoga-Miur, K, Enomoto Y, Kadono, H, Suzuki, Y. "Judgment of Loss of Contact in Men's and Women's 20km Race Walking Events," in: *Research Report of the JAAF Biomechanics Research Project on the 11th World Championships in Athletics, Osaka - Performances and Technique of the World Elite Athletes*, Japan Associations of Athletics Federations, Tokyo, 2020, pp.212-217.

Hoga-Miura K., Hirokawa R, Sugita M, Enomoto Y, Kadono H, Suzuki Y. "A Three-Dimensional Kinematic Analysis of Walking Speed on World Elite women's 20-km Walking Races Using an Inverted Pendulum Model," *Gazz Med Ital - Arch Sci Med*, 179:29-38. DOI: 10.23736/S0393-3660.18.04009-3 2020.

Hopkins, Julian. "Improving Performance in the 50 Kilometres Walk," *New Studies in Athletics,* Vol. 5:3, September 1990, pp. 45-48.

Huajing, Z. & Lizhong, G. "Marching out of Asia and into the world," New Studies in Athletics, 6(3), 1991, pp.25-33.

IAAF. *Guidance for Walking Judges*. London: IAAF, 1972.

Kantaneva, Marko. "Original Nordic Walking Article 'Sauvakävely'1997," en.markokantaneva.com/nordicwalking/original-nordic-walking-article-1997 2018. Accessed 9 October, 2020.

Kisiel, Krzysztof. *Race Walking: Methodology of Training for the Youngster to Senior Athlete*. Wydawnictwo Jarosław Kisiel: Kalisz, Poland. wbc.poznan.pl/Content/392755/Kisiel_race_walking_2016.pdf accessed October 15, 2020.

Knicker, Axel and Michael Loch. "Race Walking Technique and Judging—The Final Report of the International Athletic Foundation Research Project," *New Studies in Athletics* Vol. 5:3, September 1990, pp. 25-38.

Lassen, Palle. "The Basic Movement," in *XVI IAAF Race Walking World Cup Official Program*, April, 1993, pp. 22-26.

Lawson, Lionel. *Racewalking for Fitness and Fun*. DocTechEd Services cc, Greyville, South Africa, 1997.

Lee, James B et al. "Detection of illegal race walking: a tool to assist coaching and judging," *Sensors* (Basel, Switzerland) vol. 13,12 16065-74. 26 Nov. 2013.

Marin, Jose. "Controlling the Development of Training in Race Walkers," *New Studies in Athletics*, Vol. 5:3, September 1990, pp. 49-53.

McGovern, Dave, *The Complete Guide to Marathon Walking*, World Class Publications, Mobile, AL, 2000.

McGovern, Dave. *The Complete Guide to Racewalking*, World Class Publications, Mobile, AL, 1998.

McRobbie, Linda Rodriguez. "How Competitive Walking Captivated Georgian Britain." www.atlasobscura.com/articles/pedestrianism-george-wilson-walking/ June 29, 2017.

Menier, D.R., and L. G. C. E. Pugh. "The Relation of Oxygen Intake and Velocity of Running in Competition Walkers," *Journal of Physiology*, Vol. 197, pp. 717-721.

Murray, et al, "Kinematic and Electromyographic Patterns of Olympic Race Walkers," *The American Journal of Sports Medicine*, 1983, Vol. II.

Olan, Ben, ed. *Pursuit of Excellence: The Olympic Story*, The Associated Press and Grolier, Danbury, CT, 1979.

Padilla, Jesús Jiménez, ed. "La Caminata de Competencia," in *METAS de la Juventud y el Deporte*, Special edition, October, 1990.

Palamarchuck, Dr. Howard J., and Dr. Lawrence Kalker. "A Medical Guide for the Race Walker: Information, Recognition, Management and Self-Treatment of Common Injuries and Problems," unpublished, 1987.

Payne, A. H. "A Comparison of the Ground Forces in Race Walking With those in Normal Walking and Running," In *Biomechanics,* VIA, Vol. 2A. pp. 293-302. ed. Asmussen. E. and Jorgensen, K. University Park Press, Copenhagen, 1980.

Physical Activity Council. "2020 Physical Activity Council's Overview Report on U.S. Participation." www.aaaa.org/pac-participation-report/. Accessed 28 July, 2020.

Revord LP, Lomond KV, Loubert PV, Hammer RL. "Acute effects of walking with Nordic poles in persons with mild to moderate low-back pain," *International Journal of Exercise Science*. 2016;9(4):507-513.

Reynolds, Gretchen. "Walk Briskly for Your Health. About 100 steps Per Minute." www.nytimes.com/2018/06/27/well/walk-health-exercise-steps.html/. Accessed March 17th, 2019.

Robergs, Robert & Landwehr, Roberto. "The surprising history of the 'HRmax=220-age' equation," *International Journal of Online Engineering* - iJOE. 5, 2002.

Rudow, Martin. *Advanced Racewalking.* Technique Publications, Seattle, WA, 1987.

Rutlin, Tom. "What's the Difference?" www.walkingpoles.com/whats-difference/. Accessed October 13th, 2018.

Ryan, Jessie Guy. "The Hot 19th Century Sport That Launched Modern Athletic Betting? Competitive Walking," www.atlasobscura.com/articles/the-hot-19th-century-sport-that-launched-modern-sports-betting-competitive-walking/. February 27, 2016, Accessed September 19, 2018.

Salvage, Jeff. "The History of Race Walking" www.active.com/walking/articles/the-history-of-race-walking-870430/. Accessed September 13, 2018.

Salvage, Jeff and Westerfield, Gary. *Walk Like an Athlete*, Salvage Writes Publications, Marlton, NJ, 1996.

Summers, Harry. "Placement of the Leading Foot in Race Walking," *Modern Athlete and Coach*, Vol. 29:1, January 1991, pp. 33-35.

Trowbridge, E.A. "Walking or Running - When does Lifting Occur?" *Athletics Coach*, 1981, Vol. I, p. 15.

Tucker, Catherine B., and Hanley, Brian. "Increases in speed do not change gait symmetry or variability in world-class race walkers." www.tandfonline.com/doi/abs/10.1080/02640414.2020.1798730/ 2020, Accessed 29 July, 2020.

Tudor-Locke C, Han H, Aguiar EJ, Barreira TV, Schuna JM Jr, Kang M, Rowe DA. "How fast is fast enough? Walking cadence (steps/min) as a practical estimate of intensity in adults: a narrative review," *Br J Sports Med.* 2018, 52:776–88.

Wallace, William Gordon. *The History of Race Walking in America.* Diss., University of Texas, 1989.

Watman, Mel. *Olympic Track & Field History*, Athletics International Ltd., Ft. Atkinson, WI, 2004.

Wayman, Erin. "Sahelanthropus tchadensis: Ten Years After the Discovery." www.smithsonianmag.com/science-nature/sahelanthropus-tchadensis-ten-years-after-the-disocvery-2449553/, July 16, 2012. Accessed March 17, 2019.

Williams, Idris. "Technical Weekend in the Lake District," (British) *Race Walking Record*, No. 591, January 1992, pp. 11-13.

Woods, Rose A. "American Time Use Survey – 2018 Results (PDF)." Bureau of Labor Statistics. May 2017. Retrieved March 9, 2018.

"A Brief History of Racewalking in the United States," *Worldwide Running* www.worldwiderunning.com/racewalking_ushistory.php Accessed October 20, 2010.

Yarrow, K., Brown, P., & Krakauer, J. W. (2009). "Inside the brain of an elite athlete: The neural processes that support high achievement in sports." *Nature Reviews Neuroscience,* 10, 585-596. doi:10.1038/nrn2672.

Yoshida, T., et al. "Physiological Determinants of Race Walking Performance in Female Race Walkers," *British Journal of Sports Medicine*, Vol. 23 (4), pp. 250-254.

Yukelson, Dave and Fenton, Mark. "Psychological Considerations in Race Walking," *Track and Field Quarterly*, Spring 1992, pp. 72-76.

INDEX

About the Author

Dave McGovern is America's foremost walking coach and clinician. A 25-year veteran of the US National Racewalk Team with a master's degree in sport science/sports medicine from the United States Sports Academy, Dave has conducted up to 20 clinics and camps per year throughout North America as well as Europe, and South and Equatorial Africa, since 1991. Many of Dave's clinic alumni have lost weight, bounced back from heart disease and diabetes, and completed marathons, while others have won national championships, set age-group world records, and even made Olympic teams!

During his nearly 40-year competitive career Dave won 15 U.S. national championships and walked 20 kilometers (12.4 miles—one of the two Olympic distances for men) in 1:24:29—a 6:48 per-mile pace—which ranks him as the fastest American ever to *not* make an Olympic team. (Onward to 2024!) Dave represented the US on 20 international teams, including seven World Cup and six Pan Am Cup teams, and he is the only track and field athlete in US history to qualify for and compete in nine consecutive US Olympic Team Trials. Still competing at a high level at the age of 55, Dave won the 2016 USA Track and Field 10-kilometer Racewalk Championship, and placed 9th at the 2020 US Olympic Trials in the 50k racewalk.

As a private coach, Dave has guided 10 athletes all the way to the US Olympic Team Trials, starting with many from their first steps as racewalkers. Dave has also coached the national team of Ghana, West Africa, was the junior coach for the U.S. team at the 2008 World Cup of Race Walking in Cheboksary, Russia, and the Head Coach for Team USA at the 2012 World Cup in Saransk, Russia. Dave was for twelve years the National Coach for the Crohn's and Colitis Foundation's "Team Challenge" half-marathon team, and was Head Coach of the Newman's Own Foundation's "Team Serioüs Fun" half-marathon team. Dave was a long-time writer for *Walking Magazine* and *Walk! Magazine*, and is the author of *The Complete Guide to Racewalking, The Complete Guide to Marathon Walking,* and *Precision Walking*—all while helping to raise four great kids, aged 2 to 11, with his wife, Loretta, herself a two-time US champion.